Balkan Historiographical Wars

Diana Mishkova • Roumen Daskalov
Editors

Balkan Historiographical Wars

The Middle Ages

Editors
Diana Mishkova
Centre for Advanced Study Sofia
Sofia, Bulgaria

Roumen Daskalov
Institute of Balkan Studies and Centre
of Thracology at the Bulgarian
Academy of Sciences
Sofia, Bulgaria

ISBN 978-3-031-90112-6   ISBN 978-3-031-90113-3   (eBook)
https://doi.org/10.1007/978-3-031-90113-3

© The Editor(s) (if applicable) and The Author(s), under exclusive license to Springer Nature
Switzerland AG 2025

This work is subject to copyright. All rights are solely and exclusively licensed by the
Publisher, whether the whole or part of the material is concerned, specifically the rights of
translation, reprinting, reuse of illustrations, recitation, broadcasting, reproduction on
microfilms or in any other physical way, and transmission or information storage and retrieval,
electronic adaptation, computer software, or by similar or dissimilar methodology now
known or hereafter developed.
The use of general descriptive names, registered names, trademarks, service marks, etc. in this
publication does not imply, even in the absence of a specific statement, that such names are
exempt from the relevant protective laws and regulations and therefore free for general use.
The publisher, the authors and the editors are safe to assume that the advice and information
in this book are believed to be true and accurate at the date of publication. Neither the publisher nor the authors or the editors give a warranty, expressed or implied, with respect to the
material contained herein or for any errors or omissions that may have been made. The
publisher remains neutral with regard to jurisdictional claims in published maps and institutional affiliations.

This Palgrave Macmillan imprint is published by the registered company Springer Nature
Switzerland AG.
The registered company address is: Gewerbestrasse 11, 6330 Cham, Switzerland

If disposing of this product, please recycle the paper.

PREFACE

This book contains six studies on "historiographical wars" in the Balkans, examining some of the most emblematic cases and attempting to identify the main characteristics of this phenomenon. By "historiographical wars" we mean protracted and embittered disputes between historians of different nations, which go beyond normal difference of opinion and variance of interpretations toward a radically opposed understanding of the past attesting to deliberate and fierce political uses of history. Historiographical wars are, in our view, a species of the "history wars" understood as "cultural wars" on certain historical issues which gain wide publicity in a given society, as attested by various cases in Europe and the United States (Linenthal and Engelhardt, eds. 1996; Macintyre and Clark 2003; Bickerton, February 2006; Procacci 2003; Cajani, Lässig and Repoussi, eds. 2019).

While "history wars" attain wider visibility and publicity, historiographical wars, as we see them, are more specialized controversies between historians. Generally speaking, history wars pit against each other memory versus history, commemorative voices against mainstream academic interpretations, and invariably appeal to national loyalties. They often rest on a misunderstanding of the discipline of history and a hostility to professional history writing. Historiographic wars, on the other hand, are typically waged within the sphere of professional history writing. The difference is nevertheless relative insofar as academic historians also partake in history wars and "weaponized" arguments are drawn from specialized scholarly history writing. Besides, mainstream historiographical controversies can also resonate with the wider public if they touch upon sensitive public

v

notions and representations of history, while historians who question national narratives are also open to accusations of disloyalty. The study of both history wars and historiographical wars is important precisely because they reveal the strong emotional attitudes of society regarding its past. In our research, we approach the historiographical wars by covering a number of Balkan cases of bi-, tri-, and multi-lateral controversies. At the same time, departing from the usual focus on the professional and political biographies of scholars, we are particularly interested in the construction of narratives and strategies of argumentation involved in historiographical "warfare". To our knowledge, such a transnational study involving a variety of specific national contexts has not been conducted so far.

The question can be posed: what makes historiographical wars so bitter and differentiates them from the normal range of interpretations on certain historical issues? Some answers are suggested below.

History became a major tool in forging national identities in the Balkans and representations of the Middle Ages (along with antiquity in the case of the Greeks, the Romanians, and the Albanians) were considered crucial in this process. National(ist) educators and enthusiastic amateur historians of Romantic history "discovered" the ancestors of their peoples or nations and took pride in their deeds and works. Ethnonyms, origins, ethnogenesis, and certain political formations became extremely important in the process of sorting out one's past and disentangling it from that of others. Military glory and the establishment of a state and ecclesiastic institutions of one's own were especially treasured, as well as cultural feats of literary and artistic creativity. Present-day rivalries led to the discovery of "hereditary enemies".

Accordingly, historians assumed the role of nation-builders and "spokespersons" for the nation, of upholders of national honor and glory (Berger et al. 1999, 3–14; Berger 1997; Deletant and Hanak eds. 1988). Some national historians insisted that historical scholarship should be scientific, "objective", and "value-free" (in the Weberian sense), that is, without biases and value judgments. Others advocated taking sides and favoring a (national) "party" stand (*Parteilichkeit*). It is exactly by interrogating the national mission of historical scholarship since the early nineteenth century that the notions of "objectivity" and "freedom from values", as well as the strict separation between academic research and politics (and ideology) have been challenged. Yet, despite the academic criticism leveled against the naïve approaches and the unsubstantiated patriotic bias of Romantic historiography, the professionalization of history writing to a large extent cemented its national mission. This happened particularly in the Balkan countries. Scholarly objectivity was oddly identified with the national expediency of historiographical production. As a result, historiographical wars unfolded exactly during the period of post-Romantic critical historiography. Respectively, the attacks against alternative national approaches to the past often went together with accusations of a lack of professional ethos and methodological correctness.

Nevertheless, historiographical wars differ from normal academic disputes in both motivation and form. Unlike purely academic debates, which usually focus on an issue of specialized interest, historiographical wars address simultaneously all major points of conflict over the past provoking tensions between two or more neighboring countries. Not only do historiographical wars involve a large number of participants, but their scholarly interests and ways of doing science are dictated and financed by the academic institutions of their respective nation-states. Symptomatic is the publication of collective volumes on bilaterally disputed questions which are then usually translated into major "international" languages with the intention of reaching broader academic circles. At the same time, there are systematic attempts to win the support of foreign scholars who would lend more credibility to the national cause. Such historiographical wars are usually long-term undertakings, lasting for decades and inevitably involving scholars from several generations, often with very different academic backgrounds.

Historiographical controversies or, indeed, wars were fought on a wide range of issues and often involved several Balkan states. The disputes dealt with in this volume refer to the medieval era; a forthcoming second volume will focus on disputes regarding modern and contemporary history. They were first brought forward in the late Ottoman and early post-Ottoman period—the era of competitive and vindictive national formation in the region, and, together with it, of the political mobilization of historical knowledge. It is thus contemporary political conflict that conditioned historiographical conflict over the remote Middle Ages as a sort of "prelude" to more recent conflicts. In cases, where there are no present-day international conflicts, the distant past does not become per se the basis for heated debates between historians. Besides, as historiographical wars focus primarily on persistent and sensitive issues, they can be muted by current political circumstances but emerge again when the political situation changes. Here are some examples.

viii   PREFACE

As A. Vezenkov's chapter in this volume suggests, the Albanian narrative of the Albanians as the sole descendants of the Illyrians not only does not clash with Croatian Illyrism, but does not even ironize it, because these ideological constructions flourished at a different time and there was no contemporary conflict between the two nation-states. On the contrary, contemporary Albanian and Croatian nationalism have one main common adversary—Serbia/the Serbs. The conquest of parts of present-day Albanian lands by the medieval Bulgarian kingdoms (from the mid-ninth to the early eleventh centuries, and briefly in the first half of the thirteenth century) does not provoke a controversy comparable to the vast output of polemical writings on the Serbian rule of Kosovo, and some other territories between the late twelfth and early fifteenth centuries. After the collapse of Yugoslavia, Macedonian historiography emerged as an independent rival, whose preoccupation is, just like in the Albanian-Serbian disputes, with the "autochthony" of Albanians in the western and northwestern parts of today's Republic of North Macedonia.

Tellingly, there is no Bulgarian-Hungarian historiographical war about the Middle Ages or later, namely because of the absence of present-day political conflicts, despite a series of medieval clashes beginning in the ninth century, soon after the resettlement of the Hungarians in their present lands, and continuing almost until the fall of Bulgaria under the Ottomans. On the contrary, while there were far fewer conflicts between the medieval Bulgarian kingdom and the Wallachian principalities, in modern times one witnesses fierce tensions between nationally committed Romanian and Bulgarian historians caused by the conflict over Dobrudja. In this case, we see how a common and almost conflict-free coexistence in the past and even unity in the Bulgarian-Vlach kingdom of the Assenids can become an apple of discord (Daskalov 2015, 274–354). At the same time, the improvement of Greek-Bulgarian relations since the end of the 1960s (under authoritarian regimes in both countries) is certainly one of the reasons why there have been no protracted historiographical wars between Greek and Bulgarian academics. This fact is all the more astonishing given the numerous military conflicts between the Byzantine and medieval Bulgarian empires as well as the violent confrontation between Bulgarian and Greek nationalism since the late nineteenth century, the Greek-Bulgarian clashes in early twentieth-century Macedonia, and the Bulgarian occupations of Greek territories during the two world wars. In this case, the emergence of new priorities in the field of international politics, and the alliance against a common new or old-new "enemies" (Turkey and the Macedonian nationalism within and outside socialist Yugoslavia), ultimately prevented the eruption of bilateral conflicts and their projection onto the field of historical research.

Similarly, due to the fact that professional Macedonian historiography took shape during Tito's Yugoslavia, the Serbian medieval conquest of Macedonia did not give rise to heated disputes between historians of both nations. In contrast, the Bulgarian-Macedonian dispute over the medieval past was and is still bitter as it concerns current issues of identity and historical legacy (see Daskalov in this volume). Similar, although of more recent origin, is the case of medieval Bosnia. The "appropriation" of the Bosnian past by Serbian or Croatian history was an issue of contention only between Serbian and Croatian historians (muted in Tito's Yugoslavia) until the arrival of Bosniak historians on the academic scene, most forcefully in the aftermath of the Yugoslav wars of the 1990s, as N. Rabić's chapter in this volume demonstrates. In general, historiographical conflicts become exasperated when linked with questions of identity (over what is seen as an attribute of the "national Self") and heritage (what belongs to whom).

All these examples demonstrate the two-way interaction between academic fields of research and the realm of politics. On the one hand, political controversies determine the evolution and vehemence of historiographical wars; on the other hand, historians (and academics in general) provide narratives and interpretations that are put into play in political conflicts—including military ones, that is, in real wars. In turn, the latter generate repercussions in the field of historiography. Thus, new controversial issues arose from the Balkan Wars in 1912–1913, themselves the result of previous claims and irredentist agendas. These wars, too, were typically dealt with in light of previous conflicts and grievances by historians of the following generations, some of whom operated under authoritarian/communist regimes. Thus the "war of spirits" (*Krieg der Geister*) (Górny 2019) and real warfare feed on each other, reflecting the fact that armed conflicts are deeply implicated in the construction of master national narratives. Historiography, in this sense, presents itself as politics by other means.

The contested issues and disputes discussed in this volume are of great variety, but one can simplify the picture by arranging them into several types. To begin with, one type concerns the ethnic origins or "self-consciousness" of important historical personalities—rulers and military leaders—such as Skanderbeg, King Trvtko, and King Samuel (as treated here by, respectively, N. Clayer, N. Rabić, and R. Daskalov), and occasionally influential clerics or men of letters. Other disputes concern the origin and "national belonging" of certain institutions, including states, ecclesiastic institutions, or a literary and artistic school, and can also refer to a certain cultural phenomenon or achievement considered to be of "pan-European" value, such as the Cyrillic alphabet and Old Slavonic literature, the heretic movement of Bogomilism, and works of art (see Marinov's and Rabić's chapters in this volume). A sub-species of this kind of dispute relates to the ethnic makeup of medieval (especially short-lived) states, such as Samuel's state in Macedonia (surveyed by Daskalov), a question tied up with contemporary claims over the territory of that state based on historical right. Connected to these are disputes over the political, religious, and cultural influence of a certain medieval state upon others, especially upon neighbors, as well as disputes over the ethnic composition of certain contested territories (see Vezenkov's chapter). Characteristic is the political agenda of creating a national state whose borders coincide with the greatest territorial expansion of its supposed medieval predecessor, which inevitably implies the craving to incorporate ("recover" or "liberate") those territories that are currently part of other neighboring states ("under foreign rule"). An issue that proves especially intractable is the participation of a given ethnic group in the "ethnogenesis" of another one (e.g., Slavs and Albanians in the formation of modern Greek ethnicity)—a question that clearly involves national sensibilities, be it pride or humiliation. Other controversies concern imperial legacies, especially Byzantine and Ottoman, whose interpretation is strongly conditioned by popular attitudes to latter-day Greeks and Turks (see Mishkova's chapter).

The justification of national-political, particularly territorial, claims by "academic" means involved a wide range of arguments concomitant with historical ones: geographical, ethnographic/ethnological, linguistic, economic, and so on. Remarkably, polemical historical writings tend to resort to arguments derived from the Middle Ages and, if possible and/or necessary, from prehistory and antiquity, especially where the existing evidence from these early periods is shaky. Yet arguments from the distant past do not appear only in strictly historical studies. They are present in geographical writings, which usually go back in time to the first written sources from antiquity. The same applies to publications on folklore and, predictably, to archaeological research; contributions in linguistics and dialectology typically include, along with surveys of the contemporary linguistic situation, a long-term historical overview.

In most cases, historiographical wars take the form of explicit confrontation between different national schools of history and are expressly waged from nationally entrenched positions. This appears as a foregone conclusion since the controversies in question are themselves symptoms of the "nationalization" of historical knowledge and the use of historiography in competitive processes of nation-building. In other cases, though, and for various reasons, historiographical wars can be implicit, and the opposing positions and the interpretations issuing from them in different national historiographies may run "parallel" to and deceptively independent of each other. This was to a large extent the case of the national historiographical schools in former Yugoslavia and is still the case in present-day Greek and Bulgarian historiographies concerning a long series of conflictual issues ranging from medieval Bulgarian-Byzantine relations to the period of World War II. There are also cases when the major controversies on some topics take place within the national historiographies themselves without much reference to external contenders (such as the case of Skanderbeg in Albanian historiography discussed here by N. Clayer). Yet, even in such cases, there is a certain interplay between the "nationalized" science and transnational academic debates. In fact, as Marinov argues in his chapter, cross-national academic disputes involved not only scholars coming from different national contexts in the Balkans but also from Western and Central Europe or Russia/the Soviet Union. Their academic work was often instrumentalized in the formation of national narratives and fueled nationalist disputes in the Balkans. Whatever the particular tactics, however, professional history writing in such cases, as Mishkova demonstrates at some length, displays all the basic characteristics of heritage discourse, among preoccupation with precedence, antiquity, autochthony, uninterrupted continuity, and claims to exceptionality and uniqueness.

In order to understand the stakes involved in these controversies the authors in this book examine their changing historical contexts, including competing nation-building processes and irredentist objectives that conditioned their variable political salience. As far as space allows, these are interwoven with the personal biographies, generational profiles, professional upbringing, and political engagements of the contending authors and with the institutions in which their activities were deployed.

As can be seen from this short overview, the issues we are dealing with are not "cold" objects of research of purely academic interest. On the contrary, every now and then such latent battles break into the open and resonate strongly with the broader public. Our response to the emotionally overloaded historiographical battles is above all methodological. It invites the use of transnational or relational approaches, such as entangled history and *histoire croisée* (literally "crossed history"). The core participants in this venture have applied these approaches in their previous work (see Daskalov et al. eds. 2013–2017). The appropriateness of this methodological orientation ensues from the largely shared and intertwined character of Balkan historical "reality", itself the result of pervasive imperial (Byzantine, Ottoman) as well as authoritarian and communist legacies. Paradoxically, moreover, while striving to neatly separate ("disentangle") the pieces of a shared past and appropriate them for their own nations, Balkan historiographies could never afford to develop independently of each other as they had to constantly keep an eye on and react against the encroachments and rival claims of neighboring historical scholarship. Precisely this "duplication" of the entanglement adds fuel and personal animus to the fire of the historiographical debates and converts them into symbolic wars.

For the execution of this project, we want to express our gratitude first of all to the Bulgarian Science Fund for generously supporting our project in the framework of the "Vihren 2021" grant scheme (contract no. KP-06-DV/7). To the Institute of Balkan Studies and Centre of Thracology at the Bulgarian Academy of Sciences and, personally, to its Director, Roumiana Preshlenova, we owe thanks for hosting our team and creating the most favorable conditions for carrying out our research. We are indebted to our copy-editor, George Repper, for his meticulous and conscientious work on the manuscript and to the editor of Palgrave Macmillan for the smooth collaboration.

Sofia, Bulgaria

R. Daskalov
Tch. Marinov
D. Mishkova
A. Vezenkov

References

Berger, Stefan, Mark Donovan, and Kevin Passmore. 1999. Apologias for the Nation-State in Western Europe since 1800. In *Writing National Histories: Western Europe since 1800*, ed. Stefan Berger, Mark Donovan, and Kevin Passmore, 3–14. London and New York: Routledge.

PREFACE   xiii

Berger, Stefan. 1997. *The Search for Normality: National Identity and Historical Consciousness in Germany since 1800*. Providence and Oxford: Berghahn Books.

Bickerton, Christopher. 2006. France's History Wars. *Le Monde Diplomatique*, English edition, February.

Cajani, Luigi, Simone Lässig, and Maria Repoussi, eds. 2019. *The Palgrave Handbook of Conflict and History Education in the Post-Cold War Era*. Palgrave.

Daskalov, Roumen, Diana Mishkova, Tchavdar Marinov, and Alexander Vezenkov, eds. 2013–2017. *Entangled Histories of the Balkans*, vol. 1–4. Leiden, Boston: Brill.

Daskalov, Roumen. 2015. Feud over the Middle Ages: Bulgarian-Romanian Historiographical Debates. In *Entangled Histories of the Balkans, vol. 3: Shared Pasts, Disputed Legacies*, ed. Roumen Daskalov and Alexander Vezenkov, 274–354. Leiden, Boston: Brill.

Deletant, Dennis, and Harry Hanak, eds. 1988. *Historians as Nation-Builders: Central and South-East Europe*. Houndmills, Basingstoke and London: Macmillan Press.

Linenthal, Edward, and Tom Engelhardt, eds. 1996. *History Wars. The Enola Gay and Other Battles for the American Past*. New York: Henry Holt and Company.

Macintyre, Stuart, and Anna Clark. 2003. *The History Wars*. Carlton, Victoria: Melbourne University Press.

Procacci, Giuliano. 2003. *La memoria controversa. Revisionismi, nazionalizmi e fundamentalizmi nei manuali di Storia*. Cagliari: AM&D.

CONTENTS

1 Legacy, Tradition, Heritage and the History Writing in the Balkans — 1
Diana Mishkova
Groundwork Concepts — 1
(Historical) Legacy — 3
Heritage/Patrimoine — 15
Epilogue: Historiographical Wars in International Law — 42
References — 44

2 Controversies Over Samuel's State — 51
Roumen Daskalov
The Pre-communist Bulgarian-Serbian Debates: A Synopsis — 52
Bulgarian-Serbian Controversies During the Socialist Regimes in Bulgaria and Yugoslavia — 65
Post-Communist Bulgarian-Serbian Controversies — 69
Bulgarian-Macedonian Controversies During Socialist Yugoslavia — 78
Bulgarian-Macedonian Polemics After the Creation of an Independent Macedonian State — 90
References — 100

xv

3 Skanderbeg: Figures of Paper, Figures of Stone — 105
Nathalie Clayer
Competing Historiographies in the Age of Imperialism and Nationalism — 107
1920–1943: Albanian State-Building and the Figure of Skanderbeg — 119
Skanderbeg Redrawn in the Ink and Stone of Communism — 131
Public Controversies in the "Cosmos of Democracy" — 141
Controversies in Form, Time, and Space — 151
References — 154

4 Art Wars: The Creation of Bulgarian Art History and the Balkan Controversies Over the Medieval Heritage of Macedonia — 161
Tchavdar Marinov
What Does Bulgarian Heritage Mean? — 166
The Macedonian Question in Art History — 171
War and Heritage — 176
The Birth of "Old Bulgarian art" — 182
Traits, Trajectories, and Territories of the "Bulgarian school" — 187
Serbian Ripostes — 191
Greek Ripostes — 195
Political Uses of Medieval Painting — 198
The Macedonian Heritage—To the Macedonians — 204
Epilogue — 207
References — 211

5 Defending Our Lands in Ancient and Medieval Studies: The Albanian Case — 219
Alexander Vezenkov
Territorial Disputes and Historical Arguments — 222
Albanian Lands in Albanian Academic Historiography — 229
The Spatial Dimension of the Illyrian Hypothesis — 238
The Illyro-Albanian Continuity in All Albanian Lands — 245
Pre-Ottoman and Ottoman Albania: Interpretations and Counter-Interpretations — 255
Conclusion — 263
References — 264

6 In Search of an Acceptable Past: The Bosnian Middle Ages and National Ideologies 275

Nedim Rabić

The Development of South Slavic Historiography and the Position of the Bosnian Middle Ages 280
The Invention of Medieval Bosnia as a "Serbian Land" 283
Croatization of the Bosnian Middle Ages 288
Heresy as National Myth: The Bosniak National Perspective 295
King Tvrtko I and the Issue of His Coronation 303
Concluding Remarks 310
References 311

Index 319

LIST OF CONTRIBUTORS

Nathalie Clayer Centre d'études turques, ottomanes, balkaniques et centrasiatiques, CNRS-EHESS, Paris, France

Roumen Daskalov Institute of Balkan Studies and Centre of Thracology at the Bulgarian Academy of Sciences, Sofia, Bulgaria

Tchavdar Marinov Institute of Philosophy and Sociology, Bulgarian Academy of Sciences, Sofia, Bulgaria

Diana Mishkova Centre for Advanced Study Sofia, Sofia, Bulgaria

Nedim Rabić Institute of History, University of Sarajevo, Sarajevo, Bosnia and Herzegovina

Alexander Vezenkov Institute of Balkan Studies and Centre of Thracology, Bulgarian Academy of Sciences, Sofia, Bulgaria

CHAPTER 1

Legacy, Tradition, Heritage and the History Writing in the Balkans

Diana Mishkova

> *Every history is by nature critical, and all historians have sought to*
> *denounce the hypocritical mythologies of their predecessors. But*
> *something fundamentally unsettling happens when history begins to*
> *write its own history*
> Nora (1989, 10)

GROUNDWORK CONCEPTS

At the core of most debates among Balkan historians over national identities and the possession, by virtue of purported bequest from the past, of segments of history—populations, historical personalities, achievements, even events or phenomena—several key concepts stand out: (historical) legacies, heritage (or patrimony), and tradition.

The American Heritage Dictionary of the English Language lists three meanings of "heritage": "1. Property that is or can be inherited; an inheritance. 2. Something that is passed down from preceding generations; a

---

D. Mishkova (✉)
Centre for Advanced Study Sofia, Sofia, Bulgaria
e-mail: mishkova@cas.bg

© The Author(s), under exclusive license to Springer Nature
Switzerland AG 2025
D. Mishkova, R. Daskalov (eds.), *Balkan Historiographical Wars*,
https://doi.org/10.1007/978-3-031-90113-3_1

1

tradition. 3. The status acquired by a person through birth; a birthright" (2016, 822). *The Oxford Dictionary of English* defines heritage as "property that is or may be inherited; an inheritance," "valued objects and qualities such as historic buildings and cultural traditions that have been passed down from previous generations," and "relating to things of special architectural, historical, or natural value that are preserved for the nation." The emphasis on inheritance and preservation is important here, as is the focus on "property," "things," "buildings" and "cultural traditions" (2010, online).

"Legacy" stands for: "1. (law) Money or property given to another by will. 2. Something handed down from an ancestor or a predecessor or from the past: a legacy of religious freedom. See synonyms at heritage" (*The American Heritage Dictionary* 2016, 1003); "'an amount of money or property left to someone in a will', 'something left or handed down by a predecessor'" (*The Oxford Dictionary of English* 2010, online).

In their French usage, however, "heritage" is semantically equivalent to the English "legacy," whereas "patrimoine" carries the same meaning as "heritage" in English.[1]

"Tradition," in turn, is taken to signify: "1. The passing down of elements of a culture from generation to generation, especially by oral communication. 2a. A mode of thought or behavior followed by a people continuously from generation to generation; a custom or usage. b. A set of such customs and usages viewed as a coherent body of precedents influencing the present. Latin traditio, tradition- < traditus, past participle of tradere, to hand over, deliver, entrust. Synonym heritage" (*The American Heritage Dictionary* 2016, 1841).

All these terms, therefore, carry similar meanings—something that is passed down—and are thus often used as synonyms in popular parlance. As *scholarly concepts*, however, they have parted ways during the last decades, whereby one observes a certain bifurcation between legacy and history, on the one hand, and heritage/patrimony and tradition, on the other. Thus we are faced with semantically identical but, in recent times, epistemologically diverging concepts, which divulge different kinds of relating the past to the present and bespeak different relations to the writing of history.

---

[1] The English 'patrinomy' derives from the old French *patrimoine* and signifies 'valued things passed down from previous generations; heritage' (*The Oxford Dictionary of English* online).

This introductory chapter ventures into a conceptual investigation of the above fundamental concepts—seen here not as an end in itself, but as a means of exposing the functions they play in approaching the past, in history writing, and, by extension, historiographical wars.

(Historical) Legacy

The concept of "historical legacies" has long enjoyed intellectual appeal for scholars of different hues aspiring to understand the influence of the past in the way the present is experienced and configured. As an object of research and debates about its definition, applicability, and explanatory power, however, it became prominent during the last thirty-odd years in the burgeoning field of post-communist studies. Indeed, the study of communist-era legacies has become the dominant paradigm for explaining social, political, and economic outcomes in post-communist Eastern Europe, and the findings of individual studies have emerged into a legacy paradigm within post-communist scholarship. However, while scholars agreed that aspects of the communist era had important consequences for post-communist outcomes on many levels, and shared the intuition that these aspects could be summarized by the term "legacies," they were found to "lack a shared set of assumptions, concepts, values, and practices that govern research on legacies" (LaPorte and Lussier 2011, 653).

Within this particular study field, Mark Beissinger and Stephen Kotkin tried to formulate a rigorous ("empirical") and comprehensive common definition of the "mercurial concept" of legacy and provide "guidelines for how the study of historical legacies should be approached." They define "legacy" as "a durable causal relationship between past institutions and policies on subsequent practices or beliefs, long beyond the life of the regimes, institutions, and policies that gave birth to them" (Beissinger and Kotkin 2014, 7). Central to this definition are several elements. First, it implies "macrohistorical rupture"—a requirement that disqualifies non-disruptive continuities as legacy: "Past and present are obviously interwoven in every society," they write. "But for us, broad continuity in and of itself does not qualify as a historical legacy. Rather legacy arguments only fit situations when there has been a significant rupture between past and present—an end to one order and the beginning of another—that the legacy is supposed to straddle." Revolutions, state collapse, decolonization, or major incidents of regime change present instances of such large-scale macrohistorical transformation (Beissinger and Kotkin 2014, 7–8).[2]

The focus on legacy as a "durable causal relationship" is the other key element in a legacy argument. A correlation, historical parallel, or similarity (isomorphism), Beissinger and Kotkin argue, is unlikely to clarify the mechanisms at work that link past and present; institutions, policies, and attitudes persisting in a new historical context, moreover, often do so in a modified form.[3] Similarly, for "revivals"—that is, practices brought back to life after having been previously eliminated—to be considered historical legacies one needs to demonstrate that they are not simply functional responses to similar problems (Beissinger and Kotkin 2014, 16). The same argument can be made regarding the distinction between "survival" versus "replication" mechanisms. Such caveats indicate that explanations alternative to a legacy argument should be seriously addressed, because "the persistence of a particular practice across a macrohistorical rupture may be due to multiple mechanisms—some functional, some historical— that intertwine, making the effect of a historical legacy difficult to assess" (Beissinger and Kotkin 2014, 20).

Considering the different ways the past "operates" in the present, the main question is how we identify and conceptualize legacies or, in the words of Jason Wittenberg, "what counts as a historical legacy and how legacies differ from non-legacies" (Wittenberg 2015, 366). Beissinger and Kotkin seek the answer in what they call a "generally empirical" approach, one that "move[s] away from a focus solely on formal, outward similarities

---

[2] Indeed, the magnitude of the rupture (the extent to which it involves a disruption to ongoing societal relationships) exercises "an independent effect on the degree to which old regime practices and beliefs might endure" (Beissinger and Kotkin 2014, 10).

[3] "Legacies are not the same phenomena as those to which they are related in the past, and almost always involve something new that combines past and present or applies the past in a different way. We therefor place less emphasis on similarity than on mechanisms and inter-connections between past and present" (Beissinger and Kotkin 2014, 11–12). The authors then proceed to outline a typology of legacies which differentiates between five kinds of legacy: "*fragmentation* involves inheritance of whole parts of institutions directly from an old regime; *translation* entails utilizing old institutions or practices for completely new purposes; *bricolage* means welding together bits of old and new institutions into something entirely new; *parameter setting* signifies the foreclosing of particular institutional or policy options because of constraints left over from the past; and *cultural schemata* refer to mental frames generated by past regime practices that make certain sorts of conduct seem normal and others unthinkable, foreign, or bizarre" (Beissinger and Kotkin 2014, 16).

towards a greater appreciation of relationships and mechanisms [and] drill[s] down to explain the specific linkages between past and present within concrete spheres of activity" (Beissinger and Kotkin 2014, 19).[4] Jason Wittenberg, on the other hand, vies to demonstrate the advantages of an analytical approach, identifying three components of a legacy argument: "an outcome that is not fully explainable from causes contemporaneous with that outcome, a cause or correlate that existed prior to the outcome, and potential (or at least speculative) links between the antecedent and the outcome. ... Outcomes, antecedents, and mechanisms form the scaffolding of legacy arguments." Accordingly, "where there is no correlation between outcome and antecedent, or where the outcome is new and thus has no phenomenologically equivalent antecedent, then there is discontinuity and a legacy can be excluded" (Wittenberg 2015, 369). Yet, as he admits, why some phenomena become legacies and others do not remains a tantalizing question. One may also add the difficulty social scientists face as to how to deal analytically with different layers of legacies (e.g., pre-communist and communist), particularly when they are contradictory, and how to explain why in some cases more distant legacies seem to matter more than the recent ones.

In all these attempts at conceptualization, undertaken mostly by social scientists, the actuality and ubiquity of historical legacies are not doubted. As the editors of a recent volume discussing the Balkan legacies of violent conflicts and ideological experiments put it, "Historical legacies are there whether or not contemporary actors wish them so, defining and circumscribing their actions. Legacies can be amplified or diminished, projected, twisted, suppressed, denied, celebrated, or mourned, but they are nevertheless omnipresent" (Apor and Newman 2021, 2). Taking on board the term as formative of the "ontology" of the Balkans as a historical region, historian Maria Todorova, too, posits the totality of past experiences that has an impact on the present. Legacy, she contends, does not involve an active process of conscious selection; it encompasses everything that is handed down from the past, whether one likes it or not: "In this sense it neither betrays the past nor surrenders to the agents' active meddling." A legacy can be variously evaluated by successors; however as an abstract signifier, it is neutral (Todorova 1997, 168, 2002, 470–92, 2005, 67–68).

---

[4] Herbert Kitschelt (Kitschelt 2003, 59) and Jody LaPorte and Danielle N. Lussier (LaPorte and Lussier 2011) also consider causal mechanisms to be central to the notion of legacy if it is to claim an explanatory/analytical value.

The core aim of its analysis is to make the effects of the past visible and intelligible to the observer.

This take on legacy stops short of addressing the main questions that bedevil the researchers of post-communism (and social scientists more broadly): by which criteria should we distinguish legacy from non-legacy; what standards shall we use to discriminate between formal similitude and legacy; and why do some institutions and practices persist (become legacies) whereas others do not? Considering specifically the non-selective nature of legacy and the multiple ways in which the past is implicated in the present, which manifestations of the past in the present should qualify as legacy? Instead, Todorova introduces, with reference to the Ottoman legacy, another distinction—between "legacy as continuity" and "legacy as perception." The former is treated as "the cluster of historical continuities" after a break—in this case secession from the Ottoman Empire and the formation of independent states—which can be objectively defined and objectively analyzed. The latter is "the highly subjective insider's approach, which can be defined as the evaluative and retrospective assessment of legacy from a present viewpoint" (Todorova 1995, 53). This, she asserts, should not be interpreted as "real" versus "imagined" legacies since both categories designate social facts—just as the characteristics of the continuity are often perceptual, so the perceptions are no less a matter of continuous real social facts. Yet they are at different removes from experience: since "legacy as perception" captures the dynamic relationship between the ever-accumulating historical experiences and the ever-changing perceptions and representations of these experiences, it stands as a social fact further removed from immediate reality. Such re-evaluations amount not to reconstructing, but rather to constructing the past in works of historiography, literature, journalism, and everyday discourse (Todorova 2005, 69–70).[5] Other authors make a similar distinction between "actual" and "believed" legacy and see the two "in a relationship of tense controversy" and "constant rivalry": while the actual legacy persists in the daily life of modern citizens, the believed legacy is a product of the construction of grand national narratives and historiographies (Millas 2008, 17–18). "Legacy as perception" or "believed legacy," in this sense, closely resembles "heritage" and "tradition," as will be shown further.

---

[5] In all spheres except the demographic and the sphere of popular culture, Todorova contends, the break with the empire was completed by the end of World War I, turning thereafter into legacy as perception (Todorova 1997, 169–83).

Legacy Versus legacy discourse

Here we see a certain bifurcation of approach between present-day social science and historiography: whereas the former delves into gauging the *actual* ramifications of the past in the present, and thus uses "legacy" as a category of analysis, the latter is concerned above all with the way the past's imprints should be interpreted and evaluated, thus with "legacy discourse."[6] Legacies, write the editors of a volume dedicated to the impact of Ottoman and Habsburg rule in Southeastern Europe, "are very much open to constant reinterpretations and re-assessments according to perceived necessities in the present. The images they promote are as much shaped by the present as they are by the past" (Sindbaek and Hartmuth 2011, 2). While stepping on a fundamental agreement about the objective existence of historical legacies, historians have busied themselves with interpreting (the value or influence of) legacy—or revisiting other historians' interpretations—rather than exploring the "reality" of legacy. Contemporary takes on the phenomenon and the concept of legacy tend to "discuss 'imprints' beyond the assumption that historical or imperial legacies can be objectively defined or analysed," and treat legacy primarily as subject to different and changing retrospective re-assessments and reinterpretations, and therefore as a very flexible category (Sindbaek and Hartmuth 2011, 4; see also Gangloff 2005).

The legacies which have been crucial for the formation of the national narratives in the Balkans are those of antiquity (bound up with issues of ethnogenesis), the "national-medieval" (related to state and "nationality" formation), the imperial (above all Byzantine and Ottoman), and, most recently, the communist (combined, in former Yugoslavia, with the legacy of the wars of secession). As treated by the national historiographies, and problematized by the authors in this volume, the former two are more properly associated with the categories "invented tradition" and "heritage discourse," which will be discussed in the second part of this chapter, rather than with "legacy" and "legacy discourse." In what follows, therefore, I will try to illustrate, by necessity sketchily, the mutable and

---

[6] That being said, social scientists are not necessarily inimical to operating with variants of perceived legacy. Thus Harris Mylonas has stressed the importance of what he calls "manufactured legacy," arguing that "in some cases, what appears to be an actual legacy is rather a manufactured one resulting from governmental elites' agency acting strategically to maintain and repurpose an institution for their own purposes." (Mylonas 2019, 867).

controversial historiographical interpretations of the Byzantine and Ottoman legacies, whose strong impact was never denied.[7]

It may come as a surprise to most present-day visitors to Greece to learn that the modern Greeks' conception of their historical lineage to ancient Greece did not come about before the late eighteenth and early nineteenth centuries. In the Ottoman realm until that time, religiously determined identity, nurtured by the administrative system of the Ottoman Empire, overrode linguistic and cultural differences, and the Greek-speaking literati espoused a strictly Christian perspective on the past informed by Orthodox providentialism in the vein of a Byzantine literary convention. It was Western admiration of classical Greece that induced Greek nationalists to emulate ancient Athenians and pen their 1822 charter (the Constitution of Epidaurus) in language so archaic few could fathom it, while cleansing Greek folklore of later tales to stress continuity with classical precepts (Herzfeld 1982, 6, 20, 85–86). Under the spell of the Enlightenment, the Greek intellectuals of that time repudiated the whole Middle Ages and Byzantium as a dark period of decadence, slavery, and Roman tyranny, and deemed any reference to a Byzantine Greek legacy to be offensive to the Greeks. Medieval Greek history and that of Byzantium have nothing to do with each other, the future architect of the Greek historical master narrative, Constantine Paparrigopoulos, averred in his early writings. Around the mid-nineteenth century a confluence of international and domestic developments in politics and historiography, compounded by a hurtful foreign "provocation"—the German historian Jakob Philipp Fallmerayer's contention that the modern Greeks were Hellenized Slavs and Albanians—coalesced to wreak a major reversal. The fervor to prove Fallmerayer wrong and the felt imperative to fill in the gap between ancient and modern Greece mobilized an extensive and sustained scholarly effort. Several generations of historians, folklorists, linguists, and literary scholars exerted themselves to "expose" the Greekness of Byzantium and assert the uninterrupted continuity from ancient to modern Greece through the "middle bond" of Byzantium—the irredeemable eternal Hellenism *tout court*—which forms the backbone of the Greek grand narrative to this day.

---

[7] For a detailed account of the way the legacy of Byzantium has been interpreted and assessed in the historiographies of Bulgaria, Greece, Romania, Serbia, and Turkey from the Enlightenment to the present day, see Mishkova (2023).

The humanist writers of the seventeenth-century Romanian principalities Moldavia and Wallachia, considered to be the real founders of national Romanian historiography, showed strong attachment to the memory of Byzantium and its civilization. The national identity they sought to inculcate had an important Byzantine dimension, in that they stressed the formative connection of Romanian history with that of Byzantium, thus vindicating the "nobility" of the Romanians. The Transylvanian (or Latinist) School, which dominated Romanian history writing from the late eighteenth century through the 1860s, broke radically with this humanist tradition. Seeking to demonstrate the Latin purity of the Romanian race and its civilizational mission in "the East," the Romanian Latinists degraded Byzantium to an "Eastern empire," a "kingdom of the Greeks," who had usurped the name "Roman" and the role of custodians of the empire at the expense of its legitimate and rightful heirs—the Romanians. A new turnabout in the interpretation of the Byzantine legacy in Romanian history was executed by the great "national historian" of the first half of the twentieth century, Nicolae Iorga, who bestowed on the Romanians the role of the only real successors and perpetuators—spiritual and civilizational—of Byzantium after the empire's political demise in 1453. It was the synthesis between Byzantium and Rome, his re-interpretation drove home, that shaped the unique character of Romanian civilization, and it was this synthesis that secured the Romanians' place in world history.

The metamorphosis of opinion regarding Byzantine legacy in Bulgarian history was no less spectacular. For the nineteenth-century national "revivalists" Byzantium was not merely the political rival and, in certain periods, oppressor of the medieval Bulgarians; Byzantium and its cultural influence were held responsible for having corrupted the Bulgarian national character and caused deep cleavages in Bulgarian society. Historiography between the two world wars, as exemplified by the then foremost Bulgarian medievalist Petăr Mutafchiev, further dramatized the effects of the Byzantine legacy on the "historical fate" of Bulgaria by transforming it into the evil demiurge of all Bulgarian history and holding "Byzantinism" responsible for the abnormal dynamism of Bulgarian life with its "abrupt turns of might and weakness, contradictions, extremes and crises" (Mutafchiev 1931). After World War II the pendulum swung in the opposite direction as the Byzantine legacy became "assimilated" into the Bulgarian narrative in the form of a "Slavo-Byzantine" cultural synthesis and an institutional paragon for the medieval Bulgaria states.

The trajectory of the late Ottoman and the republican Turkish historiographies followed another course: whereas late Ottoman imperial historiography and art history were pluralistic and open to admitting Byzantine imprints on different levels, the Republican historiography, sometimes featuring the same authors, recognized no role for its predecessor other than that of a decayed rival, surrendered by the formidable Ottoman might. Similar in vicissitudes was the interpretation of the "Slavic legacy" in Romanian medieval and modern culture.

In contrast, there existed remarkably uniform and perennial discourses about the Ottoman legacy in the different Balkan countries except Turkey, notwithstanding some more nuanced assessments of certain periods or social spheres in present-day national historiographies. Conceived as having originated with an alien civilization—one that was forcibly imposed on the Balkan societies, interrupted their natural evolution, and isolated them from European developments—the legacy of the centuries-long Ottoman rule was and, in most cases, is still seen as the main source of the backwardness and all kind of deficiencies in the modern development of these societies. A product, like so many other elements of the national-historical narratives, of the age of "national revivalism" with its bedrock in romanticism and positivism, this interpretation has proved strikingly identical and stable across Balkan historiographies, engulfing nationalist and Marxist, liberal and conservative discourses alike. Albeit less dominant and uncontested, such views can be encountered even in mostly Muslim societies such as that of Albania. Addressing the lack of democracy in the modern Albanian state, Arshi Pipa, an Albanian philosopher and writer, holds that this state of affairs "can be explained by the heritage of Ottoman absolutism. The Ottoman occupation ... brought in an alien culture which caught on in Albania faster than in any other part of the Balkans (except Bosnia). The Ottoman legacy weighs heavily on Albanians' shoulders, a burden of which they will not easily be rid" (Pipa 1990, 39–40; cit. in Clayer 2005, 103).

Such extraordinary uniformity and longevity of interpretation can be ascribed not only to the violent confrontation with the Ottoman Empire in the course of the national liberation struggles in the nineteenth century. It can as well be attributed to an abiding sense of failed or piecemeal modernization and deficient "Europeanness" that permeated the empire's successor states (an issue that is hardly ever discussed in such debates is the fact that what the authors consider Ottoman legacies are often "Western" legacies filtered through the Ottoman world). Such a view, at the same time, serves to exculpate the modern Balkan institutions and societies from responsibility for their shortcomings, social and economic problems by externalizing the "guilt" to an outside force and succumbing to victimization (Sindbaek and Hartmuth 2011, 5).[8] A major problem that such treatment of Ottoman rule and its legacy entails is that the admission of a brutal historical rupture means radical discontinuity with the medieval Balkan states and the obliteration of their political, social, and economic legacies. This goes a long way toward explaining the critical weight assigned to arguments based on ethnogenesis and autochthony, on the one hand, and to the continuity of culture, identity, and (at least implicitly) race over that of statehood, on the other—issues that will be addressed in the second part of this chapter.

Although the mainstream Balkan historiographies, eager to exorcise the legacy of a fallen enemy, consider modern Turkey to be the only heir to the Ottoman Empire, the adoption of the empire's legacy in Turkey itself has been anything but unequivocal. Between the early 1920s, when the Turkish Republic was founded, and the 2000s, assessments of the legacy of the Ottoman Empire in Turkish historiography underwent a dramatic metamorphosis from oblivion to rehabilitation to full-blown resurrection. For the Kemalists, as for the nationalists in the rest of the Balkans, the Ottoman Empire was a retrograde, corrupt ancien régime, which had little to offer to a Western-oriented, secular, and modernizing nation-state and whose legacy was looked down on, ignored, or condemned. Concurrent with the political changes unleashed after World War II, the 1970s–1980s saw the crystallization of the so-called Turkish-Islamic synthesis, whereby both Islam and the Ottoman legacy were redeemed as pillars of modern Turkish identity. The latest phase in this transition was the shift toward romantic neo-Ottomanism, which started in the mid-1990s and came to the fore with Recep Tayyip Erdoğan and his Justice and Development Party's rise to power in the 2000s.

Interestingly, the 1980s also saw the memory of the Habsburg Empire undergo a similar transformation, underpinned by a notion of "Central Europe" which pursued emancipation from the Soviet sphere. Instead of being a "prison of nations," a recurring trope in both nationalist and Marxist lingos until then, it came to feature as a "multicultural" empire,

---

[8] See in this sense Milošević (2011, 76), where the author asks the provocative but reasonable question: "what can be inferred about a people that chose or were able to adopt only the negative aspects of an alien culture?"

an epitome of true European values and a superior culture, drawing on diversity and defying both the Soviet East and the consumerist West (Mishkova 2021, 53–59).

To state that the legitimacy of a new regime depends to a great extent on rejecting the old political system and manipulating its legacy appears truistic. But as the treatment of the Habsburg legacy indicates, major shifts in the international environment may also lead to shifts in the evaluation of a legacy previously rejected. The interwar Balkanologists, who strove to counter the geopolitical threats to small states by foregrounding the commonalities between the Balkan peoples, provide another eloquent example. In their writings, not only the Roman and Byzantine historical substrata feature as constitutive of a common "Balkan civilization," but the Ottoman legacy also appears in a different light: they argued that precisely the backwardness of the Ottomans made possible the preservation of the Balkan nationalities; had the empire been more advanced, that is, more like the West, these nationalities would have perished (Mishkova 2019, 78–80).

The Instrumentalization of Legacy

In contrast to heritage, as we will shortly see, legacies primarily become matters of controversy not between, but within states. Debates on (the assessment of) legacy do not, as a rule, spark wars between national historiographies but rather inside them—a phenomenon Nathalie Clayer throws into full relief further in this volume. If the debates about the meaning of the Ottoman legacy have pitted against each other Turkish and other Balkan historiographies, those concerning the legacy of World War II *within* post-Yugoslav Serbian and Croatian historiographies or those about the communist legacy in Bulgaria or Romania (often in juxtaposition to their pre–World War II legacies) have spilled far beyond the historical profession and engendered violent disagreements in politics and society.

The case of the Muslim Bosniaks is intriguing in this respect as it demonstrates how concurrent yet diverging challenges concerning identity or political choice may induce controversial assessments of legacy. As Xavier Bougarel points out, the same scholars, who may valorize the Ottoman period in order to disprove an idea dear to the Serbian nationalists—that of the "Turkish yoke"—and thus affirm Bosnian identity as distinct from the Serbian, may also disdain it when partaking in European civilization, or taking a stance between nationalists and non-nationalists, is at stake (Bougarel 2005, 65, 72; see also Hajdarpašić 2008, 715–34). A similar "double phenomenon of rejection and rehabilitation" as regards Islamic religion and identity—the most consequential vestige of Ottoman rule—exists to this day within Albanian society. Next to the narrative of the "five-hundred-year Asiatic domination," which reflected the nationalist, communist and atheistic point of view (and which after 1989 was espoused by those seeking the integration of Albania within Europe), there was another trend, which first emerged among the Albanians in Kosovo and Macedonia and was later "exported" to Albania. It stressed the positive consequences of Ottoman expansion in the Balkans and Islamization in that they had stopped the assimilation of the Albanians by the Slavs and thus preserved the Albanian national identity. This latter interpretation, which retrieved the Muslim identity of the Albanians, had everything to do with the Kosovars' opposition to the Serbs, especially following the Serbian repressions against the Kosovo Albanians in 1981 (Clayer 2005, 95–128). As in the case of Bosnia, one can see how closely the assessment of legacy hinges upon issues of identity (re-)formulation and positionality. The necessity to demonstrate distinctiveness—from the Serbs, the Montenegrins, and the Macedonians in the case of Albania, or from the Serbs and the Croats in the Bosnian case—and to advance demands for territorial autonomy on this basis ultimately shaped the (recognized) imprints of the past.

The turn in Turkey since the mid-1990s toward neo-Ottomanism—as Turkey's use of the Ottoman legacy to resolve internal socio-cultural tensions and vindicate Turkish foreign policies came to be dubbed—occurred at a time of rising ethnic and religious claims within the country, the emergence of new Turkic states in Central Asia, and the dissolution of Yugoslavia. Neo-Ottomanism was originally formulated with the double aim to increase "political and cultural tolerance for diversity [in Turkey] as in the Ottoman past" and "eliminate economic borders among the Balkan, Caucasian, and Middle Eastern countries" (Yavuz 1998, 40). It thus combined economic globalization with the formulation of a common, superior identity encompassing all Turkish citizens within an ethnic-religious affiliation. As part of this maneuver, the "neo-Ottomanist" writers took on board the idea of Ottoman pluralism, as the legal framework for the peaceful coexistence of different ethno-religious and cultural groups under a political community, and reconstructed it by linking a traditional form of pluralism (the Ottoman *millet* system) with modern liberal multiculturalism. During and after the Yugoslav wars, this "melting pot" aspect of the strategy receded in favor of its foreign application, which emphasized Islamic solidarity and the community of post-Ottoman Balkan Muslims (Çolak 2008, 147–57; Onar 2009, 1–16). This, in turn, provoked a strong reaction on the part of Balkan historians, especially in Serbia, who saw neo-Ottomanism as providing, under the pretense of concern for the fate of Muslims, a rationale to meddle in the affairs of Balkan states (particularly with respect to Bosnia and Herzegovina and Kosovo), as heralding a resurgence of the Ottoman-era violent Islamization strategy, and as part of the greater agenda of a pan-Islamic state unification to be led by Turkey (for such responses in Serbian historiography see Dević 2016, 542–6).

Interestingly, the initial construction of neo-Ottomanism in a liberal multicultural vein was accompanied by an attempt at revamping yet another legacy in the Turkish historical self-narration. In 1988, the Turkish prime minister, and later president of Turkey, Turgut Özal published, in French, a book titled *Turkey in Europe*. This seemingly non-professional work (in the production of which, however, professional historians were involved) came forth with the, from a Turkish point of view, utterly unorthodox thesis that the political, social, economic, and military structures and institutions of the Ottoman Empire had been inherited from Byzantium. Such heretical reading can only be explained by recalling that the book appeared at a time when Turkey was campaigning actively for admission into the European Community as a full member. Özal unabashedly implicated the (previously suppressed) Byzantine legacy in service to this strategic goal: "Today Byzantine culture," he wrote, "is considered unquestionably to be a part of Western civilization. In so far as we have shown that there were numerous similarities between the Eastern Roman Empire and the Ottoman Empire, one could conclude that Ottoman culture is also a part of Western culture" (Özal 1991, 169).

Some scholars, on the other hand, have pointed to the considerable risks of insisting on longer-term historical legacies, particularly with respect to symbolically denigrated regions such as the Balkans. Such an interpretative key, the argument goes, "can reinforce postcolonial cultural stereotypes about the immutable and static nature of the region, where historical change in the short- and the mid-terms is ignored or neglected, and events are explained with reference to the distant past." This kind of thinking was much in evidence during the Yugoslav wars of the 1990s, during which their immediate causes "were either neglected or elided as part of a longer-term and unbroken history of violence that dated back to the Ottoman period or even before" (Apor and Newman 2021, 5). By stressing mechanisms of "path dependency" social scientists appear particularly prone to this mode of interpreting what many of them see as a Balkan *Sonderweg* (see, as pars pro toto, Dimitrova-Grajzl 2007, 539–58). But historians in the Balkans, too, can be complicit in such representations. In a recent book, tellingly titled *The Wars of the Balkan Peninsula: Their Medieval Origins*, Romanian historian Alexandru Madgearu argues that "the ethnic changes that occurred during the Middle Ages in the Balkan Peninsula can be taken as a premise for the understanding of what happened in the nineteenth and twentieth centuries." The Ottoman Empire *"preserved in latency the ethnic and religious differences and antagonisms that rose with extreme violence in the nineteenth century. This was the distant background of the Balkan wars of 1912–1913, of the Balkan campaigns of the two world wars, and of the conflicts carried on in the Yugoslavian space after 1989"* (Madgearu 2008, 38, 97–98; original emphases). Here, as in other treatises on the Balkans, it is the invincibility and pervasiveness of legacies that stand out, marking a region incarcerated by history.

Heritage/Patrimoine

Heritage today, writes one of its prominent students, "is a broad and slippery term," a "conveniently ambiguous" concept that has been applied to many different social and political ends. It might be used to describe anything from the solid—such as buildings, monuments, and memorials ("tangible heritage"), to the ethereal—languages, ethnicity, and religion ("intangible heritage" or "heritage practices"). It is a constantly evolving concept, and the way in which it is understood is always ambiguous and uncertain (Harrison 2013, 5, 6, 14). Heritage, according to UNESCO's definition, "is our legacy from the past, what we live with today, and what we pass on to future generations. Our cultural and natural heritage are both irreplaceable sources of life and inspiration" (UNESCO n.d.). Over the past four decades there has been a process of "dematerializing" heritage by introducing an ever-increasing emphasis on the intangible aspects of heritage and tradition, those that "inform who we are as collectives, and help to create our collective social memory" (Harrison 2010, 9).

Heritage is very much culture-embedded—hence the syntagmatic "cultural" or "cultural-historical heritage"—closely linked with collective

16 D. MISHKOVA

identity and collective memory formation. As the Heritage Council, established under the Heritage Act of 1995, defines it,

> Our tangible, intangible and natural heritage and all the associated *myths, legends, traditions, and memories* provide us with a *common language and insight that enables us to communicate on a deep level with each other and to express ourselves in a unique way* to the outside world. In helping shape our identity, *our heritage becomes part of what we are.* Our expression of this identity highlights our values and priorities. Our heritage … helps us *understand and explain why we are the way we are.* Heritage is a keystone of our culture that plays an important role in our politics, society, business and world view. It informs, influences and inspires public debate and policy both directly and indirectly. (Heritage Council n.d.; emphases added)

"Having a heritage" is, in other words, an integral part of "having an identity," and it warrants the right to exist in the present and continue into the future.

A look at the internet sites of institutions and projects dealing with cultural heritage, particularly at the way they define their object of concern, displays how much the contemporary meaning of heritage has broadened its original semantics to imply something all-encompassing and almost metaphysical:

> Simply put, heritage is the past made present. Heritage is a *fundamental source of individual and group identity, vitality, and solidarity.* Heritage is a universal process by which humans maintain connections with our pasts, assert our similarities with and differences from one another, and tell our children and other young people *what we think is important and deserves to be part of the future.* Heritage is not just 'out there.' Heritage *guides each of us from within* on a daily basis. Heritage is a powerful source of practical suggestions on what to wear, what to eat, how to behave. Clothes, foods, stories, songs, and the patterned actions of the people around you influence your values and preferences. Heritage is one of the ways you *determine right from wrong, beautiful from repulsive,* meaningful from ridiculous, and so on. The preferences embedded in *what we think, say, and do* are important building blocks for communities, regions, and nations. Be mindful of your heritage, for it *helps determine your destiny and that of your descendants!* (IPinCH 2014; emphases added)

> Cultural heritage implies a shared bond, *our belonging to a community.* It represents *our history and our identity;* our bond to the past, to our present,

and the future. … But cultural heritage is not just a set of cultural objects or traditions from the past. It is also *the result of a selection process: a process of memory and oblivion* that characterizes every human society constantly engaged in choosing—for both cultural and political reasons—what is worthy of being preserved for future generations and what is not. (Google Classroom n.d.; emphases added)

It is precisely the pervasive "relics" from the past, which far outstrip material vestiges, on the one hand, and the protean discourse of heritage, on the other, that invite a juxtaposition of heritage with legacy and history. Several elements stand out in the above descriptions. First, heritage is not a "thing" but refers to a set of attitudes to, and relationships with, the past. These relationships are characterized by selection ("a process of memory and oblivion") guided by reverence ("what is important and deserves to be part of the future") and which connects with or exemplifies the past in a particular way (see in this sense also Walsh 1992; Harvey 2001, 2008; Smith 2006). Second, heritage is formed in the present and reflects inherited and current concerns about the past. It is by definition "the contemporary uses of the past," the "active processing" of the past. If "legacy" can be summarized as the force that the past exerts on the present, "heritage" can be summarized as the force that the present exerts on the past (Lowenthal 2004, 19–23; Ashworth and Graham 1997, 381; Tunbridge and Ashworth 1996, 20–21). Thirdly heritage is loaded with a sense of possession: "We value our heritage most when it seems at risk; threats of loss spur owners to stewardship. … Heritage never means more to us than when we see it inherited by someone else" (Lowenthal 1998, 24). This sense of possession explains why heritage, unlike legacy, is by default parceled or territorialized into national compartments, and as such acts in an exclusionary way: "All heritage is someone's heritage and therefore logically not someone else's: the original meaning of an inheritance (from which 'heritage' derives) implies the existence of disinheritance and by extension any creation of heritage from the past disinherits someone completely or partially, actively or potentially" (Tunbridge and Ashworth 1996, 21).

Heritage and Tradition

Both historical legacy and cultural(-historical) heritage are critical sources of group identity. Yet the difference between them is not trivial. Heritage is selective, valorized, and aestheticized legacy—a cherished, domesticated past celebrated for present minded purposes and commanding reverence and obligation. It is not a process of simply preserving things from the past, but an active process of selecting from that past what "we choose to hold up as a mirror to the present, associated with a particular set of values that we wish to take with us into the future" (Harrison 2013, 4). Contrary to legacy, where it is the donor who calls the tune, with heritage the recipients can choose to accept or reject the inheritance, or to select what they would like to preserve among what is on offer. Triumphs and achievements, or sacrifices involved in the struggle for recognition are the typical titleholders. Events and material remains which do not fit into such narratives are likely to be publicly ignored, destroyed, or "killed by silence." Thus, in most mainstream Balkan historiographies, save the Turkish and more recently the Bosnian, one can encounter references to Ottoman legacy (or "remnants," "left overs," "obsoleteness"), but not to Ottoman heritage; the latter term is preserved for prestigious bequests, such as the ancient or the "national"-medieval, and occasionally the Byzantine.[9]

This bespeaks close filiation between heritage and tradition, as the latter has been conceptualized in cultural history. Although the term "tradition" (from the Latin *tradere*—to hand over or deliver), Raymond Williams writes, has survived as a description of a general process of handing down, characteristic of its common usage is that "there is a very strong and often predominant sense of this entailing respect and duty." Considering how much has been handed down to us, it is obvious that "only some of [the many] traditions or parts of them have been selected for our respect and duty"—a discrimination that "in its own way, is both a betrayal and a surrender." As to the claims to the antiquity of tradition, "it only takes two generations to make anything traditional: naturally enough, since that is the sense of tradition as active process" (Williams 2015, 252). Intrinsic to the notion of tradition, in contrast to historical legacy, therefore, is a

---

[9] A relatively recent concept, "difficult heritage," presents a special case. Being used specifically for material remains of dictatorship—sites, buildings, and monuments closely associated with Nazism, Fascism, or State Socialism, especially heavily burdened places of "pain and shame" connected to death, trauma and suffering—it stands for unsettling and awkward pasts that *should be remembered*. It is typically considered in studies of transitional justice and the ways post-authoritarian European societies have negotiated the uncomfortable physical remains of dictatorship (See in particular Macdonald 2009 and the special section, "The Difficult Heritage of Dictatorship in Europe," in the *Journal of Contemporary History* 59, no. 1, January 2024).

1 LEGACY, TRADITION, HERITAGE AND THE HISTORY WRITING... 19

conscious selection from a cumulative mass of matters handed down and an active attitude underpinned by respect and duty; it is "a deliberately selective and connecting process which offers an historical and cultural ratification of a contemporary order" (Williams 1977, 115–16).

Like tradition, "all heritage is constructed, in the sense that people or communities have selectively assembled, defined, and validated those things that they wish to consider components of the heritage" (*Concise Oxford Dictionary of Archaeology* 2021 *online*: entry "heritage").[10] For that reason, both are positively valued (commanding "respect and duty"). Indeed, the expansive idea of "heritage" has become closely associated with the concept of tradition, such that the terms are often used interchangeably or synonymously. Already in the mid-twentieth century the properties of the interlinked notions of tradition and heritage drew the attention of some critical authors. The precursors of what was later to become "critical heritage studies" originated in the revisionist analyses of the use of the past by political power to build a sense of national identity. These analyses emerged, synchronically yet largely independently of each other, from within the fields of cultural studies, history, and archaeology.

While students of culture and cultural vocabulary devoted much energy to theorizing what was essentially selective about traditions, a contemporary generation of historians alighted upon the idea of an ever growing production of "traditions" by modern nations. In a provocative introduction to a collective volume famously titled *The Invention of Tradition* (1983), Eric Hobsbawn argued that, whatever the historic or other continuities embedded in the modern nation-state,

> these very concepts themselves must include a constructed or "invented" component. And just because so much of what subjectively makes up the modern "nation" consists of such constructs and is associated with appropriate and, in general, fairly recent symbols or suitably tailored discourse (such as "national history"), the national phenomenon cannot be adequately investigated without careful attention to the "invention of tradition." (Hobsbawm 1983a, 13–14)[11]

[10] The entry continues: "Scale is often important here, and the appropriation of a heritage is often linked to the creation of global, national, or local identity. Once defined, in whatever way, the material that is taken as being the heritage is often commodified and exploited for educational, economic, or political gain, or simply as diverting entertainment."

[11] Hobsbawm's own contribution was an exploration of the "mass-production" of traditions in Europe in the period 1870–1914 (Hobsbawm 1983b).

20   D. MISHKOVA

Hobsbawm foregrounded the key role of historians in minting and validating traditions with the object of re-interpreting past events as "national" history, of rooting a contemporary sense of nationhood in a heroic past and of cloaking the present with the respectability of antiquity:

> [T]he history which became part of the fund of knowledge or the ideology of nation, state or movement is not what has actually been preserved in popular memory, but what has been selected, written, pictured, popularised and institutionalised by those whose function it is to do so. ... [A]ll historians, whatever else their objectives, are engaged in this process inasmuch as they contribute, consciously or not, to the creation, dismantling and restructuring of images of the past which belong not only to the world of specialist investigation but to the public sphere of man as a political being. (Hobsbawm 1983a, 13)[12]

The impulse that brought together the cultural-conceptual and the historical debate lay in the "recognition of the degree to which tradition and heritage represent a means for those in the present to organize the (historical) past—sometimes for overtly ideological ends" (Schwarz 2005, 154).

A critical reflection on the contribution of archaeology to this "inventive" process, one that focuses on the political use of the discipline in nation-building, developed in parallel. In his influential article on the topic, Bruce Trigger (1984) suggested that, depending on the position of countries in the world system, there are different archaeologies—nationalist, colonialist, and imperialist—and these archaeologies provide alternative interpretations of the past. Phillip Kohl and Clare Fawcett's edited collection *Nationalism, Politics, and the Practice of Archaeology* (1995), and the work of others, testified to an increasing interest within archaeology during the 1980s and 1990s in the social construction of archaeological knowledge and the social, economic, and political contexts in which this knowledge was formed. Contemporary developments in the field of anthropology followed a similar route, as exemplified by Michael Herzfeld's influential work on the persistent manipulation of Greek

---

[12] Hobsbawm distinguishes three types of invented traditions, each with a distinctive function: (a) those establishing or symbolizing social cohesion and collective identities; (b) those establishing or legitimatizing institutions and social hierarchies; and (c) those socializing people into particular social contexts. The first type has been the most common, often taken to imply the two other functions as well (Hobsbawm 1983a).

folklore to stress continuity with classical paragons (Herzfeld 1982). This literature drew attention to the many ways in which archaeology, folklore, and "the past" were employed in nation-building and put to political use, some positive but many negative, and mostly from twentieth-century contexts. All of this work led to an acknowledgment of the need to question the social and political contexts in which historical knowledge was produced.

Heritage Versus History

Significantly, the 1980s also saw the beginnings of what was to become the burgeoning field of "(critical) heritage studies." Yet the parallelism in the development of modern notions of heritage and history (or history-writing) can be detected much earlier. Most commentators place the origins of the modern philosophies that underlie approaches to heritage and history in the context of late Enlightenment thought and the rise of nation-states in the eighteenth and nineteenth centuries. Both reflected a modern, linear notion of time that emphasized progress in its separation of past from present. By the end of the nineteenth century, contemporaneous with the institutionalization of the positivist paradigm in history, a concept of heritage had become established "as part of a broader conversation about what was important from the past in forming a set of values for the appropriate functioning of societies in the present" (Harrison 2013, 23–46). During the twentieth century heritage became increasingly controlled and defined by legislation and the state as part of the process of nation-building. The Hague Convention (1954) followed by the Venice Charter (1964) are significant in this sense in that they recognized an explicit connection between cultural heritage and national identity, and the use of heritage in nation-building. From the early 1970s on, a time that saw the rise of comparative and transnational history, the notion of "World Heritage," underpinned by belief in the existence of universal heritage value, was gaining ground.[13] The "heritage boom" that followed went hand in hand with a widespread commercialization of heritage: it ceased to be simply a part of the educative apparatus of the nation-state and became an all pervasive industry in its own right.[14]

---

[13] For this second phase in the history of heritage see Harrison (2013, 46–95).
[14] For an early critical reading of these developments see Hewison (1987).

22   D. MISHKOVA

In this context, and in communication with the aforementioned critical trends in historiography, the field of "heritage studies" began to crystalize, as signaled by the works of cultural historians Patrick Wright (1985) and Robert Hewison (1987), and above all the historian and geographer David Lowenthal (1985, 1998). Central to their arguments is the distinction they make between heritage and history. "Heritage is not history at all," Lowenthal averred; "while it borrows from and enlivens historical study, heritage is not an inquiry into the past but a celebration of it, not an effort to know what actually happened but a profession of faith in a past tailored to present day purposes" (Lowenthal 1998, x). This, however, should not be read as reifying some kind of "true history" that retrieves the past in its actual entirety against "bogus history" that swerves from the truth. *Any* history is less than the past since "three things limit what can be known: the immensity of the past itself, the distinction between past events and accounts of those events, and the inevitability of bias—especially presentist bias" (Lowenthal 1985, 214). If history is not the assembly of historical facts, "like stamp collecting or antiquarianism," Edward H. Carr once wrote, then "the facts of history do not exist until a historian creates them" (Carr 1961, 15, 21).

Objectivity remains a holy grail for even the most engaged historian. However, as Lowenthal observes, "to strive for impartiality is one thing; to achieve it another. History as actually written was usually as much moral precept as past record. ... Patriotism continues to shape much history writing and inspires most of its teaching to this day. ... National fealty remains the prime purpose of historical study." Furthermore, everything we see is filtered through present-day mental lenses, while today's perspective makes us more likely to misinterpret the past as remoteness multiplies its anachronisms. "To explain the past to the present means coping not only with shifting perceptions, values, and languages, but also with developments after the period under review" (Lowenthal 1985, 216–17, 1998, 106, 109–10, 112–15).

History, therefore, cannot avoid being incomplete, biased and present minded:

> History differs from heritage not ... in telling the truth, but in trying to do so despite being aware that truth is a chameleon and its chroniclers fallible beings. The most crucial distinction is that truth in heritage commits us to some present creed; truth in history is a flawed effort to understand the past

1 LEGACY, TRADITION, HERITAGE AND THE HISTORY WRITING... 23

on its own terms. Yet historians are also urged to make history "relevant"—in short, to turn it into heritage. (Lowenthal 1998, 119)

The two enterprises are thus inextricably conjoined, but they serve dissimilar intents and goals:

> The historian, however blinkered and presentist and self-deceived, seeks to convey a past consensually known, open to inspection and proof, continually revised and eroded as time and hindsight outdate its truths. The heritage fashioner, however historically scrupulous, seeks to design a past that will fix the identity and enhance the well-being of some chosen individual or folk. ... The aims that animate these two enterprises, and their modes of persuasion, are contrary to each other. [...] History seeks to convince by truth and succumbs to falsehood. Heritage exaggerates and omits, candidly invents and frankly forgets, and thrives on ignorance and error. (Lowenthal 1998, 87, 121–2)

The kind of history Lowenthal contrasts with heritage is a "comprehensive, collaborative enterprise, open to all—comprehensive in being part of a universal chronology, collaborative in embracing the findings of myriad colleagues, open in permitting any scrutiny. ... The idea of history as universal, and universally accessible, is widely endorsed. ... It is such history that I contrast here with heritage." Other kinds of history—tribal, exclusive, patriotic, redemptive, or self-aggrandizing as well as school history teaching "blind allegiance to nation, state, or faith"—are, by and large, "heritage masquerading as history." Therefore, "*heritage diverges from history not in being biased but in its attitude toward bias* ... while historians aim to reduce bias, heritage sanctions and strengthens it" (Lowenthal 1998, 119; original emphasis).[15]

The worst fault charged against heritage is that it breeds belligerent antagonism stemming from the fact that heritage always "belongs to someone and logically, therefore, not to someone else":

---

[15] Although history and heritage both refashion the past in present garb, Lowenthal continues, "the former does so to make the past comprehensible, the latter to make it congenial. For historians, presentist reshaping is unavoidable, a translation needed to convey things past to modern audiences. For heritage updating is not just a necessity but a virtue that fructifies links with the past" (Lowenthal 1998, 148).

24   D. MISHKOVA

> Heritage foments conflict between rival claimants, rival visions of past and present, and rival views of truth and error. … Conflict over cultural relics and rights to ancestral emblems embroils rival claimants. Rhetorical bombast inflames animus, and myopia blinds partisan rivals to their underlying affinities. … Heritage is normally cherished not as common but as private property. Ownership gives it essential worth: though heritage is now more convergent and like-mindedly cherished, it remains inherently exclusive. (Lowenthal 1998, 227–8)

Any prospect of shared history and global common heritage faces huge, often insuperable, obstacles in the possessive jealousies of particular claimants. The chief targets of the "heritage crusade" are not so much destroyers and forsakers as rival claimants to its custody and benefits. "Our severest animus is directed against those who crave our heritage or contest its claims. Confining possession to some while excluding others is the *raison d'etre* of heritage" (Lowenthal 1998, 230).

> Conflict is thus endemic to heritage. Victors and victims proclaim disparate and divisive versions of common pasts. Claims of ownership, uniqueness, and priority engender strife over every facet of collective legacies. Clashes ensue when rivals press entitlements to being first, being distinctive, or being sublimely endowed. […] Myopic rivalry is endemic to the very nature of heritage. To insist we were the first or the best, to celebrate what is ours and exclude others, is what heritage is all about. (Lowenthal 1998, 234–5, 239)[16]

Scholars of collective memory—that more encompassing category, under which heritage is often subsumed (Peckham 2003, 1–13)—have also felt compelled to draw a distinction between history and memory (and heritage for that matter) as a means of separating the mythological interpretation of the past from the historical record. Such a distinction is normative and, as Victor Roudometof avers, valid to the extent that history is sufficiently professionalized and differentiated from the state and related institutions. However, in many cases also at the present time, a distinction is difficult to draw. With reference to the Balkans, he contends that "it is necessary to integrate the pattern of scholarly production with the production of collective memory." Here forms of cultural

---

[16] It is important to note that Lowenthal's observations about (the fabrication of) heritage draw in the main on non-Balkan and non-East European material.

reproduction, such as heritage and commemorations, operate according to the logic of the national narrative:

> They aim to illustrate, highlight, and expand upon the national narrative; they respond to the narrative ... by seeking to modify or redefine it in ways commensurable with the contemporaries' values, beliefs, and predispositions. The national narrative emerges out of our forgetting of possible or alternative pasts and constructing a past that is meaningful in the present context. (Roudometof 2002, 190–91)

Put simply, where heritage and history have parted ways in their attitude to bias, be that presentist or value bias, and their openness to revision, heritage has taken on the identity-building (and emotionally-loaded) role originally performed by national historiography. Where the creation or protection of national identity remains the remit of history, heritage and historiography operate in symbiosis.

"Heritage Masquerading as History"

The question concerning the relationship between (the production of) heritage, collective memory, and national history is, in terms of our topic, not formalistic or trivial. Looking more closely into the similarities and permeations between them in the Balkan context—or any other post-imperial setting—proves revealing regarding the mechanisms that ignite and fuel the historiographical wars. Obviously, the parallels discussed below concern that dominant strand of history writing, which is steered by allegiance to a nation or a state and which partakes in shaping what is usually referred to as the master national narrative of history.

Generally speaking, this brand of history and the modern concept of heritage share the common goal of creating ethnic and national identities through specific narratives of the past, establishing continuity between what we were and what we are. Both "distil the past into icons of identity, bonding us with precursors and progenitors, with our own earlier selves, and with our promised successors" (Lowenthal 1994, 43). History *and* heritage have become defining traits of ethnic and territorial groups, above all national states, where a strong filiation presents itself between the politics of identity, the politics of heritage, and the politics of history. Here, I will demonstrate some key features of the interaction between history and heritage, and how they are utilized to forge master national narratives:

1. Political management of heritage has its counterpart in the connection between power and historical science, which in more extreme cases amounts to history's subordination to power and subservience to politics. One might say that the effects of political interference create their own "Faustian" legacy that pervades national historiographies to this day. The examples are numerous, but one of the more recent is the radical reinterpretation of the past undertaken by the historiographies of the "titular nations" of former Yugoslavia during and following the Yugoslav wars of the 1990s. Obliterating the previous narrative of Yugoslav solidarity and shared fate, the common thrust of the various national revisionisms—most conspicuously the Serbian, Croatian, and Bosnian—has been to stress the "historical grievances" of the respective nation and justify its war aims as being driven by the high intention to set "historical injustices" right (Karačić et al. 2012; Katz 2007; Stojanović 2011; Radonić 2017; Filandra 2017; see also Nedim Rabić's chapter in this volume). The close linkage of politics and historical science—more properly of politicizing history and doing politics through history—has been made conspicuous in studies of the "Macedonian Question," whether these be Greek, Bulgarian, Serbian, or Macedonian. Theories about ethnogenesis and ethnic continuity, in particular, are a favored terrain of political wrangles, in that they purportedly justify mastership over disputed territories. Thus, the Bulgarian ethnogenesis is described as including the Macedonian Slavs and as having been completed early, once and for all. Moreover, Macedonian Slavs are classified as belonging to the "Bulgarian group" of Slavs even before the advent of the name-giving Turkic Bulgars, hence their inclusion in the Bulgarian state is defined as natural and legitimate (Daskalov 2024, esp. 470–534; Marinov 2013).

When Bulgarians, Greeks, Macedonians, and Aromanians insist on their continuity in Macedonia, when Albanians and Serbs claim primogeniture in Kosovo, and when the Croats legitimate the conflicts with the Serbs by "discovering" that they are of different ethnic origin, they are less concerned with asserting ancient origin per se than with claiming rights over certain land or, as is presently more often the case, over its cultural heritage. Likewise, depending on the political climate, Romanian public discourse has been focused on either a Dacian or a Roman lineage, while the Balkan links are being marginalized. The Roman legacy was overemphasized by the Transylvanian Romanian elites in their plea for rights under the Habsburgs, as well as in times of longing for Europe (despite the Roman Empire's control over Dacia, the territory of contemporary

Romania, lasting for significantly less time than over its southern Balkan neighbors). The Dacian legacy was emphasized under the trope of resistance to the West or in times of autarchy such as during Ceauşescu's regime. As Alexander Vezenkov's chapter demonstrates, a similar role is played by the instrumentalization of Illyrianism in the Albanian historical narrative, which identifies the ancient Illyrians with modern Albanians. The Albanians are portrayed as one of the oldest European nations, having inhabited the present-day Albanian lands, including disputed territories, long before the arrival of their contemporary neighbors.

More often than not such politicization is linked to what Michael Oakeshott had called the "practical past." The distinction Oakeshott made between the practical and the historical past was meant to separate professional history from practical uses of the past for justifying actions and beliefs in the present. The historical past is a past that exists independently of our present concerns and is studied for its own sake and deserves investigation in its own right. The practical past makes sense only "in relation to ourselves and our current activities," we use this kind of past "to make valid practical beliefs about the present and the future" (Oakeshott 1983; see also Ahlskog 2016, 376–7). An apt illustration of the subordination of the historical to the practical in history is provided by Walter Leitsch in a discussion of the East Europeans who went to study at the Vienna University before 1914 with the intention of acquiring the skills needed to research the history of their own nations. These students were not interested in studying the history of their own nationality as part of the history of other nationalities. "They refused particularly to study the history of their neighbours, whom they invariably disliked. They studied history in order to be better equipped for their controversies with these neighbours." To be appropriately armed for the job they had "to master the technique of source criticism in the widest sense of the word at least as well as the envious neighbours did. The skill required for the study of medieval history was a weapon to defend the magnificence of the national past against the attacks of those who sought to deny it" (Leitsch 1988, 145).

Nationally engaged historians, no less than heritage-mongers, are prone to resort to interpretative and narrative strategies forging this kind of historical pragmatism. Unabashed "presentist" agendas are characteristic of both—presentist in the broader sense of seeking to project back to pre-modern times—and thus validate claims with origins in modern times, such as, for example, declaring present-day Macedonians present-day Bulgarians (Daskalov 2024, 560–62). This involves selection and

28   D. MISHKOVA

manipulation, whereby projected memory retains what can serve the purpose of achieving current national goals. The re-writing of Serbian history in Milošević and post-Milošević Serbia, Dubravka Stojanović tells us, involved not just a shift in interpretation, but the changing of some facts and the deletion of others, reducing the importance of some facts and foregrounding other facts with the goal of forging a mythical narrative that could vindicate the wars in the former Yugoslavia in the 1990s (Stojanović 2011, 224).

2. It is remarkable that such distortions are almost invariably accompanied by *claims to truthfulness*, objectivity, and adherence to "actual facts" and denouncement of the opposing party's "distortions," "forgeries," "appropriations," and "thefts" of someone else's history and heritage. Present-day Croatian and Bosnian historians berate each other for producing "pseudo-scientific pamphlets" and acting like "charlatans," "mythomaniacs," and "colporteurs," who are "craving for a reconquest" (Filandra 2017, 173). Lurking behind such strictures are (often mutually reinforcing) ideological instrumentalizations of the past, where the claimed "historical truth" presents, in effect, a construction that creatively commingles fact and fiction.

3. Nationally responsive history and heritage discourses ally also in evincing concerns with *precedence, antiquity, and autochthony*. The Greeks' *archaiolatreia*, the worship of antiquity, bears all the above-noted traits of "heritage." It forms the backbone of their self-awareness to this day and has been sustained through ambitious policies ranging from language reform and transfer of capital city to copying classical buildings and monument conservation to folklore "cleansing" and performative re-enactments of various kinds. For several decades after World War I, Turkish historiography operated within the fold of, and was tasked to find historical "facts" substantiating, the so-called Turkish History Thesis, the first major Turkish attempt at creating a grand national narrative. Later only slightly attenuated by variants of Anatolianism (claims to autochthony in Anatolia), it postulated that the Turks were the oldest people on earth, who initiated through migration almost all major civilizations: Chinese, Indian, Mesopotamian, Egyptian, Aegean, and so on. It had a linguistic analogue, the "Sun Language Theory," which defined Turkish as the world's oldest language.[17] Significantly, while themselves disinheriting the ancient Greeks, Turkish historians proclaimed the Greeks usurpers of the legacies

---

[17] For a discussion of the historical context of these claims, see Erimtan (2008).

of earlier and superior civilizations settled in the Aegean region. The "Thracian roots" of the Bulgarian nation, integral to the "trinal" Thraco-Slavo-Bulgarian constitution of the nation, and the "Daco-Roman" makeup of the modern Romanians are of a similar vintage. While in the early 1980s socialist Bulgaria with tremendous pomp celebrated "1300 years of Bulgaria," Ceaușescu's Romania celebrated the 2050th anniversary of the creation of the "Dacian state" under Burebista, the Dacian king, thus outdoing the Bulgarians, and even more so the Hungarians, in antiqueness. Ludicrous as such boasts of precedence and preeminence may seem, they are not innocuous, for "to be first in a place warrants possession; to antedate others' origins or exploits shows superiority. ... Claims to priority commonly derogate rivals" (Lowenthal 1998, 174–5).

4. Both heritage discourse and the national historical narrative are committed to inculcating the idea of *uninterrupted continuity*, from earliest times to the present, if not necessarily of the state, in any event of the "people." A true national history cannot fulfill this task by way of an empirical-analytical reconstruction of the past; it demands "genealogical reading" of the past, whereby the historian goes back, time and again, to the very beginnings of the national, usually located in pre-national epochs (Marinov 2001). Here the active assistance of the so-called cultural-historical archaeology—which, in our context, may be more properly called "ethnic archaeology"—deserves acknowledgment.[18]

Although it goes beyond the remit of this chapter to discuss the "national imaginations" and clashes unfolding on this professional terrain, for our purposes it is worthwhile recalling the main assignment of cultural-historical archaeology, which dominated, and still dominates, all national archaeological schools in the Balkans—namely, to provide the material signs of ownership of the national territory "from time immemorial," to underwrite the continuity of the given ethnos and, on occasion, to support policies of domination and control over neighboring lands.[19] As already noted, this endeavor has expressed itself in a perennial concern with ethnogenesis, which involves searching for ways to trace the origins of specific national groups in the archaeological record. Thus, drawing on archaeological and ethnographic artifacts, Thracian antiquity (dated to the

---

[18] On cultural-historical archaeology as an important "national discipline," see Trigger (1996, 211–313). On the nationalistically-oriented practice of archaeology in the Balkans, see Kaiser (1995).

[19] On the Bulgarian case, see Lazova (2016).

late Bronze and early Iron Age) features in the Bulgarian narrative as the heritage which the Slavs took over, whereby the focus is on demonstrating how the latter adopted the ancient culture and transmitted it to the Middle Ages—a phenomenon commonly labeled as "the Thracian heritage in Bulgarian culture" or the "Thracian substratum in the Bulgarian ethnic makeup."[20] Archaeology gradually became the main source of arguments in favor of Albanian autochthony and Illyrian-Albanian continuity, also because of the lack of historical data and the ambiguity of the linguistic evidence. The stakes in the Romanian contentions to autochthony "are the notions that Romania has never been fundamentally changed by its non-Latin neighbors and that Romanian claims to all of present-day Romania are founded in historical priority. This theme is repeated in every museum display and textbook dealing with the country's past, serving to distinguish Romania and Romanians from the surrounding parvenus— Slavs and Magyars" (Kaiser 1995, 115). Historian Lucian Boia has dealt at length with Romanian narratives' obsession with autochthony, continuity, and lineage, while othering neighbors as newcomers and usurpers (Boia 2001). In such polemics, facts often become irrelevant to or circumscribed by the narrative. As it has been pointed out with reference to the archaeological record, "that a connection to a remote antiquity is perhaps open to question is beside the point: enough 'scientific' archaeological evidence can be mustered to convince non-archaeologists of the solid basis for such claims" (Kaiser 1995, 117). On the other hand, the annihilation or neglect of Ottoman material remains across the Balkans provides a contrasting illustration of the way heritage and history are being manipulated through erasure or oblivion, and of historical monuments becoming hostages of this manipulation.

Phenomena like Christian heterodoxy, in turn, become nationalized, hence one sees the post-Yugoslav national historiographies of medieval Bosnia, for example, operating with the simplistic and anachronistic

---

[20] It is in this sense that Lowenthal writes: "Archaeological legacies become pawns of personal feuds and nationalist goals, ruins and refuse sites fashioned into metaphors of identity. What gets excavated and how reflects heritage needs more than scholarly aims. … Archaeologists are incessantly importuned to certify national and tribal sagas, testifying that this or that people came first and kept tribal faith" (Lowenthal 1998, 235). In the words of another critic, "As a consequence of the predisposition of archaeologists in southeast Europe to think about prehistory and history in terms of the categories suggested by these ideologies, it has also become possible for advocates of these ideologies to make overt use of archaeological evidence" (Kaiser 1995, 119).

taxonomy Catholic/Croatian, Orthodox/Serbian, and Bogomilist/ Bosniak. Earlier oppositions that underpinned the Greek-Bulgarian historiographic confrontations were those between Patriarchists (adherents of the Patriarchate of Constantinople), who the Greek historians counted as "Greeks," and Exarchists (those accepting the jurisdiction of the Bulgarian Exarchate), who their Bulgarian counterparts considered "Bulgarians." Similarly, all those who inhabited the one-time Bulgarian medieval states are being counted, by default, as Bulgarians; and events or actors have been declared part of Serbian, Macedonian, or Greek history on the sole ground that they took place or operated on Serbian, Macedonian or Greek soil (hence the disputes over the ownership of famed relics, including works of art coming from the territories of North Macedonia, Northern Greece, and Southeast Serbia that are still kept in Bulgarian museums, as Tchavdar Marinov indicates further in this volume); and so on. The heterotopy and "otherness" of the past are ultimately reduced to the homogeny of the national.

Typically, although rarely explicated, such claims bespeak not just cultural but quasi-racial bonds. "Biological continuity is what many Greeks really want when they say 'language and culture,' disclaimers to the contrary notwithstanding" (Kaldellis 2007, 113). This phenomenon appears in a most pronounced form in the Albanian narrative: as Alexander Vezenkov displays in this volume, the Albanians claim to be the only descendants of the Illyrians as well as descending solely from the Illyrians shorn of any significant admixture. At the end of the day race trumps, or at least begets, culture. This is especially visible in the strongly biologized notion of "ethnicity" which, albeit wrapped in cultural garb (languages, religions, customs), in effect implies kinship by blood. Hence its essentialization as something everlasting and immutable, formed once and for all in most distant times, rather than being seen as a relational and dynamic process. The lands, where this ethnic formation took place or which the already formed ethnos conquered, moreover, were those that belonged by "historic right" to the subsequent modern nation. History and the modern notion of heritage thus collaborate in mythologizing not only ethnic origins, but the sacred indivisibility of ethnos and space. This is clearly visible in the Albanian case, where the Illyrian hypothesis of the origin of present-day Albanians is also used to support their claim to autochthony in contested regions such as Kosovo and Epirus. It comes as no surprise, then, that the mutually exclusive arguments about the ethnicity of the premodern Macedonian populations should have become the main weapons with which modern Bulgarians and Macedonians fight over the right to make these populations part of their contemporary nations and states. Put another way, heritage defined by ancestry and blood aggravates chauvinism and animus. Especially in multiethnic societies of overlapping historical heritages, such as the Balkans, thinking and doing history in heritage terms and through retrospective nationalization of human activity cannot but provoke antagonism.

5. As it happens, the national-historical narratives manifestly *take on board the notion of "heritage"* in order to delimit national territory and affirm the nation's "historical rights" to it by way of an, as it were, ancestral "law of inheritance." This is a two-way relationship: as Tchavdar Marinov's chapter demonstrates, the assumption that the Macedonians are Bulgarians had shaped the imagined geography of the Bulgarian cultural heritage (with the idea of specific artistic schools and so on) and vice versa—the recognition of the Macedonians as a separate population "tears apart" the geography of their heritage from that in the larger part of Bulgaria. This kind of "heriticization" therefore bids for exclusive possession of heritage, moves away from material vestiges, and lays claim to ownership of historical personalities, political and religious formations, and other phenomena that serve to underwrite historical rights. Serbian nationalism makes prodigious use of the defeat at the Battle of Kosovo in 1389 for its territorial claims. The Kosovo conflict of 1998–1999 was largely fought about heritage, or rather violence enacted upon heritage was skillfully used by politicians to polarize coexisting communities and solidify ethnic identities. The creation of the Cyrillic alphabet, the work of Cyril and Methodius' disciples Clement of Ohrid and Naum, the heretical Bogomil movement, and the empire of Tsar Samuel (969–1018) have similarly been "privatized" and nationalized by the Bulgarian and Macedonian sides respectively—heritage debates that, in the last analysis, boil down to asserting symbolic, if not any more outright territorial, rights over Macedonia (see Daskalov's chapter in this volume and Daskalov 2024, 399–453). The Romanians' claim to "fatherhood" of all Romance-speaking (Vlach and Aromanian) populations and their heritage in the Balkans, irrespective of the countries they had been inhabiting for centuries, had long served for political trade-offs: since direct territorial acquisitions, in this case, were unrealistic, on numerous occasions Romania would exchange these populations' "right to autonomy" for other strategic concessions.

1 LEGACY, TRADITION, HERITAGE AND THE HISTORY WRITING... 33

What we are faced with here are rival claims to the same valued heritage icons. To the Macedonians' belated attempts at forging their own national narrative the Greeks and the Bulgarians have reacted with accusations of Macedonian "usurpation" of major parts of their national heritages. The Bulgarians accuse the Macedonian historians of trying to "steal" Bulgarian history and patrimony, for the lack of their own, and of deliberate lies—with the implication that the truth is reserved for the Bulgarian side (in point of fact, grounds for such accusations are not missing on either side, as the polemical works of Dragan Taškovski on the Macedonian and Bozhidar Dimitrov on the Bulgarian side amply demonstrate—Daskalov 2024, 532–34, 546–49). The perennial language question—whether Macedonians speak a Bulgarian dialect or a different Slavic language—by its very nature of being most closely interwoven with the definition of the nation, entails that any answer can only be zero-sum in that it will always be taken to mean surrendering a central part of the history of the respective people (Marinov 2010, 91–7; Brunnbauer 2004).

Consequently, to the Greek and Bulgarian intimations that they should make do with a nation without historical traditions, one that is a recent and synthetic product, Macedonian historians respond with sustained exertions to assert continuities with the ancient Macedonia of Alexander the Great—attempts that have been vehemently denounced by Greek historians (and politicians) as illegitimate appropriation, a straightforward theft of their own, Hellenic, heritage (Skordos 2011). For the contemporary Macedonians to appropriate the cultural legacy of ancient Macedonians, however, it is not even necessary to claim that the ancient Macedonians were the genealogical forefathers of contemporary Macedonians (who are, after all, a Slavic people); it suffices to assert that the ancient Macedonians were not ancient Greeks. Considering that the Greek nation-state has spent more than a century carefully constructing and propounding a national narrative based on the thesis of 3000 years of unbroken cultural continuity, alongside the idea that Macedonia falls within the legacy of ancient Greece that the modern state lays claim to and takes national pride in, one can understand the formidable stakes involved in the dispute. Their broader social consequences cannot be underestimated either, for "where there are clashing interpretations of ancestral homelands, and cultural heritages ... normal conflicts of interest are turned into cultural wars, and moral and political crusades replace everyday politics" (Smith 1999, 9). As we will see, such clashes can also shape interstate relations and provisions in bilateral international treaties.

6. Finally, to top off the above, national history and national heritage conjugate to underpin claims to *exceptionality and uniqueness.* History, like heritage, "passes on exclusive myths of origin and continuance. ... Created to generate and protect group interests, it benefits us only if withheld from others" (Lowenthal 1998, 128). Exceptionality promotes insularity, which sours both internal sameness and external difference. "We confront one another armored in identities whose likenesses we ignore or disown and whose differences we distort or invent to emphasize our own superior worth. Lauding our own legacies and excluding or discrediting those of others, we commit ourselves to endemic rivalry and conflict" (Lowenthal 1994, 41). Unique national features inculcated by historical narratives ("we treasure most what sets us apart") are, in the same stroke, often valued as having universal significance. Let me give one illustration.

In 2005 the Centre for Democracy and Reconciliation in Southeast Europe in Thessaloniki, Greece, published four volumes of historical sources from eleven Southeast European countries, where some of the most sensitive and controversial segments of the Balkan past were presented using the comparative method and different national viewpoints. The publication was the outcome of an international "Joint History Project" aimed to stimulate debate, revise ethnocentric history teaching, and subvert national stereotypes—all with the intention to contribute to conflict resolution and conflict prevention.[21] These books caused tumultuous reactions, especially in Serbia and Greece where they acquired greater visibility, and had serious consequences for some of the project participants. The focus of the attacks was, strikingly enough, the comparative approach. It was censured as a beacon of the globalization process, which, in the words of the angered Greek press, pursued the "weakening of the importance of the nation," "threatens our national identity," and wreaked a way "towards cultural homogenization," so that these books were declared a "genocide on memory" or "crime of peace" (Stojanović 2008, 159). The other target of attack was the presentation of history from different perspectives, from the point of view of various protagonists in the events. Because, as the director of the Serbian Council for Textbook Publishing, historian Radoš Ljušić, put it, "in history, there is only one truth, just as there is only one God" (Stojanović 2011, 225–6).

---

[21] The controversial themes were "The Ottoman Empire," "Nations and States in Southeast Europe," "The Balkan Wars" and "The Second World War." For the Joint History Project and the resulting workbooks, see Koulouri (2002).

To sum up, as cultivated by scholars from various disciplines, national-historical narratives and the contemporary concept of heritage conjoin and reinforce each other in their preoccupation with ethnic origins, continuity and uniqueness on behalf of creating or bolstering national identities, and laying claims to "historical heritages" and "historical rights" in the present. In the process, usually through selection and manipulation of (often inconclusive) historical sources, "historical truth" has been understood to be tantamount to national truth in the service of the national interest. Thus the boundary between historiographic reconstruction and national ideology dissolves, the result being the reproduction of a sacralized tradition (Marinov 2001). Claims to antiquity, primordiality (primordial beginnings), protochronism (precedence), unbroken continuity, autochthony (nativism), and permanence or longevity of traits and institutions are intrinsic to "invented traditions" (frequently intersecting with "believed" or "perceived legacies") *and* constitutive of heritage. The historiographical wars are waged precisely on this terrain of shared or mirrored perspectives and presuppositions (pre-emptive national position and viewpoint), premises (the preeminence of one's nation), concepts, goals, often narrative strategies, and, perhaps most importantly, selective and opinionated treatment of "facts." The ferocity of these disputes to a large extent derives from their common grounds—above all, an essentialist notion of the medieval ethnos as an archetype and (implicitly biological) forebear of the modern nation. The logical next step is the retrospective nationalization of heterogeneous populations and the patently anachronistic correlation between space and ethnos, a medieval state and a "nationality": the inhabitants for a period of time of the Bulgarian or Serbian medieval kingdoms are, respectively, "Bulgarians" or "Serbs," and the Byzantines are "Greeks" or, in the worst case, Hellenized "outlanders."

Asynchronicity in the production of the national-historical canons also plays a role. The construction of the grand narrative everywhere is a political enterprise replete with contestation, argument, and debate. However, the relatively late emergence of the Macedonian, Bosnian, and to a certain extent Albanian national-historical canons presents particular challenges to their respective historiographies and exacerbates confrontation in several critical respects. The historians in these countries have to assert their nations' "rights" on lands and artefacts already in possession of or coveted by neighboring nations on behalf of their own narratives, if not always

36 D. MISHKOVA

territorially. Often this had to be executed while drawing on the same (limited) and already processed corpus of "usable" historical records.

Therefore, in writing nationally engaged history we become involved in a process similar to the fabrication of heritage. The kind of bias ("blind allegiance to nation, state, or faith") or unreflective "presentism" (a desire to investigate history and draw or extract conclusions useful to the furthering of present purposes), which heritage production is found guilty of, is the viewpoint lodged at the heart of many historical writings. Heritage forgers and "truth-seeking" national historians end up in the same boat: "As claims to property and pride hinge on rival versions of the same experienced past, heritage-mongers feel compelled to cloak wares in historical authenticity. It is all in vain [since] adherents of rival heritages simultaneously construct versions that are equally well-grounded (and equally spurious)" (Lowenthal 1998, 249). Such rivalries, which are usually intensely righteous, pervade politics and public consciousness and ignite wars over icons of identity not only between historiographies but also states, as the Bulgarian-Macedonian, the Greek-Macedonian, the Serbian-Albanian, the Greek-Turkish, and Romanian-Hungarian rows amply demonstrate.

Why this should be the prevailing mode of writing national history in the Balkans to this day is an intricate question. There exists a widespread perception that the sense of "public immediacy" of the past in East Central and Southeastern Europe is stronger than in the older nation-states of "the West." "In few areas of the world," writes one of the most influential specialists in modern and contemporary Greek history, "is the collective historical consciousness of such acute contemporary political significance;" the study and teaching of history in the Balkans was, and remains, a highly charged political issue (Clogg 1988, 15). Let it be reminded, though, that the new nations' pursuit of "heritage" was of major importance in the development of "scientific" historiography in "the West," too, and that achievements of the professional historians later on became components of national heritages, so that now *all* national historiographies are heritages and scholarly contributions at the same time.

As for the Balkans, the belated process of nation formation and the sense of existential insecurity for the nation in this part of Europe go a long way toward explaining the perseverance of the nationally anchored matrix of history writing. "Only self-confident nations allow defections from the nationalist paradigm," cautions German historian Ulf Brunnbauer (2004, 200). It has also been held that the national question came to occupy center stage in Eastern Europe because of the legacies of overlapping imperial frameworks—not only the Habsburg, Ottoman, and Russian domination of long ago, but also, more recently, the Soviet empire and the communist experience with nationalism.[22] Complemented by consecutive crises of legitimacy and identity of political regimes and intellectual elites, it helps explain both the relentless quest for a past conferring certain dignity and the infiltration in history writing of "heritage characteristics," such as creatively commingling fact with fiction, positivist empiricism with fantasy, invention, and sometimes mystique. Or, as the arch-national Greek historian Constantine Paparrigopoulos once memorably framed it, "History is not only a science. It is at once the Gospel of the present and the future of the Motherland" (cit. in Clogg 1988, 15).

Cleavages Post-1989

The democratization of historiography and the opportunities for uncensored interpretations of the past that followed the "end of communism" did trigger critical assessment of the national history paradigm, yet failed to upset its hegemony in the historical mainstream and public consciousness. The swift overturn of the *ancien régime* and the ensuing pressure to redefine national identity breathed instead new life into the paradigm. This is true of not only newly established nation-states such as Bosnia and Herzegovina, North Macedonia, Montenegro, and Kosovo, but also "older" ones like Greece, Bulgaria, Romania, Serbia or Albania. New conservative, political as well as intellectual, elites on the left and right in these countries keep nurturing the dominant nationality's latent resentment and fear of difference and otherness that earlier nationalist, not least communist, governments were assiduously cultivating.

The post-1989 scholarly debates on collective identity serve to illustrate the leverages in the historiographic field generally. The issue is all the more germane to our subject since it is in their shared preoccupation with collective identity formation that legacy and heritage discourses to a large extent converge. The time-honored approach, as suggested by the above observations, conceives of collective identity as a "unitary and homogeneous entity, a community of shared substance, and its internal complexity and diversity disavowed"; the images it breeds are those of a "national family, a single body, shared blood, a common home(land)." The community thus envisioned maintains its specific traits—heritage, memories,

---

[22] See, among others, Bunce (2005).

values, character, particularity, and uniqueness—through time, is impervious to change and discontinuity and extols the moral force of tradition (Robins 2005, 173). As incubated by national historians and heritage-mongers the dominant and conventional discourses on identity present the collective culture and distinctiveness of a group as the expression of some inner essence or property of all members of the group. Identity thus acquires a "natural" and "eternal" quality emanating from within a self-same and self-contained collective entity.

More recent critical accounts have confronted head-on such essentialist positions, emphasizing the socially constructed status of identities. The latter are shown to be "instituted in particular social and historical contexts, to be strategic fictions, having to react to changing circumstances, and therefore subject to continuous change and reconfiguration." As such, an identity has no clear positive meaning, but an exclusionary, dark side, in that "in its strategies of differentiation, identity depends on the creation of frontiers and borders in order to distance and protect itself from the imagined threat of other cultures. … We may say, then, that there is often fear in the soul of identity" (Robins 2005, 173–4).

These two conceptions of identity bespeak a peculiar configuration of a parallel existence of two historiographical "systems" of knowledge production, which barely communicate with or bear on each other: the interpretations dominating the public sphere, which bind the toolkits of public history and school education (or, rather, which transform education into the awareness of identity), on the one hand, and those emanating from the accumulation of knowledge and the findings of critical historiography, on the other. That in this confrontation the former camp continues to enjoy unequivocal supremacy is an indication that upholding professional standards like fact-finding, heed of context, and methodologically rigorous work with sources is not sufficient to ensure a more truthful understanding of the past. What also matters, and matters critically, is the existence of effective social and cultural channels of access to knowledge that abides by such standards.

Inventing Traditions, Constructing Heritage: A Few (Synoptic) Contemporary Stories

An instance of the invention of tradition (and its fervid contestation) unfurling, as it were, in front of our eyes is the "antiquization" of Macedonia, namely the process of establishing a direct link between contemporary (North) Macedonia and the state and culture of the ancient Macedonians. It displays both the importance of the politico-ideological context and the momentous political implications of heritage politics. In the writings of intellectuals and political activists, seeking to devise some kind of Macedonian identity during the late nineteenth and the greater part of the twentieth century, there were only sporadic references to Alexander the Great.[23] Gjorgjija Pulevski (1817–1895), known today as the first author to publicly express the idea of a Macedonian "people" (*narod*) distinct from their "Bulgarian brothers" and a separate "Slavic Macedonian" language, is said to be the first Macedonian nationalist to launch the idea that the Macedonians were descendants of the ancient Macedonians. The ancient Macedonian language, he avowed, had Slavic components, and he claimed that "King Philip [II of Macedon]" and "Tsar Alexander [the Great]" were of Slavic origin. Therefore, the ancient Macedonians were the ancestors of modern Macedonians (Dokmanović 2021). It is remarkable that, drawing on these same arguments, many Bulgarian "revivalists" (representatives of the national Revival movement) in Ottoman Bulgaria claimed that the ancient Macedonians were "Bulgarians." And, around the same time, in the mid- to late nineteenth century, ancient Macedonians and Alexander the Great made it into the Greek master narrative as epitomes of Greek continuity and national unity, after decades of rejection or neglect on the part of most Greek Enlighteners, through the work of Constantine Paparrigopoulos (Marinov 2013, 280–82, 284, 315; Friedman 1975).[24] It is, however significant that the leading Macedonian nationalist writer of the early twentieth century, Krste Misirkov (1874–1926), made no reference to the ancient Macedonians in his works. Occasional references to Alexander the Great in writings of the interwar period failed to become part of the slowly crystalizing Macedonian national ideology.

The establishment of the People's Republic of Macedonia as a federal state in Yugoslavia in 1944 ushered in, for the first time, a full-fledged nation-building effort, where historiography became a key actor. The first generation of academic Macedonian historians situated the emergence of the Macedonian nation in the nineteenth century, when some intellectuals

---

[23] Until World War II only small circles of intellectuals had expressed the idea of a separate Macedonian nation (see Troebst 1983; Brunnbaurer 2004, 173).

[24] The first speculations about a Slavic character of the ancient Macedonians belong to early precursors of the Illyrian movement from Dalmatia (Marinov 2013, 280–81).

40   D. MISHKOVA

began to articulate and propagate "Macedonian" national consciousness (Brunnbauer 2004, 178). After the Tito-Stalin split in 1948 and the subsequent estrangement between Yugoslavia and Bulgaria, sustained attempts were undertaken to move the inception of the Macedonian nation to the Middle Ages (*Istorija naroda Jugoslavije*, 1953). Subsumed to the idea of Yugoslav unity, in neither official Macedonian histories nor history textbooks from the early 1950s to the late 1980s was this identity claimed to have ancient Macedonian roots. The official narrative in most historical books began with the settlement of the Slavs in the sixth and seventh centuries (see among others Ristovski 1983, 19–22, 57–60; Antoljak 1985, 161–79; Panov 1985, 7–30). It is at the same time revealing that the Macedonian historians' assertions that the birth of the Macedonian nation took place in the framework of the medieval state of Tsar Samuel came forth in the context of escalating Bulgarian anti-Macedonian propaganda during the 1970s (Daskalov 2024, 504).

That was not the endpoint of the concoction of a "Macedonian" tradition, though. The proclamation of an independent Macedonian state in 1991 was marked by two momentous symbolic acts: the selection of the star (or sun) of Vergina, associated with Philip II of Macedon, as the symbol on the Macedonian flag and the use of "Macedonia" in the official name of the state. Both met with a vehement objection on the part of the majority of Greek historians and politicians, who saw this as a theft of their ancient Hellenic heritage and suspected, on this basis, territorial designs on Greece's northern territories (Danforth 1997).[25] Indeed, both Greece and Bulgaria worried that the recognition of a state carrying the name Macedonia would not only delegitimize each side's carefully crafted national narrative but also lead to demands for minority rights for Macedonians inhabiting these two states (Roudometof 2002, 191). The coming to power of the Macedonian radical nationalists in 2006 ushered in a sweeping "antiquization" of the public space through massive construction projects of pseudo-classical state buildings and monuments. Parallel to this, a revision of the academic accounts of Macedonian history and historical textbooks was undertaken, which postulated a linkage between the ancient and modern Macedonian identities and the continuation of ancient Macedonia's statecraft tradition ("stolen" from the Greeks) via Samuel's medieval empire ("stolen" from the Bulgarians) to

---

[25] The Greek government, accordingly, opposed the recognition of the new state with the name "Macedonia" and the acknowledgment of the Macedonians as a nation.

1 LEGACY, TRADITION, HERITAGE AND THE HISTORY WRITING... 41

the present-day Macedonian nation. It also entailed the introduction of new public commemorations and celebrations and set the stage for new directions of research such as exposing parallels between the ancient Macedonian and the contemporary Macedonian language.[26] As a leading Macedonian archaeologist bluntly put it, "Macedonia will defend its name only if it proves that the Macedonian people have ancient and not Slavic roots" (cit. in Dokmanović 2021, 263). All this amounted to forceful fabrication, codification, and mass propagation of a mythical tradition, and of an attending "heritage industry,"[27] carried out with the resources of the state.

Present-day Bosnian historiography is grappling with similar reformulations. As Nedim Radić's chapter patently indicates, the newly established Bosnian and Herzegovinian state enacted a sustained effort to peg the Bosniaks' belated historical consciousness to the medieval Bosnian state, and to link the Islamization process after the Ottoman conquest with the Bogomilist spiritual substrate of the Bosnian Church. Propelling this dominant narrative of "millennial Bosnia" is the aspiration to not simply endow the Bosniaks' present identity with an ancient dimension, but above all protect it from Croatian and Serbian contestations and assert a cultural and territorial-political continuity between medieval and Ottoman Bosnia and the independent state of BiH, and thus rebuff the purported historical rights of Serbia and Croatia to "Bosnian land" (see also Filandra 2017, 165–70).[28] A Department for the Cultivation of the Medieval Heritage of Bosnia and Herzegovina was founded in 1997 with the aim to foster and propagate awareness among the Bosniaks of the medieval Bosnian kingdom as the bedrock of Bosnian and Herzegovinian statehood. Across the post-Yugoslav space, recent (World War II) and contemporary (Yugoslav) history is, predictably, what has been subjected to the

---

[26] See, among others, *Istorija na makedonskiot narod* 2008, authored by historians from the Institute of National History, which traces the distinct ethnogenesis and language of the Macedonians as well as the beginnings of their state back to the fourth century BC and draws a direct lineage with contemporary Macedonia. See also Vangeli (2011).

[27] "While the heritage industry plays an important role in the promotion of cultural identity, it is often critiqued for producing inauthentic, sentimental, nostalgic, patronising, hyperreal, and uncritical accounts wherein the past is gentrified and rewritten, often from a presentist perspective"—*Oxford Dictionary of Human Geography* 2013 (online ed.).

[28] In opposition to the untenable "millennial state continuity" of Bosnia, this author asserts a "millennial continuity of social-psychological relationships" of the Bosnian people and the latter's "ties to the Bosnian land [that] have remained as strong as ever" (172).

42   D. MISHKOVA

most radical and conflictual revisionism, especially in Serbia and Croatia. "This battle," writes professor of history at the University of Sarajevo Husnija Kamberović, "will last a long time, and may never even be finished! Stories about our history will take place once again in the coordinates of the plans for the political future of these areas (Europe, Central Europe, or the Western Balkans). This will only confirm the thesis that there is no history. There are only historians" (Kamberović 2007, 19).

EPILOGUE: HISTORIOGRAPHICAL WARS IN INTERNATIONAL LAW

As can be seen, historiographic trends have been involved in, and sometimes had serious repercussions on, the political relations between the Balkan states. From the mid-1960s on, the endemic disputes over a common history have kept relations between Sofia and Skopje tense. Relations between Skopje and Athens deteriorated considerably only with the start of the "antiquization" campaign in the 1990s. Conversely, the break-up of the two-bloc system, the radical reshuffling of the geopolitical equilibrium both outside and inside the Balkan region in the context of the violent disintegration of Yugoslavia, and the challenges brought about by the so-called transition—all these kept the issues of "national identity" and "national history" high on the agenda, which breathed new life into "history as politics" (Troebst 2022).

The international agreements between Greece and Macedonia since the 1990s provide striking instances of such connections. The "Interim Agreement" which Greece and Macedonia signed in 1995 included a suggestive article (7), stating that "if either Party believed one or more symbols constituting part of its *historic or cultural patrimony* were being used by the other Party, it should bring such alleged use to the attention of the other Party, and the other Party should take appropriate corrective action or indicate why it did not consider it necessary to do so" (United Nations 1995—cit. in Troebst 2022, 251).

The so-called Prespa Agreement of 2018 between Greece and what was henceforth to be named the Republic of North Macedonia is a strange document in that it included provisions on matters that this kind of diplomatic document is not supposed to treat, such as history and language. Thus Art. 8/2 obliged the Republic of North Macedonia to "review the status of monuments, public buildings, and infrastructures on its territory, and insofar as they refer in any way to ancient Hellenic history and civilization constituting an integral component of the historic or cultural patrimony of [Greece], to take appropriate corrective action to effectively address the issue and ensure respect for the said patrimony."[29] This obligation should be read in connection with the previous article 7/4, postulating that "The [Republic of North Macedonia] notes that its official language, the Macedonian language, is within the group of South Slavic languages. The Parties note that the official language and other attributes of the [Republic of North Macedonia] are not related to the ancient Hellenic civilization, history, culture, and heritage of the northern region of [Greece]." Finally, the agreement (Art. 8/5) envisages the establishment of a "Joint Inter-Disciplinary Committee of Experts on historic, archaeological and educational matters, to consider the objective, scientific interpretation of historical events based on authentic, evidence-based and scientifically sound historical sources and archaeological findings"; it should "ensure in each of the Parties that no school textbooks or school auxiliary material in use the year after the signing of the Agreement contains any irredentist/revisionist references."[30] As Stefan Troebst notes, "The Prespa Agreement is an attempt by Greece to impose its own historical narrative on Macedonia, which is thereby forced to considerably revise its own historical narrative. As during the Cold War, nowadays, too, governmental politics of history create a policy not only in domestic politics but also in bilateral and international relations." He then concludes that in the Balkans, "the use of historical arguments in the political realm … has proven to be a main obstacle for constructive regional cooperation. It has strongly enforced populist tendencies, fed oppositional nationalist movements, some of which even use racist hate-speech, and, in general, created a hostile climate among neighbours—with far-reaching consequences in many fields of the everyday lives of inhabitants of the region" (Troebst 2022, 254).

[29] This article concerns the sweeping antiquization of the public space in the Macedonian capital, the so-called Skopje 2014 project, initiated by the nationalist Macedonian government between 2006 and 2016 and which involved the rebuilding of its center in a lavish classical style and erecting hundreds of statues, including a thirty-three-meter statue of Alexander the Great, and a Triumphal Arch. See Reef (2018).

[30] "Final Agreement for the Settlement of the Differences as Described in the United Nations Security Council Resolutions 817 (1993) and 845 (1993), the Termination of the Interim Accord of 1995, and the Establishment of a Strategic Partnership between the Parties," June 17, 2018, 7–8 https://vlada.mk/sites/default/files/dokumenti/spogodba-en.pdf.

REFERENCES

Ahlskog, Jonas. 2016. Michael Oakeshott and Hayden White on the Practical and the Historical Past. *Rethinking History* 20 (3): 375–394.

The American Heritage Dictionary of the English Language. 2016. Fifth ed. Boston, New York: Houghton Mifflin Harcourt Publishing Company.

Antoljak, Stjepan. 1985. *Srednovekovna Makedonija*, t.1. Skopje: Misla.

Apor, Balazs, and John Paul Newman. 2021. Introduction. In *Balkan Legacies. The Long Shadow of Conflict and Ideological Experiment in Southeastern Europe*, ed. Balazs Apor and John Paul Newman, 1–17. West Lafayette, Indiana: Purdue University Press.

Ashworth, Gregory J., and Brian Graham. 1997. Heritage, identity and Europe. *Tijdschrift voor Economische en Sociale Geografie* 88 (4): 381–388.

Beissinger, Mark R., and Stephen Kotkin, eds. 2014. *Historical Legacies of Communism in Russia and Eastern Europe*. New York: Cambridge University Press.

Boia, Lucian. 2001. *History and Myth in Romanian Consciousness*. Budapest: CEU Press.

Bougarel, Xavier. 2005. L'héritage ottoman dans les recompositions de l'identité musulmane / bochniaque. In *La perception de l'héritage ottoman dans les Balkans*, ed. Sylvie Gangloff, 63–94. Paris: L'Harmattan.

Brunnbauer, Ulf. 2004. Historiography, Myths and the Nation in the Republic of Macedonia. In *(Re)Writing History. Historiography in Southeast Europe after Socialism*, ed. Ulf Brunnbauer, 165–200. Münster: Lit.

Bunce, Valerie. 2005. The National Idea: Imperial Legacies and Post-Communist Pathways in Eastern Europe. *East European Politics and Societies* 19 (3): 406–442.

Carr, Edward H. 1961. *What is History?* London: Macmillan.

Clayer, Nathalie. 2005. The issue of the conversion to Islam in Albanian politics and identity. In *La perception de l'héritage ottoman dans les Balkans*, ed. Sylvie Gangloff, 95–128. Paris: L'Harmattan.

Clogg, Richard. 1988. The Greeks and Their Past. In *Historians as Nation-Builders*, ed. Dennis Deletant and Harry Hanak, 15–30. London: Macmillan.

Çolak, Yılmaz. 2008. Neo-Ottomanism, Cultural Diversity and Contemporary Turkish Politics. In *Europe and the Historical Legacies in the Balkans*, ed. Raymond Detrez and Barbara Segaert, 147–157. Bruxelles: Peter Lang.

Concise Oxford Dictionary of Archaeology. 2021. 3rd ed. online version.

Danforth, Loring. 1997. *The Macedonian Conflict. Ethnic Nationalism in a Transnational World*. Princeton, New Jersey: Princeton University Press.

Daskalov, Roumen. 2024. *Istoriografski sporove za Srednovekovieto: Bǎlgaro-srǎbski, bǎlgaro-makedonski*. Sofia: Izdatelstvo na Sofiyskiya universitet "Sv. Kliment Ohridski".

Dević, Ana. 2016. Ottomanism and Neo-Ottomanism in the Travails of the 'Serbian National Corpus': Turkey as the Recurrent Focus of Serbian Academia. *Die Welt des Islams* 56:534–548.

Dimitrova-Grajzl, Valentina. 2007. The Great Divide Revisited: Ottoman and Habsburg Legacies on Transition. *Kyklos* 60 (4): 539–558.

Dokmanović, Mišo. 2021. The Unexpected Twist: The Historical Legacies of the Twentieth Century and the process of 'Antiquisation' in Macedonia. In *Balkan Legacies. The Long Shadow of Conflict and Ideological Experiment in Southeastern Europe*, ed. Balazs Apor and John Paul Newman, 253–273. West Lafayette, Indiana: Purdue University Press.

Erimtan, Can. 2008. Hittites, Ottomans and Turks: Ağaoğlu Ahmed Bey and the Kemalist Construction of Turkish Nationhood in Anatolia. *Anatolian Studies* 58:141–171.

Filandra, Šaćir. 2017. Instrumentalization of History in Bosnia and Herzegovina. In *Of Red Dragons and Evil Spirits. Post-Communist Historiography Between Democratization and New Politics of History*, ed. Oto Luthar, 159–185. Budapest and New York: CEU Press.

Friedman, Victor A. 1975. Macedonian language and nationalism during the 19th and early 20th centuries. *Balcanistica* 2:83–98.

Gangloff, Sylvie, ed. 2005. *La perception de l'héritage ottoman dans les Balkans.* Paris: L'Harmattan.

Google Classroom. n.d. What is Cultural Heritage. https://www.khanacademy.org/humanities/special-topics-art-history/arches-at-risk-cultural-heritage-education-series/arches-beginners-guide/a/what-is-cultural-heritage, accessed 28.12.2023

Hajdarpašić, Edin. 2008. Out of the Ruins of the Ottoman Empire: Reflections on the Ottoman Legacy in South-eastern Europe. *Middle Eastern Studies* 44 (5): 715–734.

Harrison, Rodney. 2010. What is heritage? In *Understanding the Politics of Heritage*, ed. Rodney Harrison, 5–42. Manchester: Manchester University Press.

Harrison, Rodney. 2013. *Heritage. Critical Approaches.* Abingdon, Oxon: Routledge.

Harvey, David. 2001. Heritage pasts and heritage presents: Temporality, meaning and the scope of heritage studies. *International Journal of Heritage Studies* 7 (4): 319–338.

Harvey, David. 2008. A History of Heritage. In *The Ashgate Companion to Heritage and Identity*, ed. Brian Graham and Peter Howard, 19–36. London: Ashgate.

Heritage Council. n.d. What is Heritage. https://www.heritagecouncil.ie/about/what-is-heritage, accessed 28.12.2023

Herzfeld, Michael. 1982. *Ours Once More: Folklore, Ideology, and the Making of Modern Greece.* Austin: University of Texas Press.

46   D. MISHKOVA

Hewison, Robert. 1987. *The Heritage Industry: Britain in a Climate of Decline*. London: Methuen.

Hobsbawm, Eric. 1983a. Introduction: Inventing Traditions. In *The Invention of Tradition*, ed. Eric Hobsbawn and Terence Ranger, 1–14. Cambridge: Cambridge University Press.

Hobsbawm, Eric. 1983b. Mass-Producing Traditions: Europe, 1870–1914. In *The Invention of Tradition*, ed. Eric Hobsbawn and Terence Ranger, 263–307. Cambridge: Cambridge University Press.

IPinCH. 2014. Cultural Heritage. https://www.sfu.ca/ipinch/sites/default/files/resources/fact_sheets/ipinch_chfactsheet_final.pdf

Istorija na makedonskiot narod. 2008. Skopje: INI.

Istorija naroda Jugoslavije. Prva knjiga (do početka XVI veka). 1953. Belgrade: Prosveta.

Kaiser, Timothy. 1995. Archaeology and ideology in southeast Europe. In *Nationalism, Politics, and the Practice of Archaeology*, ed. Philip L. Kohl and Clare Fawcett, 99–119. Cambridge: Cambridge University Press.

Kaldellis, Anthony. 2007. *Hellenism in Byzantium: The Transformations of Greek Identity and the Reception of the Classical Tradition*. Cambridge: Cambridge University Press.

Kamberović, Husnija. 2007. Između kritičke historiografije i ideološkog revizionizma. In *Revizija prošlosti na prostorima bivše Jugoslavije. Zbornik radova*, ed. Vera Katz, 11–21. Sarajevo: Institut za istorije.

Karačić, Darko, Tamara Banjeglav, and Nataša Govedarić, eds. 2012. *Revizija prošlosti—Politike sjećanja u BiH, Hrvatskoj i Srbiji od 1990. Godine*. Sarajevo: Friedrich-Ebert-Stiftung.

Katz, Vera, ed. 2007. *Revizija prošlosti na prostorima bivše Jugoslavije: zbornik radova*. Sarajevo: Institut za istorije.

Kitschelt, Herbert. 2003. Accounting for Postcommunist Regime Diversity: What Counts as a Good Cause? In *Capitalism and Democracy in Central and Eastern Europe: Assessing the Legacy of Communist Rule*, ed. Grzegorz Ekiert and Stephen E. Hanson, 49–86. Cambridge: Cambridge University Press.

Koulouri, Christina, ed. 2002. *Clio in the Balkans. The politics of History Education*. Thessaloniki: SDRSEE.

LaPorte, Jody, and Danielle N. Lussier. 2011. What Is the Leninist Legacy? Assessing Twenty Years of Scholarship. *Slavic Review* 7 (3): 637–654.

Lazova, Tsvete. 2016. *Antichnost, arheologiya i natsiolanlo văobrazyavane*. Sofia: NBU.

Leitsch, Walter. 1988. East Europeans Studying History in Vienna (1855–1918). In *Historians as Nation Builders*, ed. Dennis Deletant and Harry Hanak, 139–156. London: Palgrave Macmillan.

Lowenthal, David. 1985. *The Past is a Foreign Country*. Cambridge: Cambridge University Press.

Lowenthal, David. 1994. Identity, Heritage, and History. In *Commemorations: the politics of national identity*, ed. John R. Gillis, 41–57. Princeton, N.J: Princeton University Press.

Lowenthal, David. 1998. *The Heritage Crusade and the Spoils of History*. Cambridge: Cambridge University Press.

Lowenthal, David. 2004. The Heritage Crusade and its Contradictions. In *Giving Preservation a History: Histories of Historic Preservation in the United States*, ed. Max Page and Randall F. Mason, 19–44. London and New York: Routledge.

Macdonald, Sharon. 2009. *Negotiating the Nazi Past in Nuremberg and Beyond*. London and New York: Routledge.

Madgearu, Alexandru. 2008. *The Wars of the Balkan Peninsula. Their Medieval Origins*. Lahman, Maryland—Toronto—Plymouth, UK: The Scarecrow Press.

Marinov, Tchavdar. 2001. Za lăzhite na makedonizma i mitovete za bălgarshtinata v Makedoniya. *Kritika i humanizăm* 12 (3): 56–88.

Marinov, Tchavdar. 2010. *La Question Macédonienne de 1944 a nos jours. Communisme et nationalisme dans les Balkans*. Paris: L'Harmattan.

Marinov, Tchavdar. 2013. Famous Macedonia, the Land of Alexander: Macedonian Identity at the Crossroads of Greek, Bulgarian and Serbian Nationalism. In *Entangled Histories of the Balkans—Vol. I: National Ideologies and Language Policies*, ed. Roumen Daskalov and Tchavdar Marinov, 273–330. Leiden: Brill.

Millas, Hercules. 2008. Ethnic Identity and Nation Building: On the Byzantine and Ottoman Historical Legacies. In *Europe and the Historical Legacies in the Balkans*, ed. Raymond Detrez and Barbara Sagaert, 17–30. Bruxells, etc: P.I.E. Peter Lang.

Milošević, Srđan. 2011. Arrested Development: Mythical Characteristics in the 'Five Hundred Years of Turkish yoke'. In *Images of Imperial Legacy. Modern Discourses on the Social and Cultural Impact of Ottoman and Habsburg Rule in Southeast Europe*, ed. Tea Sindbaek and Maximilian Hartmuth, 69–77. Berlin: Lit.

Mishkova, Diana. 2019. *Beyond Balkanism. The Scholarly Politics of Region Making*. Abingdon: Routledge.

Mishkova, Diana. 2021. Spatial Configurations. Regional intellectual imageries in twentieth-century Central and Eastern Europe. In *The Routledge History Handbook of Central and Eastern Europe in the Twentieth Century, Vol.3: Intellectual Horizons*, ed. Włodzimierz Borodziej, Ferenc Laczó, and Joachim von Puttkamer, 1–68. London and New York: Routledge.

Mishkova, Diana. 2023. *Rival Byzantiums. Empire and Identity in Southeastern Europe*. Cambridge: Cambridge University Press.

Mutafchiev, Petăr. 1931. Kăm filosofiyata na bălgarskata istoriya. Vizantinizmăt v srednovekovna Bălgaria. *Filosofski pregled* 3/1: 27–36 [originally published as 'Der Byzantinismus im mittelalterlicher Bulgarien', *Byzantinische Zeitschrift* 30: 387–94 (1929–1930)].

Mylonas, Harris. 2019. Nation-building policies in the Balkans: an Ottoman or a manufactured legacy? *Nations and Nationalism* 25 (3): 866–887.

Nora, Pierre. 1989. Between Memory and History: Les Lieux de Mémoire. *Representations* 26:7–24.

Oakeshott, Michael. 1983. *On History and Other Essays.* Oxford: Basil Blackwell.

Onar, Nora Fisher. 2009. Neo-Ottomanism, Historical Legacies, and Turkish Foreign Policy. *EDAM/German Marshall Fund Working Paper Series* 3:1–16.

The Oxford Dictionary of English. 2010. Third ed. (online). Oxford: Oxford University Press.

Oxford Dictionary of Human Geography. 2013. Oxford: Oxford University Press, online edition.

Özal, Turgut. 1991. *Turkey in Europe and Europe in Turkey.* Nicosia: K. Rustem & Brother (1st ed. 1988 *La Turquie en Europe.* Paris: Plon)

Panov, Branko. 1985. *Srednovekovna Makedonija*, t. 3. Skopje: Misla (1st ed. 1972).

Peckham, Robert S. 2003. Introduction: The Politics of Heritage and the Public Culture. In *Rethinking Heritage: Cultures and Politics in Europe*, ed. Robert S. Peckham, 1–13. London: I.B. Tauris.

Pipa, Arshi. 1990. *Albanian Stalinism: Ideo-Political Aspects*, 1990. Boulder: East European Monographs.

Radonić, Ljiljana. 2017. Equalizing Jesus's, Jewish, and Croat Suffering—Post-Socialist Politics of History in Croatia. In *Of Red Dragons and Evil Spirits. Post-Communist Historiography Between Democratization and New Politics of History*, ed. Oto Luthar, 33–57. Budapest and New York: CEU Press.

Reef, Paul. 2018. Macedonian Monument Culture Beyond 'Skopje 2014'. *Südosteuropa* 66 (4): 451–480.

Ristovski, Blaže. 1983. *Makedonskiot narod i makedonskata nacija*, t. 1. Skopje: Misla (1st ed. 1969).

Robins, Kevin. 2005. Identity. In *New Keywords: A Revised Vocabulary of Culture and Society*, ed. Tony Bennett, Lawrence Grossberg, and Meaghan Morris, 172–175. Malden, MA and Oxford: Blackwell.

Roudometof, Victor. 2002. *Collective Memory, National Identity, and Ethnic Conflict.* Westport, Connecticut, London: Praeger.

Schwarz, Bill. 2005. Heritage. In *New Keywords: A Revised Vocabulary of Culture and Society*, ed. Tony Bennett, Lawrence Grossberg, and Meaghan Morris, 154–156. Malden, MA and Oxford: Blackwell Publishing.

Sindbaek, Tea, and Maximilian Hartmuth. 2011. Introducing images of imperial legacy in Southeast Europe. In *Images of Imperial Legacy. Modern discourses on the social and cultural impact of Ottoman and Habsburg rule in Southeast Europe*, ed. Tea Sindbaek and Maximilian Hartmuth, 1–6. Berlin: Lit.

Skordos, Adamantios. 2011. Makedonischer Namensstreit und griechischer Bürgerkrieg. Ein kulturhistorischer Erklärungsversuch der griechischen Makedonien-Haltung 1991. *Südosteuropa-Mitteilungen* 51 (4): 36–56.

Smith, Anthony D. 1999. *Myths and Memories of the Nation*. Oxford: Oxford University Press.

Smith, Laurajane. 2006. *Uses of Heritage*. Abingdon and New York: Routledge.

Stojanović, Dubravka. 2008. Balkan History Workbooks—Consequences and Experiences. *European Studies (Tokyo)* 7:157–162.

Stojanović, Dubravka. 2011. Value Changes in the Interpretations of History in Serbia. In *Civic and Uncivic Values. Serbia in the Post-Milošević Era*, ed. Ola Listhaug, Sabrina P. Ramet, and Dragana Dulić, 221–240. Budapest and New York: CEU Press.

Todorova, Maria. 1995. The Ottoman Legacy in the Balkans. In *The Imperial Legacy: The Ottoman Imprint on the Balkans and the Middle East*, ed. Carl Brown, 45–77. New York: Columbia University Press.

Todorova, Maria. 1997. *Imagining the Balkans*. New York: Oxford University Press.

Todorova, Maria. 2002. Der Balkan als Analysekategorie: Grenzen, Raum. Zeit. *Geschichte und Gesellschaft* 3:470–492.

Todorova, Maria. 2005. Spacing Europe. What Is a Historical Region? *East Central Europe* 32 (1–2): 59–78.

Trigger, Bruce. 1984. Alternative Archaeologies: Nationalist, Colonialist, Imperialist. *Man* 19:355–370.

Trigger, Bruce. 1996. *A History of Archaeological Thought*. 2nd ed. New York: Cambridge University Press.

Troebst, Stefan. 1983. *Die bulgarisch-jugoslawische Kontroverse um Makedonien 1967–1982*. Munich: Oldenbourg.

Troebst, Stefan. 2022. The Resurfacing of the 'Titanic' in the Balkan Bermuda Triangle: Political Conflicts over History between Sofia, Skopje and Athens before and after 1989. In *Instrumentalizing the Past: The Impact of History on Contemporary International Conflicts*, ed. Jan Rydel and Stefan Troebst, 245–257. Boston, Berlin: De Gruyter Oldenbourg.

Tunbridge, John E., and Gregory J. Ashworth. 1996. *Dissonant Heritage: The Management of the Past as a Resource in Conflict*. Chichester: Wiley.

UNESCO. n.d. World Heritage. https://www.unesco.org/en/world-heritage, accessed 28.12.2023.

United Nations. 1995. Interim Accord. September 13 (UN Doc. S/1995/794, Annexes I-IX)

Vangeli, Anastas. 2011. *Antička segašnost. Osvrt kon grčko-makedonskiot spor za Aleksandrovoto nasledstvo*. Skopje: Templum.

Walsh, Kevin. 1992. *The Representation of the Past. Museums and Heritage in the Post-modern World*. London and New York: Routledge.

Williams, Raymond. 1977. *Marxism and Literature*. New York: Oxford University Press.

Williams, Raymond. 2015. *Keywords. A Vocabulary of Culture and Society*. New York: Oxford University Press.

Wittenberg, Jason. 2015. Conceptualizing Historical Legacies. *East European Politics and Societies and Cultures* 29 (2): 366–378.

Wright, Patrick. 1985. *On Living in an Old Country: The National Past in Contemporary Britain*. London: Verso.

Yavuz, M. Hakan. 1998. Turkish Identity and Foreign Policy in Flux: The Rise of Neo-Ottomanism. *Middle East critique* 7 (12): 19–41.

CHAPTER 2

Controversies Over Samuel's State

Roumen Daskalov

Tsar Samuel's (in Bulgarian—Samuil) state was founded between 969 and 976 by Samuel and his brothers, the *kometopuli* (meaning sons of a *komes* or comes, regional governor) in Macedonia on the territory of the former Bulgarian state, which had been conquered first by Prince Sviatoslav of Kievan Rus and then by Byzantium in 971. It engaged after 976 in fierce and protracted warfare against Byzantium and reached the peak of its might toward the end of the tenth century, when it included most of the Balkans. Then it was forced onto the defensive until it fell under Byzantine rule in 1018. Samuel himself died in 1014 after the routing of his troops in the Battle of Kleidion (in the Belasitsa mountain, village of Klyuch) and the blinding of 14,000 of his men by the Byzantine Emperor Basil II the Bulgar-Slayer, but the state survived four more years under his successors.

Samuel's state has been the subject of numerous controversies between Bulgarian, Serbian, and Macedonian historians. These concern when and how the state was created, the rather enigmatic provenance of Samuel's family, his relations with the eunuch Roman (the last legitimate heir of the fallen Bulgarian state), and the way Samuel was crowned. But the most controversial of all is the ethnic composition of his state and its relation to

---

R. Daskalov (✉)
Institute of Balkan Studies and Centre of Thracology at the Bulgarian Academy of Sciences, Sofia, Bulgaria

© The Author(s), under exclusive license to Springer Nature Switzerland AG 2025
D. Mishkova, R. Daskalov (eds.), *Balkan Historiographical Wars*, https://doi.org/10.1007/978-3-031-90113-3_2

51

the fallen Bulgarian state, especially its eastern part in today's northern Bulgaria. While it is not the only historical controversy over Macedonia, concerning the Middle Ages, it is the most central.

These controversies have always been embedded in a particular socio-political context and, in this case, several contexts: from the establishment of the Bulgarian Exarchate in 1870 until the Balkan Wars and World War I; the interwar period; the communist era; and the post-communist transition until today. They began as a protracted Bulgarian-Serbian controversy, joined after the creation of a Macedonian republic in Tito's Yugoslavia by Macedonian historians. The controversies had various extra-scientific stakes and motivations, particularly a rivalry for the possession of heritages connected with national identities, and for the validation of "historical rights" over territories. The historiographical clashes came from opposing interpretations of the same events, personalities, institutions (especially the state and the church), and other phenomena.

In this work I will deal primarily with controversies between professional historians, though they were also highly politicized and can hardly be qualified as unbiased, scientifically distanced or purely professional. In fact, they attest to the close intertwining of science and politics, historiography and ideology—a veritable "politics through history" or *Geschichtspolitik* in German (Troebst 2007, 426–27; Höpken 1999, 210–43).

The Pre-communist Bulgarian-Serbian Debates: A Synopsis

I will begin reviewing the points of contention by using the Bulgarian national (and more pointedly nationalist) interpretation, put under attack by Serbian historians, as a sort of "measuring rod" and orientation for the stakes of the controversy. I will pay special attention to what is "ideally" most favorable from the point of view of the Bulgarian national narrative, which is concerned mostly with the continuity and identity of institutions, but especially regarding ethnicity, though there were differences on these issues between the Bulgarian historians themselves.

There is controversy, to begin with, on how Samuel's state emerged. One view is that it emerged through "secession" from the Bulgarian state with a revolt against the legitimate Bulgarian ruler Tsar Peter (or Petăr) while he was still alive, with the wrong dating of this revolt by the Bulgarian historian Marin Drinov in 963, purely for reasons of power (Drinov 1971a, 396, 403–06, 431, 1971b, 523, 548–49). Or, somewhat more acceptably from a Bulgarian national point of view, through a revolt in 969 (the correct date) already after his death against his absent sons, but again motivated by a striving for power (Balaschev 1929, 11), or still more acceptably, because of the pro-Byzantine policies of the tsar's court and the separation of the ruling circles from the people (Zlatarski 1927, 630–32). Alternatively, Samuel's state emerged through a Bulgarian uprising against Byzantium after emperor Tzimiskes' death in 976 (Anastasijević 1927, 5–8). We will later see the use of the 969 revolt by Macedonian historians in an anti-Bulgarian sense and its rejection by most Bulgarian historians in favor of a single uprising in 976.

What made the date and number of the revolts so crucial is that a revolt in 969 could only be against the legitimate Bulgarian dynasty, whether motivated by a striving for power or because of the incompetent and pro-Byzantine Bulgarian rule (Zlatarski 1927, 630–2), or even for the salvation of the Bulgarian state (Mutafchiev 1943, 278–79). On the other hand, a single revolt in 976 could only be directed against Byzantium. However, according to the Serbian historian Dragutin Anastasijević, it did not lead to the restoration of the Bulgarian state, but to the formation of a different state (of Samuel): that is why he puts Samuel's Macedonian (or Ohrid) Bulgaria everywhere in inverted commas and speaks of Moesia (today's northern Bulgaria) as the "real Bulgaria" (Anastasijević 1927, 6), in contrast to Macedonia. Therefore, this date in itself is not unambiguous and can also have a dual meaning. Besides, there then arises for Bulgarian historians the awkward task of accounting for the time between 971 (the fall of the eastern Bulgarian lands) and 976, lest Bulgarian continuity is interrupted.

Did the western part of the Bulgarian state preserve independence after the fall of the eastern part? The prevailing opinion amongst Bulgarian authors is that it remained free or de facto free, but according to Anastasijević it fell under Byzantine supremacy until 976 (1927, 5–8, 11). According to the Serbian historian Božidar Prokić it was free until 973 when it was subjugated for two years (Prokić 1908, 248–56). From a Bulgarian point of view, it would be better if the western part remained independent in order to preserve continuity with the Bulgarian state, and that it then took the initiative for the war against Byzantium in 976.

Another disputed issue is over the place from which the 976 uprising against Byzantium began—from the free western part (Drinov 1971a,

430–31, 1971b, 547–48) or from the subjugated eastern part (Mutafchiev 1943, 281), or from both together in unison. This final suggestion may mean that the western part was free (as with Zlatarski 1927, 642–44), but not necessarily so (according to Anastasijević, mentioned above, it was not free). The scenario of an "agreement" between the two regions suits the Bulgarian national position best, but the other scenarios are also acceptable.

What was the attitude of the *kometopuli* toward the eastern part of the state? Did they liberate it first as a priority (Zlatarski 1927, 642–44; Mutafchiev 1943, 281—though untrue) or did it remain secondary for them, hence their first actions in other directions—the campaigns to the south in Macedonia, Thessaly, and Greece (Gil'ferding 1866, 202–04) and later easy renouncing of the eastern part (Serbian and Macedonian authors below)?

Another disputed question is how the *kometopuli* assumed power. Was it on their own initiative, either with an emphasis on self-will, most extreme in Balaschev as "usurpation" (Balaschev 1929, 28–29) or justified by Blagoev as a temporary "taking over" of the authority with the establishment of a regency based on kinship ties with the former Bulgarian dynasty (Blagoev 1931, 30–32, 1942, 33) (untrue). Or, the authority was "entrusted" to them, and therefore the further question is whether this was done also by the Bulgarians from the eastern part (as with Zlatarski 1927, 642–44) or not. It is clear that the "entrusting" of the *kometopuli* with authority serves Bulgarian state legitimacy better, the more so if Bulgarians (actually, boyars) from the eastern part also participated. In Mutafchiev there is also the further idea of a manifest leadership of the *kometopuli*, who twice (in 969 and 976) took initiative in cases of danger and assumed responsibility, but at the same time showed loyalty to the dynasty (Mutafchiev 1943, 279, 282).

The origins of the *kometopuli* was also debated. Were they Slavicized Bulgarians (i.e., Turkic Bulgars mixed with Slavs) or even "pure" Turkic Bulgars (Blagoev 1926, 25–27, 1942, 28–30 with followers under the communist regime); "pure" Slavs from the *Berzetes* or *Brsiak* tribe in Macedonia (Irechek 1976, 127; Prokić 1908, 236–37 and Macedonian authors after him); half Armenians through their mother Ripsimia (Ivanov 1925, 55–62, Adontz 1965, 381–94), Persians from the Vardariotes (Petković 1919, 23–5); or even Vlachs (Iorga 1927, 7–9). The Bitola inscription of the last Bulgarian Tsar John (Joannes, or Ivan in Bulgarian) Vladislav, where he declares himself "Bulgarian by birth", and that he repaired the fortress for the safety of the Bulgarians, was discovered later in 1956. Ethnic origin is of particular importance from a national and nationalist point of view. From this perspective, the most desirable (though improbable) interpretation is that Samuel's family was of direct Bulgar descent, followed by the Slavicized Bulgars or Bulgarianized Slavs interpretation (which is implied by the term "Bulgarians" in most Bulgarian authors). Arguing that they were "pure Slavs" is problematic from the Bulgarian nationalist point of view as it opens the door for a Macedonian ancestry through the *Brsiak* tribe, as in Prokić. From a nationalist Bulgarian point of view, the other possibilities, such as the Armenian one, are undesirable, though Yordan Ivanov offered the option of "Bulgarianized" Armenians, while the Persian hypothesis remained exotic (besides being refuted).

Of particular significance from the point of view of legitimacy, and more broadly continuity, is the question of whether the castrated Roman, the son of Tsar Peter, was recognized as tsar by Samuel after he fled from Byzantine captivity. If he was recognized as tsar (Zlatarski 1927, 656–58, 693; Blagoev 1931, 28–29, 34; Mutafchiev 1943, 282) this would present a strong argument in favor of the Bulgarian thesis of continuity. If not (as with many authors), the change in dynasty seems to hint at illegitimacy and even a "new state" of Samuel. Nonetheless, justifications existed. For example, it has been argued that Roman was not enthroned because according to the then valid principle eunuchs could not become tsar (Gil'ferding 1866, 196–97; Irechek 1976, 141, 144; Prokić 1908, 280–81, 284). It has also been argued that he was not enthroned because he was seen by the *kometopuli* as a Byzantine puppet (with some socialist authors, e.g., Yonchev 1965, 45–48). An intermediary position also exists—that he was recognized by the *kometopuli* as co-tsar in order to bolster their own authority and to prevent the resentment of the boyars (Balaschev 1929, 40, 42).

Did Samuel become tsar, and if yes (the opinion of most authors), when was he crowned: before or after the death of Roman, and by whom? If he was crowned before Roman's death, this resembles usurpation because of the availability of a living heir to the dynasty who was also the grandson of the great Tsar Simeon, expressed most strongly by Balaschev above (although in his opinion Roman was accepted as co-ruler). If Samuel was crowned after Roman's death, or at least after his second captivity, irrespective of whether the latter was tsar or not, this shows respect for the Bulgarian royal tradition (Zlatarski 1927, 695, 700–02; Blagoev 1942, 38–39; Mutafchiev 1943, 285).

56   R. DASKALOV

By whom was Samuel crowned? That he was not crowned by the Byzantine Patriarch is clear, because he was not recognized as a legitimate ruler by Byzantium, according to whose ideology he was a "rebel", "usurper", and "tyrant", but this is not important for the Bulgarian thesis. The argument that he was crowned by the Bulgarian patriarch is best for the Bulgarian thesis, as it asserts the church and royal tradition (Snegarov 1919, 7, 1924, 21 and similar opinions by other Bulgarian authors later on). The argument that he was crowned by the Pope (Gil'ferding 1866, 224–25; Rački 1931, 22–23; Balaschev 1929, 28–29) is still acceptable insofar as he received a Bulgarian crown and became a Bulgarian tsar, which ensures a continuity of the royal institution. But this belittles the significance of the Bulgarian Patriarchate that fled to him and weakens, even disrupts, the Bulgarian church continuity. If Samuel was not legitimately crowned as with Ferluga (see below) in the sense of not being recognized by Byzantium (Ostrogorski and Barišić, eds. 1966, 64n, 79–81n) then the Bulgarian "thesis" also suffers. Yet this allows for a certain qualification in the sense that even if he was not formally crowned, he actually ruled as a sovereign and therefore he considered himself, and was in effect, tsar.

Some of the controversies also concern the Ohrid Patriarchate/ Archbishopric. Was it a continuation of the Durostorum Bulgarian Patriarchate and identical with it? Or did it originate in the much older Justiniana Prima? This thesis spread with the church's Hellenization under Byzantine rule, but found later expression in the historiography, especially with some Serbian and Macedonian authors. Or, finally, was it a new institution, founded by Samuel to complement the new state and aid in his elevation to tsar (Prokić 1912, 201–02, 261–62, and other Serbian and Macedonian authors after him)? The major arguments in favor of a continuity and identity with the Bulgarian Patriarchate are that the Bulgarian Patriarch fled there after the fall of the eastern Bulgarian lands and that Basil II later recognized the Ohrid Archbishopric as autocephalous, within the older Bulgarian diocesan boundaries even expanded in Samuel's era, though he degraded it to an archbishopric.

The ethnic composition of Samuel's state is also a major point of contention. According to all Serbian authors it had a small number of Turkic Bulgars and was made up mostly of Slavs, who were "pure" Slavs, that is, not assimilated with Bulgars, and more precisely ethnically indeterminate Slavs from Macedonia, called also "Macedonian" Slavs in a regional sense, not ethnically separate. Later on, Macedonian historians would speak of ethnically distinct "Macedonian" Slavs (see below). If a mixed ethnic composition of Macedonian Slavs, Bulgarians from Moesia (today's northern Bulgaria), Serbs (after the Serbian statelets fell under Samuel's authority), Greeks, Vlachs, Armenians, and Jews within Samuel's state is admitted, then the debate is about who prevailed, and the Bulgarians are often ranked in the third place after the Macedonian Slavs and the Serbs (e.g., Prokić 1906, 7, 25, 1908, 213, 256, 282). It has to be added that in a deliberate strategy of reducing the number of Bulgarians in Samuel's state what most (but not all) Serbian authors categorize under "Bulgarians" are only Turkic Bulgars and eventually Bulgarianized Slavs (Slavicized Bulgars) from Moesia. This is contrary to the Bulgarian understanding that all Slavs in medieval Macedonia were Bulgarians not only because they are called so in the sources but also because they were biologically mixed with Bulgars or Slavicized Bulgars from Moesia or culturally Bulgarianized under the earlier Bulgarian rule.

The main stake in the controversies around Samuel's state revolve around its "character" or identity: whether and to what extent it was a Bulgarian state (as a continuation of the previous Bulgarian state or identical with it) or an entirely new state. One can also encounter statements by Romanian authors about the great role of the Vlachs in Samuel's state. Thus, according to Nicolae Iorga, its military forces were primarily made up of Vlachs and Albanians (Iorga 1912/1913, 79, 1927, 9). Petre Panaitescu even affirms in polemics with Mutafchiev that the Vlachs (Rumanians) played the primary role in Samuel's kingdom (Panaitescu 1929, 23).

How Samuel's state is named expresses these controversies in a condensed way. It has been named the Western Bulgarian Kingdom, the Ohrid Kingdom, Samuel's state (or Kingdom), Samuel's Bulgaria, the "Slavic State" in Macedonia, or the Macedonian State (in an ethno-national sense). One can generally say that until World War II Samuel's state was typically called the Western Bulgarian Kingdom by Bulgarian historians (under Drinov's influence) or Samuel's Kingdom and, more rarely, the Kingdom of Ohrid. This would become politically incorrect under communism, which preferred the unambiguously Bulgarian designation Samuel's Bulgaria. In the same era Samuel's state was called Macedonian in an ethno-national sense by the Macedonian authors.

The causes of the controversy are varied. On one level they came from the heterogeneous and contradictory sources and from gaps and incongruities even within the same source. An extreme example is the use of falsified and entirely erroneous sources, such as the so-called *Dalmatian List* of Pincius and the *Zograf Memorial List* of the Bulgarian Tsars, which misled Drinov and others as to the identity of Samuel and his family and their place of origin. An example of varying reliability are sources with a more distant (Armenian, Arab) origin with gaps, distortions of data and contradictions, yet containing new information which puts some points in the Byzantine sources into question. But even the Byzantine sources, usually seen as the most reliable, are not devoid of their biases and intentionality or gaps. For example, the basic source, Joannes Skylitzes' Chronicle, rendered literally by Kedrin, says nothing on Basil II's campaign of 991 to 995, which was reported by the Arab author Yahya.

Changes in views were also connected with later discoveries and the introduction of new authentic sources, such as Samuel's tomb inscription from the village of German near the Prespa Lake, the additions by Michael of Devol to Skylitzes-Kedrin's Chronicle, and the later discovery of the Bitola inscription of Joannes Vladislav. Finally, some of the questions that interest the national historians simply did not enter the perspective of the medieval authors, and so are not explicitly addressed.

There then begin the attempts of historians to reconstruct historical events from the available sources, accompanied also by hypotheses and conjectures to get at the meaning of the events. Preference is given to one source over another or several sources are used, which results in different reconstructions of what happened. During these logical operations gaps are filled in, often from "clues" or judgments from subsequent developments, so that contradictions are smoothed over and explained away. An example is the issue of two rebellions according to Skylitzes: some historians eliminate the first one as literary "anticipation" of the second one, while others accept both.

Given this situation, even the most conscientious and unbiased historians can create different reconstructions of the events contained in the sources and adduce differences in the motivations of the participating personalities. It is widely recognized that these reconstructions already contain interpretations that reflect the historian's own, in this case mostly nationalistic, preferences. There are also freer and arbitrary interpretations which add to what is said in the sources. The historian's own narrative orders the events in a meaningful way that lays additional signification on the narrated course of events. This seems unavoidable and only the juxtaposing and "clashing" of different interpretations of the kind I am trying

2 CONTROVERSIES OVER SAMUEL'S STATE   59

to conduct here in a sort of meta-historical reflection makes possible their explication, through comparing and relativizing, if not neutralizing, them.

The controversies that are the subject of the present work are conditioned by the nationalist orientation of the interpretations in the first place. An example from the present work is the various interpretations of the 969 movement of the *kometopuli*: was it a pure usurpation against the legitimate authorities, an anti-Byzantine move, or even an action for the salvation of the Bulgarian state? Or was it an expression of feudal separatism as in the dogmatic Stalinist years later on with Dimitãr Angelov (Kosev et al. 1954, 144), or a Macedonian attempt to break with Bulgarian rule (see in the relevant section)? The sources are drawn into a game of nationalist interpretations and used for proving nationalist historical theses and the creation of national master narratives. In these national narratives, the continuity and identity of Samuel's state (and church) is the main stake: was it a continuation of the Bulgarian Kingdom, a new Slavic state in Macedonia, or a state of the Macedonian Slavs and later to-be Macedonians?

We can delineate here the most consistent pro-Bulgarian interpretation, proceeding from Bulgarian national tenets. It would harden into a national truth later on with the evolution of the socialist regime toward communist nationalism, accompanied by newer considerations and arguments. According to this interpretation, there was only one uprising, in 976, and it was unambiguously directed against Byzantium; in case a previous 969 attempt is admitted, it was against the pro-Byzantine policies of the state. The 976 uprising broke out simultaneously in the eastern and the western parts of Bulgaria, and if it broke out first in the western part, it immediately rushed to the liberation of the eastern part and not in other directions. The uprising was led by the *kometopuli*, especially by Samuel, who were of Bulgar descent or at least descended from Slavicized Bulgars. Samuel was entrusted with the rule by the Bulgarian boyars both from the east and the west. Tsar Peter's son Roman was recognized as tsar upon his flight from Byzantine captivity to Samuel, although he had been castrated. Samuel was proclaimed tsar only after Roman's death and received the crown from the Bulgarian Patriarch of the Bulgarian Durostorum Patriarchate, who had fled to Macedonia and thus continued the tradition of the Bulgarian church and kingdom. The directions of expansion of Samuel's state were the same as those of Simeon's empire, namely toward Albania, the Adriatic coast, and Serbia, and the objectives were similar— anti-Byzantine and to "unify" the kindred Slavs from the "Bulgarian group". Samuel's state was Bulgarian in its ethnic composition (with some lesser ethnic groups of no significance), as expressed in the names "Bulgarian" and "Bulgaria" in the sources. It was entirely identical to the Bulgarian state of Tsar Simeon and Tsar Peter (and of the khans before them) with only a transfer of the center of the state to the west because of the fall of its eastern part and the old capitals.

This is the most hardline pro-Bulgarian view. It was not worked out into a Bulgarian "position" (the very word implies extra-scientific rigidity that rests on faith) immediately, but evolved, most consistently during the late socialist era and after it. At the start was Drinov who, given the then-available sources and incipient controversies, did not find anything wrong with a secession of the western Bulgarian lands via a revolt of Samuel's family against Tsar Peter motivated by a purely selfish desire for power. Neither did he find fault with the creation in this way of a separate Western Bulgarian Kingdom in Macedonia parallel to the Bulgarian Eastern Kingdom.

For Zlatarski and Mutafchiev, later on, this would not suffice. They also thought that there was a previous attempt before the 976 uprising, correctly dated in 969, directed against the Bulgarian state of Tsar Peter's heirs, whatever the justifications (anti-Byzantinism, patriotism, etc.). For them the *kometopuli*, whatever their origins, were continuators and renewers of the Bulgarian royal institution, if not necessarily of the Bulgarian dynasty, and Samuel waited until the extinction of the old dynasty and the vacancy of the crown before sitting legitimately on the throne as founder of a new Bulgarian dynasty. The Western Bulgarian Kingdom (or more rarely, "Ohrid Kingdom") is for them the continuation of the Bulgarian state, whether it "overlapped" with it for a time (Zlatarski) or was created after its fall (Mutafchiev), and consequently it stands as a successor state. But even this means a certain degree of separation of the western Bulgarian lands (Macedonia), which would later be deemed unacceptable by socialist authors, themselves under similar nationalist pressures. The Ohrid Patriarchate is for Bulgarian historians similarly and without doubt a continuation of the Bulgarian Durostorum Patriarchate, regardless of whether it crowned Samuel (Snegarov, Zlatarski above) or not (Balaschev).

The Serbian historiographical attack against the Bulgarian position was first launched by the Serbian politician, historian, and diplomat Stojan Novaković (1842–1915) at the end of the nineteenth century. Concerning Samuel's state his argument is as follows. After Tzimiskes' death the Bulgarian state moved from its old center in Eastern Bulgaria to a new hearth, with a different ethnographic basis among "pure Slavs". In this region were Slavic people, who had nothing Bulgarian (meaning Turkic Bulgar), but had assumed the Bulgarian name and the Bulgarian statehood because of its political significance, and because of the state concept, which they opposed to the Byzantine state concept (Novaković 1893, 188–89). The center of the "new state" was located in Ohrid, where a hundred years earlier Clement had laid the center of the Slavic letters (Novaković 1893, 143–44). The strengthening of the Bulgarian Kingdom under Samuel reoriented the Bulgarian state toward the Adriatic coast and it conquered Serbian Zeta (today's Montenegro) and even Dyrrachium (or Dyrrachion, today's Durrës, Albania), while the former Bulgarian Kingdom that also expanded in those territories could not conquer Dyrrachium (Novaković 1893, 189–90). Novaković explains the transfer of the capital from Preslav to Ohrid with the strengthening of Byzantium and with the unfavorable conditions in the north, such as vulnerability to invasions (Novaković 1893, 206). Novaković is ambiguous in characterizing Samuel's state in its new place as Bulgarian and one can trace here some of the ideas concerning the difference between this new state and the old that would be taken up by subsequent Serbian and Macedonian authors.

The Serbian attack was expanded in the first decade of the twentieth century by the Serbian Byzantinist historian Božidar Prokić (1859–1922), who considered Samuel's state as a new creation—"a great Slavic kingdom" in the Balkans, although he did not deny its ideological ties with the fallen Bulgarian Kingdom, whose traditions it took up. Leaving aside other things, he attacked Drinov's notion of Samuel's state as a "Western Bulgarian state" and the historians influenced by him. According to Prokić, Samuel's state was namely a "new Slavic state", called by him also "Slavic Kingdom", "Bulgarian-Slavic Ohrid Kingdom", and "Macedonian Kingdom" (Prokić 1906, 7, 25, 51, 1908, 213–15, 256, 268, 270, 282, 290–91, 297–98), built upon the southwestern remnants of the state of Tsars Peter and Simeon. This new state still bore the name Bulgaria, but its ethnic circumstances and political center were different: in Prespa and Ohrid, in western Macedonia, in a "new ethnographic milieu" among the Slavic tribes there, which for a century had been included in the Bulgarian state (similar to Novaković above). This new state managed to unite politically all south Slavs in the Balkans. Samuel also succeeded in spreading his authority beyond the Slavs in Macedonia over the Bulgarians between the Danube and the Balkan range (Stara Planina), the Serbs, and the South-Slavic tribes in Epirus, Thessaly, Middle Greece and the Peloponnesus.

62 R. DASKALOV

Meanwhile the Greeks were pushed south of the Balkan range (in Thrace) and along the coast. Given its geographic location and ethnic composition, this "great Slavic kingdom" could have created a political union of the Balkan Slavic tribes that would have been able to uphold its independence against its previous Byzantine master. The question then was whether the Balkan Peninsula should be Slavic or remain Greek. But as the better organized and stronger state, Byzantium succeeded in destroying the "Macedonian state" (Prokić 1908, 213–15).

It has to be highlighted that, contrary to some later assertions by Bulgarian authors, for Prokić Macedonia and Macedonians do not feature as Macedonian political and ethnic units, although he often designates the kingdom as "Macedonian". Instead, he means "Macedonia" in a geographical sense, and talks of "Macedonian Slavs", but only as a Slavic element, not as an autonomous political agent—quite understandably for 1908.

According to Prokić, Samuel's state differed from Simeon's Bulgarian Kingdom both geographically and ethnically. Simeon's kingdom included all Bulgarian lands and the lands south of the Balkan range and only part of the Serbian lands, east of the Kolubara River. Thus, ethnically it included the whole Bulgarian population and only part of the Serbian tribes. The Macedonian Kingdom, in contrast, included all Serbian tribes and all Serbian lands and only those Bulgarians who lived between the Danube and the Balkan range, but not the Bulgarians from present-day South Bulgaria (south of the Balkan range in northern Thrace). The Bulgarians prevailed in the Bulgarian Kingdom while the Serbs were the mightiest element in the Macedonian Kingdom (Prokić 1908, 291). Implied is that Serbia has historical rights over Macedonia.

Prokić faces the inevitable question: why was the Macedonian or Slavic Kingdom called Bulgarian, its rulers were called Bulgarian tsars and its inhabitants were called Bulgarians? According to him this was a purely political name and it was not in agreement with its ethnic composition, in which the Bulgarians (from Danubian Bulgaria) came third in number after the Macedonian Slavs and the Serbian Slavs. Besides, the ethnic name Sklaveni or Slavs was weaker than the state name Bulgaria, in a similar fashion to how the name "Roman" imposed itself on the citizens of the Byzantine Empire and the name French (from Franks) over the Gallo-Romans of the Frankish Empire. Prokić describes how imposing and ubiquitous the political name "Bulgarian" became during the Bulgarian conquests (Prokić 1908, 290, 297–307). We will see the argument for a purely political, not ethnic, name in later Serbian and Macedonian authors. It should also be noted that when "counting" the strength of the various ethnic elements, the Serbian author means Bulgarians in the eastern (Danubian) part of Samuel's state, after it was liberated, while all Bulgarian authors mean that the Macedonian Slavs had become (ethnic) Bulgarians during the preceding Bulgarian rule.

Prokić's views present a frontal assault on all basic points of the Bulgarian master national narrative, and it became synonymous with the "Serbian position" (until World War II). The Bulgarian reaction to his views continued for decades and there were rebuttals even under socialism. I will limit myself here to one typical response to his views, from the Bulgarian church historian Ivan Snegarov (1883–1971), from Ohrid. Snegarov rejected Prokić's view that Tsar Samuel was not a Bulgarian, but a Slav, and even nearer to the Serbs, as well as the argument that the Slavs in his kingdom did not see themselves as Bulgarians. According to him, if that were the case, it is not clear why Samuel would declare himself a Bulgarian tsar and appoint a Bulgarian Patriarch as head of the church in his state. It is also not clear why he would name his kingdom Bulgaria and not Serbia, although he conquered all Serbian lands. The Serbian name would be more logical according to his "tribal instinct" if he were nearer to the Serbs, and would also suit better the majority of his subjects. Snegarov does not accept Prokić's consideration that Samuel named himself a Bulgarian tsar only because the Bulgarian Kingdom was internationally recognized in the absence of a Serbian state recognized as a kingdom. Instead, Samuel aspired to restore precisely the kingdom of the Bulgarian Tsars Simeon and Peter, which means that he and his soldiers considered themselves Bulgarians. Finally, Snegarov rejects the comparison with the titles of Charlemagne (Charles the Great) and the basileus of Byzantium as "Roman emperors" because these were empires with universal political strivings, while the Bulgarian Kingdom was "national". Besides, the Roman title of Charlemagne did not apply to the Franks as a national name. According to Snegarov, the Bulgarian name had already become a national name for the Moesian Slavs and the Macedonian Slavs, who had accepted the same name because they had a Bulgarian consciousness similar to the Moesian Slavs. In conclusion, he affirms in a somewhat circular manner that "[t]he Bulgarian kingdom was strictly national and the name 'Bulgarians' for every Slavic tribe, which wore it, was a national name". This is why the Macedonian Slavs from Samuel's kingdom called themselves, and were called by other peoples, Bulgarians, and Samuel's kingdom and its soldiers were called Bulgarian (Snegarov 1919, 15–16n, 1924, 15–17n,).

The Balkan Wars and World War I left Bulgaria resentful. The greater part of the intelligentsia, among it a considerable share of Macedonian emigres, joined efforts in defense of the Bulgarian cause, and rebuffed Serbian (and Greek) claims that what they had acquired during these conflicts rightly belonged to them. They argued along historical, linguistic, ethnographical, and geographical lines that Macedonia had been and continued to be Bulgarian, and that the Macedonians were Bulgarians. To support these efforts the Macedonian Scientific Institute was founded in 1923 with a publication of its own, "Makedonski Pregled" (*Macedonian Review*), to which eminent scholars contributed.

Against this background a second phase of the Bulgarian-Serbian historiographical controversy began during the interwar period. It started with an article by the Serbian historian Dragutin Anastasijević, in which he decisively rejected Drinov's hypothesis and its modifications with Zlatarski and Blagoev that there existed a Western Bulgarian state before the 976 uprising. In his view, no such state existed that would rush to liberate the fallen Eastern Bulgarian state. The whole Bulgarian Kingdom fell under Byzantine rule (Anastasijević 1927, 5–8, 11). At the same time, Anastasijević defined Moesia (north-eastern Bulgaria) as the "real Bulgaria", prava Bulgarska (Anastasijević 1927, 6), and referred to Samuel's Bulgaria with inverted commas, implying that it was not a continuation of the Bulgarian Kingdom. He was answered by Petăr Mutafchiev, who refuted Anastasijević's arguments about the conquest of the whole of Bulgaria, defended Zlatarski's argument for two uprisings, and affirmed the existence of a West Bulgarian state before 976 (Mutafchiev 1928, 121–29).

In the last analysis the Serbian historiographical attack aimed at, and to an extent succeeded in, detaching medieval Macedonia from the Bulgarian historiographical ground and the Bulgarian symbolic appropriation. If not directly appropriating it for the Serbs, it at least made it a disputed historiographical ground. In any case, the polemic shattered the Bulgarian scholarly monopoly, including over Samuel's state and the Ohrid Archbishopric.

It has to be noted that the Serbian attack on the Bulgarian tenets paved the way for later Macedonian historians, who found in it arguments that allowed them to insert Macedonian national identity into discussions around Samuel's state. This distancing and a seeming "neutralization" of the object of study opened the possibility for Macedonian authors to claim the terrain for themselves and try to "lodge" themselves onto it. For example, the Macedonian Slavs by place of living in Serbian arguments would become Macedonian Slavs by ethnicity; the Slavic state in Macedonia would become the Macedonian state of Samuel; and the Ohrid Archbishopric would lose its Bulgarian exclusivity and be appropriated by the Macedonians.

BULGARIAN-SERBIAN CONTROVERSIES DURING THE SOCIALIST REGIMES IN BULGARIA AND YUGOSLAVIA

The Bulgarian-Serbian controversies continued in the altered context of state socialism under different kinds of communist regimes in Yugoslavia and Bulgaria. Vardar Macedonia remained within the (second) socialist Yugoslavia as an autonomous republic, declared as such by the Anti-Fascist Assembly for the National Liberation of Macedonia that took place in St. Prohor Pčinjski Monastery symbolically on August 2, 1944—the first day of the 1903 Ilinden Uprising. The Yugoslav communist leadership renounced the unsuccessful Serbianizing policies of interwar Yugoslavia toward the population of Macedonia, and embarked on a course of recognition and support toward the Macedonian nation and language, in this way integrating it into the new federative Yugoslavia. Accordingly, there began the establishment of Macedonian national institutions, including those connected with the study of history.

During the late fifties and the early sixties something like a Yugoslav consensus concerning Samuel's state emerged. It was based on the work of Georgi Ostrogorski (1902–1976), a Russian-born Yugoslav historian of Byzantine studies, a professor at Belgrade University and founder of the Institute for Byzantine Studies at the Serbian Academy of Sciences and Arts in 1948 and its director until his death. His writings were foundational in the formation of the new school of Serbian Byzantinists. He was the author of *History of Byzantium*, which was translated into many languages (Ostrogorski 1959, 1969). In this work he expressed his opinion on Samuel's state:

> Politically and ecclesiastically, the new empire was the direct descendent of the empire of Simeon and Peter, and it was regarded by Samuel and the Byzantines alike as being simply the Bulgarian empire. For apart from Byzantium, only Bulgaria at that time possessed a tradition of empire with a

patriarchate of its own. Samuel was entirely committed to these traditions. But in reality, his Macedonian kingdom was essentially different from the former kingdom of the Bulgars. In composition and character, it represented a new and distinctive phenomenon. The balance had shifted towards the west and south, and Macedonia, a peripheral region in the old Bulgarian kingdom, was its real center. (Ostrogorski 1969, 301–02)

According to Ostrogorski, if Samuel's goal was to restore the old Bulgarian Kingdom, he would have directed himself toward the Bulgarian lands and would have aspired to liberate them first. The interest that he exhibited toward the old Bulgarian regions east of Serdica (Sofia) was quite weak and the expansion of Samuel's kingdom was oriented most of all toward the south (Ostrogorski 1959, 288).

After the initial dogmatic period in Bulgaria, when the emergence of Samuel's state was treated as feudal separatism, at the beginning of the 1960s there appeared several works of Bulgarian medievalists about Samuel's state which defended the Bulgarian position in a purer and pointed way, and proposed a corresponding interpretation of the sources. These were, among other things, directed not only against earlier Serbian authors but also against Bulgarian "bourgeois" authors who now did not seem patriotic enough, that is, not nationalistically correct. Mihail Voynov, was the first to explicitly reject any notion of a separate Bulgarian Kingdom in the west, followed by Lyubomir Yonchev(Voynov 1963, 122–32, 1979, 5–25; Yonchev 1965, 29–48). By speaking about a Western Bulgarian state, even if it is conceived as a continuation of the First Bulgarian Kingdom as an emergent state (concurrently or successively), it still implies some difference between the two. The socialist authors grasped for new interpretations which would better serve the Bulgarian national "position" or "cause". In short, continuity alone did not suffice and had to be replaced by something stronger, like identity. This was expressed with the idea of just "moving the political center" from the conquered east to the unconquered west (Voynov 1963, 125, 1965, 34).

The best solution proved to be positing only one uprising in 976, when it was unambiguously directed against Byzantine rule. Yonchev was the first among the Bulgarian authors to argue this (Yonchev 1961, 107–10). But then the problem arose that without a concept of a Western Bulgarian state the continuity between 971 (or 969) and 976 would be disrupted. Hence the various speculations about what happened in Macedonia in the meantime: unconquered de facto, but only "formally", and without a state until 976 (Voynov 1963, 128) or that it isn't clear what was going on there in the absence of evidence by Byzantine and Latin authors, but the *kometopuli* "obviously" prepared an uprising there (Yonchev 1965, 33–34, 41–45). It is clear that the notion of continuity was hard to reconcile with the idea of full identity.

In 1966 there appeared in Yugoslavia the four-volume "Byzantine Sources of the Peoples of Yugoslavia" (a counterpart of the Bulgarian series "Greek Sources for Bulgarian History"). Samuel's era is treated in the third volume by the Slovenian historian Jadran Ferluga in numerous and long footnotes equivalent to a whole book (Ostrogorski and Barišić 1966). Below I will summarize only his opinions on some major controversial questions.

Concerning the designation of the 976 uprising, insurgents and state as "Bulgarian", Ferluga says the Byzantine authors named the inhabitants after the name of the state or the later administrative *thema* (large unit) Bulgaria, transferring the name onto the whole population. The views of the Byzantine authors on the ethnic problems were very different from ours and we have to avoid applying modern views to medieval conditions. The Greek authors of the tenth century understood "Bulgarian" as the population within the Bulgarian state, and not of the *thema* Bulgaria, created later in the eleventh century after Basil II (the Bulgar-Slayer) conquered Samuel's state. Before that the designation was restricted to the Bulgars and from them it was projected onto the state and its entire population—the old Slavic tribes and the Bulgars still differing. Concerning Bulgarians Skylitzes in particular (end of the eleventh century) still meant the population of Tsar Peter's state without making ethnic distinctions and that is why his words cannot be used to identify such differences. According to Ferluga, the state that emerged in 976 was not determined by ethnicity. Yet, he thinks that there were ethnic differences, because in the region of Sklavinia (i.e., Macedonia), which was joined to the Bulgarian state in the mid-ninth century, there was little ethnic mixing compared to the territory between the Balkan range (Stara Planina) and the Danube (Ostrogorski and Barišić eds. 1966, 59–60n).

Concerning the ethnic aspects, according to Ferluga they are "often exaggerated" (*predimenzionirani*) because they are considered according to nineteenth- and twentieth-century views. The differences between the Slavic tribes in the Balkans were not as deep as in modern history: "In the new state, created through the 976 uprising, the ethnic aspect was of second-rate and third-rate significance". Of much greater importance was

68   R. DASKALOV

the development of feudal forces, which "carried, organized and represented the state" (Ostrogorski and Barišić, eds. 1966, 65n). The great conquests during the beginning of the uprising show that behind the *kometopuli* there stood powerful boyars (*velikaši*) interested in acquiring new lands and greater revenues, who supported the uprising for that reason. In other words: "Samuel's state was a new creation, which based itself on new feudal forces from one part of the former Bulgarian kingdom, but it was new also because these feudal forces operated on a new and higher stage of development" (Ostrogorski and Barišić, eds. 1966, 65n).

Did Samuel become tsar, and how? Most Greek sources do not attribute to him the title tsar (basileus) but reference him only by name or refer to him as tyrant or ruler; only Nicephorus Bryennius (or Nikephoros Bryennios) attributes to him the title tsar. Basil II's charter about the Ohrid Archbishopric calls Peter basileus, but not Samuel. Especially important is Skylitzes-Kedrin, who nowhere calls him tsar, but in one place seems to forget when he says that the "royal palaces" were found in Ohrid (but Zonaras reformulates this as "archon's palaces"). Ferluga takes this to mean that Ohrid was the capital of the Bulgarian tsars, but that they were self-proclaimed, de facto tsars, unrecognized by Byzantium. This is because Samuel was not only a rebel against Byzantium, but the royal title of Simeon, Peter, and Boris II could not be transferred to him without the empire's permission because the Bulgarian Kingdom ceased to exist in 971. According to Ferluga, it has been rightly noted that Samuel leaned on the Bulgarian state tradition, which alone gave him the opportunity to take a tsar's crown, but he also considers correct these authors who see Samuel's state as a new creation. In the eyes of the Byzantines there was no continuity between Samuel's and Peter's states as seen also in the fact that they did not name him tsar. Thus it is hard to say whether he was tsar or de facto ruled as tsar, but not formally as Byzantium did not recognize him as such (Ostrogorski and Barišić, eds. 1966, 64n, 80–81n). In other words, Ferluga accepts that Samuel was crowned but takes the Byzantine point of view that because he was unrecognized by Byzantium, he was therefore illegitimate.

After this followed a Bulgarian reaction to the comments of the Yugoslav historians on the "Byzantine Sources", especially to the third volume about Samuel (Voynov et al. 1968, 113–18). One objection relates to Ferluga's considerations of whether Samuel was a tsar or not. According to him he was not recognized as tsar by Byzantium and could not receive the royal title of Peter and Boris II without its consent. The Bulgarian reviewers refuted this with Skylitzes' words about the "palaces of the Bulgarian tsars" (where Basil II found "crowns with pearls") as well as Psellos' words that Samuel and Aaron "ruled and reigned" (pointed out by Ferluga as well). This the Bulgarian reviewers took to mean (very dubiously) that the Byzantines "recognized de facto the royal dignity of Samuel" (Voynov et al. 1968, 115). They also added the convincing argument, pointed out by Snegarov before, that Byzantium's consent for the crowning of the Bulgarian ruler was not needed because he had at his disposal a Bulgarian Patriarch with his own rights to coronate.

Further on—and this is the main point—Ferluga erroneously interpreted the fact that Samuel is not called basileus (tsar) in most Greek sources as an important argument that there was no continuity between the state of Simeon, Peter, and Boris II, and that of Samuel. Thus Ferluga aimed to reinforce his thesis that "Samuel's kingdom was not the traditional Bulgarian one, but some new state creation, whose subjects were not Bulgarians, that is, Bulgarian Slavs, but some other Slavs". According to the Bulgarian reviewers, however, there was a clear political continuity, expressed by Basil II in his second charter about the Ohrid Archbishopric, whose Archbishop was granted the right to rule all Bulgarian bishoprics, which were under the rule of Tsar Peter and Samuel. Apart from the political continuity, there is a clear church continuity, expressed by Basil II also in his second charter that narrates about the transfer of the Bulgarian Archbishopric from Durostorum through several intermediary residences to Ohrid (Voynov et al. 1968, quote on 116).

Post-Communist Bulgarian-Serbian Controversies

In 2000 a very significant book (Pirivatrić 1997) about Samuel's state was published by the Serbian historian Srđan Pirivatrić (born 1966), translated also into Bulgarian (Pirivatrich 2000). As pointed out by the author, the literature on Samuel's era is strongly influenced methodologically by the "idol of nationalism", created during the period of the national revivals and especially during the phase of so-called mass nationalism. According to him, it would be interesting to show from methodological and other points of view in what ways and to what extent such idols enter the historical scholarship and what their impact is. What happens in particular when the issues are approached from a preconceived conceptual and value system or one seeks in the sources answers to questions that they cannot give (Pirivatrić 1997, 26–27)?

This is precisely the guiding interest of the present work, namely to research the impact of "extra-scholarly" biases, especially nationalist ones, upon the presentation of Samuel's era. Besides, like Pirivatrić, and even more radically than him, I doubt to what extent the purely scientific can be separated from the extra-scholarly elements, which apart from being biased, set the framework for interpreting the facts and their arrangement in overall narratives. Below I will consider at some length only the debated issues, tackled by the Serbian author, which provoked a (positive or negative) Bulgarian reaction.

What were the actions of the *kometopuli* in 969? According to Pirivatrić, "[a]ll combinations for a supposed split of the western areas from the Preslav court, whatsoever inventive and not contradicting the sources, do not find the necessary corroboration in them" (Pirivatrić 1997, 68). The Bulgarian Kingdom was destroyed in 971, but its entire territory was not militarily occupied. What was going on in Western Bulgaria (i.e. Macedonia) from 971 until Tzimiskes died in 976? Had the western part of the destroyed kingdom, which survived, continued to act as a Bulgarian state? The silence of the sources on Western Bulgaria and the fate of the four brothers after 969 (their failed attempt at assuming central authority) and after 971 (the fall of the eastern part of the kingdom) opened the possibility for various conjectures. The answer, according to Pirivatrić, remains in the sphere of speculation. Still, the later development of events shows that there remained in the western areas of the Bulgarian Kingdom state-building forces. Consolidating authority required a certain amount of time and it was presumably going on until the outbreak of the 976 uprising. Yet the view that a certain Western Bulgarian Kingdom was created in 969 by way of a split is not corroborated by sources. As to the question of whether a supreme Byzantine authority existed in these border areas, it was quite nominal, if it even existed at all (Pirivatrić 1997, 68–71).

There is no doubt for Pirivatrić that Samuel's state took up the state and church tradition of the Bulgarian state that ceased to exist in 971: "First of all it is evident that Samuel and his descendants act within the framework of the Bulgarian Kingdom, discontinued by Joannes Tzimiskes in 971. In the new state two institutions gave themselves a meeting, which in a different way and along different paths were transferred to it from the previous one" (Pirivatrić 1997, 133). These were the royal institution and title, which Samuel appropriated, and the Bulgarian church, which, after the conquest of Bulgaria through several migrations, established itself in the new state (Pirivatrić 1997, 133–48, 161–68).

Regarding the royal title, Pirivatrić makes a distinction between the official Byzantine point of view and the Bulgarian one. From a Byzantine point of view the creation of a Bulgarian state after the destruction of the Bulgarian Kingdom in 971 was not legitimate, and its ruler was not entitled to a royal title. The official contemporary Byzantine view of Samuel is most clearly seen in the two *sigillia* of Basil II from 1019 and 1020, where Samuel's name does not possess a title while Peter is titled basileus (tsar). This is why the uprising of the Bulgarians is defined by Skylitzes as a "mutiny" or "falling away" (*apostasia*) in the sense of renouncing the legitimate authority of the emperor. Such an act according to Byzantine law required blinding as Basil II did with the captured Bulgarians. Skilytzes, who wrote toward the end of the eleventh century, called Peter and Boris II basileus (and so recognized by Byzantium), but did not assign the title to Samuel. According to Pirivatrić, this means that the ideological atmosphere of the Bulgarian-Byzantine wars influenced Skylitzes through the sources he used, even though he wrote quite later. This was not so much the case with other contemporaries of Skylitzes such as Michael Psellos and later Byzantine authors, more so as Samuel's descendants became integrated into the Byzantine elite (Pirivatrić 1997, 133–39).

Here Pirivatrić (in contrast to Ferluga) turns toward the view of Samuel himself, according to which the title Tsar of the Bulgarians had become an internal affair of the Bulgarians, and therefore was ideologically independent of official recognition from Constantinople. From a Bulgarian point of view such recognition was not necessary for him, because he considered himself as a continuer and restorer of the legitimate Bulgarian Kingdom (which from a Byzantine point of view was destroyed in 971). In the Bitola inscription the last Bulgarian ruler Joannes Vladislav is titled *samodărzhets*, a Slavic translation of the Greek "autocrator", but not a tsar (maybe because he was not yet crowned) and Samuel's name is accompanied by "*(samodr)zhavnogo*", which means literally that he does not owe his authority to the Byzantine emperor (Pirivatrić 1997, 139–44).

Pirivatrić believes that Samuel's crown had a domestic Bulgarian origin and that he did not have to seek either a royal crown or recognition from either Constantinople or Rome. The development of the church and civil institutions in Bulgaria created the possibility for a renewal of these same institutions, abolished in 971, in the new state based on precedent. Such a precedent for the coronation of a Bulgarian ruler by a domestic head of the church was the bestowing of a royal title by Byzantium on Tsar Peter, together with the elevation of the head of the Bulgarian church to the rank of patriarch. Especially important was that the latter probably crowned Tsar Peter's son Boris II in 969 too (Pirivatrić 1997, 164–68).

The question of the ethnic composition of Samuel's state, so important for the national historians, was of secondary importance for his era, as explicitly stressed by the author (Pirivatrić 1997, 180–86). According to him, the problem of the ethnic structure has often been put simplistically in the form of what people lived on the territory of Samuel's state. To this question the Byzantine sources always give the same well-known answer—they call its population Bulgarians (or in an archaizing style, Moesians), and likewise in the eastern sources. Most importantly, in the Bitola inscription Joannes Vladislav calls himself "Bulgarian by birth" and that he repaired the fortress "for refuge and rescue of the life of the Bulgarians". This view of the Byzantine and other sources was endorsed with few exceptions in the historiography. It is also endorsed by Pirivatrić, who explicitly states that "there is no reason why the inhabitants of Samuel's state should not be called Bulgarians and the state itself—Bulgaria, as many times in the present work without special substantiation" (Pirivatrić 1997, 180).

Yet the data from the sources requires a certain clarification, namely: "who were the Bulgarians, mentioned by the Byzantine authors?" According to Pirivatrić, they owed their name to the state they inhabited, which in turn received it from the Turkic people, who established a state between the Danube and the Balkan range in 681, where several Slavic tribes lived. Thus we see a seemingly paradoxical phenomenon:

> The state called after the name of the people that founded it becomes a 'framework', which parallel with its territorial expansion extends also the name of the people—it begins to refer also to the population of the conquered areas. This is precisely what happened with the Slavic population of Macedonia and southern Albania, which the Bulgarian rulers gradually included in their state from the mid-ninth century onwards. For the Byzantine authors of the tenth and the eleventh century they are all 'Bulgarians'. This is also valid for all other sources. (Pirivatrić 1997, 181)

He then polemicizes with the explanation of the ethnic phenomena along the established Bulgarian line (exemplified by Dimităr Angelov). According to the Bulgarian authors, with the extension of Bulgarian rule over the Balkan Peninsula there occurred a process of merging between the Bulgars and the Slavs. The Bulgars were less numerous but they

2 CONTROVERSIES OVER SAMUEL'S STATE   73

created the state, subordinated the Slavs and gave them their name. But they were exposed to gradual "Slavicization". According to Angelov, the formation of the Bulgarian nationality (narodnost), for which this ethnogenetic process was of key importance, was completed by the end of the ninth and the beginning of the tenth century, and from then on one can speak of a Bulgarian people with its own language, material and spiritual culture, and national self-consciousness (Angelov 1971, 1973, 49–64).

Pirivatrić says (obviously with disapproval) that it is not his intention to engage with the question of the Bulgarian ethnogenesis and when this stage ended. But he emphasizes that it was more intensive between the Balkan mountains and the Danube River and much less so in the southwest, in Macedonia. There it was shorter and different in character because the Bulgar layer in the state was at that time in the process of vanishing. That is why one should underline the predominantly Slavic character of Samuel's state with centers in Prespa and Ohrid, in contrast with the old Bulgarian Kingdom of Simeon and Peter, which had Preslav as its center (Pirivatrić 1997, 181–82, 195–96).

Yet Pirivatrić considers the Bulgarian character of the state as beyond doubt, especially the monarchical institution, taken up from the kingdom destroyed in 971, as well as the church institution. The two Bulgar institutions of *kavhan* and *ichirgu-boila* also attest to the Bulgar tradition. Finally, the Bitola inscription shows that Joannes (Ivan) Vladislav considered himself a Bulgarian and his subjects Bulgarians. This has a legal sense but not only, and there is a qualitative difference between the Bitola inscription (of domestic provenance) and other sources of foreign origin. While the latter simplify the ethnic problem, the former expresses ethnic self-consciousness. But it is the single such source and we can only surmise what was the vertical extension of this self-consciousness (i.e., according to social layers) and the horizontal one, which refers to its extension on the territory of the Bulgarian state (Pirivatrić 1997, 182–83).

In Pirivatrić's view, the process of ethnic amalgamation on the basis of the Bulgarian state and church tradition occurred at a relatively slow pace in comparison with the era of the national revivals. This was mostly as a consequence of the organization of the state as a Christian kingdom, and not as a goal. On the level of the state institutions the process was disrupted with the subjugation of Bulgaria in 1018 and state discontinuity was accompanied by a systematic resettlement of the social elite—Samuel's boyars—in the eastern part of Byzantium. The local elite as the potential carriers of ethnic self-consciousness declined, and in the absence of a

Bulgarian state the ethnogenetic processes were slowed down, which allowed for a "comparatively painless later introduction of a similar Slavic tradition as that of the medieval Serbian state" (Pirivatrić 1997, 184). Thus these early centuries were significant for the formation of the Bulgarian nation, but not decisive. The later centuries from the sixteenth to the nineteenth had a much greater significance for it and for each of today's nations in the Balkans (Pirivatrić 1997, 183–84).

Pirivatrić opposes in principle debating ethnicity in the Middle Ages with standards from the era of the national revivals. During the Middle Ages there existed other kinds of communities as well, from the Roman Empire, which was universal in every aspect, including nationality, to communities that stood lower in the hierarchy of universality, such as Samuel's Bulgarian Kingdom. Samuel's kingdom cannot be seen to hold universalism of nationality (*narodnost*) as an ideological tenet, but according to Pirivatrić universalism did exist as a consequence of the concurrence of circumstances. In Samuel's kingdom, there lived the (Slavicized) Bulgarians themselves, the Slavs (of various Slavic tribes), but also the non-Slavic (Illyrian) inhabitants of the Albanian mountains, the Serbs under his rule, Rhomios, and Armenians. However, this "universalism" was a consequence of conquests and practical necessity, and it was not an ideological ambition. The decisive factor in the creation of Samuel's state was not its ethnic "character", but other factors—the traditions of the destroyed Bulgarian Kingdom and the Bulgarian church as well as a proper social structure capable of taking them up and renewing them. The ethnic question was of much less significance in comparison with these (Pirivatrić 1997, 184–85).

In the conclusion of the book Pirivatrić writes that the state created after 976 followed the traditions of the destroyed Bulgarian Kingdom. The same applied to its internal structure, for example, the Bulgar institutions of *kavhan* and *ichirgu-boila*, the division into "internal" and "external" areas, and so on. Yet the author, who follows in this respect most of the Serbian authors beginning with Novaković, and most notably Ostrogorski, Samuel's state was a new creation with a different political center and center of gravity, hence its different state interests, determined by its location (Pirivatrić 1997, 192–93).

Pirivatrić's book elicited several reactions from Bulgarian historians. In his introduction to the Bulgarian translation the eminent Bulgarian medievalist Vasil Gyuzelev gave a very high evaluation. He defined the book as a "new and objective view of the Serbian medieval and Byzantinist studies on the history of Samuel's Bulgaria; it is a phenomenon in the Balkan historiography"; and stated that after Vasil Zlatarski it is the very best writing on this era of the Bulgarian history (Gyuzelev 2000, 10). Gyuzelev agrees with Pirivatrić on several counts.

As can be expected, in line with the Bulgarian tenets Gyuzelev disagrees with Pirivatrić's treatment of the ethnic question, namely, that the population of Samuel's state was called Bulgarian after the state, while it consisted of Slavicized Bulgars, Slavs, Illyrians (i.e., Albanians), Serbs, Rhomios and Armenians. Also, unacceptable according to Gyuzelev is the view of the author that despite following the traditions of the Bulgarian Kingdom destroyed in 971, Samuel's Bulgaria was a "new creation" with a new political and church center and different state interests (Gyuzelev 2000, 11).

The eminent Bulgarian medievalist Ivan Bozhilov (1940–2016) also wrote a review of Pirivatrić's book which, despite some agreements is, in fact, deeply critical (Bozhilov 1999, 190–202). His disagreements apart from some factual questions are mostly related to the ethnic question. Most importantly, Bozhilov rejects Pirivatrić's approach, which is not content with the fact that, according to the sources on the territory of Bulgaria and of Samuel's state in particular, Bulgarians lived there, but furthermore asks who these Bulgarians were. And he answers that they were ethnically heterogeneous due to circumstances, such as conquests, so the universalism of the name Bulgarians was not ideological, but factual, in contrast to the ideological universalism of the name Rhomios, which designated all subjects of Byzantium.

Bozhilov does not agree with this equalization between the meaning of the term Bulgarians, who for him obviously were ethnically homogeneous, and the term Rhomios, who were ethnically heterogeneous. According to him, Pirivatrić placed "almost a sign of coincidence in an ideological sense" between them, whereas the Rhomios and all other foreigners in Bulgaria were "Bulgarians" and the Bulgarians in Byzantium and all other peoples in it were Rhomios. Yet as we saw, Pirivatrić underlines precisely the factual, in contrast to the ideological aspect of the designation "Bulgarians" for a population almost as heterogeneous as the "Rhomios". Here Bozhilov, known for his writings on the imperial ambitions of Simeon and the most important Bulgarian rulers after him (Daskalov 2021, 250–54), paradoxically advocates the view of an ethnically homogeneous ("national") Bulgarian state. According to him, the imperial ambitions of Bulgaria, which, however, were not universalist, found their best expression under Simeon in the title "Basileus of the Bulgarians and Rhomios" or "Tsar and samodărzhets of all Bulgarians and Greeks" (in the thirteenth and the fourteenth centuries), which he interprets (rather casuistically) as including also all Bulgarians who did not live within the confines of the kingdom, plus the Greeks (Rhomios), who were subjects of the Bulgarian tsar. After that he asserts that it would be difficult to "persuade" Skylitzes to designate all subjects of Tsar Samuel as "Bulgarians" similar to the designation "Rhomios" for all subjects of the basileus, that is, to transfer the principles of Byzantine ideology to a foreign milieu (Bozhilov 1999, 201–02). In other words, Skyzlitzes could not but make a difference between Bulgarians proper and other subjects of Samuel, if there were such (apart from the Greeks), but obviously there were not.

I went into this question in some detail to demonstrate the casuistic means to which Bozhilov resorts in his striving to prove some untenable ethnic homogeneity of the subjects of Samuel's Bulgarian medieval state. Finally, in one convoluted sentence he opines that the process of forming a unified Bulgarian nationality proceeded evenly across Bulgaria, because Khan Asparuh's Bulgars did not remain where they initially settled. He ends by saying that "the attempt to look beyond the clear term Bulgarians in the sources would be a violence upon them" (Bozhilov 1999, 202). All this shows is the terminological fetishism of the Bulgarian position which bars asking inconvenient questions, such as going beyond the term "Bulgarians" in the sources.

Further on, Bozhilov does not agree with the treatment (following Ostrogorski) of Samuel's state as a "new creation" with a different political seat and different state interests. According to him, there is nothing unusual in a new capital after the eastern areas fell under the Byzantines as this new capital was necessary in order to continue the war of independence. Likewise, he argues that the political aspirations and state interests of Samuel's Bulgaria were the same as those of Simeon's Bulgaria, namely, the restoration of the wholeness of the Bulgarian Kingdom. Bozhilov also does not agree with the terms "uprising" and "creation of the state", because they allegedly express the Byzantine point of view, though he himself in other places took precisely this point of view, namely, that the action is best expressed as "falling away" from the emperor's authority (apostasia). But here he prefers the Bulgarian point of view of today's national and nationalist historians, expressed in terms such as "war of independence, a continuation of the war of 971, a war for the restoration of the breached territorial, political and national unity" (Bozhilov 1999,

197). He makes one more consideration regarding terminology that implies an underlying national position: Pirivatrić was right in rejecting the term "Western Bulgarian state", but he also had to abandon the term "Samuel's state", which was abused in Skopje, and prefer the term "Samuel's Bulgaria" instead (Bozhilov 1999, 197–98). Here the connection between terminology and the idea of continuity, in this case identity, is clearly stated.

In the conclusion, Bozhilov acknowledges the high professionalism of the author and calls the book "a good medicine, which cures, if not entirely, at least to a great extent the wound called Samuel's Bulgaria" after decades in which "many wounds were unjustly inflicted upon the body of the Bulgarian medieval state, and on the later centuries of Bulgarian history" (Bozhilov 1999, 202–03). In other words, taking a position different from the Bulgarian one is likened to inflicting "wounds" on the body of Bulgarian medieval and later history—a bodily metaphor in a nationalistic style.

Later on, in his own account, Bozhilov rejects not only the idea of a Western Bulgarian state (and a 969 revolt by extension), but also abandons the search for the legitimacy of Samuel's ascension to the throne by not making him wait for the death of Roman. According to him, Samuel crowned himself after he killed his brother Aaron around 987, without connection with Roman's fate (Bozhilov and Gyuzelev 1999, 312, 317–18). For a pointed nationalism not only does identity trump continuity (through the omission of a Western Bulgarian state after 969) but also personality beats legitimacy.

Another strongly negative review was produced by Petăr Petrov as seen in the title "A Timid Step in the Right Direction" (the right one is, of course, the Bulgarian national position and his view in particular). For this author the greatest merit of the book is that it recognized for the first time in Serbian/Yugoslav historical scholarship that the population of Macedonia in this era was Bulgarian and that the state was Bulgarian. Thus, he subjected to critique Prokić's "unscientific theses" about a "Slavic kingdom" endorsed by authoritative scholars such as Ostrogorski, Ferluga, Božidar Ferjančić, etc. as well as the theses of the "Skopjan historians" and a great number of amateurs about a population of Macedonian Slavs and a Macedonian state (Petrov 2002, 158, 167).

Petrov then begins to critique Pirivatrić. According to Pirivatrić (as earlier in Ostrogorski) Samuel's kingdom "only" took over the traditions of the Bulgarian Kingdom and Patriarchate, but it was new and different in its ethnic composition and character. Besides, Pirivatrić underrated the formation of a consolidated Bulgarian nationality (*narodnost*) at the end of the ninth and beginning of the tenth century with a Bulgarian name and a Slavic self-consciousness, and regarding Macedonia he asserted that the process of Bulgarian ethnogenesis was weaker. Consequently, he affirmed wrongly that the Slavic tradition of the medieval Serbian state was painlessly received. Petrov also strongly disagrees with Pirivatrić's assertion that the times of Samuel's state were important but not decisive for the formation of the Bulgarian nation (Petrov 2002, 163, 167–68). In conclusion:

> What S. Pirivatrić has said with many circumlocutions, namely, that the state was Bulgarian and its population was not Macedonian, is only a timid step in the Yugoslav historiography for overcoming a great delusion and falsification [...] But at the same time the author adheres blindly to all theses and views expressed by the Serbian scholars, which did not allow him to take a firm scientific stand. The book is a historiographical review rather than a scholarly monograph. One can say in conclusion that S. Pirivatrić's book not only does not give the Bulgarian reader anything new but can bring him into delusion. (Petrov 2002, 168–69)

Bulgarian-Macedonian Controversies During Socialist Yugoslavia

The radical turn in Bulgarian politics toward the Macedonian question took place at the beginning of the 1960s with a return to traditional Bulgarian nationalism. The turn began at the Plenum of the Central Committee of the Bulgarian Communist Party on March 11–12, 1963, at which Todor Zhivkov presented several historical "theses", some concerning medieval history, including Samuel's state. According to him, in the ninth century a Bulgarian nationality (*narodnost*) was formed in Danubian Bulgaria, Thrace, and Macedonia, which in the eighteenth and nineteenth centuries was transformed into the Bulgarian nation. No Macedonian nationality existed in the medieval past and the Macedonian falsifications on this question should be rejected; Tsar Samuel's state was Bulgarian.

There followed a Politburo Plenum of the Central Committee of the Bulgarian Communist Party in April 1967, which worked out a position on the Macedonian question that did not recognize the existence of a Macedonian nation and a Macedonian language until 1945 and postulated that only then did Macedonian national consciousness begin to form. In 1967 Todor Zhivkov's so-called theses for the activities of the Komsomol (the communist Youth organization) and the "patriotic upbringing of the youth" ushered in the return of nationalism in all directions of national self-consciousness and the rejection of "national nihilism" (Troebst 2007, 74–77, 85; Marinov 2010, 113–120). This altered Bulgarian historiography too.

In accordance with my task, I will limit myself to the historiographical debates between professional historians. Macedonian historians gradually grew in importance during the controversies, while the Serbian authors in general supported their Macedonian colleagues. I admit a certain artificiality in separating the Macedonian historians from the Serbian (and some Croatian) historians in the common Yugoslav context. Still, I think this is appropriate because of the peculiarity of the Macedonian views and positions due to their striving for "national affirmation" and the emergence of an autonomous Macedonian national historiography.

The Macedonian attack against the Bulgarian historiography began in earnest at the celebrations of the 1050th anniversary of the death of Clement of Ohrid in 1966. It was initiated by an article by Dragan Taškovski (1917–1980) under the title "Clement of Ohrid and His Times" in the newspaper *Nova Makedoniya* (Taškovski 1965, December 14, 19, 20, and 21), which provoked a strong and lasting Bulgarian reaction. The article is dedicated mostly to the activities of Clement in Macedonia in spreading the Glagolitic alphabet created by Cyril of Thessaloniki. However, Taškovski elaborates the idea that this missionizing was in opposition to the educational and cultural school of the capital Preslav in northern Bulgaria, which embraced the Greek-modeled Cyrillic alphabet (in use today), therefore betraying the deeds of Cyril and Methodius. This opposition between the two cultural centers was, according to Taškovski, only the first step in a series of struggles of the Macedonian Slavic people against Bulgarian rule. The "cultural particularism" grew into the Bogomil heresy after Clement's death and ended in the 969 uprising against Bulgaria, when Knez (Prince) Nikola with his four sons laid the foundations of the first "Slavic-Macedonian state". These ideas were further elaborated by the author and we will return to them. But it is evident that the issue was about historical heritage, especially the deeds of Clement and his Ohrid school, the Bogomils (a dualist Christian heresy), and Samuel's state with the Ohrid Patriarchate, which were appropriated by Taškovski for the present-day Macedonians.

80   R. DASKALOV

As a Bulgarian reaction (partly to these articles) Mihail Voynov published an article under the telling title "To the Question of the Bulgarian Nationality in Macedonia" (Voynov 1966, 61–72). In it, he is especially sympathetic to the Slavic element of the Bulgarian nationality, though ironically in other works he sympathized strongly with the Turkic Bulgars. He points out that the strongest reaction against the pro-Byzantine politics of Tsar Peter came from Macedonia. But according to Voynov, the *kometopuli* did not revolt against Bulgaria, nor did they split from it, and if they revolted earlier in 970 (in fact, in 969), this was not against Bulgaria, but against the pro-Byzantine policies of the court. This is clearly seen in the events of 976, when the same Bulgarians, and more precisely the Bulgarian boyars, entrusted them with the supreme authority of the state when they threw off Byzantine rule. Samuel made "titanic efforts in order to rescue and renew the Bulgarian Kingdom" and his nephew Joannes Vladislav "carved with chisel that he is by birth a Bulgarian". Thus, it is naïve to think that "because of state, political, and legal considerations he would hide his ethnic ('Macedonian') origin", as Taškovski tries to persuade the reader with his article (Voynov 1966, 63–64, quote on 64) (It is important to note that Taškovski thinks otherwise, namely, that Samuel came from "Macedonian Slavs").

Voynov means that the Macedonian Slavs had become, in essence, ethnic Bulgarians. That is why he disagrees with Taškovski that all medieval authors were "misled by the state-political designation 'Bulgarians' and put it as an ethnic name of the Slavic population in Macedonia", although they noticed many different ethnic groups in Macedonia, such as Vlachs, Pechenegs, Kumans, etc., but (with irony) not Macedonians. Thus, they did not name "Macedonians", the presumably mightiest group of the population. Samuel himself, who presumably accepted Bulgarian state traditions because of tactical considerations, did not add to his title "Tsar of Bulgarians and Macedonians" as (due to political considerations) Kaloyan (Kaloiannes) did during the Second Bulgarian state, who titled himself "Tsar of Bulgarians and Vlachs" in order to please the Pope (Voynov 1966, 65, quote included). In fact, Taškovski does not affirm that the population of Macedonia consisted of "Macedonians", but that this name was taken much later by the Macedonian Slavs as an ethnic name. According to him, the population consisted of "Macedonian Slavs", distinct from the "Bulgarian Slavs" in Moesia, and entirely different from the Bulgars.

The Bulgarian medievalist and Byzantinist Dimităr Angelov (1919–1996) entered a polemic with Taškovski in 1966 (Angelov 1966, 7–24, 61–109). He first outlined his ethnogenetic theory, namely about a "Bulgarian group" of kindred Slavs that included the tribes from Moesia, Thrace, Macedonia, and part of Albania and Greece; the unifying policies of the Bulgar khans for the inclusion of these kindred tribes within the Bulgarian state; and that "they were included on their own will within the borders of the Bulgarian state, because it was for them their natural center, where their brothers of the same kin and language lived" (Angelov 1962, 35–38, 1966, 7–8, 14). There followed the formation of a unitary Bulgarian nationality through the merger of heterogeneous ethnic elements: Slavs from the "Bulgarian group" and Bulgars but also older surviving (Hellenized or Romanized) Thracians. The numerous Slavs prevailed over the other ethnic elements and the Slav language imposed itself while the Bulgars gradually melted and their language vanished (Angelov 1966, 9–12).

Angelov puts the end of the process of the formation of the Bulgarian nationality as early as the end of the ninth century, obviously in order to include the Macedonian Slavs at the time of their joining and long before Samuel's state. Terminologically the ethnogenetic process found expression in the vanishing of the initial differentiation between "Slavs" and "Bulgars" by the Byzantine authors and the imposition of the unified name "Bulgarians" for the already formed nationality in Moesia, Thrace, and Macedonia after an intermediate and transitional phase. The term Slavs was later used only for those who were not included in the Bulgarian state (Angelov 1966, 13–18). In other words, according to Angelov the replacement of the dual usage with "Bulgarians" as the only name means that the ethnogenetic process in the three regions was complete and as a result a unified Slavic nationality under a Bulgarian name was formed.

According to Taškovski the Bulgarian name came much later to Macedonia with the crowning of Samuel in 997 and Basil II's *sigillia*. Angelov gives a few examples of an earlier use. In other sources from the tenth to the twelfth century the terms Slavs and Bulgarians were considered equivalent, after which the dual usage disappeared and the Bulgarian name imposed itself. The duality of terminology is explained by Angelov along the above-indicated lines: "the nationality, created on the territory of Bulgaria was in essence Slavic and in name Bulgarian". That is why the terms "Slav" and "Bulgarian" could be used interchangeably (Angelov 1966, 16–17).

82   R. DASKALOV

Not so with the Macedonian authors. For them, it is exactly the first period of their existence, that is, the two centuries before the Bulgarian conquest, which is of central importance as a period of separate existence. They interpret the "generic" Slavs as a particular ethnic designation for themselves, although not quite determinate and undifferentiated from the common Slavic name, but still contrasted enough with the Bulgarian name (and the Serbian and Croatian name) in order to lend it distinctiveness and specificity among the southern Slavs. The argument is that after the explicit separation of these three peoples, the so to say "residual" Slavs were precisely the Macedonian Slavs, future Macedonians.

The various views on Samuel's state have been considered above. Here I will present only some specific Macedonian interpretations. Taškovski, though more of a popularizer, is perhaps most representative of the Macedonian position because of his consistent ideological elaboration on Samuel's state, and because of his emphatically nationalistic and polemical style (Taškovski 1970, 88–103, 1985, 40–45). So, I will expand on him in some detail.

Taškovski dates the emergence of Samuel's state in 969 through an uprising of the *kometopuli* in Macedonia against Bulgarian rule, which according to him led to the liberation and independence of Macedonia. The year is chosen because of its anti-Bulgarian implication, similar to how 976 is preferred by most present-day Bulgarian historians (together with the rejection of the concept of a Western Bulgarian state) for its clearly anti-Byzantine orientation. The fall of the "Preslav regime" in 971 left Macedonia unconquered. The 976 uprising thus refers not to Macedonia but to north-eastern Bulgaria (Taškovski 1970, 100–07). After Tzimiskes' death in 976, the north-eastern Bulgarians took arms against Byzantium, but they were weak and their leaders decided to hand over their authority to the *kometopuli* because the legitimate heirs were in Constantinople. The *kometopuli*, according to Taškovski, assumed rule over the Bulgarians "out of necessity". But they headed south to Serres and Larissa in Thessaly in order to join the Macedonian Slavic tribes there, and to Epirus to include other Slavic tribes, all of whom formed an "ethnic whole" with the already liberated tribes, and to get support from them (Taškovski 1970, 112–13, 119).

When the legitimate Bulgarian heir Roman fled to Samuel, the latter appointed him as governor of Skopje, which Taškovski sees as another proof that Samuel's state was not a continuation of the Bulgarian state under the name "Western Bulgarian Kingdom", but "a new state, over which the Bulgarian rulers did not have rights" (Taškovski 1970, 117–18n). After Samuel killed his brother Aaron on suspicion of conspiring with Byzantium, he became an independent ruler. Roman was taken captive by Basil II in 991 and even fled to him, obviously as befits a Bulgarian dignitary. After Roman's death, Samuel usurped the Bulgarian royal crown in 997 and declared himself tsar. According to Taškovski, he received it from Rome, with uncritical reference to the correspondence between Kaloyan and Pope Innocent III (Taškovski 1970, 132–34). As one can see, the events are the same, but the explanations provided for them are diametrically opposed to those given by Bulgarian authors, as are the motivations ascribed to the same personalities.

Taškovski then explains the Bulgarian name of the kingdom and its population, namely, that the name did not have the ethnic meaning ascribed to it by Bulgarian historians today, but rather was a political state name. The medieval names and concepts cannot be identified with those of today and filled with today's national contents. According to the era, they have different contents. "People" in particular is an ethnic category that cannot be equated with nation (although it is a latent nation) and still less with being subjects of a state, which is a legal category. Within a state the ethnic development is not interrupted, but continues in combination with the new territorial forms of relating, in which ethnicity acquires other aspects. Administrative and political inclusion in one state is not enough for the various tribes to become one people, especially if the state lasts for a short time and comprises ethnically alien groups (Taškovski 1970, 135–38, 1974, 149–52, 155n).

Such was the case with the Bulgarian state, where the Bulgars in their expansion held under their rule various peoples, including the Macedonian Slavs. During the relatively short time of Bulgarian rule over Macedonia, it was not possible that the Macedonian Slavs and the Bulgars were assimilated into one people, especially considering that Bulgarians (meaning primarily Bulgars) neither colonized Macedonia, nor resettled Macedonian Slavs (Taškovski 1970, 138–40).

By detaching the Macedonian Slavs from the state name "Bulgarian", Taškovski claims that he reveals an ethnic process that remained invisible under the surface of the state name and thus strongly ethnicizes and in the end nationalizes the medieval times and Samuel's state in particular. Of course, the Bulgarian authors do the same in favor of the Bulgarian ethnos or nationality during the Middle Ages (with the advantage of having the name in the sources), and because of that—contrary to Taškovski—they have to identify the state with ethnicity or nationality. But in the end, the ethnic dimension proves to be basic in both strategies.

On the question of the name of the state, Taškovski refers to other medieval dynasties and crowns. The states in this era were monarchies (princedoms or kingdoms) in which titles and the crown played an enormous role. The Bulgarian royal title, taken by Samuel, is a strong argument of the Bulgarian historians in favor of state continuity and dynastic legitimacy. To counter this argument, Taškovski explains why Samuel adopted the Bulgarian title by going into the medieval views on monarchical titles (following Franz Dölger). Simeon aspired to the Byzantine imperial crown, but after he failed and still declared himself "Basileus of the Rhomios", he was reluctantly recognized by Romanos Lekapenos as "Tsar of the Bulgarians". Yet Byzantium recognized his son and heir Peter's title and position as tsar, and the Bulgarian Archbishopric was elevated to Patriarchate (Taškovski 1970, 143–53).

Samuel usurped the Bulgarian royal crown, which was vacant after the death of Roman, and according to Taškovski asked the Pope for a king's crown and a blessing. He received a blessing (untrue), which was most important, but whether the Pope sent his legate for the crowning is not known. In any case, it is the Pope and not the Bulgarian Patriarch, who here lends legitimacy to the coronation. With the usurpation of the Bulgarian crown, one of the three recognized imperial crowns, Samuel pursued its state-political (not ethnic) significance, as it went together with the right to claim all lands which were once under it, that is, to embrace under his scepter most Balkan peoples. He couldn't declare himself Tsar of the "Sklavinii" and still less "Tsar of the Macedonians" because the Macedonian Slavs then did not call themselves Macedonians and their rulers did not assume royal, but princely titles (of *knez*). In this sense, and not without pathos, Taškovski says that the ancestors of today's Macedonians, who were the pillar of Samuel's kingdom, were at the same time its victims in the sense that they could not "affirm" themselves under their name (Taškovski 1970, 154–63). (We will see a similar idea about a "blinded state" with Mitko Panov below.) To quote:

> That is why Samuel in his striving toward the resonant title tsar attached himself to a past, which was only a legend, without bearing upon the ethnic composition of the masses, which presented the spine of the kingdom. The dead body of the Bulgarian kingdom 'came back to life' with the coronation of Samuel as king of 'the Bulgarians', same as how the dead body of the

Roman kingdom lived in the theoretical grounding of the Byzantine kingdom. In fact, this magic 'coming back to life' of the Bulgarian kingdom, which occurred with this coronation, was only in name, but not in substance. The magician of this seemingly coming back to life was the Pope's blessing and gift of the royal crown, which Samuel wore on his head and declared himself a 'Bulgarian' tsar. (Taškovski 1970, 161–62)

If one departs from the medieval views, and not from the modern (ethno)national ones, as theoretically appealed to by Taškovski, the most important would be the dynasties and the crowns with their names and hereditary territories as well as the state and church traditions, but not the ethnic composition of the state and ethnic belonging. But with him it turns out exactly the opposite, namely, that in the case of Samuel's state the most important element was its ethnic make-up, and the rest were "only" political (state or administrative) names and the ruler's title.

Taškovski further explains why the later Byzantine chroniclers called Samuel and his subjects "Bulgarians" with the fact that after its conquest Basil II organized the central part of the kingdom—Macedonia—as an administrative *theme* with the name "Bulgaria". In this way, the Bulgarian name in Macedonia acquired also an administrative and military meaning, so that long after the fall of Samuel's kingdom the Byzantine historians found it proper to call the population of mostly Macedonian Slavs "Bulgarian" (Taškovski 1970, 164–66).

Finally, Taškovski pays special attention to the "ethnographic" views of the Byzantines about the peoples in the Balkans and points out how confused and different from today's national views they were, because they looked at them through the prism of the universalism of the Byzantine empire. He strives to demonstrate the "conditionality" of "Bulgarian" and "Bulgaria", which sometimes embraced other ethnic groups and sometimes did not cover the authentic Bulgarians themselves. Moreover, the Bulgarians themselves then appeared under other names as well, which do not designate the Bulgarian ethnos or nationality, such as "Vlachs", "Moesians", "Scythians", etc. The conclusion from all that is that one cannot judge directly from names the nationality of a people, and that one should not judge the Macedonian Slavs in particular by state and political designations (Taškovski 1970, 142, 166–70).

Discussing the relation between the Bulgarian name during the Middle Ages and the ethnic composition of the population, for which it is used in the sources, Taškovski exhibits hyper-criticism and de/constructionism.

This is in full contrast with the ethnic "essentialism" of the Bulgarian concept of ethnicity, where every mention of the Bulgarian name is associated with an eternal and unchangeable Bulgarian ethnic (*narodnostna*) essence and with uninterrupted continuity, and thus smoothly flows into the present-day Bulgarians, blocking all questions of difference with a medieval people. The issue is that all criticism by Taškovski of this approach applies only to the Bulgarian view. Regarding the Macedonian people in the Middle Ages he shows a lack of criticism and a proclivity toward ethnicizing the Macedonian Slavs' peculiarity, and postulating continuities of the Macedonian people. Here lies the paradox that in spite of the methodologically and theoretically sound tenets regarding peoples, states, and titles during the Middle Ages in contrast to the era of nations, in practice Taškovski proceeds from the same assumptions as the Bulgarian historians, coming from the era of Romanticism (the national Revivals in the Balkans). Namely, they all essentialize nationalities and postulate continuities regardless of conditions. Precisely the shared nationalist (and some Marxist) presuppositions of the Macedonian and the Bulgarian historiography make the rivalry especially embittered (Troebst 2007, 42).

The Croatian historian Stjepan Antoljak (1909–1997) from Skopje University published a book on Samuel's kingdom in 1969 (Antoljak 1969). It is written in his characteristic scattered style and without a clear or strong Macedonian message, which is weakened further by some involuntary pro-Bulgarian interpretations. I will only note some characteristic points. According to him, it was easier for the Bulgarians (under Tsar Peter) to rule Macedonia, because the center of Bulgarian rule was nearer to it than the center of Byzantine rule in Constantinople (undervaluing Thessaloniki and the sea route) and because both spoke the Slavic language. Antoljak accepts here the Bulgarian ethnogenetic vision in contrast to Taškovski, who thinks of the Bulgarians primarily as the dominating Bulgars and opposes them to the Slavs in language and race. There were, according to Antoljak, in the time of Tsar Peter various nationalities in Macedonia apart from the Slavs, and they all were called by the Byzantine authors from the tenth century onward not only "the more expansive name Bulgarians", but also "Macedonians". In his examples of the latter, this author confuses geographic Macedonia with the *theme* Macedonia in Thrace, for example, in saying that Macedonia became a *theme* as early as the eighth century, and that Khan Krum resettled the "Macedonians" from it (actually from Adrianople, in Thrace) to the north of the Danube. In fact, in the best case the name was used in an archaizing manner. For example, in one instance, Theophylact of Ohrid says that he lived in Macedonia. In Simeon's time the Bulgarians were the strongest of the Slavs, and after they conquered Macedonia they succeeded in imposing themselves through the Slavic language over the Macedonian Slavs, who were considered Bulgarians, whether they wanted or not, by the Byzantines, who did not acknowledge another people on the Balkan peninsula besides themselves and the Bulgarians. According to Antoljak this is why many events were ascribed by the Byzantine authors to the Bulgarians, including the uprising of the *kometopuli* (Antoljak 1969, 10–12, 78, 119–21). But his striving to discover the present-day Macedonians under the Macedonian name in the medieval sources is quite hopeless.

Antoljak (following Taškovski) accepts 969 as the year of the *kometopuli* uprising, who wanted to secede from the Bulgarian state, but interprets this as feudal secession after Tsar Peter's death, that is, without a clear pro-Macedonian national message. Then he strays into the origin of Samuel and his brothers and endorses the Armenian version. According to him, during the war between Sviatoslav and Tzimiskes the *kometopuli* waited and then recognized the latter's supremacy (as in Anastasijević) because they did not want to be overrun by him as Serbia. They found it easier to obey because Tzimiskes was also of Armenian origin and left them in peace without violating their autonomy, and even implicitly favored them—a rather naïve statement (Antoljak 1969, 12–18, 20–21).

Most numerous in Samuel's state were the Macedonians (specified in brackets as Macedonian Slavs) and then in descending order (as if there had been a census) Greek Slavs, Bulgarians, Serbs, Croats, Rhomios, Albanians, Romani (Vlachs), Vardarioti-Turks, and Armenians. "The Tsar of Bulgaria" (or "Tsar of the Bulgarians") stood at the head of this conglomerate of peoples, but according to Antoljak the name did not have a connection with the Bulgaria of Simeon and Peter. Yet this new kingdom could have a tsar only as a continuation of the First Bulgarian Kingdom, and so thought Samuel, although his state was a "completely new creation" with a different nucleus and center and different domestic and foreign policies (here the author follows the Serbian tradition). It would be more appropriate if he had called himself "Tsar of the Bulgarians and the Slavs" (but regrettably for Antoljak he did not). Samuel received his crown from the Pope, but a princely one with the title rex, yet he could consider himself a tsar like his predecessors Simeon and Peter, notwithstanding that Byzantium did not recognize him. The Ohrid church was presided over by an archbishop (not a patriarch) also with the Pope's approval (Antoljak 1969, 80–82).

As pointed out by the Macedonian historian Mitko Panov, with the thesis of two uprisings in 969 and 976 Antoljak deviated from the Yugoslav scholarly consensus of one uprising in 976, based on Ostrogorski's authority. His positions became the basis of a Macedonian historiographical consensus (it is not clear why Taškovski's priority is not mentioned here) in viewing Samuel's state as part of the national history of the Macedonian people. It was established by an anti-Bulgarian uprising by the *kometopuli*, who were of Armenian origin, and was based on a population of a non-Bulgarian ethnic character. The Bulgarian royal title was assumed because of its prestige, and even then the crown was received from the Pope. The same line was followed later by Antoljak's follower Branko Panov and other Macedonian historians (Panov 2019, 364–67).

The Macedonian cultural historian Blaže Ristovski (1931–2018) was the author of something approaching a manifesto in 1968 about the formation of the Macedonian nationality. It was listed among the "classified" books in the Bulgarian National Library during the socialist regime, access to which was barred (Ristovski 1983, 15–36). Here I am only interested in his treatment of Samuel's state and the problem of the Macedonian name.

Ristovski justifies the right of the Macedonians as a people to have their medieval history, although not under a name of their own. There are other historical cases of a common development of two or more peoples, followed by a separation, foreign languages and names being adopted, and state territories and borders changing. For example, the old Gaul (Gallia) was conquered by the Germanic tribes, expanded to include most of Western and Central Europe by Charlemagne, then split into three states: France, Germany, and Italy. Ristovski's idea is that this was the case with the Bulgarians and Macedonians, who possess a common past, but then parted and went their own way. He also says that the present-day peoples should not identify themselves with old feudal states with short-lived borders and claim the one-time territories of these states that carried their name (in the Macedonian case: "Greek lands", "Bulgarian lands" or "Serbian lands"), given that feudal states had ethnically heterogeneous subjects. The right approach according to him is to depart from the history of individual peoples (not states) such as Greeks, Serbs, Bulgarians, etc., which in different eras entered other states. Thus, the Macedonian people in its historical development had various masters, but forged its own identity, from which a Macedonian nation later evolved (Ristovski 1983, 15–18).

According to Ristovski, the Macedonians had political and state formations of their own in the past, but these "were either not fully developed, or remained on a smaller territory, or wore a foreign name, so that in the modern histories they turned out to be on somebody else's pages" (Ristovski 1983, 60). He points out that after the inhabitants of the Bulgarian state became "Bulgarians", the name "Slovenes" or "Slavenes" in the Byzantine sources is meant exclusively for the Macedonian Slavs. Thus, the first name of the Macedonian people was "Slovenes" or "Slavenes" and this name remained until the eleventh century, notwithstanding that alien names started to impose themselves politically and administratively (Ristovski 1983, 57–60).

Ristovski considers Samuel's state as the first state of the Slavs in Macedonia, through which the uniting of the Macedonian Slavs in a people's unity against Byzantium took place, and which extended its territory on much of the Balkans. Despite the "complications" with its naming, the Macedonian nation started to "affirm itself as a people" with a unified Slavic state language, Ohrid as a literary and cultural center, and an autonomous church organization, the Ohrid Patriarchate. There also developed a "Slavic people's (*narodno*) self-consciousness, but with a double naming: with the people's name 'Slavs' and the state name 'Bulgarians'" (Ristovski 1983, 34). The next two centuries as a Byzantine administrative unit under the name "Bulgaria" eclipsed the people's name still more and the name "Bulgarian" was asserted. The fall under Serbian rule led to a new eclipse of the national name, and with the Ottoman conquest and its specific religious order other designations such as *rayah*, *giaour*, "Christian", etc. came to the fore. The "deconstitution" continued until the formation of the modern Macedonian nation. (Ristovski 1983, 34–35).

Branko Panov followed Antoljak and the established Macedonian consensus. Thus the 969 uprising of the Macedonian Slavs against the Turano-Bulgarian rule led to the elimination of Bulgarian rule and the creation of the first state of the Macedonian Slavs. Although Tzimiskes' supreme power in Macedonia was recognized after the destruction of the Bulgarian state in 971, the *kometopuli* preserved considerable self-rule. After Tzimiskes' death in 976, they launched a new uprising, this time against Byzantium, and joined all territories of the former Slavic-Macedonian princedoms to the new Macedonian Slavic state, whose core was the Macedonian-Slavic ethnic group. It also included non-Macedonian

90 R. DASKALOV

territories and grew into a kingdom. In the Macedonian state the Macedonian tribal princedoms were consolidated, and they were transformed into a people. Thus, the ethnogenesis of the Macedonian people was complete. Samuel's state was treated as "Bulgarian" even though it had nothing in common with the First Bulgarian Kingdom because of the former Bulgarian rule over Macedonia (nothing is said here about the Bulgarian crown). After its conquest by Basil II (his nickname "Bulgar-Slayer" is not mentioned) there were several uprisings by the Macedonian Slavs, who did not resign themselves to their fate (Panov 1985, 23–26).

Bulgarian-Macedonian Polemics After the Creation of an Independent Macedonian State

After the creation of an independent Macedonian state in 1991 the Bulgarian-Macedonian polemics intensified. Some publicly active Bulgarian historians and historicizing politicians such as the leader of the IMRO nationalist party Krasimir Karakachanov thought that the time had come to launch a decisive attack in the changed international conditions, which placed the Republic of (now North) Macedonia in a difficult situation, and to exert pressure upon it to acknowledge the Bulgarian "truth" on all historical matters. This was in "propaganda" works, such as the ones published by the renewed Macedonian Scientific Institute in its publication "Macedonian Review" (since 1991), which does not concern us here. A special joint Historical and Educational Issues Commission between Bulgaria and North Macedonia was created, which held its first session on July 4, 2018, and whose activities remain fruitless to this day. As for the properly historiographical "scholarly" works, one can observe a recycling of the facts and arguments. Exceptions are a few critical and reflexive works of a small number of Bulgarian historians, who distanced themselves not only from the Macedonian tenets but also from the Bulgarian position in order to trace a more neutral and balanced view by pointing out weaknesses on both sides. Most importantly, beyond a simply "balanced" view, they problematize and try to overcome the nationalist assumptions in the historical narrative. But these works have a more principled character and do not treat specifically the Middle Ages, and some are available only on the internet.

After Antoljak and Panov, Milan Boškoski took up the enterprise of looking for the Macedonian name in the Slavic past of Macedonia, with special attention to the ethnic meaning. He did this in a special study of the uses of the names "Macedonia" and "Macedonian" in the medieval sources with a parallel translation in English (Boškoski 2003). His objective was to trace every mention of these names and their particular meaning from the late Roman/early Byzantine era to the fourteenth century. We are concerned here only with the part that deals with the Bulgarian rule over Macedonia.

With the Bulgarian conquest of Macedonia (without Thessaloniki) and especially with the 927 peace treaty between Tsar Peter and Byzantium, which recognized most of the Bulgarian conquests, the common terms for the region and its inhabitants became "Bulgaria" and "Bulgarians". In Boškoski's opinion this was a designation for the inhabitants of the area without regard for their ethnicity as Macedonian Slavs, Vlachs, Greeks, Serbs, Albanians, etc., after the name of the state. This name continued during Samuel's state because of the preceding Bulgarian rule and the state and legal traditions taken up from the fallen Bulgarian Kingdom. For similar reasons, the Ohrid Archbishopric first usurped the name First Justiniana (untrue), and after the fall of the First Bulgarian Kingdom in 971, the church rights of the Bulgarian church itself (Boškoski 2003, 81, 105–06, 210).

Yet even when Macedonia was under Bulgarian rule in the tenth century, Constantine VII Porphyrogennetos, in his desire to show his erudition, used the terms Macedonia and Macedonians in an archaizing manner, according to Boškoski "in their ancient meaning with a certain reminiscence of the new inhabitants—"the Slavs" (Boškoski 2003, 82). Leo the Deacon called the inhabitants of the "new Macedonian state" of Samuel (besides Bulgarians) also "Scythians" and "Moesians" while he used the term "Macedonians" to designate the Macedonian Slavs from southeastern and southern Macedonia who remained in the Byzantine empire. According to Boškoski this term was a "negation" of the term Bulgaria for the territory of Macedonia under Bulgarian rule (Boškoski 2003, 98–99). For example, Leo the Deacon says that the basileus led his army against the Moesians, that is, the *kometopuli*, who caused damage to the Byzantine state and ravaged the part of Macedonia under Byzantine rule (Beshevliev, ed. 1964, 275).

Boškoski wants thusly to demonstrate the continuity of the Macedonian name not only as a name of the classical geographic region, but most of all for its medieval population in an ethnic sense, though no such thing is seen in the sources. However, when the name Macedonia (or the adjective

Macedonian) is used, it is either in an archaizing sense as in Constantine VII Porphyrogennetos in the tenth century, or with later authors during the decay of the *theme* system (e.g., Nikephoros Gregoras, Joannes Kantakouzenos) it means the whole region, or parts of it, or towns and villages in it, or Byzantine soldiers recruited from it. On the rare occasion when the name "Macedonians" is used by contemporary authors, it is not in an ethnic sense as Boškoski would like, but denotes people from the region, for example, with the routed Macedonian troops of Petăr Deljan in the uprising of 1041, who passed to Italy (Duychev et al., eds. 1960, 359).

The other major objective of Boškoski is to delink the Macedonian Slavs from the Bulgarian name. That is why he is especially attentive to the use of the Macedonian name when the Bulgarian one prevailed, and he wants (in vain) to interpret it not only with the archaizing geographic meaning, but in reference to the actual territory, and to the actual population. But most of all he is keen on seeing some kind of differentiation from the Bulgarian name during the decay of the *theme* system and the rise of the Second Bulgarian Kingdom after 1185. The logic here is that even if the Macedonian Slavs were not directly called Macedonians, they were differentiated from Bulgarians.

To summarize, while Taškovski and Ristovski frankly acknowledged the strategic adoption of the Macedonian name as a nationality during the Macedonian revival (prerodba), we can see in Boškoski another strategy, following Antoljak and Branko Panov, whose views he often quotes. This rather unconvincing strategy aims to establish a link between the medieval uses of the name "Macedonian", and the present-day Macedonians, that is, to show the present-day Macedonian people as existing in the medieval sources under its present name, and not only as Macedonian Slavs "hiding" under other names. One has to say that the first strategy is more convincing in its frankness than the second strategy, which arbitrarily interprets medieval sources. We will see yet another strategy further on with Mitko Panov.

In 2000 the first volume of the five-volume "History of the Macedonian People" was published. The section on medieval Macedonia is written by Branko Panov, which broadly follows the Macedonian line.

The wars against Kievan Rus and Byzantium in Danubian Bulgaria weakened the Bulgarian position in Macedonia, and created the conditions for a liberation movement against Bulgarian rule. It broke out after Tsar Peter's death in southwestern Macedonia, the former sklavinia of the

Berzetes (Brsiaks), where a "new Slavic state in the Balkans was created, known as Macedonian [sic!] or Samuel's state after the founder of the Macedonian royal dynasty" (Panov 2000, 358). Although Macedonia was not conquered by Byzantium, it recognized Tzimiskes' supreme authority and after 971 existed as a dependent state (following Anastasijević). After Tzimiskes' death in 976 the *kometopuli* rose to arms, this time against Byzantium. When the uprising succeeded, Macedonia became fully independent. In the same year, the Bulgarians of Moesia also took up arms and handed authority to the four brothers, and so the territory of Bulgaria was also included in the Macedonian state. After Roman's arrival in Macedonia he was appointed governor of Skopje by Samuel, which "convincingly testifies that the Macedonian state was not a continuation of the First Bulgarian Kingdom, but a new Slavic state in the Balkans" (Panov 2000, 358–62, quotes on 358 and 361).

Samuel could not take the Bulgarian royal crown, which was carried by Tzimiskes in 971 to Constantinople (as if royal authority lay with the specific material crown) and so could receive a crown only from Rome. The correspondence between Tsar Kaloyan (of the Second Bulgarian Kingdom) and Pope Innocent III is uncritically used as proof that Samuel received his crown from the Pope, though only as rex, as only the German emperors could be crowned kings. Samuel did not belong to the prior Bulgarian dynasty, but founded a new Macedonian royal dynasty. The newly created Macedonian church (the ending "and of all Bulgaria" is passed in silence) was raised to the rank of archbishopric, again with papal permission, in the presence of papal legates. Thus, the Macedonian Kingdom received a royal title and international recognition (Panov 2000, 272–74).

The Macedonian state was multinational in its ethnic composition, and alongside the ruling Macedonian people it comprised Bulgarians, Serbs, Albanians, Croats, Vlachs, Vardariotes-Turks, Armenians, and Greeks. Although many contemporary Byzantine authors called the Macedonian state "Bulgaria" and its inhabitants "Bulgarians", with the creation of the new Macedonian state they started to make a certain difference (which isn't explained) between Macedonia and Bulgaria, Macedonians and Bulgarians. The more frequent use of the names "Macedonia", "Macedonian land", and "Macedonians" (we saw the state of affairs with the names, especially the latter) and the vanishing of tribal names attests to the fact that in Samuel's time "the long and complex ethnogenetic process of unifying the Macedonian Slavic tribes into a unitary Macedonian people finished definitively" (Panov 2000, 384–85, quote on 385).

One Bulgarian reaction to this history (and the other volumes) came from Milen Mihov. His objection is that by ignoring the numerous historical testimonies of the name "Bulgarian", the conclusion is drawn that the rare mention of "Macedonia" in Greek sources is enough to demonstrate that in Samuel's time the process of forming a Macedonian people was accomplished. More generally, the exposition of ancient and medieval history emphasizes that Macedonia and the Macedonians, the land and the people, are inextricably linked and present a constant unity throughout the centuries (Mihov 2006, 130–35). In other words, continuity and unchangeable identity, based on the coexistence of land and its inhabitants.

Lastly, I will consider the work of the medievalist Mitko Panov (son of the medievalist Branko Panov) whom I quoted a number of times above, published in English under the title *The Blinded State*. It consists of two large parts, but I am primarily interested here in the first one. Panov elaborates on the idea that in their adherence to the Byzantine imperial ideology, the Byzantine authors committed a huge injustice to Samuel's state by distorting and even "blinding" it (the metaphor of the title) when they named it Bulgarian and disguised the identity of its population at the time (Panov 2019, 4, 5, 391–93, 397–98). Something like a Byzantine conspiracy existed against it. This of course presupposes that it had another real, authentic character, although Panov avoids directly saying that it was Macedonian. Yet in one place he is more explicit when he affirms that the Macedonian revolutionaries and intelligentsia resurrected "an authentic Macedonian Samuel naturally belonging to the Macedonians, demonstrating their innate historical right to the territory" (Panov 2019, 395).

Panov considers in the first place Byzantine and other sources concerning Samuel's state during its existence and further on until Ottoman rule. His basic idea is that per Byzantine ideology, Byzantine authors concealed the entirely different character of Samuel's new state. What was this ideology and what did it require? According to Panov it required that Samuel's state was not recognized as a new entity but was treated as a continuation of the Bulgaria destroyed in 971, in order to make it look illegitimate, the result of throwing off Byzantine authority, under which it legitimately belonged after the fall of the Bulgarian Kingdom. In this way, according to him, Byzantine sovereignty over this former Roman province as well as Byzantine supremacy and prestige were asserted, the imperial conquest was legitimized, and an idea of an uninterrupted Byzantine imperial domination was created, which in reality never existed (Panov 2019, 5, 6, 10, 11, 12, 392).

With the contemporary Byzantine authors Leo the Deacon, Joannes Geometres, and others, this was done by avoiding any (ethnic) designation and even concealing Samuel's name and calling the adversaries of the Byzantines older names, especially "Moesians" and the more general "Scythians" or "barbarians", while Samuel and his brothers were called *kometopuli* (Panov 2019, 22, 28–68). But Panov evades the fact that by these names, and especially "Moesians", the Byzantine authors unambiguously meant Bulgarians, and wants to persuade the reader that the Moesians of Leo the Deacon, in particular, were not the Bulgarians subjugated in 971, but had another (Macedonian?) ethnic identity. They were a foreign people with "Scythian" characteristics (meaning Samuel's troops), who mercilessly devastated the "lands of the Macedonians", that is, of the Slavs remaining under Byzantine rule. The rare mention of "Bulgaria" and "Bulgarians" by contemporary Byzantine authors presumably referred (very doubtfully, though Panov stubbornly tries to prove it) to the subjugated eastern part, later conquered by Samuel, or to (present-day) Greece (Panov 2019, 32–34, 37–38).

The main culprit for disguising or veiling Samuel's state was, according to Panov, Basil II. With his *sigillia* establishing the Ohrid Archbishopric, he connected it with the Bulgarian Patriarchate under Samuel. Thus, Basil II connected the new state with the patriarchal tradition of the Bulgarian state destroyed in 971. All this was an expression of Byzantine ideology and propaganda, denying the independent character of Samuel's state with an identity of its own by treating it as part of the already destroyed state with a degraded tsar (Panov 2019, 8, 9, 12, 22–23, 75, 79–83, 392–93).

Regarding the Ohrid Archbishopric, Panov's view is that it was different from the Patriarchate of the former Bulgarian Kingdom (abolished by Tzimiskes). Basil II in his *sigillia* created a false impression of continuity and it is not true that the archbishopric moved from place to place, while it was established by Samuel (Panov 2019, 82–86, 116–17, 392–93). All in all, according to Panov the Bulgarian name of Samuel's state was an imposed identity and an invention of tradition by Basil II, who established a fictitious continuity through the administrative *theme* and church name. The name "Bulgaria" in this case did not have an ethnic meaning (same as with all Macedonian authors), while the name "Macedonia" could not be used because it was already used by another *theme* in Thrace. In this way a "projected identity" of Samuel's state as Bulgarian was established, which misled subsequent Byzantine and other medieval authors, as well as modern scholars (Panov 2019, 5, 10, 85–89, 392–94). After the initial falsified concept by Basil II of Samuel's state as Bulgarian, there followed new layers of construction over construction over construction or, actually, one and the same ideological construct repeating itself in new eras and under new conditions, which distorted the historical realities.

However, Panov does not reveal the (implied) Macedonian character of Samuel's state as a similar construct, but (implicitly) considers it as a restoration of the historical truth about the state of affairs. Samuel's state and the duel between Samuel and Basil II in general are rightly conceived as "symbols" and appropriation of Samuel's legacy by various forces, but it is implied that it belongs to today's Macedonians. One can note the one-sidedness and asymmetry in Panov's exposition in the sense of deconstructing only the identification of Samuel's state as Bulgarian, without similarly criticizing the Macedonian construct of the state as Macedonian.

Likewise, he does not change perspectives on the ethnic question as seen by his panicked rejection of the Bulgarian name and his numerous references to "Macedonian land" in the sources, but plunges deeper by expanding it with new ideas about medieval ethnicity and Byzantine ethnographic views with references to Florin Curta, Anthony Kaldellis, Guy Halsall, Walter Paul, Patrick Geary, etc. Panov thinks of himself as a "revisionist" of the traditional view that Samuel's state was a direct continuation of the First Bulgarian Kingdom, or even an independent state which continued the Bulgarian imperial and church tradition (Panov 2019, 4–6, 11). However, instead of revisionism, we get the same in an updated and more concealed and indirect form.

There is a basic problem in Panov's repetitive insistence on the distorting Byzantine imperial ideology and its layering and passing on by later authors until today. It comes from the indiscriminate use of the term "ideology" in the negative Marxist sense of distortion, manipulation, disguising, veiling, masking of the "truth", etc. (Ricoeur 1986). The problem lies in the (if implicit) claim of the author to be able to discern behind the ideological constructs the truth of the matter, in this case the Macedonian-Slavic character of Samuel's state and how its subjects had felt and identified themselves and how they thought about their polity. Although, according to Panov, there is no clue coming from the historical personalities as to their identity (ignoring "Bulgarian by birth" of Joannes Vladislav's Bitola inscription), he rejects any identification with the Bulgarian one and implies some "Macedonian" self-consciousness (Panov 2019, 3, 88, 391–92). The Bitola inscription is according to him damaged and its deciphering was guided by the modern imagination. Besides, the mention of an ethnic origin was unusual for the eleventh century, which suggests (most improbably) that it was written later by another person who wanted to impose a Bulgarian origin on the former ruler (Panov 2019, 3, 74, 391). Panov does not mention Samuel's Bulgarian crown and asserts that it is unknown when and how he received the royal title, and from where he received legitimacy, but asserts in contrast to many authoritative authors that he did not associate himself and his state with the preceding Bulgarian state and did not strive to continue its traditions (Panov 2019, 9, 11–12, 392).

All of the above adds a new twist to dealing with the absence of a Macedonian name in the Middle Ages. Namely, its absence is explained by the pro-Bulgarian Byzantine ideology that would be taken up in the modern era by various ideologies such as the pan-Hellenism, pan-Slavism (i.e., of imperial Russia), and especially nationalism. The "imposed" Bulgarian identity on the region of Macedonia is explained as administrative and church terminology invented by Basil II only after conquering Samuel's state, without prior roots in the past Bulgarian domination or in Samuel's state itself.

The 1000th anniversary of the death of Samuel in 2014 was solemnly celebrated in Bulgaria through numerous events in Sofia, Blagoevgrad, Petrich, and Odrin (Edirne). The central event was an international conference on "The European Southeast in the Second Half of the Tenth—the Beginning of the Eleventh Century", which took place at the Bulgarian Academy of Sciences, and from which a volume was published (Gyuzelev and Nikolov, eds. 2015). It was accompanied by the laying of flowers at the monument of Samuel's warriors in the presence of the President and the Prime Minister of the Republic of Bulgaria, a liturgy by the Bulgarian Patriarch in memory of Tsar Samuel, and church music in the aula of Sofia University "St. Kliment Ohridski". Finally, there was a trip to Rila Monastery and Samuel's (reconstructed) fortress near Petrich. In connection with the celebrations a number of monographs and collective volumes were published, as well as special issues of journals, catalogues of exhibitions, works of fiction, and materials in the daily press, and there were broadcastings on Bulgarian national television and other mass media. As noted by the author of the review of the celebration, the eminent medievalist Gyuzelev: "One has every reason to affirm that there has hardly been another medieval ruler, to whom such great attention was paid by the Bulgarian public with such different and varied events" (Gyuzelev

2014, 110–13, quote on 113). It is not difficult to answer why, given that there was a similar celebration in the Republic of Macedonia, though with less pomp. This was one more episode of the Bulgarian-Macedonian controversy over Samuel's belonging and legacy.

To conclude, the question of whose is Samuel's state is so controversial because it is in the last instance a question of heritage or more broadly of legacy. Thus Taškovski, chosen here for being the most outspoken and militant, rejects any continuity between the Bulgars of the First Bulgarian state (who according to him did not even get Slavicized) and the modern Bulgarian nation formed by other Slavs on other territories. Moreover, he also thinks that the Bulgarian nation is not entitled even to the legacy of the Moesian Slavs, who led a "non-historical" existence under the domination of the Bulgars, while many fled to Byzantium (Taškovski 1974, 11, 84–87). Taškovski concludes that the present-day Bulgarians have no right to claim the Bulgar legacy. He is absolutely explicit with a clear awareness of the stakes, and uses the term "patrimonium" to refer to historical heritage, that is, inherited from the fathers (*bashtina*, *babalăk*). According to him, today's Bulgarian people cannot appropriate the non-Slavic Turano-Bulgarian Kingdom as their patrimonium only because it has taken its name as a national name (similarly to how the Macedonians, who have taken the name of the old Macedonians, cannot claim their legacy). In particular, today's Slavic generations in Bulgaria cannot consider the Bulgar king's crown as their "heritage", or think that everyone who has attained it, such as Samuel, can automatically be considered a Bulgarian in today's sense of the word (Taškovski 1974, 67, 87).

In his counterattack, Taškovski accuses Bulgarian historiography of falsification and appropriation as patrimonium of the present-day Bulgarian people not only of the Turano-Bulgarian legacy, but also of the Slavic Macedonian legacy. To quote, Bulgarian history is an "artificial synthesis or combination of two very alien historical heritages, which had as its objective to create at any price a Slavic nationality under [the] Bulgarian name at the expense of the Slavs in the western half of the Balkan peninsula and at the expense of the Macedonians in the first place" (Taškovski 1974, 10–13, quote on 11–12).

According to Taškovski, the historical legacy of today's Macedonian people is the Slavic one, especially on the cultural plane: first the Slavic script, created by Cyril and Methodius based on the language of the Slavs in Macedonia, then the educational activities of their disciples Clement of Ohrid and Naum, then the heretic Bogomils, then Samuel's kingdom and the earlier anti-Byzantine uprisings in Macedonia, which all occurred on Macedonian terrain. By appropriating the Macedonian Slavic history and the Turano-Bulgarian legacy today's Bulgarian generations, according to Taškovski, not only pose as a great historical people with a glorious medieval past, but also claim Macedonia, which after the failure of the San-Stefano fiction of a "Greater Bulgaria" became a political ideal of the Bulgarian Principality. Thus, Bulgarian historical views are tied to broader national interests, which makes them extremely resistant to any critique, including scholarly (Taškovski 1974, 12–14).

We see here an inverted image of the assertions of Bulgarian historians about the theft of Bulgarian history by Macedonian historians. The issue is that the latter don't have a terrain from which to take resources for their own medieval (and later) history and in this way a building material for their identity, except from the perimeter already occupied and appropriated by Bulgarian historians for the Bulgarian nation. The medieval past especially was common and shared, if we look at it from today's point of view of two already-existing nations, but it has passed under the Bulgarian name and Bulgarian state-church traditions. Hence the mutual accusations of "theft of history", falsification, and the like. This makes the clash over "owning" medieval personalities, events, and phenomena frontal and, given the strong nationalism in both societies and statesmen, dramatic, a veritable historiographical war.

More broadly, historical legacies are tied to identity building and are often accompanied by claims of "historical rights" to territories. Both Bulgarians and Macedonians were formed in a modern national sense not during the Middle Ages—the medieval "peoples" were different—but during the modern era, and retrospectively they looked for a past of their own. This is the same need for creating an identity through the past: the question "who are we?" leads to the questions: "where do we come from?, "what have we been?", "what deeds have our ancestors accomplished?". These are universal identity questions, asked by the national (and nationalist) historiographies launched during Romanticism. Present-day generations strive through their professional or amateur historians to adopt fathers and forefathers as their predecessors and to seek a historical "heritage" from them. The Bulgarian historians gave their answers to the above questions earlier in time, because of Bulgaria's earlier national formation and creation of the new Bulgarian state, and they succeeded in persuading scholars abroad (Russian scholars were less impressed). Not to forget, they had the advantage of the Bulgarian name and the Bulgarian state and church tradition. Faced with this the Macedonian historians either denied it or tried to diminish its importance along Serbian lines. Both Bulgarian and Macedonian historians were interested in the ethnic composition of Samuel's state not only for identity building, but also to establish a sort of "historical right" over its territory in modern times. In fact, the debates on the distant medieval past arose precisely during the Balkan national revivals in the nineteenth century, first with the rivalry over the division of Macedonia and later with the appearance of a Macedonian historical agent, claiming history and rights of its own. The Bulgarians had the name, but the Macedonians countered this with the land, now in Macedonian possession, and the people, who inhabited it then in spite of the name. Also, with the idea that everything which happened on this land belongs to them. And the clash goes on.

REFERENCES

Adontz, Nicolas. 1965. Samuel l'Armenien, roi des bulgares. In *Etudes Armeno-byzantines*, 347–407. Lisbonne: Libraria Bertrand (first published as: Nikoghayos Adonts. 1938. Samuel l'Armenien, roi des bulgares. Brussels: Extrat, de Mémoirs publiés par l'Académie royale Belgique. Classe des lettres. Collection 8, vol. 39).

Anastasijević, Dragutin. 1927. Hipoteza o 'Zapadnoj Bugarskoj'. *Glasnik Skopskog naučnog društva*, 3, 1–11.

Angelov, Dimităr. 1962. Po văprosa za naselenieto v Makedoniya prez srednovekovnata epoha (7–14 vek). *Izkustvo* 12 (4–5): 35–38.

Angelov, Dimităr. 1966. Bălgarskata narodnost i deloto na Kliment Ohridski. In *Kliment Ohridski. Sbornik ot statii po sluchay 1050 godini ot smărtta mu*, ed. Bonyu Angelov, 7–24. Sofia: BAN. An English translation: Angelov, Dimiter. 1966. "Clement of Ochrida and Bulgarian Nationhood." *Etudes historiques*, no. 3, 61–109.

Angelov, Dimităr. 1971. *Obrazuvane na bălgarskata narodnost*. Sofia: Nauka i izkustvo.

Angelov, Dimiter. 1973. Formation and Development of the Bulgarian Nationality (Ninth to Twelfth Centuries). *Bulgarian Historical Review*, 1, 49–64.

Antoljak, Stjepan. 1969. *Samuilovata država*. Skopje: Institut za nacionalna istorija.

Balaschev, Georgi. 1929. *Bălgarite prez poslednite desetgodishnini na desetiya vek, chast 1*. Sofia: P. Glushkov.

Beshevliev, Veselin, ed. 1964. *Grătski izvori za bălgarskata istoriya*, t. 5. Sofia: BAN.

Blagoev, Nikola. 1926. Kriticheski pregled vărhu izvestiyata na Yoana Skilitsa za proizhoda na tsar Samuilovata dărzhava. *Makedonski pregled* 2 (4): 1–64.

2 CONTROVERSIES OVER SAMUEL'S STATE   101

Blagoev, Nikola. 1931. Bălgarskiyat tsar Roman. *Makedonski pregled* 6 (3): 15–34.

Blagoev, Nikola. 1942. Bratyata David, Moysey, Aron i Samuel. In *Godishnik na Sofiyskiya universitet. Yuridicheski fakultet*, t. 37, кniga 14, 28–41. Sofia: Sofiyski universitet 1942.

Boškoski, Milan. 2003. *Iminjata Makedonija i Makedonci vo srednovekovnite izvori*. Skopje: Republički zavod za zaštita na spomenicite na kulturata.

Bozhilov, Ivan. 1999. Bălgariya v epohata na tsar Samuil. S. Pirivatrich, Samuilovata dărzhava. Obhvat i harakter, Belgrad, 1997. *Istoricheski pregled* 55 (5–6): 190–202.

Bozhilov, Ivan, and Vasil Gyuzelev. 1999. *Istoriya na srednovekovna Bălgariya VII–XIV vek*. Sofia: Anubis.

Daskalov, Roumen. 2021. *Master Narratives of the Middle Ages in Bulgaria*. Leiden-Boston: Brill.

Drinov, Marin. 1971a. Nachaloto na Samuilovata dărzhava. In *Izbrani săchineniya*, ed. Ivan Duychev, vol. 1, 388–433. Sofia: Nauka i izkustvo (1st ed. 1874–1876).

Drinov, Marin. 1971b. Yuzhnye slavyane i Vizantiya v X veke. In *Izbrani săchineniya*, eds. Ivan Duychev and Marin Drinov, vol. 1, 434–586. Sofia: Nauka i izkustvo (1st ed. 1875).

Duychev, Ivan, Mihail Voynov, Strashimir Lishev, and Borislav Primov, eds. 1960. Annales Barenses. In *Latinski izvori za bălgarskata istoriya*, t. 2, 359. Sofia: BAN.

Gil'ferding, Aleksandr. 1866. *Sobranie sochineniy*, vol. 1, *Istoriya Serbov i Bolgar*, 3–280. St. Petersburg: Pechatnitsa V. Golovina.

Gyuzelev, Vasil. 2000. Za tazi kniga. Za neyniya avtor. In Sărdzhan Pirivatrin, *Samuilovata dărzhava. Obhvat i harakter*. Translated by Stefan Stoyanov, 9–12. Sofia: Agata.

Gyuzelev, Vasil. 2014. Natsionalni i mezhdunarodni nauchni proyavi, posveteni na 1000–godishninata ot smărtta na tsar Samuil (October 6, 1014 g.). *Spisanie na BAN* 127 (6): 110–113.

Gyuzelev, Vasil, and Georgi Nikolov, eds. 2015. *Evropeyskiyat Yugoiztok prez vtorata polovina na X—nachaloto na XI vek. Istoriya i kultura. Mezhdunarodna konferentsiya (Sofia 6–8 okt. 2014)*. Sofia: BAN.

Höpken, Wolfgang. 1999. Vergangenheitspolitik im sozialistischen Vielvölkerstaat: Jugoslawien 1944–1991. In *Umkämpfte Vergangenheit. Geschichtsbilder, Erinnerung und Vergangenheitspolitik im internationalen Vergleich*, ed. Petra Bock and Edgar Wolfrum, 210–243. Göttingen: Vandenhoeck & Ruprecht.

Iorga, Nicolae. 1912/1913. Notes d'un historien relatives aux événements des Balcans. *Académie roumaine. Bulletin de la Section historique* 1, 57–101.

Iorga, Nicolae. 1927. *Histoire des Roumains et de la romanité orientale*, vol. 3, *Les fondateurs d'état*. Bucarest: L'académie roumaine.

Irechek, Konstantin. 1976. *Istoriya na bălgarite*. Edited by Vasil Zlatarski. Sofia: Strashimir Slavchev (1st ed. in Czech and German in 1876).

102   R. DASKALOV

Ivanov, Yordan. 1925. Proizhod na tsar Samuiloviya rod. In *Sbornik v chest na Vasil Zlatarski po sluchay 30-godishnata mu nauchna i profesorska deynost*, 55–62. Sofia: no data on publisher.

Kosev, Dimităr, Dimităr Dimitrov, Zhak Natan, Hristo Hristov, and Dimităr Angelov. 1954. *Istoriya na Bălgariya*, t. 1. Sofia: Nauka i izkustvo.

Marinov, Tchavdar. 2010. *La Question Macédonienne de 1944 à nos jours. Communisme et nationalisme dans les Balkans*. Paris: L'Harmattan.

Mihov, Milen. 2006. Review of *Istorija na makedonskiot narod. Skopje, t. I, 2000; t. II, 1998; t. III, 2003; t. IV, 2000; t. V, 2003. Makedonski pregled* 29, no. 3, 130–142.

Mutafchiev, Petăr. 1928. D. N. Anastasijević, Hipoteza o 'Zapadnoj Bugarskoj'", Glasnik Skopskog naučnog društva 3 (1927), 1–11. *Makedonski pregled* 4 (4): 121–29.

Mutafchiev, Petăr. 1943. *Istoriya na bălgarskiya narod*, chast parva [part one]. *Părvo bălgarsko tsarstvo*. Sofia: Hemus.

Novaković, Stojan. 1893. *Prvi osnovi slovenske književnosti među balkanskim Slovenima. Legenda o Vladimiru i Kosari*. Beograd: Srpska Kraljevska Akademija.

Ostrogorski, Georgije. 1959. *Istorija Vizantije*. Beograd: Srpska Književna zadruga.

Ostrogorski, George. 1969. *History of the Byzantine State*. Revised ed. New Brunswick, New Jersey: Rutgers University Press.

Ostrogorski, Georgije, and Franjo Barišić, eds. 1966. *Vizantijski izvori za istoriju naroda Jugoslavije, t. III*. Beograd: Naučno delo.

Panaitescu, Petre. 1929. *Les relations bulgaro-roumains au moyen age (à propos d'un livre récent de Mr. P. Moutaftchiev). Extrait de la Revista Aromănească*, I, 3–25. Bucureşti: Institutul de arte grafice "Bucovina" I. E. Torouţiu.

Panov, Branko. 1985. Za etnogenezata na makedonskiot narod. In Branko Panov, *Srednovekovna Makedonija*, t. 3, 7–30. Skopje: Misla, 1985 (1st ed. 1972).

Panov, Branko, ed. 2000. *Istorija na makedonskiot narod. Tom prvi. Makedonija ot praistoriskoto vreme do potpaganjeto pod turska vlast (1371 година)*. Skopje: Institut za nacionalna istorija.

Panov, Mitko. 2019. *The Blinded State. Historiographic Debates about Samuel Cometopoulos and His State (10-th–11-th Century)*. Leiden-Boston: Brill.

Petković, Vladimir. 1919. *Une hypothèse sur le Car Samuel*. Paris: L'Émancipatrice.

Petrov, Petăr. 2002. Plaha stăpka văv vyarna posoka. Review of *Samuilovata dărzhava. Obhvat i harakter*, by Sărdzhan Pirivatrich. *Makedonski pregled* 25 (3): 157–169.

Pirivatrić, Srđan. 1997. *Samuilova država. Obim i karakter*. Beograd: Vizantološki institut Srpske Akademije nauka i umetnosti.

Pirivatrich, Sărdzhan. 2000. *Samuilovata dărzhava. Obhvat i harakter*. Translated by Stefan Stoyanov. Sofia: Agata.

Prokić, Božidar. 1906. *Die Zusätze in der Handschrift des Johannes Skylitzes. Ein Beitrag zur Geschichte der sogenannten westbulgarischen Reiches*. München: H. Kutzner.

2 CONTROVERSIES OVER SAMUEL'S STATE   103

Prokić, Božidar. 1908. Postanak jedne slovenske carevine u Makedoniji u X veku. *Glas Srpske Kraljevske Akademije* 76, *Drugi razred* 46: 213–307.

Prokić, Božidar. 1912. Postanak Ohridskog patrijarhata. *Glas Srpske kraljevske akademije, Drugi razred* 53:175–267.

Rački, Franjo. 1931. *Borba Južnih Slovena za državni neodvisnost. Bogomili i patareni.* Beograd: Srpska Kraljevska Akademija (1ˢᵗ ed. 1873).

Ricoeur, Paul. 1986. *Lectures on Ideology and Utopia.* New York: Columbia University Press.

Ristovski, Blaže. 1983. Makedonskiot narod i makedonskata nacionalna svest. In Blaže Ristovski, *Makedonskiot narod i makedonskata nacija,* t. 1, 15–87. Skopje: Misla (1ˢᵗ ed. 1969).

Snegarov, Ivan. 1919. *Ohridskata patriarshiya.* Sofia: Al. Paskalev.

Snegarov, Ivan. 1924. *Istoriya na Ohridskata arhiepiskopiya (ot osnovavaneto i do zavladyavaneto na Balkanskiya poluostrov ot turtsite.* Sofia: Koop. Pechatnitsa Gutenberg.

Taškovski, Dragan. 1965. Kliment Ohridski i negovoto delo. *Nova Makedoniya,* December 14, 19, 20 and 21, 1965.

Taškovski, Dragan. 1970. *Samuilovoto carstvo.* Skopje: Naša kniga (1ˢᵗ ed. 1961).

Taškovski, Dragan. 1974. *Kon etnogenezata na makedonskiot narod.* Skopje: Naša knjiga.

Taškovski, Dragan. 1985. *Makedoniya niz vekovite.* Skopje: Naša kniga.

Troebst, Stefan. 2007. Geschichtspolitik und historische 'Meistererzählungen' in Makedonien vor und nach 1991. In *Das makedonische Jahrhundert. Augewählte Aufsätze,* ed. Stefan Troesbt, 425–42. München: R. Oldenbourg Verlag (1ˢᵗ ed. 2002).

Voynov, Mihail. 1963. Petăr Hr. Petrov, Văstanieto na Petăr i Boyan v 876 g. i borbata na komitopulite s Vizantiya, *Byzantinobulgarica,* t. 1, Sofia, 1962, 121–144. *Istoricheski pregled* 19, no. 2, 122–32.

Voynov, Mihail. 1966. Kăm văprosa za bălgarskata narodnost v Makedoniya. *Istoricheski pregled* 22 (5): 61–72.

Voynov, Mihail. 1979. Bălgarskata dărzhavna priemstvenost i Samuilovata dărzhava. *Istoricheski pregled* 35 (6): 5–25.

Voynov, Mihail, Vasilka Tăpkova-Zaimova, and Lyubomir Yonchev. 1968. Review of *Vizantijski izvori za istoriju naroda Jugoslavije, t. III, 1966. Istoricheski pregled* 24 (3): 113–118.

Yonchev, Lyubomir. 1961. Nyakoi văprosi ot bălgarskata srednovekovna istorija v 'Istorija naroda Jugoslavije', Beograd, 1953. *Istoricheski pregled* 17 (6): 106–114.

Yonchev, Lyubomir. 1965. Nyakoi văprosi văv vrăzka săs Samuilovata dărzhava. *Istoricheski pregled* 21 (1): 29–48.

Zlatarski, Vasil. 1927. *Istoriya na bălgarskata dărzhava prez srednite vekove,* t. 1. *Părvo bălgarsko tsarstvo,* chast [part] 2. *Ot slavyanizatsiyata na dărzhavata do padaneto na Părvoto tsarstvo (852-1018).* Sofia: Dărzhavna pechatnitsa.

CHAPTER 3

Skanderbeg: Figures of Paper, Figures of Stone

Nathalie Clayer

Long celebrated by Christian Europe as a prominent figure in the struggle "against the Turks", George Kastriot Skanderbeg (1405–1468) led a 25-year rebellion against the Ottoman sultans from 1443 until his death. The son of a lord in today's central Albania, he had been taken as a hostage, converted to Islam—hence his name Iskender Bey/Skanderbeg—and trained at the Imperial Palace before embarking on a career in the Ottoman army. However, he defected and returned to his native region to fight the Ottomans and competing powers (other landlords, Venice) in shifting alliances with other local lords, other Balkan powers (Hungarian and Serbian), or those present on the Italian peninsula (the Kingdom of Naples, the Papacy). With the political emancipation of the Balkan nations from the Ottoman Empire, Skanderbeg became in the nineteenth century one of the main symbols of this emancipation, as much in literature and the arts as in historiography and public debate. While the figures of national heroes are classic, that of Skanderbeg is special in that, at least in

---

N. Clayer (✉)
Centre d'études turques, ottomanes, balkaniques et centrasiatiques, CNRS-EHESS, Paris, France
e-mail: nathalie.clayer@ehess.fr

© The Author(s), under exclusive license to Springer Nature Switzerland AG 2025
D. Mishkova, R. Daskalov (eds.), *Balkan Historiographical Wars*,
https://doi.org/10.1007/978-3-031-90113-3_3

the nineteenth and beginning of the twentieth century, he was claimed by several Balkan nations: Greek, Serbian, Montenegrin, and above all Albanian because of the territory to which he was eventually linked. This competition was favored and nourished by the fact that his image strongly remained that of a Christian hero, but also because the affirmation of Albanian sovereignty was late, fragile, and contested, notably by other Balkan powers. Even if Skanderbeg took from the end of the nineteenth century a significant place in the Albanian national-historical narrative (Clayer 2007), the consolidation of an Albanian historiography really took shape only after the Second World War, at a time when other topics such as the Partisans' struggle became a central theme of this historiography. Non-Balkan historiographies (Austro-Hungarian, Russian, Italian, etc.) were also important in the shaping of Skanderbeg's figure, also because of imperialist and irredentist visions at different periods.

In addition, the paucity of sources from the medieval period and their very gradual discovery could only fuel a degree of uncertainty and lead to divergent interpretations. Beyond his ethno-national affiliation (Albanian, Greek, or Slav), Skanderbeg's religious affiliation (Orthodox or Catholic Christian, Muslim) as well as other aspects of his biography and his actions (for instance his region of origin, his youth, the motives for his defection or his internal and external alliances), have given rise to debate, and continue to do so even within Albanian society itself. The "figures of paper", or "figures of stone" in the case of monuments, that have been associated with him since the early nineteenth century are consequently diverse and often contradictory.

Beyond political issues and the question of sources and their use, the debates have been linked to the development of interdependent historiographical fields through the circulation of authors, texts, artifacts, and methods in an area that is not limited to the Balkans, including Europe— from Russia to Great Britain—and as far afield as the United States, particularly because of imperialism and of the Albanian diaspora. But they have also been strongly marked by their relationship with politics and media, which have characterized the spaces in which these historiographies have developed. Without going into a history of studies on Skanderbeg (on this subject, see Schmitt 2009, 348–52), I shall attempt here to analyze the main debates, their contexts, and their functions. Following the sociology of controversies proposed by Cyril Lemieux (2007), we need to pay attention to the arenas in which controversies develop, involving not only one or more authors, but also public, whether specialized or not, depending on the media in which they take place. In addition, we need to consider that debates are not only indicative of social and institutional developments and power relations, but that they also play a part in these transformations and power relations.

Even if the timing of these controversies has not always coincided with the major political events in Southeast Europe, three turning points seem decisive here: the formation of an Albanian nation-state at the beginning of the twentieth century between 1912 and 1920, the establishment of Communist regimes in 1945 in the Balkans, and their collapse in 1989–1991. We should therefore distinguish four main periods for which the historiographical controversies concerning Skanderbeg presented different overall patterns: the second half of the nineteenth century, a period of imperialism and irredentist national constructions and the formation of national historiographies in the absence of a specifically Albanian scene; the first half of the twentieth century, a time of the creation of an Albanian state with contested sovereignty and as yet non-existent academic institutions; the period of Communist regimes and the real institutionalization of an Albanian historiography; and finally, the post-1990 period leading to political pluralism and neoliberal globalization.[1]

COMPETING HISTORIOGRAPHIES IN THE AGE OF IMPERIALISM AND NATIONALISM

Controversies concerning Skanderbeg arose in the second half of the nineteenth century within national and transnational academic spaces that were in a formative process from both an institutional and a methodological point of view. These debates sometimes spilt over into the public arena, especially as they were situated at the crossroads of both scientific and socio-political processes. The construction of Balkan historiographies on the medieval period, in close interaction with German, Russian, and Habsburg historiographies, as well as Italian, French, and English historiographies on the Balkans, was fueled or influenced by the confrontation between imperialism and the construction of new Balkan states, which fostered irredentism toward the Ottoman Empire. Until the beginning of

---

[1] I would like to warmly thank the organizers and participants of the project for their discussions, as well as Leonidas Embiricos, Nikos Sigalas, Etleva Domi, Mario Kreuter, Artan Puto, Julia Popovic, and Tchavdar Marinov for their help in collecting the material and in the discussion concerning some points of the analysis.

the twentieth century, these debates on Skanderbeg had two main facets: on the one hand, the question of the nature of the sources (narrative sources vs. archival documents) and their reliability; and on the other, the question of Skanderbeg's ethno-national origin.

The man who until then, through a biographical and literary tradition, had been the hero of Christianity in the Middle Ages "against the Turks" easily became, at the beginning of the nineteenth century, the hero of the liberation of the Christian Balkan peoples against those same Turks. Yet, through new historiographical and political dynamics, he was becoming a Greek hero for some people and a Slavic hero for others. This was not without tensions and challenges. In particular, it was the German-speaking (and Russian-speaking) historiography, in terms of its results and methods, which through reactions or appropriations in the Balkans and Europe led to a number of polemics about the figure of Skanderbeg, first in the 1870s in the Greek public arena, and later in French and Serbian academic circles.

The Greek Controversy

In January 1876, a text by the famous Greek historian Konstantin Paparrigopoulos (1815–1891) on the life of Skanderbeg appeared in the brand-new Athenian literary magazine *Estia*. This publication in a periodical aimed at a wide readership sparked a controversy that lasted for over a year (Jochalas 1975, 40–44). This controversy revolved mainly around the question of ethnic origin: Slavic, Greek, or Albanian. In this way, it undermined the image that had prevailed until then in Greek public opinion and historiography of a national hero serving as a model for the fight against the "Turks" and fueling irredentism toward the Ottoman Empire, in connection with the "Great Idea". Twenty years earlier, in the first version of his *History of the Hellenic Nation* (1853) written for schools, K. Paparrigopoulos had himself presented the character as Greek (Jochalas 1975, 40–41). In so doing, he was following in the footsteps of the biographical genre that had developed since the beginning of the nineteenth century on the subject of Skanderbeg (Georgios Kastriotis in Greek), starting in France, in a transnational space stretching from Russia to Italy via Greece and Romania.

In 1812, a Greek translation of the book by the French Jesuit father Jean Nicolas Duponcet (*Histoire de Scanderbeg Roy d'Albanie.* Paris: Jean Mariette, 1709) appeared in Moscow, before being translated into Russian,

Romanian, and Italian (Jochalas 1975, 21–39). The amended Italian version, the work of the physician and writer Andreas Papadopoulos-Vretos (1800–1876), published in Naples in 1820, had itself been translated into Greek and published several times from 1848 onward, becoming an important source of inspiration in Greek literature. The latter disseminated the image of a Skanderbeg who was Christian and Epirote, and therefore Greek, even if the work of Papadopoulos-Vretos also became a tool for asserting a certain Albanian identity (Zanou 2018, 146–8; Clayer 2007, 192). In the early 1860s, another biography began to circulate: that of the politician and writer Nicolaos Dragoumis (1809–1879), founder alongside K. Paparrigopoulos of the journal *Pandora*. The work was a translation of a book by the French politician Camille Paganel, published in 1855 at the time of the Crimean War. Published in 1861 and republished in Smyrna in the Ottoman Empire in 1880, N. Dragoumis's biography portrayed a figure who, for Paganel, had been "the last representative of ancient Greece", "the most eminent precursor of the heroes of modern Greece" and "the unshakeable defender of Christianity" (Paganel 1855, "Foreword").

However, in 1874, in the 5th volume of the newly expanded version of his *History of the Hellenic Nation*, K. Paparrigopoulos altered this account by questioning Skanderbeg's Greek origin. What had happened? As a professional historian, he had followed the latest findings of European historiography, with which he was in constant discussion. The German historian Carl Hopf (1832–1873) had put forward the idea of Skanderbeg's Slavic origin in his *History of Greece* published in 1868 (Hopf 1868, 122), and in 1873 he had just published a new collection of sources (*Chroniques gréco-romanes inédites ou peu connues*) in which one of the chronicles on which he relied was included (Hopf 1873). Hopf and his Russian colleague Vikentij Makušev (1837–1883) began to make systematic use of European libraries and archives in order to shed light on medieval Greek and Balkan history from the time of Skanderbeg onward (Lapteva 1982). The Austrian consul Johann Georg von Hahn (1811–1869), a pioneer of the new Albanology with his work *Albanesische Studien* published in Jena in 1854 (Hahn 1854), testifies to the impact of the discovery of these new sources for his field:

> Indeed, Mr Hopf's typically German zeal for research, which did not leave him during his journey of several years through Italy and Greece to gather material for a history of Greece in the Middle Ages, also enabled him to

gather a mass of documentary evidence on Albania and on the Kastriot family, which opens up entirely new points of view on the history of Skanderbeg. He gave them to me during his stay in Syra, with permission to make full use of them. They are collected in the appendix to this work. The result is that the Kastriot, as Fallmerayer had already assumed, were of Serbian origin. (Hahn 1867, 22)

In contrast to the authors who contributed to the biographical genre, adapting and designing works that had more to do with literature, art, and politics, K. Paparrigopoulos was critically involved in the no less politicized European arena of new historical studies that favored, and now relied on, the editing and use of primary sources, chronicles, or archival documents. After studying in Odessa, Greece, France, and Germany, he became one of the founders of a new historical school in Athens. Another controversy with the German journalist and historian Jakob Fallmereyer (1790–1861), for whom there had been a break in Greek history due to the settlement of Slavic and Albanian populations in Greece from late antiquity, led him to formulate as early as 1843 what was to become the dominant thesis in the country. K. Paparrigopoulos had succeeded in imposing a new national narrative that defended the continuity of the Hellenic nation from antiquity to the modern era, placing the Byzantine period at the heart of this narrative. As a professor at the University of Athens from 1851, he occupied a central position in Greek academia (Sigalas 2000; Curta 2011; Märtl and Schreiner 2013; Grivaud and Nicolaou-Konnari 2021).

However, when he presented Hopf's thesis of a Slavic origin for Skanderbeg, while asserting himself an Albanian (and therefore non-Greek) origin in 1874 in his magnum opus on the history of the Hellenic nation (Paparrigopoulos 1874, 355–6), there was no reaction. The controversy was only triggered when the debate left the academic arena and entered the public arena, via its publication in *Estia*. One might think that, for those reacting, it was a question of defending Greek identity, which had hitherto been widely accepted concerning Skanderbeg and prevented it from being called into question. As T. Jochalas pointed out (2019, 89–90), the memoirs of certain figures of the period show that the image of George Kastriot was then shaped throughout the Orthodox Christian space by biographies such as those of Papadopoulos-Vretos and Dragoumis, which presented the deeds and actions of a Greek and Christian hero.

However, it seems that if the controversy sparked by Paparrigopoulos's article in 1876 helped to shake the figure of Skanderbeg as the hero of Greekness, it was not only because of Paparrigopoulos's position but also, paradoxically, because of the responses of his opponents. For them, or at least for some of them, the question of an Albanian identity arose in one way or another, even if this one was more or less strongly linked to a Greek and/or Orthodox Christian identification. Since the beginning of the century, in an Orthodox Christian space stretching from Italy to Romania via the Balkans, we can see the emergence of Albanianism, and the affirmation of Albanian identity. This was a consequence of the emergence of a Western Albanology, of the action of Protestant missionaries who favored the use of the vernacular language, of the search for their origins of the Arbëresh (the Albanian-speaking people of southern Italy who had retained the Greek rite), and of the Ottoman reforms which, along with the question of schools and the development of the press, also led to the identification of Albanian-speaking populations. The emancipation of the nations of Southeast Europe, the autonomy and even independence of certain Ottoman provinces, were also powerful factors in the development of Albanianism, either by imitation or reaction. In particular, within Hellenism itself, the idea of an Albanian identity developed in line with the Pelasgian theory, which held that the Albanians were descended from the mythical population that had preceded and also fathered the Greeks on the Peninsula, namely the Pelasgians. Hence, there was a relationship between Greeks and Albanians, but it was eventually called into question through a later exclusive identification of the Pelasgians with Albanians (Clayer 2006, 157–240). In 1876, this relationship was in the process of being re-articulated as a result of the serious crisis in the region, in which the Slavic populations were primarily involved, following the outbreak of revolts in Herzegovina the previous year. These were followed by insurrections in Bulgaria in the spring of 1876, repression by the Ottoman authorities, the declaration of war by Serbia and Montenegro against the Empire in June, and the introduction of Ottoman constitutional rule at the end of the year (Georgeon 2003; Grandits 2021).

It was during this time of uncertainty, confrontation, and the opening up of possibilities—for Russian and Austria-Hungarian imperialism and irredentism in the Balkans in particular—that the controversy developed. It involved scholars and identity-building entrepreneurs participating in the construction of irredentist Hellenism, almost all of whom came from territories that were still Ottoman at the time and were therefore all the

112   N. CLAYER

more sensitive to events. However, their position in Greek academia and their sensitivity differed. The first was Athanasios Petrides (1830–1911). Originally from the Greek-speaking village of Dhrovjan, near Sarandë in Epirus (a region that was still Ottoman at the time), he had studied in Athens, devoting himself to the history of his native region. In 1871, he had just published an edition of an ancient *Chronicle of Argyrokastro*, a metropolis in northern Epirus. A teacher and scholar, he was clearly influenced by the Great Idea (Proikakis 2000) and, for him, Skanderbeg was Greek and Epirote. His criticism was deontological, in that he criticized K. Paparrigopoulos for not specifying the sources that enabled him to put forward a Slavic origin (Jochalas 1975, 42–43).

Two other figures weighed more heavily in the controversy because of their position in academia. Practicing in Athens, they were at the forefront of a movement to institutionalize various scientific disciplines in the country because of the political role they assigned to them. Antonios Miliarakis (1841–1905), a historian, lawyer, and geographer born and educated in Athens, was interested in the history of the Cyclades and of the Despotate of Epirus. In 1879, putting into practice his desire to use history in politics, he was part of a Greek delegation to establish the new border with the Ottoman Empire in the Epirus region of Preveza (Peckham 2000; Vlachos 2020). In a pamphlet published in 1876, he replied to his colleague Paparrigopoulos, refuting any Slavic origin for Skanderbeg. In doing so, he was not content to simply argue with his Greek colleague, but he also criticized the German-speaking historians C. Hopf, on whom Paparrigopoulos relied, as well as J. Fallmerayer, and above all J.G. von Hahn, both on the subject of ethnic origin and on that of the family's region of origin, called Emathia in the sources, which in his view corresponded not to Macedonia but to Albania. He also questioned the sources that spoke of a Slavic origin, in the absence of the original manuscripts. He preferred to give renewed importance to the history of Skanderbeg published by Marinus Barletius (Barletius 1508–1510) in Latin at the very beginning of the sixteenth century (one of the main sources of all subsequent biographies), as well as to Venetian sources, thus concluding that the Kastriots were of "Greek race", but that George Kastriot Skanderbeg himself was Albanian. Beyond this Albanian-Greek duality, which could already exist in the biographical genre (remember that C. Paganel wrote: "Moreover, while recognizing the Albanians as a distinct race, we must also note their very great affinity with the Greeks. Obviously, one day, Albanians and Greeks will become a single people" [1855: introduction, lvii]), at a time when Slavic irredentism seemed to be reawakening in the Balkans, it was Slavicness that was rejected. This motivation seems to have been even more present in Margaritis Dimitsas (1829–1903), who played a more prominent role in the controversy.

A Vlach (or Slav) from Ohrid in Ottoman Macedonia, Margaritis Dimitsas (1829–1903) was a historian and geographer whose career was highly transnational. After studying philology in Athens, Berlin, and Leipzig, he pursued a teaching career, first in the Ottoman Empire, in Bitola/Manastir, and then Salonika/Thessaloniki, and from 1869 in Athens, Greece. In the spirit of legitimizing territorial claims against the Ottomans and also the Slavs in the name of Hellenism, his work focused on his hometown and, more generally, on the geography of Macedonia. In 1870, he published a book in Thessaloniki on the ancient geography of the region (Peckham 2000; Daskalov 2013; Vlachos 2021). Throughout 1876, he repeatedly took part in the polemic in Athenian newspapers and eventually wrote a book that came out at the beginning of 1877. Entitled *Critics argue over the origin and ethnicity of Georgios Kastriotis Skanderbeg*, the book reviewed the ongoing controversy. From the very first pages, the author highlighted the dangerous Panslavist dimension that he saw in the thesis Paparrigopoulos was advocating. To alert the readers, he compared the controversy to that which existed over the ethnic origin of Copernicus between Poles and Germans. Then, going back over the details of the 1876 controversy, his arguments were based on historical geography, anthropo-geography, onomastics, and source criticism. He concluded that Skanderbeg, the "hero of Albania", was an Epirote Albanian. In the text, M. Dimitsas set out to criticize his colleague K. Paparrigopoulos, whom he repeatedly referred to as "the wise historian", "the wise professor" or "the national historian", thus perhaps also calling into question his position in the academic field. But, like A. Miliarakis, he also attacked the German-speaking historians on whom Paparrigopoulos had relied: von Hammer, J. Fallmerayer, J.G. von Hahn and C. Hopf, turning the controversy into an arena in which the empowerment of the Greek academic field was at stake. Hopf and other outsiders must not be left to their own devices, as in the case of the question of Copernicus's nationality, he explained (Dimitsas 1877, 55).

Another spillover from the strict Greek academic field occurred three years later. The controversy resurfaced in 1880 when Efthim Brandi/Efthimios Prantis (1817–1882), an Albanian identity entrepreneur (who had no academic position), originally from Korçë in the Ottoman Empire but part of the Orthodox Christian diaspora in Egypt, published a book in Athens entitled *Alvanika Parapona* (The Albanian Complaint) (Prantis 1880). Among the grievances directed at the Greeks, the author referred to the article by K. Paparrigopoulos and denounced the attempt to give the Albanian hero a Slavic origin, whereas Albanians and Greeks were brothers through their common Pelasgian ancestry. In the meantime, the political crisis had deepened with the Russo-Turkish War in 1877–1878, the Treaty of San Stefano in March 1878, which briefly outlined a Greater Bulgaria, and then the Treaty of Berlin in July of the same year, which further redrew the map of the Balkans. The voice of the Albanians was increasingly heard in the Greek public arena, as illustrated by the publication of a newspaper entitled *The Voice of Albania* (*I foni tis Alvanias*) in 1879–1880, in which the editor, Anastas Koulourioti, had begun to publish a history of Skanderbeg (Jochalas 1975, 50; Clayer 2007, 291–3). At this time, Albanian mobilization was also becoming increasingly visible in the Ottoman Empire against the territorial claims of the Balkan countries. Thanks to the research of Dhori Qiriazi (2020), however, we know that Efthim Brandi had actually wanted to react to K. Paparrigopoulos's comments as early as 1877. After reading an article in the Greek Constantinople-based newspaper *Neologos*, he tried to publish a response in an Athenian newspaper with the help of Thimi Mitko (1820–1890), an important member of the Albanianist network, who was also based in Egypt. Mitko likely thought it would be a delicate matter to publish such a text in 1877. In any case, it was only in a version corrected and toned down by Mitko himself that it was finally reproduced in the book published in 1880. Dh. Qiriazi also notes that, in his correspondence with Th. Mitko, E. Brandi even mentioned the idea of erecting a statue of Skanderbeg in Athens, this figure of stone intending to symbolize and seal Panhellenic brotherhood (Qiriazi 2020, 16–17).

At a time when the Eastern Crisis was shaking the Balkan Peninsula, the refutation of the Slavic origin that had been put forward by German-speaking historians and then adopted by the most important Greek historian had led to a certain questioning of the balance of power within the Greek academic field, both personal and disciplinary. With D. Dimitsas and A. Miliarakis, the political role of geography and ethnography was affirmed at the same time as Greek historiography asserted itself vis-à-vis foreign historiography. Moreover, the polemic paradoxically led to Skanderbeg's Albanian (and therefore non-Slavic, but also not exclusively Greek) origins being asserted, even though they were closely linked to

Hellenism and Orthodoxy, as we can see from E. Brandi's contribution. With the development of Albanianism from the 1880s onward, and especially after the new crisis of the mid-1890s, however, a Skanderbeg emerged more and more clearly as a figure of Albanianism emancipated from Hellenism (Clayer 2007, 441–4).

Greece was not the only country to react—positively or negatively—to this new historiography, notably from the German-speaking world, which emerged at the end of the 1860s, debated the origin of a figure forged above all by literary works and the biographical genre, starting with the text of Marinus Barletius (1508–1510). The Slavic character derived from this evolution was also refuted by a part of the historiography, both outside and within the Balkans, beyond Greece.

Disputing the Slavic Skanderbeg and the Question of Sources

Before questioning the figure of the Greek hero, the debate that erupted in Greece in 1876 first a foremost revolved around a rejection of a Slavic Skanderbeg constructed by German-speaking historiography. The thesis of a Slavic origin was supposed to stem from a denial of the reliability of narrative sources and a preference for other documents. Carl Hopf himself wrote:

> We have a large number of biographies of this Albanian national hero, but almost all of them are based on the fabulous story of the leader, written by Marino Barlezio of Shkodër. [...] A critical comparison of all subsequent works on the history of Skanderbeg, from Pontanus to the most recent by A. Papadopoulos Vretos and Paganel (in Greek by Dragumis, Athens, 1861), clearly shows that their authors completely lacked documentary sources, and that they consequently wrote novels rather than histories. This has been emphasized at length by Fallmerayer [...] Happier than him [Fallmerayer], we are in a position, with the help of the history of the Musachi family and Venetian documents, to draw up here a more reliable biography of the great chief. (Hopf 1868, 122)

Like C. Hopf and his Russian colleague V. Makušev, who had been the pioneers, scholars, particularly in Austria-Hungary (M. Šufflay, L. von Thalloczy, K. Jireček), Romania (N. Iorga), and Serbia (S. Ljubić), were endeavoring at the turn of the twentieth century to continue this collection of sources on the medieval history of the region, more or less in accordance with political imperial and national agendas. Concerning the Slavic origin of Skanderbeg that was supposed to result from this, some of their colleagues felt obliged to follow them. At the beginning of the biography of Skanderbeg that he wrote in 1894, the Austrian consul Julius Pisko, who has himself been criticized for not going far enough beyond narrative sources (Caro 1896; Zhugra 2014), wrote, without really insisting, that the hypothesis of these recent historians seemed to be based on the fact that Skanderbeg's father was married to a certain Voizava and that some of his children bore Slavic names (Pisko 1894, 7).

Other historians, however, rejected this hypothesis, especially in French Catholic milieus. In the 1890s, two French historians denounced the "legends" and "errors" spread about Skanderbeg. Specifically, they both criticized on this point the Austrian historian Ludwig von Pastor, whose *History of the Popes* had been published in German in 1886 (Pastor 1886) and translated into French in 1888. The first to intervene in 1891 was the abbot Paul Pisani (1852–1933). He belonged to the Catholic circles to which Pastor also belonged, and was particularly interested in Napoleonic Dalmatia and the Orient, working at the Catholic Institute in Paris where he later became a professor. The second, who in 1896 wrote an article entitled "Les deux Skanderbeg. Solution d'un problème historique" (The two Skanderbegs. Solution of a historical problem) was Pierre Coquelle (b. 1858), archivist and librarian in Meulan, near Paris, and author of a *History of Montenegro and Bosnia* in 1895. These two specialists, who belonged only to the fringes of Balkan medieval studies, maintained that Pastor, concerning the Slavic origin of Skanderbeg, had followed the three authors C. Hopf, V. Makušev, and K. Jireček, who made this claim because they were Slav themselves (in the case of the latter two at least). On another point, namely the idea that Skanderbeg had never been given as a hostage at the sultan's court and had spent his youth in the Albanian mountains, Pisani and Coquelle explained that this was also to be rejected and that, on this point, L. Pastor was in contradiction with Hopf and Makušev, as only Jireček put forward such a hypothesis. Pisani and Coquelle concluded that Barletius was not necessarily disqualified, as Hopf, Makušev, and Jireček would have readers believe. Interestingly, Pisani suggested reading Ottoman sources, in particular the chronicler Saadeddin, who mentioned the fact that Skanderbeg had been raised at the sultan's court (Pisani 1891, 13–14). As for P. Coquelle, he tried to understand how Jireček could have made a mistake on Skanderbeg's youth, and for that he appealed to the history of Montenegro on which he had worked. He explained that there had been a misunderstanding about two "Skanderbegs": George Kastriot and a later figure, Skanderbeg Czernovitch (Crnojević), a Slav who, for his part, had not been given as a hostage to the Ottoman court, but had lived later in the late fifteenth and early sixteenth century (Coquelle 1896).

In the new revised and expanded edition of his opus published in 1901 (pp. 720–721), Louis Pastor, who had been aware of Pisani's criticism, went back on his own assertions, admitting an error and referring to his French colleague on the subject of Skanderbeg's childhood. However, when it came to the Slavic origin of Skanderbeg, he was only halfway there, as he pointed out that Paul Pisani admitted "that a lot of Serbian blood runs in the veins of the hero of the Albanians".

In Serbia, if the Slavic origin was also contested, it was, on the contrary, in the rejection of Barletius and the preference for the sources brought to light by Hopf and Makušev. Moreover, the polemics that developed about Skanderbeg cannot be understood in isolation. They are largely to be seen in the context of the many controversies which, from the 1870s onward, pitted what was then considered to be the father of critical historiography, the archimandrite Ilarion Ruvarac (1832–1905), against the representatives of "Romantic historiography", to adopt the terms generally used. Born in Sremska Mitrovica, educated at the high school in Sremski Karlovci in the Habsburg Empire, then at the University of Vienna in law and history, I. Ruvarac studied theology at Sremski Karlovci. He was no less a historian than a theologian, and he was inspired by German historiography, in particular Leopold von Ranke (1795–1886) and his defense of "objectivity" and the critical use of the most "authentic" sources. In a highly polemical style, I. Ruvarac rejected Serbian historiography based on epic poetry and narrative sources, and fought against the appropriation of various historical figures in the name of nationalism. As Michael Antolović (2016) has shown, in the jousts that pitted him against his opponents, starting with Pantelija Srećković, the leader of the Romantic school, there were also power stakes within the Serbian academic field, which had long been dominated by them. The controversies eventually contributed to a shift in favor of critical historiography, professionalization, and a greater emphasis on the younger generation.

In these debates, which focused on medieval history and the question of the second battle of Kosovo in 1448, the figure of Skanderbeg, who had been widely appropriated by Serbian and Croatian literature following the works of the Croat Franciscan friar Andrija Kačić-Miošić (1704–1760) and the Serb writer Jovan Sterija Popović (1806–1856) (Schmauss 1966, 1969; Puchner 2015; Lazarević 2018), was present. In two articles published in 1901 and 1902, I. Ruvarac attacked some of his colleagues who wanted to Serbianize Georges Kastriot Skanderbeg, just as they had Serbianized Jean Hunyadi or the saintly Sveta Petka. In the first contribution (Ruvarac 1901; Radojčić 1934, 520–3), in which he aimed to refute the thesis of John Hunyadi's Serbian origin, he broadened his argument by attacking the young Nikola Vulić (1872–1945), a Serb from Shkodër, author of the work *Djuradj Kastriotić Skenderbeg, Historical Study* published in Belgrade in 1892 (Vulić 1892), as well as Jovan Djordjević, professor of history at the Velika Škola, the forerunner of Belgrade University. He criticized them for their patriotic impulse, which led them to see in Skanderbeg a Serbian blood figure, which Serbian historiography had to seize upon. In the second article on "Djuradj Vuković, Serbian despot, and Djordje Kastriot- Skenderbeg, Albanian chieftain, year 1444" (Ruvarac 1902), I. Ruvarac criticized first the Croatian historian Vjekoslav Krajić, and then N. Vulić again. He gave them a lesson in the critical analysis of sources, categorically rejecting in particular the use of Barletius's text:

> What the Albanian-Latin priests relate about the exploits of Djordje Kastriot during the fourth quarter of the year 1444 is nothing but myth and fable that deserves no credence. We can therefore only admire the credulity of the Serb Čedomilj Mijatović and the young Serb N. Vulić, who take myth for truth. (Ruvarac 1902, 13)

However, Ruvarac relied in particular on Hopf and Makušev (Ruvacac 1902, 7) to delegitimize the use of Barletius, without considering their thesis of the Serbian origin of Skanderbeg.

We do not know whether these criticisms elicited an immediate response. Forty years later, however, one of I. Ruvarac's affiants, Jovan Radonić (1942, VIII), came to the defense of N. Vulić by explaining that his work, even though it was a student's work, had all the scientific qualities required: "high-quality and conscientiously collected historical material, as well as the conscientious use of professional literature". In his view, Ilarion Ruvarac had been wrong to criticize his use of Barletius as a source, whereas N. Vulić had been cautious and had, for this reason, used other sources, including the work of the Italian priest from Brescia, Giammaria Biemmi (*Istoria di Giorgio Castrioto detto Scander-Begh*) published in 1742—which was not yet known to be based on a forgery. In a way, in this reply, the question of sources and method masked that of Skanderbeg's ethnicity, which had also been at the heart of the controversy. But after the turning point of the Balkan Wars and the First World War, other themes came to the fore in the controversies that emerged.

1920–1943: Albanian State-Building and the Figure of Skanderbeg

The long decade of wars that shook the region between 1912 and 1923 changed the geopolitical map of Southeastern Europe. On the western fringe of the Balkans, the independence of an Albanian principality was recognized in 1913 under the guarantee of the Great Powers. At the end of the First World War, after various military occupations, Italy, the last occupying power, did not obtain an international mandate over Albania, the territories that included Skanderbeg's "homeland", and the country's independence was once again recognized. However, this new sovereignty was fragile due to Yugoslav and Greek irredentism, as well as the new Italian imperialism that was being deployed in Africa, the Mediterranean, and the Balkans.

The affirmation of this new sovereignty, fragile though it was, gave rise to new dynamics in the historiographical landscape of Southeastern Europe. Following on from the writings inspired by the development of Albanian nationalism prior to the creation of the state itself, the figure of Skanderbeg was affirmed in the writings of new authors as the national hero symbolizing independence. Significant in this sense was the fact that, when he was proclaimed king in 1928, Ahmet Zogu, who had succeeded in regaining power at the very end of 1924, took the name of Skanderbeg III for a time. In the absence of academic and research institutions, the nascent Albanian historical production on Skanderbeg nevertheless remained underdeveloped, polycentric, and fragmented. More patriotic than critical, it was also a controversial part of a regional and European historiographical landscape whose poles were no longer Greece, Germany, and Austria-Hungary, but were now shifting from Vienna and the United States to Albania, as well as Yugoslavia, Romania, and Italy.

Before being stifled by Italian historiography, the formation of this composite historiography passed, significantly, through two moments of controversy on the subject of Skanderbeg. While the types of debate differed because of their arena—scientific on the one hand, more public on the other, as we shall see—the two moments were both closely linked to sequences of national and state affirmation: the early 1920s, when Albania was to be recognized once again on the international stage, and 1937, when the 25th anniversary of the declaration of independence was celebrated at a time when Italian tutelage was becoming increasingly burdensome. Independence and union were the main topics of discussion.

Under the Banner of Independence

Situated at the crossroads with the previous era, the first moment of the new debate was marked by the publication of a polemical work produced by Xhevat Korça (1893–1959) as a thesis defended in the former capital of the Habsburg Empire in 1922. A native of southern Albania, where he had joined the ranks of young Albanianists in the final years of Ottoman sovereignty, Djevat Kortsha/Xhevat Korça had been sent to Vienna in 1917 to study for a higher education. The Austro-Hungarian authorities, who occupied a large part of Albanian territory at the time, supported a degree of Albanian national affirmation under their tutelage. Despite the collapse of the Dual Monarchy, Xhevat Korça defended his thesis in 1922. Entitled *Drei Fragen aus dem Leben Skender Begs* (*Three Questions about the Life of Skanderbeg*), the work was published in Albanian the following year in Tirana, when the author became head of the state secondary school in Shkodër in the north of the country. The text was presented as a radical refutation of three historians who, at the end of the previous period, had contributed to the writing of medieval history in the Balkans in various ways, also touching on the figure of Skanderbeg: the Austro-Hungarian historian and Slavist Constantin Jireček, this time with his two-volume history of the Serbs (*Geschichte der Serben*, Gotha 1918); the Byzantinist Klaus Roth with his *History of Albania in 1914*; and the famous Romanian historian Nicolae Iorga, in his history of the Ottoman Empire (*Geschichte des Osmanischen Reiches*, 5 vols. 1908–1913), in which the figure was mentioned in Volume 2.

The three questions underlying Xh. Korça's study were: did Skanderbeg pay annual tribute to the sultans or not? Had Skanderbeg abandoned Krujë to the Venetians in 1450? Had the Albanian chiefs betrayed Skanderbeg, forcing him to take refuge in the mountains to save his life? So, it was no longer a question of Skanderbeg's ethnicity or his childhood, but rather one of national unity and independence from the Ottomans and the Venetians (and therefore the Italians) that was at stake: two crucial themes in the early 1920s. The integrity and independence of the Albanian state had to be reaffirmed on the international stage, particularly in relation to Greece and Yugoslavia, and even more so in relation to Italy. Addressing his Albanian readers, Xhevat Korça wrote in his preface:

> The dedicated historian Constantin Jireçek, the Byzantinist Karl Roth and the Romanian historian Nicola Jorga, by answering yes to the three questions, have made a serious mistake. These three historians have relied on unfounded sources and have painted a picture of Skanderbeg's life that does not correspond at all to the truth. The writings of these historians on these points have helped to spread such faulty ideas in the civilised world that it was our patriotic duty to refute their claims with historical facts. (Kortsha 1923, 1)

The idea was that Skanderbeg had always been an "independent prince" (Kortsha 1923, 3). In order to advocate that, the author discussed the way in which the aforementioned historians had used sources: either they had not really cited any sources, or they had failed to criticize them when they were unreliable, or they had failed to understand the situation at the time and the psychology of the "Albanian hero" (*fatosi shqiptar*). In his rebuttal, Xh. Korça emphasized the preponderance of political factors linked to the question of the country's independence (Kortsha 1923, 10 and 53 ff.), as well as Skanderbeg's value, bravery, and strength, drawing on numerous sources, but also on numerous analyses and psychologizing hypotheses. Being the product of an Albanianism initially favored by Austro-Hungarian imperialism and deployed within the framework of the new Albanian state that was to assert its independence, Xhevat Korça's work was to have a concrete consequence for a wider public: based on his idea, a room dedicated to Skanderbeg was created within the first national museum, designed in Tirana in 1923 by one of his Viennese professors, Carl Patsch, who had been called in by the Albanian government as an expert (Clayer 2012). The figure of paper, symbolizing union and independence from any outside power contrary to what some historians had claimed, thus became a figure of museum for the first time in the Balkans.

Apart from this episode, Xh. Korça's work had very little impact, but three years later in Yugoslavia it was critically reviewed in a specialist journal. There were two reasons for this: the fact that an Albanology was being forged there as a combination of Yugoslav domestic and foreign policy interests and the legacy of Austro-Hungarian Albanology, and that Xh.

Korça himself was taking part in it in situ. The journal *Arhiv za arbanašku starinu, jezik i etnografiju* (Archives of Albanian Antiquity, Language and Ethnography) was published in Belgrade from 1923. Interest in Albanian studies had been sparked by the famous Serbian geographer Jovan Cvijić, rector of Belgrade University in 1907, following an initial attempt to introduce a course in Albanian in 1905. But it was only after the long period of war that a course in Albanian linguistics was opened in 1920–1921 by Henrik Barić (1888–1957), a specialist in comparative Indo-European grammar trained in Graz and Vienna, and the same man who launched the journal. It was also under the aegis of H. Barić that Xh. Korça in 1925, a refugee in Belgrade after A. Zogu's return to power, had been given a position as a reader (Mandić and Sivački 2015, 271). It was the following year that the journal published two critical reviews of works on Skanderbeg.

One of them was a notice concerning the book by Xh. Korça (*Arhiv*, III, 296). The highly critical Serbian historian Vladimir Ćorović (1885–1941) criticized him for not making use of specialist literature in Serbian, such as the work of Jovan Radonić about Western Europe and the Balkan peoples in the first half of the fifteenth century (1905). Above all, on the basis of various sources, he thought that Skanderbeg's dependence on various centers of power could not be minimized, as Xh. Korça did. He concluded by calling into question the idea of Skanderbeg's independence, and probably that of Albania at the beginning of the twentieth century. It should be noted that he considered the book as belonging to a "patriotic historiography", in a way echoing the words of the author who had made it his patriotic duty, as we have seen. V. Ćorović wrote:

> Patriotic historiography cannot make of Skanderbeg anything other than a poor little Balkan dynast, who also had a great deal of heroism and love of freedom, but who, with his insignificant struggles, could not support himself other than by bending over and seeking the support of the most powerful. (*Arhiv*, III, 296)

The journal *Arhiv*, which was certainly keen to keep abreast of everything to do with Albanian studies, also gave Xh. Korça (III, 1926, 241–43) the opportunity, not to reply, but to publish his own review of another work on Skanderbeg written in Albanian and which had in fact preceded his own. Written by Fan/Theofan Noli (1882–1965), an Orthodox Christian intellectual from Ottoman Thrace, a former theater actor turned journalist, bishop, and founder of the Albanian Orthodox Church in the

United States, this book entitled *The History of Skanderbeg (Gjerq Kastriot) King of Albania (1412–1468)* (Historia e Skenderbeut (Gjerq Kastriotit) Mbretit i Shqiperise 1412–1468) was published in Boston in 1921. It can therefore be seen as the foundation stone of this patriotic historiography. The book was the product of a competition launched in 1919 by Albanian émigré societies in the United States: the pan-Albanian society *Vatra* (The Home) and the society *Arësimi* (Instruction) of migrants from Korçë in Boston. The aim was to write a biography of the national hero for them (Jorgaqi 2005, vol. 1, 412–14).

Produced in six months at the request of his sponsors, 6000 copies were printed and distributed free of charge in Albanian schools (in Albania). Meanwhile, Fan Noli was playing a leading role in the political negotiations for full recognition of Albanian independence, particularly with the League of Nations. In his approach, the author was not as polemical as Xhevat Korça. Like the protagonists of the 1870s polemic, his main point of disagreement with authors of the previous period such as C. Hopf and J.G. von Hahn concerned the question of Skanderbeg's ethnic origin: Skanderbeg was not an Albanianized Slav, he was Albanian. This time, the Albanian identity being defended had nothing to do with Hellenism (Noli 1921, 47–59).

To return to Xh. Korça's report, it did not deal with this last point, which he felt was not worth discussing. He preferred to return to the two themes he had emphasized in his own thesis. So he insisted on the notion of union and stressed that he agreed with Fan Noli's image of a Skanderbeg who wanted to centralize the country and abolish feudalism. On the other hand, his own efforts to minimize any help from foreign powers led him to criticize Fan Noli for giving too much importance to Skanderbeg's relations with Italy. His criticism also took on another dimension when Xh. Korça gave a positive assessment of Fan Noli's contribution to "Albanian national science", that is, to the creation of a specifically Albanian historiography, despite his errors, his excesses (when he went so far as to compare Skanderbeg to Joan of Arc) and his methodological limitations (the fact that he did not really use archival documents, but only literary sources).

Albanian Historiography Under Debate

It was not until 1937 that this patriotic Albanian historiography of Skanderbeg, which was gradually developing, once again became the subject of controversy, this time in the face of a wider Albanian public made up of readers of cultural journals. Since Ahmet Zogu had established an authoritarian regime, reforms had not led to the creation of higher education or research institutes in Albania (Idrizi 2020; Schmitt 2005). As a result, specialists were trained abroad, and publications, if not books, often appeared in newspapers and magazines published by various private actors. The 25th anniversary of the declaration of independence on 28 November 1912, which was celebrated throughout 1937, gave rise to numerous publications looking back at the period of the "renaissance" (*Rilindja*) in the late nineteenth and early twentieth centuries, and more generally at national history.

It was against this backdrop that a polemic erupted around the figure of Skanderbeg, publicized at first by three magazines: a new cultural magazine, *Kombi* (The Nation), published in Vlorë in the south by an intellectual of Muslim origin by the name of Ali Kuçi; the Jesuit organ, *Leka*, and the Franciscan journal, *Hylli i dritës* (The Star of Light), both published in Shkodër in the north of the country. Kuçi was reacting to an anonymous article that appeared at the beginning of a special issue of *Leka* (no. 8–12, August–December 1937, part II). The article was entitled "*Gjergj Kastrioti pasqyra e atëdhétarit shqiptár*" (Georges Kastriot. The Mirror of the Albanian Patriot) (535–46). In reality, the author was none other than the editor, the Italian Jesuit father Giuseppe/Zef Valentini (1900–1979) based in Shkodër (Kamsi 2008, 89). Trained in Italy in philosophy and theology, but later also developing a work as an Albanologist and Byzantinist in Albania, he would become secretary of the first institute of Albanology founded in Tirana in 1940, during the Italian occupation (Instituti Mbretnuer i Studimeve Shqiptare) (Faja 2012). Father Valentini, who did not sign the text, was therefore both an outsider and an insider. He was Italian, but had learned the Albanian language perfectly and was already playing a central role in the 1930s in the publishing of one of the country's most prominent journals, where historical contributions were commonplace. On the occasion of the anniversary of the declaration of independence, his text emphasized, among other things, that Skanderbeg could not have had a "centralizing" will (here he used Fan Noli's expression), and that it was wrong to project the patriotic ideal and nationalism of the nineteenth and twentieth centuries onto the figure and times of Skanderbeg:

3 SKANDERBEG: FIGURES OF PAPER, FIGURES OF STONE 125

If we want to take history as a teacher of life and not make ourselves a teacher of history, we will not take into account the efforts of some who project the modern mind onto the world of the past: These people try to turn Gjergj Kastrioti into a kind of racist [nationalist] 1900, in such a way that they stylize the national idea in a Hegelian fog, taking him to heaven on the one hand, and on the other emptying him of that moral and spiritual life that only religion and the historical tradition of centuries give. (*Leka* no. 8–12, August–December 1937, part II, 540)

Ali Kuçi (*Kombi* no. 5, June 1938, 23) criticized the person behind the article for presenting Skanderbeg as someone who would only have defended his own principality and the "family institutions" that were at its heart, without any "centralizing ideal", the guiding idea of patriotic historiography as it had developed over the previous few years. In Ali Kuçi's view, as long as certain overly romantic elements were removed, the only valid study was that of Fan Noli, who had developed this idea of a unifying and centralizing will.

But the controversy also took on a new dimension, this time a religious one. Valentini had criticized those who were rejecting any spiritual factor in the analysis of Skanderbeg's actions. Ali Kuçi criticized him for the opposite, that is, for proposing an eminently religious interpretation. By pointing out that the author of *Leka* was basing his analysis on a work by the Franciscan Father Athanas/Athanase Gegaj (1904–1988), he was referring to a way of presenting things that would have been peculiar to a certain "Shkodër group", by which he meant the Catholic clergy. Let us remember that the magazine *Leka* was the organ of the Jesuits. In his brief reply (*Leka* no. 6–7, June–July 1938, 254–55), Father Valentini refuted, again anonymously, both the idea of a homogeneous Catholic vision and the fact that the importance of the religious dimension in Skanderbeg was the result of this supposed Catholic interpretation. There was no Catholic unity, especially as he was arguing based on documents kept in the archives of the Jesuit Convent and not on the book by his Franciscan confrere, which he quoted merely for the convenience of the reader. Moreover, he made it clear once again that he did not agree with A. Gegaj (as with Fan Noli) that Skanderbeg had centralizing aims. Following another Franciscan, Marin Sirdani (1885–1962), who wrote various studies on Skanderbeg in the 1920s and 1930s, he thought this was not the case. For him, the religious dimension emerged through an objective, not subjective, study of the documents.

Although he had not been directly targeted by Ali Kuçi's notice, Athanas Gegaj, one of the main contributors to the Franciscan review *Hylli i dritës*, also responded. His contribution introduced a new aspect to the controversy: the question of legitimacy and competence, and more broadly that of the construction of an Albanian historiographical field. Originally from the mountainous areas of Montenegro close to the Albanian border, and having studied at the Franciscan college in Shkodër, he had just defended his thesis at the University of Louvain in 1936 and, at the beginning of the following year, published in French in Paris, via the famous orientalist publisher Geuthner, the monograph *L'Albanie et l'Invasion turque au XVe siècle* (Albania and the Turkish invasion in the fifteenth century, 1937), which was largely devoted to the figure of Skanderbeg. In his article, entitled "Dilettantisme historique" (*Hylli i dritës* 1938, no. 10, October 1938, 549–55), he first denied any historical legitimacy to Ali Kuçi and other Albanians who ventured into the field of historical studies without taking a sufficiently critical approach. He also contrasted the studies done in Albania with those done abroad, which were "paradoxically" more advanced and more critical. In his view, Fan Noli's study put forward by Ali Kuçi was not sufficiently critical and scientific. A. Gegaj also distanced himself from Father Valentini, whom he severely criticized from a methodological point of view—the references he gave (such as his own book) were not in line with the content; the chroniclers were presented as eyewitnesses when they had not been. He also criticized Valentini's conclusions. On the main point of disagreement, namely the question of Skanderbeg's centralizing agenda, A. Gegaj invoked foreign historiography as irrefutable proof: authors such as the Italian F. Cerone and the Romanian C. Marinesco/Marinescu, who was quoted at length at the bottom of the last page, were cited to prove that, in his actions and ideals, Skanderbeg was working toward the unification of the country.

It is clear that Athanas Gegaj, a recent graduate of a European university and author of a book published in French, presented himself to his opponents as the sole representative of scientific Albanian historiography, having studied at a European university. He also did so by emphasizing the importance of using archival documents. In a second article entitled "Historical sources from the time of Skanderbeg" (*Hylli i dritës* 1939/1, 49–53), in which he continued his polemics (even though he had been advised not to do so), Athanas Gegaj once again took a methodological approach by explaining to "public opinion" the supposed objectivity of archival documents, which made it possible to go further than literary sources, such as the history of Barletius, which were supposed to be more subjective. Still with the idea of developing a critical history, he returned to the idea that Fan Noli's book could not be fully integrated into this category, contrary to what Ali Kuçi had suggested. Kuçi, who had been accused of dilettantism, reacted this time to the question of competence and legitimacy: he demanded the right of those who had not studied at university to intervene in historiographical debates, particularly in the debate in question, which he did not want to see as a religious polemic, but as a properly scientific one (*Kombi* November–December 1938, 16–18).

Meanwhile, Branko Merxhani (1894–1981), one of the intellectuals at the forefront of neo-Albanianism—a movement inspired by the sociology and Turkish nationalism of Ziya Gökalp—was debating with other southern Albanian periodicals (*Demokratia* and *Drita*) about how to write Albanian history. While his magazine *Përpjekja Shqiptare* (13, January 1938, 66) had published a rather favorable notice of the publication of Athanas Gegaj's book, a few months later, in a short essay entitled "History and historiography" (*Përpjekja Shqiptare*, 18–24, December 1938, 409–411), Branko Merxhani argued for the empowerment of an Albanian historiographical field and the systematization of the collection of material. He used Athanas Gegaj as an example, without naming him: "a young doctor from Shkodër [who] recently published a 'dissertation' on fifteenth-century Albanian history, which a foreign specialist described as '*grund-saetzlich ein Missgriff*'". He did not translate this expression in German, which means "a fundamental error", but explained that the German-speaking scholar had pointed out the problem of sources: Gegaj had ignored Biemmi's falsification and completely ignored Ottoman sources. B. Merxhani concluded that it would have been better for the author to devote himself first and foremost to collecting historical material relating to this period before getting down to writing the history. This criticism led him to set out what, in his opinion, would be necessary to build an Albanian historiography: to found an institute of Albanology; to create a "circle for historical studies on the Gjergj Kastrioti period" along the lines of the idea of the French archaeologist Léon Rey; to ask the German Turkologist Franz Babinger to systematize sources in Turkish, Arabic, and Persian, as other Balkan countries had already done; and finally, more broadly, to develop Balkan studies in the country.

Indeed, without such institutions and initiatives, what might be called an Albanian historiography—on Skanderbeg in particular—remained extremely tenuous and highly composite, given the heterogeneous and highly transnational profile of its main protagonists: an Orthodox bishop who had emigrated to the United States and was trying to play a political role in Albania; a former student of the University of Vienna, headmaster of a secondary school in Shkodër, then a reader in Belgrade; an Albanian Franciscan who had studied in Graz; another Albanian Franciscan who had defended a thesis in Louvain and published a monograph in Paris, then returned to Shkodër; and even an Italian Jesuit father who had settled in Albania. However, this historiography seemed to take hold with the controversies of 1937–1939. In the absence of an institutionalized academic field, those directly involved in these polemics disputed its limits, methods, key figures, and main theses.

At the end of the 1930s, in this field, Skanderbeg's Albanian identity was no longer claimed or discussed; it remained implicit. Moreover, explicitly or otherwise, Fan Noli's book, the first and only biography of Skanderbeg in Albanian, was often placed at the center of the debate, whether for its (insufficient) scientific value or for the ideas it put forward. The issue of centralization and the end of feudalism put forward by Fan Noli in 1921 was now at the heart of the controversy. It conjured up an image of Albania governed by a leader who wanted to put an end to local powers, or on the contrary leave them in place; this echoed the debates that were then taking place on the cantonalization of Albania, so dear to certain members of the Catholic clergy, and above all on the problem of the power of the beys and the agrarian reform that had largely failed (Clayer 2022, 135–67 and 365–96; Halimi 2013). As a book written by an Albanian, Athanas Gegaj's book was part of this debate. Published in French by a prestigious Parisian publishing house, it was also discussed in the field of international historiography on Skanderbeg, which, as we have seen, resonated in Albania. This historiography was evolving as a result of geopolitical changes, and in particular Fascist Italy's policy toward Albania.

Albanian Historiography, the Nicolae Iorga School, and Italian Imperialist Historiography

As we have seen, the integration of Albanian historiography and the creation of the figure of Skanderbeg into a wider space had already taken place in Belgrade in the 1920s due to the birth of Yugoslav Albanology that was in the process of being institutionalized. In the 1930s, it spread further, through criticism of A. Gegaj's thesis, and then of the Italian historiography that had taken up this theme.

Let us take as our starting point a central figure in the global historiographical field that was developing around Skanderbeg, rather than a polemic. Of Transylvanian origin, Francisc Pall (1911–1992) was a Romanian Byzantinist and medievalist who studied at the University of Cluj, where he was for a time secretary and librarian at the Institute of History, before taking up residence at the Romanian School in Rome in 1934–1936 and at Fontenay-aux-Roses in France in 1937. His career was therefore European, and he published in Romanian as well as in French, Italian, and German. He had been a pupil of the famous Byzantinist and professor of world history Constantin Marinescu (1891–1982)—himself a pupil of Nicolae Iorga—author of a study on Alfonso V, King of Aragon and Naples, and Skanderbeg's Albania (1923). F. Pall succeeded him at the University of Cluj. From 1933 onward, F. Pall worked on the history of the Crusades and was the author of several publications dealing directly or indirectly with the figure of Skanderbeg: on Skanderbeg and Hungary (1933), on Gegaj's book (Pall 1937), on Barletius (Pall 1938), and on Italian historiography (Pall 1942) (Suma 2003). In these texts, he politely but severely criticized Albanian patriotic historiography, and Italian historiography produced within an imperialist framework.

Francisc Pall was not the only one to report on the new study represented by Athanas Gegaj's work in 1937. Reviews appeared in various general and specialist historical journals (*American Historical Review, Revue historique, Jahrbücher für Geschichte Osteuropas, Echos d'Orient*). Opinions were very divided: while the American William L. Langer, who was not a medievalist, was all praise, the German albanologist Georg Stadtmüller wrote an extremely critical dry note (in fact a summary of a review that had appeared in the *Revue internationale des Etudes balkaniques* in Belgrade). Ambiguity was also the rule, as in Jovan Radonić's introduction to the collection of documents he published in 1942: he judged the book to be much better than Fan Noli's, while referring the reader to F. Pall's highly critical review.

In 1937, F. Pall published a long review in the leading Romanian journal of Balkan studies, *Revue Historique du Sud-Est Européen* (n°10–12, 1937). While welcoming the work because it was based on a variety of sources and therefore did not simply rely on Barletius's account, he nevertheless described it as "more or less critical". In his opinion, the way in which the author cited his sources did not correspond to historical criticism. Above all, for F. Pall, the problem was that A. Gegaj had not taken into account the studies of German scholars Franz Babinger (1931) and Kurt Ohly (1933). They had suggested and demonstrated that one of the narrative sources used by A. Gegaj, in this case the anonymous fifteenth-century writing by a person from Bar/Antivari reproduced in the chronicle of Giammaria Biemmi (1742), was a forgery from the eighteenth century by the same Biemmi. F. Pall showed how, as a result, some of A. Gegaj's assertions were completely false. He therefore highlighted not only the inadequacy of the work in terms of the requirements of the scientific method but also a problem of disconnection between Albanian historiography and the development of studies in Western Europe.

A few years later, the rise of an Italian historiography on Skanderbeg, largely stimulated by the annexation of the small state to the Italian Empire, did not escape F. Pall's attention either. Pall was no stranger to the country, as he had spent several years at the Romanian School in Rome and was a regular visitor to its archives. In 1942, he wrote an article in German entitled "Die Geschichte Skanderbegs im Lichte der neueren Forschung" (The History of Skanderbeg in Light of the Most Recent Research) in which he quickly listed the contributions that had appeared in Italian from 1939 to 1940, including that of Gennaro Mari Monti, on Skanderbeg's expedition to Apulia (1939), the importance of which he emphasized. But apart from this study, F. Pall was far more critical of other contributions, which were the pure fruits of a historical policy aimed at creating a bridge between Italy and the recently annexed Albania to underline the historical links between the two shores of the Adriatic; a policy made tangible in the public space by the erection in 1940 in the Italian capital of the first statue of Skanderbeg that had ever existed (Belli Pasqua 2019). Even the work by Alessandro Cutolo (1899–1995), a medievalist in Rome, Naples, and then Milan, had little scientific value in his eyes. Entitled *Scanderbeg* (1940), it was an unannotated biography, preceded by a brief introduction in which the author reviewed historiography and sources, particularly in light of the work of F. Pall. However, Pall was extremely critical, as it did not consider his own work and followed too closely, sometimes word for word, Fan Noli's work, or rather the translation that had been made in 1924 by an Italian-Albanian, Francesco Argondizza. As the Second World War raged on, Francisc Pall's assessment of the situation was still that there was no "real critical biography" in existence.

SKANDERBEG REDRAWN IN THE INK AND STONE OF COMMUNISM

The Communist seizure of power after the Second World War in the Balkans (except in Greece) had a major impact on Balkan historiography, both ideologically and institutionally. As far as debates on Skanderbeg are concerned, the most important development was the structuring of academic fields in Albania in the postwar period, and later in the southern provinces of Yugoslavia (Kosovo and Macedonia). This led to a kind of magnetization of the global field of Skanderbeg studies, through a desire on the part of Albanian actors—primarily in Albania—to impose a narrative in line with the new Marxist and nationalist ideology and to place themselves at the heart of the production of this narrative. The debates that ensued, however, took on particular forms, which did not exclude more complex dynamics and controversies, albeit of particular types. Firstly, there was a process of critical re-appropriation of existing historiography and of a new production coming from the United States. Secondly, after 1968, because of the break between Albania and the Soviet Union, which led to its relative isolation in Europe and an increasingly nationalistic rhetoric highlighting past struggles against "foreigners", the celebrations marking the five hundredth anniversary of Skanderbeg's death constituted another form of often contradictory re-appropriation of scientific contributions at the international level.

Aleks Buda, the Critical Re-appropriation of Fan Noli, and the Institutionalization of the Historiographical Field

According to the historian Kristo Frashëri (1920–2016), in the aftermath of the Second World War Skanderbeg was not viewed positively by Albania's Communist leaders. Considered a bey by virtue of his name—Skanderbeg, that is, Iskender Bey—he was associated with the large landowners, against whom the new regime set itself up with agrarian reform from 1946. The figures of the "national revival" of the late nineteenth and early twentieth centuries, and above all those of the Partisans, played the leading roles in the new politics of history (*Aleks Buda* 2012, 15). The man who was then asserting himself as the leader of an Albanian historiographical field that was still confused and in the process of being institutionalized (Idrizi 2020), that is, Aleks Buda, would nevertheless elevate the figure of Skanderbeg to the top of the national historical pantheon.

Aleks Buda (1911–1993) was born in Elbasan, in central Albania, into a family of merchants belonging to the urban bourgeoisie. His father, a pharmacist, had been a very active Albanianist. He sent his son to study for many years in Italy, then Austria, at the Salzburg secondary school and the University of Vienna. There, A. Buda trained as a historian and attended the Institute of Balkan Studies between 1930 and 1935. After teaching at secondary schools in Tirana and Korçë, he returned to Italy in 1941 to study at the linguistics department of Padua University. He only stayed for a year, joining the ranks of the Partisans in Albania in 1942. After the war, as one of the few Albanians with a university education in the humanities, he was appointed director of the National Library and helped set up the Institute of Sciences in 1947. He was also behind the founding of the Institute for History in 1955 and was the chair of history at the new university in 1957. He even became president of the Academy of Sciences after its creation in 1972, a position he held for 20 years, from 1973 until his death in 1993 (Idrizi 2020).

So, it was from this dominant position in the academic field that Aleks Buda drew the figure of Skanderbeg in the ink of the new regime, largely through a process of critical re-appropriation. Indeed, controversy seems to have been one of the foundations of the new narrative he was proposing in the national and international arenas, as his disciples and colleagues recall (*Aleks Buda* 2012, 35–36, 44, 45, 74). Before the great celebrations of the late 1960s, to which we shall return, Buda constructed his Skanderbeg by criticizing the existing historiography, and above all by positioning himself in relation to Fan Noli's work. This was not the 1921 work, but the revised version of a thesis defended in 1945 at Boston University and published in 1947 (*George Castrioti Scanderbeg*) (Noli 1947), of which there was also a popular version published in Albanian in the United States in 1950 (*Historia e Skënderbeut. Kryezotit të Arbërisë (1405–1468)*, Boston).

The critical dialogical construction with Fan Noli took place on several occasions, and varied considerably, in front of different audiences and in changing political and scientific contexts. It began in January 1949, shortly after the break between Albania and Yugoslavia, at a public conference held in Tirana, the text of which was published a few days later in the newspaper *Zëri i popullit* (The Voice of the People). According to Kristo Frashëri, this was the first conference of its kind in Enver Hoxha's Albania. As a young intellectual, he was captivated by the speaker's rhetoric:

3 SKANDERBEG: FIGURES OF PAPER, FIGURES OF STONE 133

> In his lecture, he developed, among other things, a debate with the views Fan Noli had presented on this theme [the socio-economic context in fifteenth-century Albania] in his thesis in English on Skanderbeg, published in New York two years earlier. The debate with this brilliant work made the conference very interesting, because of the critical point of view it addressed to Fan Noli's contribution. (Frashëri 2014, 186)

K. Frashëri was also fascinated by Buda's interpretation, which saw no contradiction in the fact that a movement of free peasants could have been led by a leader belonging to the feudal class (Frashëri 2014, 186). According to him, in the name of the objective use of documentary sources, Aleks Buda initially rejected both the historiography that surrounded Skanderbeg with legends and praise, and that which denigrated him. He insisted on the importance of the economic and social context for understanding history: in this case the existence of a free peasantry. This led him to highlight Noli's new work, which went in this direction. Buda, however, raised a number of major objections to Noli's work, both in terms of the use of sources—since Noli relied on the forgery written by Biemmi—and in its substance. In particular, he criticized Noli's assumptions about Skanderbeg's childhood and the social dimensions of the revolts. For Kristo Frashëri, "the style of the debate showed the way to be followed by historians and scholars of Communist Albania, in a way quite different from the debates that journalists and partisan activists conducted on political issues" (*Aleks Buda* 2012, 15–19). The holding and content of this conference would therefore have represented a certain assertion of the academic sphere vis-à-vis the political sphere.

Two years later, in 1951, in a scientific article published in the *Bulletin of the Institute of Sciences*, a showcase for Albanian Communist science in the making (Buda 1951), Aleks Buda this time addressed his colleagues directly, but still in a relatively ambiguous way with regard to Fan Noli. Taking up the same argument, but with a more assertive Marxist approach, he judged the existing historiography in terms of the attention paid to the socio-economic conditions of Skanderbeg's actions and the character of the struggles led by the population. In a more nationalistic vein, he paid particular attention to the three monographs written by Albanians. He felt that Noli's 1921 monograph was more a patriotic and literary history than a critical one. Athanas Gegaj's work was "worthy of the profession" because of his analysis of the sources despite using Biemmi's forgery, but it was "bourgeois historiography" in that it said nothing about the socio-economic context. Finally, he felt that Fan Noli's most recent study, whose analysis emphasized the "role of the popular masses in the struggles of Skanderbeg" (Buda 1986, 167), was the only step in the right direction, as it broke free from the patterns of bourgeois historiography. More generally, it was considered an interesting contribution through the use of new sources (notably Byzantine and Ottoman), and because Fan Noli addressed questions that had not been asked until then: the importance of the revolts, the factors that had made their success possible, and the way in which Skanderbeg had known and been able to imagine his victorious tactics.

This positive assessment certainly led to the translation and publication of Fan Noli's work in Tirana in 1967 and to the publication on several occasions (1962, 1967) of his more popular 1950 work, as well as the production in 1962—the year of the fiftieth anniversary of the declaration of independence—of another work made up of extracts, intended for the country's schools, not to mention editions in Kosovo. Yet, paradoxically, in the same text Aleks Buda did not hesitate to reject—sometimes ambiguously it is true, out of ideology and/or nationalism (Dani 2014)—important elements of Fan Noli's account, as he had already done at the 1949 conference. Thus, while he considered Noli's work on Skanderbeg's youth to be the most interesting, he showed that his theory on that part of his life, during which he would not have been at the sultan's court, did not hold water. Above all, he insisted at length on the fact that Fan Noli did not adequately characterize the social class to which Skanderbeg belonged, because he described him as a patriarchal rather than a feudal ruler, close to the peasantry. This approach did not correspond to the Marxist schema and corresponding periodization followed by Buda in presenting fifteenth-century Albanian history. This schema suggested that Skanderbeg and his family were part of the feudal system characteristic of the period, as feudal lords. Contrary to what Noli might have thought, this did not prevent him from arriving at the same analysis of the struggle as a popular struggle. On the contrary, for Buda, "only a Skanderbeg who was a member of the ruling class" could simultaneously lead the peasant masses, counter the centrifugal dynamics within the feudal class, and find allies outside. He concluded by highlighting the Marxist interpretation of the controversy:

> The result of [Fan Noli's] misinterpretation of this important phase is that it does not make clear the role Skanderbeg played in our history and its function, which is to overcome feudal anarchy and move towards the

formation of a centralised feudal monarchy, a necessary precondition for more advanced political formations, for the creation of a national state, as universal history teaches us. (Buda 1986, 167)

This tension between praise and criticism—and between Marxism and nationalism—even appeared in the preface to the translation of Fan Noli's work, published in Tirana in 1967, which he also concluded in a very ambiguous way:

> This does not mean that we are devaluating the work of the historian F.S. Noli, but we have concentrated on a number of points which raise remarks and objections and which, in our opinion, should be considered by readers of the book which is now being given to Albanian readers. It is true that 'The History of Skanderbeg' of 1947 cannot be considered as a work that can fully satisfy the scientific requirements, as well as those of the broader masses of our new intelligentsia. [...] But despite these remarks, Fan S. Noli's work before us has the merit of once again posing the problem of Skanderbeg on a new, higher plane, from a more advanced point of view. And this is one of the merits, and not the least, that the history of Albanian culture rightly recognizes in our famous poet and patriot, historian and thinker, Fan S. Noli. (Buda 1986, 336)

In other texts, Buda would focus less on Fan Noli's work in constructing his own point of view, which was increasingly becoming that of an official historiography under the control of the political sphere (Idrizi 2020). By 1957, for a Russian-speaking audience, he was no longer focusing on Fan Noli or Albanian authors. In the text entitled "The struggle of the Albanian people under the leadership of Skanderbeg against the Turkish invaders" (Buda 1986, 192–225), he denounced more generally the "feudal and bourgeois" historiography that had ignored the popular masses (Buda 1986, 193) and the "fascist" historiography represented by the German M. Braun who, in 1941, had situated the masses as simply passive. He went on to say that "[t]he historian, whose aim is to decipher the meaning of history scientifically and in a Marxist manner, will certainly reject such opinions, which openly distort and falsify historical facts" (Buda 1986, 194). The rest of the article simply offered a narrative in which the only references discussed were those of the Russian historian Makušev, and Fan Noli on the subject of Skanderbeg's youth (Buda 1986, 205).

In 1967 it was the new political and social situation created by the break with the Soviet Union in 1961 and the regime's ban on religion that prompted him to cater his criticism to a national audience. In an article published in *Studime historike* (1967/4, 3–22) entitled "On a few problems about the Skanderbeg era", Buda qualified his remarks in order, in a way, to contribute to the anti-religious struggle: Athanas Gegaj, who had been a Franciscan priest, was no longer mentioned, and Fan Noli was criticized for having quoted him. A reference to the work of the Jesuit Father Zef Valentini made its appearance, because he had wrongly seen only religious motives in the uprisings. Above all, Buda now refuted Fan Noli's analysis of external factors. In particular, he greatly overestimated the role of the Pope and religion (Buda 1986, 226–53). In the preface to the edition of Fan Noli's book that he was writing at around the same time, largely based on his 1951 text, he added a paragraph on the same subject.

In the *Studime historike* article, however, a new critical dimension had more to do with the development of contemporary historiography, regarding which Albanian institutions were acting as censors. Buda strongly criticized the Turkish historian Halil Inalcik for playing down the peasantry's involvement in the fighting, focusing on feudal lords and their reactions against the introduction of the new Ottoman system (Buda 1986, 229). Halil Inalcik, who had been responsible for the most significant historiographical advances since the early 1950s thanks to the exploitation of hitherto unexploited Ottoman archives, was also invited to Tirana the following year for the celebrations organized by the Albanian authorities to mark the five hundredth anniversary of Skanderbeg's death in 1968.

Celebrations and International Historiography

We met Professor H. Inalcik personally and spoke with him when he came to Albania in December 1967, a month before the meeting of the second conference of Albanological Studies in Tirana, dedicated to the five-hundredth anniversary of the Hero's death. Despite his qualities as a historian, during the discussions we had with the Turkish professor, we noticed that we disagreed on many subjects. He defended the Ottoman Empire, and barely painted a picture of Albanian resistance, because he sang the glory of Sultan Fatih (the Conqueror). Albanian historians, on the other hand, defended Skanderbeg's actions and called Sultan Fatih an invader of Albania. (Frashëri 2009, 170)

Kristo Frashëri recalled the exchanges with Halil Inacik when he came to Tirana in late 1967 or early 1968. He added that a meeting had been organized at the university in his honor, during which he had given a lecture followed by shorter talks from Albanian colleagues. The ensuing exchanges were reportedly heated, particularly over the notion of "Albanian resistance". H. Inalcik is said to have reacted by telling his colleagues that they were wrong, as many Albanians had held high positions in the Ottoman administration. Through the figure of Skanderbeg, the wider question of the relationship—submissive or not—between "Turks" and "Albanians" throughout the Ottoman period was at stake. K. Frashëri concluded by writing that they parted "as friends", but that Inalcik never returned (Frashëri 2009, 170–71). After these closed-door controversies within the walls of the university and before the departure, there was nevertheless another side, that of the "friendly" public controversies at the major international conference to mark the 500th anniversary of Skanderbeg's death in January 1968.

The same year, scientific and non-scientific events were held to celebrate this anniversary also in Yugoslavia (in Kosovo in May, at the initiative of the recently reopened Institute of Albanology in response to the new political situation) and Italy (in Rome in April and Palermo in December). In this last case, different actors were involved around the university-based Institutes of Albanian Studies, generally belonging to the circles of exiled Albanians since the Communist take-over such as Ernest Koliqi, intellectuals and politicians from the Italian Arbëresh community, and representatives of the Catholic Church (Ndoja 2013). Other events took place later in the Albanian diaspora (United States and Belgium) and in Bulgaria at the Academy of Sciences.

These celebrations, which sometimes gave rise to publications and reports, provided few opportunities for direct polemics. They were more theaters where the presentation of scientific advances was at least as important as ideological, political, national, and religious statements. In Tirana and Prishtina, a Marxist and nationalist interpretation was dominant, although in Prishtina the Ottomanist approach was more present, while in Rome and Palermo, where one of the main organizers was the Jesuit Father Giuseppe Valentini (now in Italy), the Catholic dimension was central (*La Civiltà cattolica* 1969/1, 57–61). In all cases, what mattered above all was the presence of recognized specialists from different countries—these "friends"—who contributed to the worldwide prestige of the figure of Skanderbeg, of the nation, and of the organizers. In this way, these celebrations became arenas for re-appropriation, beyond the more or less fundamental differences illustrated by the case of Halil Inalcik in Tirana, to which I will return later. The critical character was less marked in Prishtina, where national affirmation and the development of an Albanian historiography were only just taking shape after the end of the period of oppression by the Yugoslav Minister of the Interior Aleksandar Ranković, who was opposed to Albanian autonomy (Krasniqi 2020). The case of the Palermo colloquium shows that the national affirmation and legitimization of the local or national Albanian field that were being achieved through these celebrations were more important than the ideological aspects:

> Researchers from all over the world were invited to Palermo to commemorate the five hundredth anniversary of the death of Gjergj Kastriot. They came from America, France, Germany, Yugoslavia and, of course, all over Italy. The International Centre for Albanian Studies, the organizer of these Kastriot cultural events, saw it as a way of linking these symbols to the Fifth Conference of [Albanian] Studies. Today, this organization has gone beyond the narrow circle of Arbëresh in Italy; its name is known throughout the cultural world. (Karl Gurakuqi, "Kongresi i pestë i Studimevet Shqiptare dhe pesëqindvjetori i Skandërbeut në Palermë", *Shejzât* 13/1–3 1969, 15)

The Bulgarian historian Strašimir Dimitrov, who took part in the Tirana congress, concluded a report of the meeting by stressing that although Albanology had been born outside Albania, the second Tirana conference had shown that this country should henceforth be considered its center (*Istoričeski Pregled* 168, 135–37). Indeed, the "friendly" debates during the celebrations were generally due to the desire of Albanian specialists to set the pace from their central position. The proceedings of the Tirana conference included a section entitled "Discussions and additional material" (*Konferenca e dytë* 1969, 586 ff.). These were mainly remarks made to foreign "friends" by the main Albanian historians working on the Skanderbeg period: A. Buda, K. Frashëri, and Selami Pulaha. The remarks of the latter—at the time one of the few Ottomanists in the country— were the most radical, since he accused the Turkish historian H. Inalcik of having transformed the struggle of a people and the popular masses against an invader into an uprising of a few feudal lords seeking to defend their own economic interests. This idea of a "heroic struggle for freedom against the Turkish invaders", which had become the leitmotif of Albanian historiography, had already been criticized by Franz Babinger, one of the representatives of this new international historiography on the Ottoman Empire. Pointed out by Babinger as an anachronism on the occasion of a conference held in 1962 to celebrate the declaration of independence, Buda had responded to him in a relatively straightforward manner. Buda's somewhat contradictory reply was that, while there was no national state or national feeling in the modern sense at that time, there was a struggle against foreign occupiers, a union of different regions under the political and military guidance that strengthened Skanderbeg's central power, and thus the existence of a strong popular patriotism based on an Albanian national feeling (Buda 1986, 294–9).

Conversely, the internationalization of the treatment of Skanderbeg in scientific circles prompted certain actors to voice criticisms and counter-proposals, but in other arenas. In the diaspora, Abas Ermenji (1913–2003), a former leader of *Balli Kombëtar* (The National Front), one of the groups opposed to the Partisans during the Second World War, published a history in France entirely dedicated to Skanderbeg. Entitled *Skanderbeg's Place in Albanian History* (1968), the account was produced outside the official historiographical field and was intended as an alternative history of Albania "for the free world", that is, a non-Communist history liberated from Marxist ideology, imbued instead with national values. The book—not limited to the period of Skanderbeg—aimed to show the greatness of the hero and its people, who fought without external help to defend Europe.

Publicity also reopened the question of ethnic origin in very marginal arenas, but probably revealed unexpressed opinions. Thus, in a review of the publication of a selection of contributions from the Tirana conference in the French-language Albanian journal *Studia Albanica*, published in the *Bulletin of the Modern Greek Studies Association* (1969, 1, 492–493), a certain John Demus noted that the question of Skanderbeg's origin had not been addressed. He took the opportunity to cast doubt on his Albanian identity: his real name would have been Greek (*Georgioi Kastriotis*), just as his father and wife would have been Greek. Two years later, it was a historian from southern Serbia, T.P. Vukanović, who wrote in a local magazine that Skanderbeg was the product of a Slavo-Albanian symbiosis due to marriage ties, the purely Slavic names borne by part of his family, and the large bequests made by his father to the Serbian monastery of Hilandar ("Slovenska simbioza porodice Đurđa Kastriota Skenderbega", *Vranjski glasnik*, knj. VII, Vranje 1971).

Apart from the celebrations, there were also internal confrontations in Albania itself, where it would be wrong to imagine an academic field devoid of polemics due to its constraints by political power. From the 1960s to beginning of the 1970s, two of the main historians working on Skanderbeg, Kristo Frashëri and Kasem Biçoku, clashed in articles on the question of Skanderbeg's childhood and the period before 1443, about which little was known, as Doan Dani has shown (2016, 384–91). In 1974–1975, another controversy erupted, this time not in scientific journals but in the pages of the newspaper *Mësuesi*, the organ of the Ministry of Education and Culture. The local origin of the Kastriot family was discussed. Kasem Biçoku contradicted Kristo Frashëri's claim that they hailed from the Dibra region and not Has, a little further north. The medium chosen for the controversy provided an opening outside the circle of professional historians, as two local historians from Dibra, Hazis Ndreu and Ali Hoxha, the former a teacher and the latter an artist, also took part in the debate.

However, the discussions were not always publicized, as Kristo Frashëri testifies when he talks about plans to erect a statue or a museum dedicated to Skanderbeg, which led to exchanges within commissions bringing together politicians, historians, and artists. According to him, there had already been discussions about the representation of Skanderbeg for the statue that was erected in Tirana in 1968 to replace that of Stalin, which had been enthroned since 1953: should he look like a warrior or a statesman? In what position should he be? With which clothes? In the commissions that met to design the museum that was to be built a decade later, there were also several opposing visions. On the one hand, Aleks Buda, who was responsible for sketching out a design for the museum, imagined the figure of a legendary warrior who was to embody the freedom fighter and liberator, while K. Frashëri expressed reservations, preferring to see the figure of a statesman, the "first to have created a national Albanian state". The balance of power within the scientific and political field favored Buda's interpretation (Frashëri 2014, 247–56), and it was not until the fall of the Communist regime and the advent of political pluralism that Kristo Frashëri set out his vision for the public (2002).

3 SKANDERBEG: FIGURES OF PAPER, FIGURES OF STONE 141

PUBLIC CONTROVERSIES IN THE "COSMOS OF DEMOCRACY"

Seven years after the publication of his book *Skënderbeu. Jeta dhe vepra* (Skanderbeg. Life and Work, 2002), K. Frashëri was involved in one of the biggest controversies to erupt in Albania over the figure of Skanderbeg after the fall of Communism. Following the publication in Tirana, in Albanian, of a book by the historian Oliver Schmitt, professor at the University of Vienna (*Skënderbeu* 2008), he responded with a book whose title set the tone: *Skanderbeg Disfigured by a Swiss Historian and a few Albanian Analysts*. While conceding, in the conclusion, that in the "democratic cosmos" all opinions were permissible, he appealed to the State to defend this symbol (Frashëri 2009, 195–8). For almost two decades, the relationship between power, academia, historiography, and the media had been turned upside down in Albania, as in other countries in the region that had experienced Communist regimes. The opening up to the outside world, the introduction of a multi-party system, the liberalization and reconfiguration of the academic and media fields, as well as socio-economic upheavals, armed conflicts, increased mobility, and the reaffirmation of religious identities, had all contributed to major historiographical transformations. These were linked in particular to the loss of the monopoly on the writing of history by official institutions, as well as to greater transnational circulation, for which the development of the internet was only one factor.

Without going over all of the new controversies that have erupted since the turn of the 1990s around Skanderbeg—one of the major narrative figures produced during the communist era—I will first focus on the controversy that arose around Oliver Schmitt's book, to show that there was a strong overlap between the international controversy and national controversies. Secondly, I will look at the proliferation of polemics and controversies in Balkan public spaces.

Intertwined International and National Controversies

In his monograph published first in Albanian and then in German, Oliver Jens Schmitt attempted to draw up an anatomy of Skanderbeg's rebellion, using new sources, incorporating knowledge of the terrain, considering what we know about the societies of that time, as well as trying to grasp Skanderbeg's personality beyond the mythical figure (Schmitt 2009, 7–12). In so doing, he proposed an analysis that would provoke reactions from various circles in Albania on different points. Michael Schmitt-Neke (2010) highlights four of them. The first is the fact that Oliver Schmitt not only underlines the Slavic family origin of Skanderbeg's mother, but also uses the first name "Ivan" for his father, that is, the Slavic form of John (Gjon in Albanian), which would imply that he gives Skanderbeg a Slavic (and not Albanian) ethnicity. For Oliver Schmitt, however, this is irrelevant in terms of ethnicity and, for him, Skanderbeg belongs to a family of the "Albanian minor nobility under Byzantine-Slavic cultural influence" (Schmitt 2015, 1079). Another point concerns his religious affiliation, which fluctuated over time, but which was initially forged by a link with the Orthodox Church. The third point concerns the reasons for his defection, which, although multiple, were primarily personal (the desire to avenge the execution of his father by the sultan), and not political or moral. The fourth and final point concerns the consequences of the twenty-five years of fighting, which Oliver Schmitt depicts as having had a heavy impact on the region, which was notably depopulated.

Indeed, reactions soon occurred in the media, political, and historical fields within the Albanian space, starting with that of the famous writer Ismail Kadare, who denounced the book in the press as an attack on the image and freedom of the Albanian nation, as well as on Albania's European future. The highest authorities of the Albanian state and, to a lesser extent, some politicians in Kosovo made declarations condemning the attempts to downplay the action of Skanderbeg toward the formation of Albanian statehood and its belonging in Europe. However, there were also other reactions, in a way using Schmitt's new propositions: the intellectual Fatos Lubonja, to whom we will come back, reacted promptly to Kadare in order to stress the need for a demystification of Albanian history, while the politician Abdi Baleta, defending a Muslim sensitivity, found an opportunity to disconnect the Albanian national identity from Catholicism and Europe.

Kristo's Frashëri's criticism clearly introduces two targets with his aforementioned title *Skanderbeg Disfigured by a Swiss Historian and a few Albanian Analysts*. On the one hand, the people targeted are Oliver Schmitt, characterized by his membership of a foreign academic field, and, on the other, "analysts", that is, people who took part in the debate, not necessarily as historians, but as Albanians. K. Frashëri was therefore first and foremost following the numerous critiques that had arisen in Albanian political, media, and scientific circles following the publication of O. Schmitt's book, polemics revolving in particular around the ethnicity of Skanderbeg's family, its motivations, alliances, and successes, as we have seen. At the same time, however, Frashëri was targeting some of his colleagues, as well as other Albanians involved in the debate. But this was no mere juxtaposition. Frashëri developed cross-arguments that showed the extent to which the international controversy was linked to controversies between Albanian actors. While maintaining a boundary between Albanian historiography and foreign historiography, Frashëri targeted, for example, those Albanians who had given a positive reception to Schmitt, those who had been influenced by him, or those upon whom Schmitt had relied, or those who were moving in a similar direction.

As one of the most important representatives of the historiography of the previous era, now retired but continuing to publish, Frashëri drew up, in the second part of his book, an alarming general assessment of post-Communist Albanian historiography:

> The crisis facing Albanian historiography today is truly worrying. Worrying, but explicable. It is the result of the transition from a system of controlled and disciplined historiography to a system of free, open historiography, without injunction from above. There is open discord among historians today, because their methodology, in most cases, is guided by a lack of methodology. Most of them are unfamiliar with the historiographical schools that flourished in the modern era. Some of them are guided by partisan motives, some by personal grudges, some by a penchant for a particular protagonist, and some by total ignorance. (Frashëri 2009, 146–7)

This observation did not prevent Frashëri from rejecting the questioning of the historiography of the previous period and of some of its foundations. Questioning based on its association with Enver Hoxha and Communist ideology was, in his view, unfair. On the other hand, the importance given to the figure of Skanderbeg had had nothing to do with the desire to create a civil religion, and the historians of the Communist era, like him, had been patriots and not nationalists (Frashëri 2009, 30–37).

To structure his refutation, Frashëri categorized the main groups who questioned the principles of Communist historiography as "xenomaniacs", "globalists", "Ottomanists", and "anti-Europeanists". Xenomaniacs were par excellence those who supported Schmitt because he belonged to a foreign historiography, supposedly superior to the existing Albanian historiography. Globalists were those who criticized "Albanian Skanderbegian historiography for being a slave to E. Hoxha's national-communism"

(Frashëri 2009, 151), and thus for having been not only Marxist but also too narrowly nationalist. The Ottomanists, for their part, were those who, through their approach, now rejected the leitmotiv of the struggle against the Ottoman invaders. The anti-Europeanists were those who rejected another central idea of the historiography of the previous period, namely that of the role played indirectly by Skanderbeg in the defense of Europe against the "Turks".

Behind, or beyond, these labels, Frashëri more specifically targeted several actors in the controversies, representative of one or more of these categories. Rather than focusing on the labels, we need to look at the profiles of these figures, which will help us to understand the tensions that existed in the aftermath of Communism between the several types of actors now present in a complex historiographical field, only partially institutionalized and spread across an increasingly varied range of media.

Thus, in criticizing the bibliography on which Schmitt was relying, Frashëri went on to expose multiple disagreements with his former colleague Kasem Biçoku (Frashëri 2009, 115–24). Also a member of the historical field since the 1960s, K. Biçoku had later become director of the Institute of History (1993–1997), then director of the National Museum (2008–2009), and had published several books on Skanderbeg between 1990 and 2000 in which he took up some of his works done (and not always published) during the Communist era. Frashëri did not label him, probably because he also came from the pre-1990 historical field. But the pages he devoted to what he called the "nonsenses" (Frashëri 2009, 124) of his former colleague bear witness to the divergences that existed from the Communist era onward, either in earlier works (particularly on the question of the geographical origin of Skanderbeg's family, but not exclusively) or on the subject of new studies published after 1990. For example, Frashëri was particularly critical of the "conjecture" allegedly made by Biçoku in an article published in 2005 on "Alexander the Great in the historical memory of Skanderbeg and the Albanians" (*Studime historike* 1/2, 2005, 7–29), and which Schmitt was inspired by.

Frashëri also attacked Dritan Egro, a young Albanian Ottomanist, thereby denouncing a new generation of historians (he himself uses the expression "young historian", *historian i ri*) who trained abroad and returned to Albania to practice, contributing to the opening up and evolution of the Albanian historical field and to a new interaction between national and international academic spheres. They also helped develop a new vision of the history of Albania in its relationship to imperial histories.

Having become Halil Inacik's student in Ankara, D. Egro, who served as an example to Frashëri for the category of "Ottomanists", was accused of "using the methodological and ideological parameters of Turkish historiography" and of applying the frameworks of Ottoman history to Albanian history, whereas the question of Skanderbeg involved relations between the dominant and the dominated (Frashëri 2009, 161). According to Frashëri, Egro's book *History and Ideology. A Critical Approach to Ottoman Studies in Modern Albanian Historiography* published in 2007 (Egro 2007), that is, shortly before Schmitt's book, sought to integrate Albanian historiography into Ottoman historiography (Frashëri 2009, 164), implying that the study of five centuries of Ottoman domination could be treated as something other than an imperial history.

In his controversy with Hysamedin Feraj, presented as "anti-Europeanist", Frashëri again defended the Albanian historiography of the Communist era, but this time in the face of transformations due to the development of political science, and more broadly in the face of new interactions between history and the humanities and social sciences. Hysamedin Feraj had been involved in debates on Skanderbeg since the late 1990s, well before the publication of Schmitt's book. He was a political scientist, born in Kosovo, with a degree from the University of Tirana and specialized at the University of Bern in 1993–1994. He was also a political activist and essayist who made frequent appearances in the media. His criticism of Albanian historiography, which he developed in his *Sketch of the Albanian Political Thought* (1998) and in a series of articles published in the press ("About the Skanderbeg debate", *Rimëkëmbja*, 2000), rehabilitated the Ottoman period, but not in the same way as that of Dritan Egro. What distinguished his approach from the historiography of the Communist years was not his Ottomanist approach, but his very schematic politicist interpretation which placed religious factors at its center, and in particular the supposed negative consequences of any alliance with Christian (Balkan and European) powers at the time of Skanderbeg, as in Albanian history in general. We will return to the question of the religious dimension he introduced. It should be noted here that, for Frashëri, this positioning was also in alignment with other foreign historiographies, more exactly the Muslim and Serbian historiographies.

Finally, Frashëri highlighted another category of actors now involved in debates on history: intellectuals. For him, Fatos Lubonja, whom he considered to be both a "xenomaniac" and a "globalist", was a case in point. A former political prisoner during the Communist era, he was then a journalist and writer. He appeared in various media outlets, but also created a cultural magazine called *Përpjekja* (The Effort), in reference to Branko Merxhani's magazine *Përpjekja shqiptare* from the interwar period. Lubojna and his collaborators claimed, at the very heart of their work, a critical approach to history and more specifically to Albanian historiography:

> The magazine is structured around three main themes: Current Affairs-Society; Albanian Letters; Historical Consciousness. The first section publishes articles dealing with topical issues affecting post-communist Albanian society; the second section aims to provide a high-quality collection of contemporary Albanian literary production, as well as publishing critical articles on literature; the third section includes writings on the history of Albania, which aim to view the country's history through a critical lens, thus providing an alternative to the 'official' romantic-nationalist history. (https://revistaperpjekja.org/index.php?option=com_k2&view=item&layout=item&id=67&Itemid=58&lang=en)

Frashëri denied Lubonja any legitimacy to intervene in the debates because he was not a professional historian and went looking for references outside the Albanian historiographical field. For him, the introduction of philosophical, sociological, and historical concepts was also the result of "xenomania" (Frashëri 2009, 150). Questions of method therefore went beyond the usual question of sources (particularly concerning the use of Barletius, Biemmi, and the Ottoman chronicles). Following on from the criticism of the relationship between "legend" and "history" that had characterized many classic studies of Skanderbeg, those involved were now arguing about the relationship between myth and history, and about the qualification of different historiographies (past/present, Albanian/foreign) in relation to these two notions (Frashëri 2009, 22 and 89–100; *Përpjekja* 2012, 28–29, and in particular the contributions by A. Puto 2012, 18–23 and F. Lubonja 2012, 24–48). Lubonja made the deconstruction of myths (and in particular those of National Communism) a condition for knowledge and freedom, specifying that it was not a question of being against myths, but of understanding their formation from the nineteenth century onward in particular. This constructivist approach went beyond Skanderbeg and was concerned with the question of the nation and its relationship to its hero. This is also why Lubonja was, in the eyes of Frashëri, the promoter of a globalization that tended to erase any national character. For Doan Dani, a historian of the younger generation specializing in the medieval period who studied in Shkodër (in the north of Albania) and Turin in Italy, the problem was precisely the omnipresence of an othering "Us/Them" interpretative framework, which post-Communist Albanian historiography had inherited and was unable to rid itself of (Dani 2016).

This cross-debate between Kristo Frashëri and Oliver Schmitt and between him and various critics of Albanian historiography was, however, only the climax of a constellation of controversies and debates about Skanderbeg that took place in the post-1990 Balkans.

Polemics on the Fringes of Academic Circles

In Southeastern Europe, the fall of the Communist regimes put an end not only to the monopoly of the party-states in the political field, but also to the monopoly of history writing where it existed. The emergence of private universities, scientific journals, and publishers, as well as the possibility of self-publishing, led to a fragmentation of the field of historical production. The privatization, multiplication, and evolution of the media sphere—with the emergence of the internet in particular—have enabled multiple interactions with political fields undergoing reconfiguration, in a context of profound economic and social transformations. The result has been a new relationship between the academic sphere, the partisan political sphere, and the public sphere, all three of which are not separate.

Thus, in the case of Skanderbeg, controversies and exchanges multiplied in Albania (as well as Kosovo and North Macedonia) and throughout the region, because they contributed to transformations and tensions within the academic field, as we have just seen, but also because they were part of wider socio-political transformations in which historians of different generations and statuses competed or collaborated with other types of actors, whether political entrepreneurs or identity entrepreneurs.

Political entrepreneurs have not failed to seize upon this symbol which they have been able to reshape according to their needs. For example, statues have been erected in public spaces: in Prishtinë, in Kosovo, in 2001, two years after the end of the war; in Skopje, in 2005, four years after the Ohrid Agreements, which were intended to seal the armed conflict that had taken place in Macedonia. In the latter case, as Nadège Ragaru (2008) has shown, while the stone figure symbolized the assertion of new rights for the Albanian minority through inscription on the territory, in the speech by political leader Ali Ahmeti it also represented struggle, unification, wisdom, and European values to which the Albanians of Macedonia now aspired. In reality, controversy surrounded the statue and its design, which betrayed a multi-layered, local, national and regional, inter-ethnic and intra-ethnic, political competition. The figure of Skanderbeg also appeared at the heart of the political arena when, in autumn 2017, Edi Rama, who was beginning his second term as prime minister of Albania, declared 2018 "the year of Skanderbeg on a national scale" to mark the 550th anniversary of the hero's death. Events were organized in Albania, Kosovo, Macedonia, and elsewhere, from an exhibition at the National Museum in Tirana to a scientific conference at the Academy of Sciences, for which historians were convened. As well as asserting the Albanian nation beyond the borders of the Albanian state, the aim was to emphasize the unity of the Albanian people and their democratic and European aspirations, which were supposed to be embodied by the figure of Skanderbeg. A first commemorative scientific conference, organized in Tirana in 2005 to mark the 600th anniversary of Skanderbeg's birth, in the tradition of the previous conferences, had already been entitled "Skanderbeg and Europe"; and it was under this title that the proceedings were published the following year, thus recalling Skanderbeg's role in the defense of Europe, even if the texts brought together dealt with much more diverse subjects (*Skënderbeu dhe Evropa* 2006).

However, these two central dimensions—Albanian and European—in the political field have been contested and discussed by identity-based entrepreneurs, often located on the fringes of the historical field, as well as on the fringes of the Albanian space, and have in turn provoked strong reactions. Debated in the context of the controversy surrounding Schmitt's book, the question of ethnic origin once again became a sensitive issue after the fall of the Communist regimes. In Macedonia, an essayist named Petar Popovski published a book in 2006 in which he referred to Skanderbeg as a Macedonian and criticized the authorities for not promoting him as such, sparking debate in the press, the academic world, and internet forums (Ragaru 2008, 532–3). In Serbia, in the aftermath of the conflicts linked to the dissolution of Yugoslavia, a historian from the Belgrade faculty, Olivera Milosavljević (2002, 218 ff.), showed how a certain tradition among Serbian nationalist intellectual circles had been constructing altering and devaluing stereotypes since the end of the nineteenth century. In particular, this trend tended to deny Skanderbeg's Albanian identity and turn him into a Serb, thereby denying the Albanians' ability to have a state. Fifteen years later, this trend had a representative in the person of Predrag R. Petrović, a retired engineer from Montenegro, who in 2016 published a study seeking to prove the Serbian origin of George Kastriot and his family, and asserting that the Albanian origin had been an idea developed in the nineteenth century under Austro-Hungarian imperialism (https://predragrpetrovic.com/). His thesis was relayed in the Serbian press and led to "Albanian" reactions, particularly on social networks.

As for the European dimension promoted by political leaders, this has provoked reactions even in Albania. As Enis Sulstarova has pointed out (Sulstarova 2006), Skanderbeg is strongly associated with an *ante murale* myth: thanks to him, the Albanians defended European civilization against the Turks in the fifteenth century, and therefore deserve to be accepted into the European political family in the twenty-first century (http://www.respublica.al/2016/12/14/mitet-antemurale-dhe-sk%C3%ABnderbeu). Originally, the myth had a Christian religious dimension: the hero of the Renaissance was the "Athlete of Christ". During the Communist era, the image of Skanderbeg defending Albania and Europe against the Turks was widely used to promote the Albanian nation and legitimize its independence. The new geopolitical situation and, above all, the rehabilitation of religion in Albanian society gave this myth new dimensions. For, as Cecilie Endresen (2010, 249–50) has shown, since 1990 religious leaders have remodeled the figure of Skanderbeg in their own image, re-emphasizing the links that the figure may have had with each of their denominations (Catholicism, Orthodoxy, Islam, and even mystical Islam), while others preferred to continue to insist on his Albanian identity.

The close association with Christianity and Europe that has nevertheless prevailed has led some actors (particularly of an Islamic sensibility) to challenge this interpretation of history, and even to reject Skanderbeg as a hero of the Albanian nation. As we have seen, H. Feraj criticized the existing historiography as early as the late 1990s. He portrayed Skanderbeg as someone who had chosen the wrong path by allying himself with European Christian princes, Serbs, Bulgarians, and Greeks, while other Albanians, by integrating into the Ottoman Empire, had prevented assimilation with other neighboring Balkan peoples. The debate on Skanderbeg, launched by Feraj and others, gave rise to a response devised by the circles formed around Franciscan cultural magazine *Hylli i dritës*, which reappeared in 1993. Aurel Plasari, an historian and specialist in comparative literature, who was editor-in-chief of the magazine at the time and went on to become director of Tirana's National Library for many years, preferred to respond in an unhurried and scientific, rather than media-friendly, manner. He then set about writing a book that was published only in 2018 (Plasari 2018): *Skanderbeg. A Political History* (see his interview in *Exlibris* 7/12/2018). In this voluminous work, however, the critique is not direct; it seeks to impose itself through the new narrative of a political history, in which the character of Skanderbeg finds himself at the heart of the confrontation between a Christian Europe and a Muslim threat. This approach, which also revisits the doxa of the Communist era, has, in turn, attracted criticism, notably from the medieval historian Doan Dani already mentioned, as being too culturalist and exclusionary (*Përpjekja*, 2012, 28–29, 89–141).

In 2016, another controversy erupted when a Turkish popular historian, Talha Uğurluel, during a visit to Albania, compared Skanderbeg to the "Kurdish terrorists of the PKK" to denounce his betrayal of the Ottoman Empire. There were two types of reaction. Albanian historians representing academic institutions intervened in the media to disqualify these remarks by rejecting their author from the academic sphere: his remarks did not correspond to scientific standards, and international historiography testified to the positive role played by Skanderbeg (https://sot.com.al/kultura/marenglen-verli-roli-i-sk%C3%ABnderbeut-i-njohur-dhe-nga-historiografia-bot%C3%ABrore-prononcimi-i). On the other hand, Olsi Jazexhi, who was trained in history and was already a protagonist of polemical debates in the media, took the opportunity to reiterate his condemnation of the figure of Skanderbeg, in extreme terms:

The fact that today's Albania, for better or for worse, regards Skanderbeg as a hero imposed by the Catholic imperialism of Austria and Italy in the past, and the fact that behind Skanderbeg today are lined up hundreds of nationalist thugs and Catholic fanatics, who defend him with religious devotion, cannot change the nature of Skanderbeg. Even if the Turkish historian should not have expressed himself so openly in front of the fake Skanderbeg memorial in Lezhë, I nonetheless remain of the opinion that the debate he has provoked is a healthy one for Albanian society, which is today confronted with the phenomenon of Wahhabi terrorism in Syria. In the same way that we condemn the religious terrorism of the Islamic State, we must review the historical accounts of Albania that support a horrible religious war waged by Skanderbeg. The religious war waged by Skanderbeg in the name of the Pope and Jesus Christ was ultimately a Catholic terrorist war and in no way secular or national. (https://olsijazexhi.wordpress.com/2016/07/07/skenderbeu-si-hero-terrorist-i-shqiptareve/)

Analyzing this same type of radical rejection of Skanderbeg among certain Muslim political activists in Kosovo, Fatos Lubonja (2014) again insisted on the need for Albanian society to discuss myths and reconsider its history to get rid of nationalist myths and find other myths that look not to the past but to the future. Be that as it may, the polemics caused by reintroducing the religious dimension show that, more than ever in the 30 years following the fall of the Communist regimes, there has been a blurring not only between past and present, but also between the historiographical, political, and media spaces.

CONTROVERSIES IN FORM, TIME, AND SPACE

Shapes

In the preceding pages, we have seen that the Skanderbeg controversies have taken a variety of forms in terms of tone, medium, and degree of publicity. From the most bitter polemic to silence, we discover, unsurprisingly, a range of ways of opposing and refuting other theses. In the case of the figure of Skanderbeg, however, it should be emphasized that the Communist era gave rise to ambiguous and paradoxical forms of critical re-appropriation: Aleks Buda constructed a new figure of Skanderbeg by promoting Fan Noli's approach, while criticizing him on numerous points, and international conferences were organized, welcoming foreign "friends" who more or less erased their disagreements and contributed to the historiographical and political influence of the figure of Skanderbeg.

The issue of publicity is a central one, even before the internet. From the second half of the nineteenth century onward, specialized journals and scientific works were the media chosen by the protagonists in the academic field (in Serbia, as in Europe at the end of the nineteenth century; in interwar Yugoslavia with the development of Albanology; in Albania from 1945 to 1990 following the institutionalization of the academic field, etc.). But controversies also often took place in the general media. This was the case in Greece in 1876–1877; it was the case in Albania in the 1930s, admittedly in the absence of an academic alternative; it was also the case in the Albania of Enver Hoxha, not only when Buda's lecture was reproduced in the Party organ in 1949 but also when the debates between historians on certain points moved to the journal of the Ministry of Education and Culture in the 1970s. This was also the case after 1990, when many debates took place not only in the general press, but also on television and the internet. It should be added that the question of the language of publication (i.e., a European or a Balkan language) also contributed to greater or lesser publicity.

The controversies analyzed also took different forms in terms of the themes addressed by the protagonists. Six broad themes can be distinguished: the question of sources; the relationship between myth and history and the heroic nature of the figure of Skanderbeg; his origin and belonging; the character of his struggle (individual or collective); his relationship with the powers of the time; and finally his unifying aims, or even his action toward the creation of a state. As we have seen, apart from the question of sources and myth, which has been around since the nineteenth century (albeit in different ways, but very often as a delegitimizing tool), each period has seen the emphasis placed on one or other of these themes depending on the general context, the positioning of the protagonists, and the socio-political function that the controversy may have had. Thus, while Skanderbeg's ethnicity was being debated in Greece in the 1870s against a backdrop of irredentism toward the Ottoman Empire and confrontation with Panslavism, the same was true in Serbia at the turn of the century in the context of the confrontation between critical and romantic historiography. Twenty years later in Albania, the issues of independence and union were given greater prominence to legitimize the founding of the new Albanian state. In the 1930s, the religious factor and the relationship with Italy gained importance in the debates, while after 1945, and even more after 1961, the social dimensions, independence, and the relationship with the Ottoman Empire were placed at the heart of the controversies as symbols of the Albanian people's ongoing struggle against their surrounding enemies. After 1990, the questions of ethnicity and religion made a powerful comeback.

Beyond these themes, through the figure of Skanderbeg, the question of the past relationship to Ottoman sovereignty is constantly debated, and with it the question of Ottoman sources and historiography, as well as that of the supposed civilizational and confessional frontier that this sovereignty would have shaped.

Time and Space

The preceding pages show, however, that the division into periods should not mask the existence of more specific moments, as we have seen (1876–1877, 1920, 1937, 1968, etc.), but also of continuities between periods. In fact, controversies were not always synchronic, but often diachronic. Predecessors were criticized, as was the case with Xhevat Korça's criticism of German-speaking historians at the very beginning of the twentieth century, or Aleks Buda's criticism of bourgeois and fascist historiography, or the more recent critical approaches to the historiography of the Communist era. On the other hand, certain actors such as Francisc Pall, Fan Noli, Kristo Frashëri, and Kasem Biçoku appeared in successive periods.

Some temporalities differ from purely political time, such as the processes of uncovering and collecting sources (e.g., with its first phase in the 1860s and 1870s as far as European and Byzantine sources are concerned, and the first phase of exploiting Ottoman archival sources in the 1950s) or the individual trajectories of key figures in the controversies.

Among the Albanian protagonists in particular, a notable dimension of these debates was their gradual inclusion in a genealogy of Albanian "Skanderbegian historiography", to use the term coined by Albanian historians. This could sometimes be accompanied by the vision of continuities between authors to which an opposition is built. For Frashëri, Schmitt would have followed in the footsteps of previous German historians (such as G. Stadtmüller and F. Babinger) who would have scorned the historiographies of small nations. Pëllumb Xhufi, an Albanian medievalist, drew a parallel between Schmitt and Edward Gibbon, the eighteenth-century English historian (Xhufi 2013). Processes of nationalization of historiographies are therefore at work beyond the processes of institutionalization. Controversies have regularly served to assert the need to form a national historiography or to reinforce its boundaries, especially in relation to European historiography, rather than in relation to the historiographies of neighboring Balkan countries, with which polemical interaction seems to have remained relatively limited in the case of Skanderbeg. We have seen that, concerning the most sensitive issue of ethnicity, the critical Greek and Serbian historiographies, already at the turn of the twentieth century, abandoned their claims on Skanderbeg, leaving it to marginal historiographical (and political) milieus. This is one of the reasons why there was no Albanian-Greek or Albanian-Serbian polemics, although it does not mean that the respective national narratives are convergent.

Also of note are the strong links between national and international historiographies since these debates started. In the early controversy, K. Papparigopoulos was as much a target as German-speaking historians. At the beginning of the twenty-first century, Frashëri attacked Oliver Schmitt as much as some of his Albanian compatriots. Moreover, the careers of the protagonists were almost always transnational: local historians often studied abroad and sometimes wrote in other languages. During the Communist era, the new historiography, although strongly constrained by political power, was nonetheless the result of complex circulations within the Eastern bloc, and also in the West. Buda had spent a large part of his early years in Italy and above all in Austria, where he had been trained; he decided to promote the work of Fan Noli, produced in the Albanian diaspora in the United States. And, as I have already stressed, at that time legitimization by a foreign presence during celebrations was central. In recent years, we are witnessing the emergence of a degree of globalization. For example, a Korean specialist, Jayoung Che, has published an article in a Greek scientific journal based on a partial review of Oliver Schmitt's book (Che 2017).

Finally, the developments studied in the preceding pages were not always located within academic institutions, which did not always exist (e.g., in the case of Albania between the wars). They also took place on their margins, and the media and public spaces were also arenas for them. We have also seen that the boundaries between these spaces have often been crossed and blurred. If politics and historiographies have always been strongly tied, the historiographical field was never totally linked to the political field, as the internal debates testify.

References

Aleks Buda. Një jetë për Albanologjjinë (Konferencë Skencore. 2012. Tirana: Akademia e Shkencave e Shqipërisë,

Antolović, Michael. 2016. Modern Serbian Historiography between Nation-Building and Critical Scholarship: The Case of Ilarion Ruvarac (1832–1905). *The Hungarian Historical Review* 5 (2): 332–356.

Babinger, Franz. 1931. Die Gründung von Elbasan. *Mitteilungen des Seminars für Orientalische Sprachen* XXXIV (2): 1–10.

Barletius, Marinus. 1508–1510. *De Vita Moribus Ac Rebus Praecipue Aduersus Turcas, Gestis, Georgii Castrioti, Clarissimi Epirotarum Principis.* Rome.

Biçoku, Kasem. 2005. Aleksandri i Madh në kujtesën historike të Skënderbeut e të shqiptarëve. *Studime Historike* 1 (2): 7–29.

Biemmi, Giammaria. 1742. *Istoria di Giorgio Castrioto detto Scander-Begh*. Brescia: Bossino.

Buda, Aleks. 1951. Fytyra e Skënderbeut në dritën e studimeve të reja. *Buletini i Institutit të Shkencave*, 1951/3–4: 139:164 (reproduction in Buda 1986, 161–191).

Buda, Aleks. 1986. *Shkrime historike, 1*. Tirana: Akademia e Shkencave.

Caro, J. 1896. Review of *Skanderbeg*, by Julius Pisko. *Historische Zeitschrift* 77 (3): 525–527.

Che, Jayoung. 2017. The Socio-political Meanings of the Conflict between the Muslims and the Christians around the Western Balkan in the 15th Century. Centering on the Heroic Kastrioti-Skanderbey of Albania. *Athens Journal of History* 3 (4): 297–320.

Clayer, Nathalie. 2007. *Aux origines du nationalisme albanais*. Paris: Karthala.

Clayer, Nathalie. 2012. Carl Patsch et le Musée national de Tirana (1922–1925). *Revue germanique internationale* 16:91–104.

Clayer, Nathalie. 2022. *Une histoire en travelling de l'Albanie (1920–1939)*. Paris: Karthala.

Coquelle, Pierre. 1896. Les deux Skanderbeg. Solution d'une question historique. *Revue de la Société des Études historiques* 3–4:137–183.

Curta, Florin. 2011. *The Edinburgh History of the Greeks, c. 500 to 1050*. Edinburgh: Edinburgh University Press.

Cutolo, Alessandro. 1940. *Scanderbeg*. Milano: Istituto per gli studi di politica internazionale.

Dani, Doan. 2014. Marxism and Nationalism in the Albanian Historiography School: The Position of the National Hero. *Mediterranean Journal of Social Sciences* 5 (6): 251–254.

Dani, Doan. 2016. *Shpikja e Mesjetës. Vetja dhe Tjetri në medievistikën shqiptare*. Tirana: Pika pa sipërfaqe.

Daskalov, Roumen. 2013. Bulgarian-Greek Dis/Entanglements. In *Entangled Histories of the Balkans*, ed. Roumen Daskalov and Tchavdar Marinov, vol. 1, 149–239. Leiden: Brill.

Dimitsas, Margaritis. 1877. *Kritikaí érevnai perí tis katagoyís kai ethnikótitos Yeoryíou Kastriótou tou Skendérmpei*. Athens: Villar.

Egro, Dritan. 2007. *Historia dhe ideologjia : një qasje kritike studimeve osmane në historiografinë moderne*. Tirana: Maluka.

Endresen, Cecilie. 2010. 'Do Not Look to Church and Mosque'? Albania's Post-Communist Clergy on Nation and Religion. In *Religion und Gesellschaft im albanischsprachigen Südosteuropa*, ed. Oliver Schmitt, 233–258. Frankfurt: Peter Lang.

Ermenji, Abas. 1968. *Vendi që zë Skënderbeu në historinë e shqipërisë.* Paris/Rome: Komiteti Kombëtar Demokrat 'Shqipnija ë Lirë'.

Faja, Xhoana. 2012. The Role of the Institute of Albanian Studies in Albanological Research. *Journal of Educational and Social Research* 2 (6): 173–178.

Feraj, Hysamedin. 1998. *Skicë e mendimit politik shqiptar.* Tirana: Koha.

Frashëri, Kristo. 2002. *Skënderbeu. Jeta dhe vepra.* Tirana: Toena.

Frashëri, Kristo. 2009. *Skënderbeu i shpërfytyruar.* Tirana: Dudaj.

Frashëri, Kristo. 2014. *Jeta e një historiani.* Tirana: Akademia e Shkencave.

Gegaj, Athanas. 1937. *L'Albanie et l'Invasion turque au XVe siècle.* Paris: Geuthner.

Georgeon, François. 2003. *Abdülhamid II. Le sultan calife.* Paris: Fayard.

Grandits, Hannes. 2021. *The End of Ottoman Rule in Bosnia. Conflicting Agencies and Imperial Appropriations.* London: Routledge.

Grivaud, Gilles, and Angel Nicolaou-Konnari. 2021. Aux origines de la 'frankokratia'. Genèse, péripéties idéologiques et apologie d'un néologisme de l'historiographie néo-hellénique (Seconde partie). *Frankokratia* 2:1–30.

Hahn, Johann Georg von. 1854. *Albanesische Studien,* 3 vols. Jena: Friedrich Mauke.

Hahn, Johann Georg von. 1867. *Reise durch die Gebiete des Drin und Wardar.* Wien: KKHS Druckerei.

Halimi, Redi. 2013. Il *dibattito* intellettuale e politico in Albania tra le due guerre mondiali: Mehdi Frashëri tra 'i vecchi' e 'i giovani'. *Halimi, Redi.* Venice : Phd University Ca'Foscari.

Hopf, Carl. 1868. Geschichte Griechenlands vom Beginn des Mittelalters bis auf unsere Zeit. In *Ersch-Grubers Encyklopädie,* vol. 85 et 86, Leipzig: Brockhaus.

Hopf, Charles. 1873. *Chroniques gréco-romanes inédites ou peu connues.* Berlin: Librairie de Weidmann.

Idrizi, Idrit. 2020. Between Subordination and Symbiosis: Historians' Relationship with Political Power in Communist Albania. *European History Quarterly* 50 (1): 66–87.

Jochalas, Titos. 1975. *O Georgios Kastriotes-Skentermpees eis ten neoelleniken istoriographian kai logotecnian.* Thessaloniki: Institute for Balkans Studies.

Jochalas, Titos. 2019. Gjergj Kastrioti—Scanderbeg in the Modern Greek Historiography and Literature. *Studia Albanica* 56 (1): 89–134.

Jorgaqi, Nasho. 2005. *Jeta e Fan S. Nolit.* 2 vol. Tirana: Ombra GVG.

Kamsi, Willy. 2008. *'Hylli i Dritës' 1913–1944. Bibliografi kronologjike.* Shkodër: Botime Françeskane.

Konferenca e dytë e studimeve albanologjike me rastin e 500-vjetorit të vdekjes së Gjergj Kastriotit-Skënderbeut: Tiranë, 12–18 Janar 1968, vol. 1, 1969. Tirana: Universiteti shtetëror, Instituti i historisë dhe i gjuhësisë.

Kortsha, Djevat. 1923. *Tri pyetje nga jeta e Skender Beut.* Tirana: Nikaj.

Krasniqi, Elife. 2020. Kosovar Albanian Historiography Reflects a Long History of Oppression... In *Memory Landscapes in (Post)Yugoslavia,* ed. Milica Popović. Sciences Po CERI and University of Ljubljana and Natalija Majsova, University of Ljubljana. http://www.istorex.org/post/elife-krasniqi-kosovar-albanian-historiography-reflects-a-long-history-of-oppression-1

Lapteva, Ljudmila. 1982. Vikentij Makušev und Karl Hopf. Ein Beitrag zu den russisch-deutschen Wissenschaftsbeziehungen im 19. Jahrhundert. *Jahrbuch für Geschichte der sozialistischen Länder Eiropas* 25 (2): 107–122.

Lazarević, Persida. 2018. Jovan Sterija Popović and George Castriot Skanderbeg. *Studia Albanica* 50 (2): 109–120.

Lemieux, Cyril. 2007. À quoi sert l'analyse des controverses? *Mil neuf cent. Revue d'histoire intellectuelle* 25:191–212.

Lubonja, Fatos. 2012. Bëhu i ditur të jesh i lirë (Mbi debatin për Skënderbeun). *Përpjekja* 28–29:24–48.

Lubonja, Fatos. 2014. Myslimanët, historia dhe miti i Skënderbeut. Panorama, 20/3/2014. http://www.panorama.com.al/myslimanet-historia-dhe-miti-i-skenderbeut/.

Mandić, Marija, and Ana Sivački. 2015. Jezik i etno-politički sukob: Slučaj albanskog u savremenom Beogradu. In *Figura neprijatelja: preosmišljavanje srpsko-albanskih odnosa*, ed. Aleksandar Pavlović, Adriana Zaharijević, Gazela Pudar Draško, and Rigels Halili, 261–280. Belgrade: KPZ Beton/ Institut za filozofiju i društvenu teoriju.

Märtl, Claudia, and Peter Schreiner, eds. 2013. *Jakob Philipp Fallmerayer (1790–1861). Der Gelehrte und seine Aktualität im 21. Jahrhundert*. Munich: Verlag der Bayerischen Akademie der Wissenschaften.

Milosavljević, Olivera. 2002. U tradiciji nacionalizma ili stereotipi srpskih intelektualaca XX veka o 'nama' i 'drugima'. *Ogledi* no. 1, The Helsinki Committee for Human Rights in Serbia.

Monti, Gennaro Maria. 1939. La spedizione in Puglia di Giorgio Castriota Scanderberg. *Japigia* Ser. NS, vol. 10, 275–320.

Ndoja, Leka. 2013. Albanian Literary Circles in Italy. *Global Challenge. International Journal of Linguistics, Literature and Translation* 1/2.

Noli, Fan S. 1921. *Historia e Skenderbeut (Gjerq Kastriotit) Mbretit i Shqiperise 1412–1468*. Boston: Dielli.

Noli, Fan Stylian. 1947. *George Castrioti Scanderbeg: 1405–1468*. New York: International University Press.

Ohly, Kurt. 1933. Eine gefälschte Ratdoltinkunable. *Gutenberg Jahrbuch* 8:53–61.

Paganel, Camille. 1855. *Histoire de Scanderbeg ou Turks et Chrétiens au XVe siècle*. Paris: Didier.

Pall, François. 1937. Une nouvelle histoire de Scanderbeg (Remarques sur le livre de M. Gegaj). *Revue Historique du Sud-Est Européen* 114 (12): 293–306.

Pall, Francesco. 1938. Marino Barlezzio. Uno storico umanista. *Mélanges d'histoire générale* 2, ed. C. Marinescu, 135–318.

Pall, Francisc. 1942. Die Geschichte Skanderbegs im Lichte der neueren Forschung. *Leipziger Vierteljahrschrift...* 6:85–98.

Paparrigopoulos, Konstantinos. 1874. *Istoria tou Ellinikou Ethnous*. Vol. 5. Athens: Passari.

Pasqua, Belli, and Roberta. 2019. Il monumento equestre di Giorgio Castriota Scanderbeg a Roma. In *La simbolicità di Scanderbeg ponte tra l'Albania e l'Europa cristiana*, ed. Rovena Sakja and Franco Tagliarini, 219–246. Roma: IL Vetro.

Pastor, Ludwig. 1886. *Geschichte der Päpste seit dem Ausgang des Mittelasters*. Freiburg im Bresgau: Herder.

Peckham, Robert Shannan. 2000. Map Mania: Nationalism and the Politics of Place in Greece, 1870–1922. *Political Geography* 19 (1): 77–95.

Pisani, Paul. 1891. 'La Légende de Skanderbeg.' *Compte-rendu du Congrès International des Catholiques tenu à Paris du 1er au 6 1891*, 5–14. Paris: Alphonse Picard.

Pisko, Julius. 1894. *Skanderbeg: Historische Studie*. Vienna: W. Frick.

Plasari, Aurel. 2018. *Skënderbeu. Një histori politike*. Tirana: IDK.

Prantis, Efthimios. 1880. *Alvanika parapona*. Athens: Mellontos.

Proikakis, Panagiotis. 2000. *Critical Edition of the 'Chronicle of Argyrokastro'*. University of Birmingham, Master Thesis.

Puchner, Walter. 2015. *Die Literaturen Südost-Europas 15. bis frühes 20. Jahrhundert*. Vienna: Böhlau.

Puto, Artan. 2012. Nga Skënderbeu mitik në atë historik. *Përpjekja* 28–29:18–23.

Qiriazi, Dhori. 2020. Një shtatore e Gjergj Kastriotit në Athinë … (Autori, parateksti, teksti dhe konteksti i një dokumenti-polemikë me historianin grek K. Paparigópulos, për origjinën etnike të Skënderbeut). http://ikee.lib.auth. gr/record/312188/files/this%20Kyriazis-Qirjazi%20Ligjerata%20per%20 Skenderbeun%20REVISED%20FINAL%20VERSION%20A%20Jan.%20 2020.pdf.

Radojčić, Nikola, ed. 1934. *Zbornik Ilariona Ruvarca*. Belgrade: Srpska Kraljevska Akademija.

Radonić, Jovan. 1905. *Zapadna Evropa i Balkanski narodi prema Turcima u prvoj polovini XV. veka*. Novi Sad: Izdanje Matice Srpske.

Radonić, Jovan. 1942. *Djuradj Kastriot Skenderbeg i Arbanija u XV veku (istoriska gradja)*. Belgrade: Srpska Kraljevska Akademija.

Ragaru, Nadège. 2008. The Political Uses and Social Lives of "National Heroes": Controversies over Skanderbeg's Statue in Skopje. *Southeast Europe. Journal of Politics and Society* 2008 (4): 528–555.

Ruvarac, Ilarion. 1901. Poreklo Sibinjanin Janka. *Kolo 1*. Reprinted in Radojcić, ed. 1934. *Zbornik ilariona Ruvarca:* 510-523.

Ruvarac, Ilarion. 1902. Djuradj Vuković, despot srprski i Djordje Kastriot-Skenderbeg, vodj arbanaški, godine 1444. *Letopis Matice Srpske* 212:1–13.

Schmaus, Alois. 1966. Der Skender-beg-Zyklus bei Andrija Kačić-Miošić. *Shéjzat* 1966 (9–12): 320–335.

3 SKANDERBEG: FIGURES OF PAPER, FIGURES OF STONE 159

Schmaus, Alois. 1969. Skanderbeg in der serbischen Literatur. In *Studia Albanica Monacensia*, ed. Alois Schmauss, 146–175. Trofenik: Munich.

Schmidt-Neke, Michael. 2010. Skanderbegs Gefangene: Zur Debatte um den albanischen Nationalhelden. *Südosteuropa* 58 (2): 273–302.

Schmitt, Oliver Jens. 2005. Genosse Aleks und seine Partei oder: Zu Politik und Geschichtswissenschaft im kommunistischen Albanien (1945–1991). In *Beruf und Berufung. Geschichtswissenschaft und Nationsbildung in Ostmittel- und Südosteuropa im 19. und 20. Jahrhundert*, ed. M. Krzoska and H.-Ch. Maner, 143–166. Münster: Lit.

Schmitt, Oliver Jens. 2008. *Skënderbeu*. Tirana: K&B.

Schmitt, Oliver Jens. 2009. *Skanderbeg. Der neue Alexander auf dem Balkan*. Regensburg: Friedrich Pustet Verlag.

Schmitt, Oliver Jens. 2015. Skanderbeg. In *Dictionnaire de l'Empire ottoman*, ed. François Georgeon, Nicolas Vatin, and Gilles Veinstein, 1079–1080. Paris: Fayard.

Sigalas, Nikos. 2000. Hellénistes, hellénisme et idéologie nationale. De la formation du concept d' "hellénisme" en grec moderne. In *L'Antiquité grecque au XIXe siècle. Un exemplum contesté?* ed. Chryssanthi Avlami, 239–291. Paris: L'Harmattan.

Skëndërbeu dhe Evropa: përmbledhje kumtesash. 2006. Tirana: Akademia e shkencave.

Sulstarova, Enis. 2006. *Arratisje nga lindja*. Tirana: Dudaj.

Suma, Mircea. 2003. Particularităţi ale discursului istoric la Francisc Pall. *Annale Universitatis Apulensis* VII:377–383.

Vlachos, George L. 2021. To Make a Land Hellenic: Toward a National(ist) Landscape in Southern Macedonia, 1896–1932. *National Identities*. https://doi.org/10.1080/14608944.2021.1872516.

Vulić, Nikola. 1892. *Djuradj Kastriotić Skenderbeg, istorijska rasprava*. Belgrade: Parna štamparija Narodne radikalne stranke.

Xhufi, Pëllumb. 2013. Skanderbeg et Alphonse V de Naples: Vassalité ou alliance? *Studia albanica* 2013 (1–2): 3–20.

Zanou, Konstantina. 2018. *Transnational Patriotism in the Mediterranean, 1800–1850: Stammering the Nation*. Oxford: Oxford University Press.

Zhugra, A. B. 2014. Iz istorii albanovedeniya v Rossii. *Acta Linguistica Petropolitana* X (1): 565–587.

CHAPTER 4

Art Wars: The Creation of Bulgarian Art History and the Balkan Controversies Over the Medieval Heritage of Macedonia

Tchavdar Marinov

The present chapter tackles identity discourses and national(ist) interests embedded in the emergence and development of medieval art history in the Balkans. Its ambition is to disentangle the historical formation of a particular ideological construct named "Old Bulgarian art" (*starobălgarsko izkustvo*) against the background of Balkan polemics regarding the medieval cultural heritage of the geographical region of Macedonia. Thus, the main intention of this text is to present critically the construction of "national" medieval pasts as well as the development of related ideological conflicts—in particular, to show how political disputes over Macedonia shaped mainstream theses and arguments in Bulgarian and, in general, in Balkan art history. The chapter's main focus is on academic works

---

In memory of Ada Hajdu

T. Marinov (✉)
Institute of Philosophy and Sociology, Bulgarian Academy of Sciences,
Sofia, Bulgaria

© The Author(s), under exclusive license to Springer Nature
Switzerland AG 2025
D. Mishkova, R. Daskalov (eds.), *Balkan Historiographical Wars*,
https://doi.org/10.1007/978-3-031-90113-3_4

161

produced during the first half of the twentieth century. Hence, it examines mostly, but not exclusively, the formative period of canonical interpretations that are still, to a large extent, commonly accepted in academia and sometimes within the broader public.

While it dwells mainly on the interpretation of architectural heritage, the present study likewise sheds light on heated arguments about mural painting, applied arts, and epigraphic monuments dating back to the pre-Ottoman Byzantine era and partly to the Ottoman period. At the same time, the chapter intends to go beyond the analysis of ideological arguments and to present the direct involvement of Balkan (art) historians and archaeologists in state politics, particularly during wartime periods when "history wars" turned into real military conflicts. By tackling this involvement, the chapter reveals the ways in which scholarly expertise has been mobilized precisely to justify military occupations and to substantiate post-war territorial claims.

Expectedly, the main protagonists of the studied debates are Bulgarian, Serbian, Greek, and other Balkan (art) historians and archaeologists. With the fashion of medievalism in the nineteenth century, European countries "manufactured" narrowly national cults to medieval past and canons of medieval historical monuments (Geary and Klaniczay 2013). Yet, in reality, heritage has been from the outset an eminently transnational field of academic expertise: conservation and restoration of monuments was a topic of European debate opposing figures such as Viollet-le-Duc and Ruskin, and it became a matter of increasingly internationalized notions, standards, and institutions in the twentieth century.[1] The first Balkan medievalists often received their academic training in major centers of art history and of Byzantine Studies such as Munich, Paris, or Vienna, and sometimes collaborated for a long period of time with their Western and Central European mentors.[2]

Moreover, since the second half of the nineteenth century, the ancient and medieval monuments of the Balkans (to the north of Classical Greece)

---

[1] On the notions of "heritage" and "legacy," see Diana Mishkova's contribution to the present volume.

[2] On the case of Josef Strzygowski, leading figure of Vienna School of Art History, and his contacts with Serbian and Bulgarian scholars: see Makuljević (2013) and Gargova (2017), respectively.

have been studied first by foreign travelers,[3] then by representatives of Western European academic institutions (such as the French and other foreign archaeological schools at Athens) acting as "soft power" agents in Southeast European academic and cultural contexts. Extremely important was also the activity of the Russian Archaeological Institute of Constantinople (established in 1895). Its mission was to compete with Western scholarship on ground where Russia seemed to be culturally better prepared: the history of Orthodox Christianity, and in particular of Balkan Slavs, to whom Russia presented itself as a "role model" in science (Mishkova 2023, 82).

Therefore, in the case of the Balkan art histories, it would be inevitable to discuss the formative role played by non-Balkan experts: archaeologists and (art) historians, in particular proponents of Byzantine Studies—another transnational field of research that has been nevertheless marked by scholarly nationalism (Maufroy 2010). As we shall see throughout this chapter, "foreign" specialists to a large extent structured Balkan national canons and notions of medieval heritage, and they proved to be no less militant actors of Balkan "history wars." Thus, they made these look less akin to a *querelle de clocher*—although, in some cases, the Balkan quarrels were literally *de clocher* as they concerned, in particular, the origin of medieval church towers.

Firstly, a few words on heritage and the construction of medievalism in the Balkans are necessary. As elsewhere, concerns about heritage in the Balkans have been for a long time focused on "antiquities" (*archaiotites* in Greek; *starine/-i* in the Balkan Slavic languages) and "monuments" (variably named "historical," "cultural," etc.)—that is on immovable or movable objects classified in this way because of their outstanding or exceptional historical and aesthetic value. The assignment of these categories to objects from the past developed into an expansive process of construction of heritage which was parallel to the nation-building itself. At its onset, was the adoption of the first legislative acts defining "antiquities" as public goods and prerogatives of the state authorities—something which was done relatively early in some Balkan countries (1834 in Greece, ten years later in Serbia). Medieval heritage was progressively assigned national importance through the nineteenth and the beginning of the twentieth century.

---

[3] Here, the name of the Austro-Hungarian Felix Kanitz cannot be missed—with his descriptions of Bulgaria's antiquities and his work on what he termed "Byzantine monuments of Serbia" (Kanitz 1862).

In Greece, the establishment of the Christian Archaeological Society in 1884 marked a movement away from the initial exclusive emphasis on the preservation of monuments of Classical Antiquity (Chlepa 2022, 68–71). In 1910, the first Ephor (curator) of "Byzantine antiquities" was appointed and, four years later, the creation of the Byzantine and Christian Museum in the Greek capital crowned the efforts of the Christian Archaeological Society to dignify "medieval Hellenism." This concept and the one of "Helleno-Christian civilization" were introduced decades earlier in the Greek historical narrative by the national historian Constantine Paparrigopoulos and by his colleague in the field of history and philology Spyridon Zambelios. Their activity was decisive in the process of canonizing Byzantium as a continuation of ancient Hellenism, but also as a prefiguration of the modern Greek nation and an inspiring source of an imperial project—the famous *Megali Idea* (Kitromilides 1998; Mishkova 2023, 45–54). Formulated in the aftermath of the Balkan Wars in 1913, the project of a "Byzantine Museum" in Salonika/Thessaloniki materialized only eight decades later, thus definitively confirming the identity of the place not only as the "capital" of geographical Macedonia but also as Greece's "Byzantine city" *par excellence.*

In the cases of Serbia and Bulgaria, the "nationalization" of Antiquity and the Classical tradition was much more difficult than in Greece or Romania, although by no means impossible.[4] Artifacts from Antiquity were (and are) exposed in the key institutions endowed with the mission to articulate the idea of national heritage and to address domestic and foreign audiences: the National Museum in Belgrade (founded in 1844) and the one in Sofia (1892). Yet, both Serbian and Bulgarian historical canons were clearly dominated by the narrative of the medieval era focused on the history of states, rulers, Orthodox Christian saints, and enlighteners identified as "Serbian" or "Bulgarian" either in the historical records, or retroactively.

Meanwhile, the academic study of medieval cultural heritage, of architecture and art in particular, followed uneven dynamics in the Balkan countries. In Serbia, it clearly started in the nineteenth century with Mihailo Valtrović and Dragutin Milutinović, the founding fathers of art history in the country. The latter headed a chair of "History of Architecture and Byzantine Style" at the Technical Faculty of Belgrade as early as 1897

---

[4] On the cases of Bulgaria and other Southeast European countries, see Klaniczay et al. (2011).

(Ignjatović 2016, 158). The first chair of Byzantine art and archaeology at the University of Athens opened no earlier than 1911 (Chlepa 2022, 64). Although courses in art history were taught at the National Academy of Arts in Sofia (created as the State School of Painting in 1896), a distinct academic major of Theory and History of Art was established only in 1970.[5] In addition, students of architecture have been trained in Sofia's State Polytechnic School only since 1943. Bulgarian museography of medieval art and culture also remained relatively weak: while a church-historical collection was officially designated as a museum in 1923, a specialized Museum of Christian Art opened in Sofia in 1965 in order to display indiscriminately icons of different provenance and historical periods.

In fact, at least from an academic point of view, the construction of medieval heritage in the Balkans largely depended on a specific ideological cluster. Against the background of the transnational development of Byzantine Studies, it depended on the dominant interpretation of Byzantium and its legacy and on the capacity of national canon-builders to symbolically "assimilate" and compete with it. While, in the Greek national narrative, Byzantium was progressively celebrated as the "medieval Hellenic" empire, the Byzantine legacy was both rejected and appropriated in various ways in other Balkan ideological contexts. The Serbian case seems to be the least antagonistic with its dominant "Serbo-Byzantine discourse" (Ignjatović 2016, 110–22) whereby medieval Serbia was deemed both an alter ego and a legitimate successor and rejuvenator of the Byzantine imperial dignity. As Aleksandar Ignjatović argues, Serbian academic attitudes toward Byzantium varied from a complete identification of "Serbian" and "Byzantine" to the mainstream thesis of the cultural superiority of Serbia over Byzantium, the rejection of the Byzantine imprint on medieval Serbian culture being quite rare. Serbia was imagined as a symbolic daughter of Byzantium but one that exceeded its parent in political vigor and cultural creativity (Ignjatović 2016, 603–745).

From this point of view, the Bulgarian case seems to be more straightforward: with its clear anti-Greek overtones, the Bulgarian national narrative emphasized the political antagonism between the Byzantine and the medieval Bulgarian states and remained for a long period of time clearly hostile to what was seen as harmful Byzantine influence. Only since the 1970s, a parallel trend in Bulgarian historiography, inspired by the

---

[5] For an overview of Bulgarian art history from its origins to nowadays: see Bakalova (2012).

medievalist Ivan Duychev, has tended to rehabilitate the Byzantine cultural impact on medieval Bulgaria and to appropriate it in terms of a "Slavo-Byzantine synthesis" (Daskalov 2021, 162–4; Mishkova 2023, 219–63). As will be demonstrated, the ideological rejection of Byzantium entailed a "de-Byzantinization" of medieval art in Bulgaria (less so in Serbia) and the invention of specific medieval "national schools" and "styles." In this way, the medieval past was ultimately "nationalized" in the field of material heritage as well. Yet, this process was far from obvious as a closer look at the Bulgarian case confirms.

What Does Bulgarian Heritage Mean?

The construction of medievalism in the Balkans was by no means a purely academic or intellectual occupation: as elsewhere in Europe, it had also clear political tasks and entailed the adoption of certain politics of heritage. Thus, the destiny of "antiquities" in the Balkans was largely decided at the intersection of different ranges of cultural and political phenomena—of national narratives and transnational academic interest, of raising heritage awareness and the evolution of practices of heritage protection,[6] of archaeological expertise and construction of art historical canon. In this conjuncture, Ottoman heritage was most often associated with foreign oppressive rule and oriental backwardness, and it was massively destroyed in the Balkan countries with an Orthodox Christian majority (Lory 2015). Yet, Byzantine/Christian medieval heritage did not remain intact either. A notorious case is nineteenth century Athens: in an effort to restore the Greek capital to its Classical Hellenic splendor, the city authorities pulled down dozens of churches and other monuments from the Byzantine and "post-Byzantine" eras.[7] Similar was the case of Sofia—since 1879, the

[6] Regarding the evolution of these practices, a characteristic episode is the activity of the French architect André Lecomte du Nouÿ (disciple of Viollet-le-Duc) who was invited in the 1880s by Romanian King Carol I to restore a series of medieval Wallachian and Moldavian churches and monasteries. The French expert not only significantly altered the architecture of these monuments, but in some cases demolished and rebuilt them from scratch, with the aim of restoring what he believed to be their "original" Byzantine appearance (Minea 2022, 51–52).

[7] See Chlepa (2022, 40) and Samara (2016, 549–550). "Post-Byzantine" is to date the official Greek term denoting periods of Ottoman or Venetian domination. Its ideological mission is clear: it both avoids mentioning undesired foreign rule and tacitly pretends that its heritage is a mere continuation of the Byzantine one.

capital of the newly proclaimed Bulgarian Principality—where the de-Ottomanization of the urban fabric and the mass destruction of buildings did not spare several medieval churches (Todorov 2001). Later exalted as great masterpieces of Bulgarian medieval painting, the thirteenth-century murals in Sofia's Boyana Church (nowadays, a UNESCO World Heritage Site) were still endangered in 1912, as the church was scheduled for demolition.

While the first law on antiquities in post-Ottoman Bulgaria was passed in 1889, one had to wait until 1911 and a second law for a clearer definition of immovable and movable heritage. The first "tangible activities" aiming to protect cultural monuments were launched only in 1927 (Denchev and Vasileva 2010, 216). It was already too late for some of these: the most important medieval paintings that had survived in the city of Tărnovo—those of the Church of Saints Peter and Paul (thirteenth–sixteenth centuries)—were largely destroyed as the temple collapsed in 1913 in an earthquake. It must be noted, that between 1187 and 1393, Tărnovo was the capital of the Second Bulgarian medieval state and—as it was also perceived as the last one before the Ottoman conquest—the city had a foremost symbolic value in the modern Bulgarian context. The fate of historical sites in Bulgaria lacking this reputation was even worse: pre-Ottoman material heritage that had survived there under/despite Ottoman rule was often destroyed as a result of neglect or sheer vandalism (Kiel 1985, 49–50).

This was the case of the mostly Greek town of Meleniko/Melnik in the Pirin region which was annexed by Bulgaria as a result of the Balkan Wars. By the end of the Ottoman period in Macedonia, the French archaeologist Paul Perdrizet attested the existence of dozens of churches that were still in use in the town (Perdrizet 1907). These included a number of Byzantine temples as well as the thirteenth-century monasteries of Saint Charalambos and the one of the Mother of God by the Cave (Panagia Spiliotissa). Many of these monuments, including the two monasteries, were reduced to ruins after the "liberation" of the town by Bulgaria: as Meleniko's Greek population left in 1913, they were abandoned and used as building material by the local and the refugee Bulgarian population that was installed there (Marinov 2015). As this case suggests, one has to take into account the political upheavals in the Balkans while analyzing the fate of heritage—in particular wartime periods that tended to focus the public attention on "undesired" sites and monuments. In this respect, a characteristic case is the fourteenth-century church of Spasovitsa near the city of Kyustendil in southwest Bulgaria. As the building was commissioned by the Serbian King Stefan Uroš III Dečanski to mark his victory over Bulgarian Tsar Mihail III Shishman in the Battle of Velbăzhd (1330), it was dynamited by a Bulgarian military unit in 1913 (Kiel 1985, 28–29).

This destruction of traces of the past certainly reduced Bulgarian medieval immovable heritage, which seemed in any case relatively poor to foreign observers (Kiel 1985, 216) and even to some of its first Bulgarian researchers.[8] Despite the existence of (ruins of) a number of monumental buildings from the early Christian and medieval era, Bulgaria was not famous for clusters of still-standing churches, monasteries, and other structures like those of Raška or Morava in Serbia, of Athens and Attica or Mystras and Meteora in Greece. With its numerous medieval monuments in the cities of Salonika, Ohrid, Prilep, Kastoria, or Veroia, around Skopje and Kumanovo, in the areas of the Prespa lakes, etc.—not to mention Mount Athos—geographical Macedonia was in clear contrast to Bulgaria. What is more, as the aforementioned examples demonstrate, some antiquities from the medieval period in Bulgaria were initially regarded as traces of foreign presence. This was also the case of the important cluster of Byzantine monuments in Mesimvria (nowadays, Nesebăr), a city on the Bulgarian Black Sea coast, which retained its Greek ethnic character until the interwar period. In the first outline of Bulgarian architectural heritage, published by the architect Yanaki Shamardzhiev in 1904, "Messemvria" was presented as a Byzantine fortress destined to protect the empire against the Bulgars. Its churches were characterized as *perles d'architecture bysantine* (sic) (Chamardjieff 1904, 5, 7).

Against this background, it would be hardly surprising to find skeptical declarations of leading Bulgarian intellectuals regarding the importance and cultural value of architectural heritage in the country. In 1895, Konstantin Velichkov, writer and Minister of Public Instruction, stated bluntly: "Our ancestors from the former Bulgarian tsardoms left us no artistic creations, no monuments … only some pitiful, poor walls of churches and monasteries, small reminders of a great cultural past, without any artistic value" (Denchev and Vasileva 2010, 115). Decades later, the architect and writer Chavdar Mutafov declared that there was no "great architecture" in Bulgaria's past: in medieval Bulgarian architecture

---

[8] "[I]n general, it must be noted that there are much fewer preserved art monuments in Bulgaria than in other Balkan countries, like for instance in Macedonia or Serbia" (Filov 1930b, 58).

he detected "mighty domination" and faithful copying of Byzantine models, which were later replaced by Ottoman ones (Mutafov 1927). Apart from the general lack of valorization of medieval heritage in Bulgaria, such statements betray also a particular kind of distrust, namely, in the national originality of this heritage.

Similar to Serbia and Romania (Minea 2022), during the first decades of the existence of the modern Bulgarian state, it was not exceptional to identify the "Byzantine style" as the idiom of medieval architectural heritage in the country and also as the right formal expression of modern projects pretending to represent "national architecture" (Hajdu 2017, 430–5). Against the background of the negative evaluation of Byzantium in the Bulgarian historiography and national narrative, the perception of Bulgarian medieval heritage as "Byzantine" was even more problematic than the corresponding trend in Serbia.[9] But not only Bulgarian heritage was conceptually hazy. It must be remembered to what extent, in the late nineteenth and the first decades of the twentieth century, research on Byzantine art and cultural heritage was also still a history in the making with its difficult emancipation from both Classical Studies and the fashion of orientalism (Angelov 2003). As we shall see, the evolution of this field of research was one of the contexts that made possible the construction of the theory of a particular Bulgarian medieval art/architecture within or outside the realm of Byzantine art. The other one was certainly the development of medieval archaeology in Bulgaria with its important discoveries made at the turn of the twentieth century.

In 1899–1900, the Czech scholar Karel Škorpil, founding father of Bulgarian archaeology (although lacking university training in this field), excavated the first Bulgarian medieval capital Pliska. Škorpil had correctly identified its site near the ethnic Turkish village of Aboba in Northeast Bulgaria.[10] Funded by the Russian Archaeological Institute of Constantinople and co-directed by its president Fyodor Uspensky, the discovery of Pliska changed substantially the scholarly perception of the First

---

[9] In the interwar period, this perception reoriented Bulgarian architects to a somewhat paradoxical appropriation and "nationalization" of heritage from the Ottoman period (Marinov 2017, 554).

[10] On Karel and his brother Hermenegild Škorpil, their relative Konstantin Jireček (one of the founders of modern Bulgarian historiography with a major contribution to the Serbian one) as well as the other Czech scholars and intellectuals who shaped to a great extent Bulgarian culture by the end of nineteenth and the beginning of twentieth centuries, see Curta (2013).

Bulgarian state (founded in the late seventh century). Among the most spectacular discoveries made in Pliska, as well as in Preslav and other centers of this state, were the foundations of monumental palaces and temples (the most grandiose one being the "Great Basilica" of Pliska), original buildings with intriguing plans (e.g., the "Round Church" of Preslav), fine polychrome ceramics, surprising water supply systems, and heated baths.

From the outset, the unearthed "Pliska-Preslav culture" provoked debates related to its origin—in particular, regarding aspects that were quite untypical for contemporary Byzantine architecture like the impressive manner of building using huge accurately cut limestone blocks (*quadrae*). Up to the present time, opinions have varied from the thesis that the pagan Bulgars who erected those structures brought Oriental architectural traditions to the idea that they actually used building material from ancient Roman constructions.[11] While these controversies remained mostly confined to the study of medieval Bulgarian history and heritage, they did have an ideological "spill-over" in at least one neighboring country. This was Romania, where sites with similar archaeological material were excavated but were conceptualized instead as "Dridu culture"— whose allegedly (Proto-)Romanian character was suggested (Madgearu 2007). More importantly, the discoveries in Pliska, Preslav, and the adjacent areas conferred legitimacy to the Bulgarian historical narrative claiming the imperial grandeur of the First Bulgarian state, particularly under Tsar Simeon in the late ninth and early tenth century when Bulgaria had its largest territorial expansion, while its culture experienced a "Golden Age" (Daskalov 2021, 249–54, 266–9).

A key part of its supposedly vast territory and illustrious culture was Macedonia, in particular Ohrid, where the Bulgarian rulers had sent the disciples of Cyril and Methodius after their arrival in Pliska following the debacle of their mission in Great Moravia.[12] By the 970s, after the Russian and Byzantine conquests of Preslav, the Bulgarian splendor largely darkened, while the centers of medieval Bulgaria allegedly moved southwestwards toward Ohrid and Prespa in Macedonia, where the ruler Samuel

---

[11] Although the interpretation of the site near Aboba as Pliska was questioned, this identification is nowadays largely accepted—despite some disagreements about the dating of the site (Henning 2007).

[12] On the national sacralization of Cyril, Methodius, and their disciples in Bulgarian and South Slavic context, see Daskalov (2021, 197–203, 257–61) and Rohdewald (2022, 36–66, 246–401, 597–737).

(who reigned between 997 and 1014) continued the heroic struggle against the Byzantine invasion.[13] Thus, in the Bulgarian national imagination, Macedonia had acquired the halo of a sacred hearth of the "Old Bulgarian" culture, being also the last bastion of the Bulgarian struggle for independence.

Against this narrative, Bulgarian medieval archaeology and art history had to face significant problems on the level of both geographical coverage and historical continuity of medieval Bulgarian heritage. First, the material culture of Pliska-Preslav was rather restricted to the Lower Danube region—in particular, to Northeast Bulgaria—hence far from Macedonia. Second, after nearly two centuries of Byzantine domination, even the resurrected Bulgarian state around Tărnovo demonstrated quite different patterns of architecture—in general it was far from the monumentality characterizing the period of the first state.[14] These and other circumstances questioned the idea of an original "national" art covering all "Bulgarian territories" and possessing essentially the same identity through the centuries of Bulgaria's medieval existence. As far as the material heritage of Macedonia is concerned, there were also other and mighty pretenders.

The Macedonian Question in Art History

Dating back to (pre-)Greek and Roman Antiquity, the rich cultural heritage of Macedonia was first studied and, in some cases, appropriated by travelers and scholars coming from Western Europe but also from the Russian Empire, the latter being particularly interested in Byzantine and Balkan Slavic antiquities. Characteristic cases include the Russian/Ukrainian philologist Viktor Grigorovich who, during his tour of Bulgaria and Macedonia (including Mount Athos) in the 1840s, collected and brought to Russia dozens of old manuscripts, or the antiquary Pyotr Sevast'yanov who somewhat later exported from Mount Athos in the same direction hundreds of original icons and other artifacts as well as

---

[13] On the controversies surrounding Tsar Samuel who is claimed by both Bulgarian and Macedonian historical narratives, see Roumen Daskalov's contribution to the present volume. Featured in different national claims, Samuel's capital Ohrid is a nice example of "history wars" and controversies also focused on the famous Monastery of Saint Naum in the city's vicinity (Lory and Nathanaili 2002; Todorov 2021).

[14] As noticed by some of the leading Bulgarian specialists, for example, Krăstyu Miyatev: see Kiel (1985, 213).

Greek and Slavic manuscripts (Pyatnitsky 2011). By the end of the nineteenth century, the Russian Archaeological Institute of Constantinople navigated between demanding tasks: maintaining friendly cooperation with Ottoman authorities and with the Constantinople Patriarchate, while pursuing a research activity ideologically underpinned by the idea of Russia as heir of the Byzantine imperial legacy and protector of Balkan Orthodox Christians (Üre 2014). It was the co-founder of the institute—Nikodim Kondakov—who elaborated the first canonical description and analysis of Byzantine and medieval Slavic monuments of Macedonia during his "archaeological journey" in the region (Kondakov 1909).

Regarding the local Christian population, the Russian "protective" mission was certainly difficult given the background of the current conflicts opposing different national agendas in the Balkans. It coincided with the tense period of the "Macedonian question": the last decades of Ottoman rule in the western Balkan territories saw the ultimate formation of Greek, Serbian, and Bulgarian irredentist agendas, whereby the geographical region of Macedonia turned out to be the "apple of discord" coveted by the three Balkan states. Athens, Sofia, and Belgrade justified their territorial claims in front of foreign and domestic audiences with ethno-linguistic, ethnographical, and historical data. Historical monuments were also mobilized as political weapons (Kiel 1985, 26–32). In different ways, Russian scholars took sides in these controversies. The historical and archaeological studies produced by them were often combined with "ethnographical" descriptions supporting certain national causes—in some cases, consciously—as demonstrated by Pavel Milyukov,[15] collaborator with the institute in Constantinople, and partisan of the Bulgarian cause. Kondakov (who moved to Sofia for a couple of years after the October Revolution) is even nowadays referred to in Bulgarian nationalist publications regarding Macedonia. Yet, Kondakov seems to be more useful to the Bulgarian cause with his data on the population of late Ottoman Macedonia than with his descriptions of the region's medieval monuments. In fact, the Russian scholar had discovered much more Serbian medieval heritage in Macedonia: while he acknowledged Bulgarian political primacy in the medieval Balkans, he considered that old Serbian art was "after Russian art, the most important branch of Byzantine art" (Kondakov 1909, 290).

---

[15] See his much-quoted description of "Christian antiquities" of Western Macedonia (Milyukov 1899).

As suggested by this case, the inclusion of Macedonia in Bulgaria's canon of cultural heritage was far from obvious and swift. As early as 1896, the Ohrid-born philologist and teacher Margaritis Dimitsas published a 1046-page study on the ancient heritage of Macedonia (Dimitsas 1896). Next to historical sources, he focused on epigraphic materials and archaeological discoveries in the region made by other scholars. By presenting *Macedonia in Speaking Stones and Surviving Monuments* (as the book's title reads), Dimitsas's purpose was to demonstrate the purely Hellenic character of the region since time immemorial. In the conclusion to his monumental work, Dimitsas fiercely attacked the Bulgarian claims regarding Macedonia's history as well as their advocates in other Slavic countries. Dimitsas had first-hand impressions from the "Pan-Slavic" activism in his native Ohrid, including that propagated by his relatives (Naxidou 2019). Dimitsas's work was known to the Bulgarian intelligentsia, both in Bulgaria and Macedonia, and clearly presented a challenge to its national aspirations and narratives.

The Bulgarian answer came twelve years later with a (less monumental) publication by the philologist Yordan Ivanov, himself of Macedonian origin (Ivanov 1908). His study similarly focused on epigraphic monuments (inscriptions, manuscript notices) but included also medieval charters, hagiographies, and other documents either published by other (in particular, Russian) scholars or discovered by Ivanov himself during his diplomatic service in Salonika. The title of Yordan Ivanov's work—*Bulgarian Antiquities in Macedonia*—is telling about the author's aims: the publication presented written traces of Bulgarian medieval presence and rule in the hotly debated region. The cases of Dimitsas and Ivanov are representative of early attempts of the "nationalization" of Macedonia's heritage. Yet, none of them focused specifically on the region's medieval architectural and, in general, artistic monuments. The same heritage entered prominently the works of non-Balkan specialists of Byzantine Studies such as Kondakov and the French art historian Gabriel Millet.

Founding father of Byzantine archaeology and art history as an academic discipline in France, Millet was also a tireless traveler who used photography as the primary medium in his research. Following a series of fieldwork studies of Byzantine monuments from the Peloponnese to Macedonia and Serbia, and from Trebizond to Italy, his first groundbreaking monographs appeared during the Great War. One of these advocated the existence of a particular "Greek school" (*école grecque*) in Byzantine architecture, distinct from the Constantinopolitan models

(Millet 1916a). Thus, the idea of provincial but also nationally determined "schools" within Byzantine art was clearly legitimated in international scholarship.

According to Millet, the "Greek school" flourished in the period following the destruction of the Bulgarian state at the beginning of the eleventh century. Its monuments were to be found throughout Greece, from Laconia to Arta, the churches of Kastoria in Western Macedonia being notable among its first and most characteristic examples. While Salonika remained under strong Constantinopolitan influence, Ohrid represented the extreme northwest limit of the "Greek school." Millet's description of its distinctive features referred to specific plans of temples (basilicas, cross-in-square churches, and their subtypes), methods of construction, structural elements, and forms (vaults, porticos, arcatures, apses, domes). On the basis of plans, Millet concluded the considerable difference between Greece and Constantinople—dissimilarity, which was even more visible in the building techniques and decorations. Thus, while Constantinople's architecture was characterized by constructions in bricks only or in *opus mixtum* consisting of alternating layers of bricks and stones, the "Greek school" employed the *cloisonné* technique: the framing of stones in bricks. Opposition to Constantinople was attested also by the rich ceramic decoration of the churches in Greece: Greek and pseudo-Kufic characters, rosettes, lozenges, stars, and other elements made of bricks, glazed cups, etc. make the church walls there look like "real carpets hung over the façades" (Millet 1916a, 258).

It must be noted that Millet attributed the distinctive elements of the Greek/Helladic medieval architecture to Oriental influences. In the spirit of his indirect interlocutor Josef Strzygowski,[16] he proposed numerous comparisons of Greek medieval constructions with the architectural heritage of Armenia and Anatolia, Georgia, and even Mesopotamia: we shall see how similar analogies made possible the "de-Byzantinization" of heritage in the Bulgarian case as well. By contrast, Millet supposed that the architecture of the Byzantine metropolis followed Hellenistic traditions.

Considered "unsurpassed work" by Greek specialists even nowadays (Chlepa 2022, 64), *L'école grecque* was not Millet's only contribution of this kind. Three years later, the publication of his monograph *L'ancien art serbe. Les églises* standardized the canon of "Old Serbian architecture" and

[16] On Strzygowski's *furor orientalis* and the turn-of-the-century German/Austrian interpretation of "Oriental art," see Marchand (2009, 387–426).

its mainstream interpretation to this day. What is more, in the Serbian intellectual context, Millet's monograph achieved a "mythic status" (Ignjatović 2016, 679)—it "coalesced with the subject to which it was dedicated" (Stevović 2021, 289). Millet did not simply produce an academic study of churches and monasteries related to medieval Serbian statehood and history: he left a true apotheosis of medieval Serbian art. On the one hand, the French scholar situated it in the context of Byzantine art and at the crossroads of influences coming from different centers: from Constantinople and Greece, from the Orient (again), but also—and more importantly—from the West. On the other hand, he emphatically concluded that Serbian art/architecture was neither a simple branch of the Byzantine one, nor a mere synthesis of traditions coming from elsewhere. It was an original art—daring, free, clearly exceeding the limits of Byzantine models: Serbian architects were always searching for "an expression that is more powerful than the one of their Byzantine teachers" (Millet 1919, 201).

Nevertheless, the very definition of "Old Serbian art/architecture" was not without problems. The French Byzantinist had to face the striking architectural variety of medieval churches qualified as "Serbian" in reference to the sovereigns who either commissioned their construction or restored existing (Byzantine) buildings (Pantelić 2016, 442)—or simply on the basis of their chronological dating and stylistic features. While the oldest group of monuments—those of Raška—are stone-built constructions with Romanesque features, the churches of Kosovo and Macedonia are clearly characterized by Byzantine and "Greek school" building techniques such as the *cloisonné*; finally, the late fourteenth- and fifteenth-century churches in central Serbia are unique with their fine layers of perfectly cut stones and bricks and impressive stone-carved decorations.

Based on typological and stylistic features, Millet's solution was to classify the Serbian medieval heritage into three sub-national "schools" corresponding to specific historical periods and geographical localizations: the earliest one was the "Raška school" (twelfth-thirteenth century), while the last cluster of monuments—the one of central Serbia—belonged to the "Morava school." The intermediary "school" was designated by Millet as *école de la Serbie byzantine*. It referred to the period of the greatest territorial enlargement of medieval Serbia in the late thirteenth and fourteenth centuries and to monuments located mostly in "Old Serbia"—Millet used the standard Serbian designation of Kosovo and the northern parts of geographical Macedonia. Millet's "Byzantine Serbia" reached southward as far as Mount Athos and the monasteries of Meteora in Thessaly.

Definitively, the authoritative monographs of the French academic did not leave room for "Bulgarian antiquities" in Macedonia. Moreover, medieval monuments on Bulgarian territory such as the churches of Nesebăr, of Stenimachos (later Asenovgrad), and even of the capital Tărnovo were discussed only as offspring of Byzantine architecture. By all means, the historical moment of Millet's publications should be taken into account. In the foreword to *L'école grecque*, Millet referred to the "epic" of the Byzantine emperor Basil II the Bulgar Slayer who reduced to ruins the First Bulgarian state. He did not miss to thank for his hospitality Germanos Karavangelis—the Greek Metropolitan bishop of Kastoria, one of the masterminds behind the Greek anti-Bulgarian struggle in late Ottoman Macedonia. *L'ancien art serbe* clearly pursued a political agenda: on its front page, Millet left a dedication "to the Serbian people" and a quote from *The Mountain Wreath* by the Serbian/Montenegrin national poet Njegoš. Millet's work reads often like a panegyric on the Serbian "genius," on the ardor, the bravery, and the tenacity of this "admirable people" who were—not least—faithful friends of his native France in the Great War (Millet 1919, 10).

War and Heritage

Lasting longer in the Balkans than in the West, the destructive wartime period that ended the "long nineteenth century" was also a formative moment in many aspects. Apart from new forms of warfare, the crystallization of new identities and ideologies, and the creation of new states, it also marked the emergence of new sensibilities: in the sphere of human rights and philanthropy through international humanitarian action, but also in the field of heritage. The Great War was the occasion to elaborate new patterns of valorization of what was regarded as "treasures" of culture and civilization. Facing accusations of barbarity, the German-speaking Central Powers launched the so-called *Kunstschutz*—practices of preservation of enemy's art and cultural monuments (Kott 2006)—whose results were ambiguous. They were criticized as propaganda and even as "robbery" of heritage, while the art historians engaged in them were also described as "apologists of annihilation" (Born and Störtkuhl 2017). In any case, World War I encouraged fieldwork archaeological and art historical studies—including in the Balkans.

Both Central Powers and Entente countries sent to the area scholars and entire academic missions, whereby the military mobilization of scholarly expertise merged together the study and protection of heritage with colonial and "soft power" practices. Under the auspices of the *Armée d'Orient*, Hellenists from the French School at Athens combined their archaeological work in Macedonia with counterintelligence and propaganda activities (Baric 2017). The Austrian *Balkanexpedition* in occupied Montenegro and Albania between May and August 1916 brought together specialists in the fields of Balkan *Volkskunde*, linguistics, archaeology, and art history (Marchetti 2013, 153–86). German academia was represented by another interdisciplinary *Mazedonische landeskundliche Kommission* whose members undertook in particular excavations at the archaeological site of ancient Stobi.[17] Yet, these kinds of missions were not hitherto unknown to Balkan scholars: Bulgarian academic expeditions had taken place in occupied Macedonia and Thrace already in 1912–1913, during the First Balkan War.

The most important wartime mission of Bulgarian scholars was organized between July and September 1916 by the General Staff of the Bulgarian Army in the reoccupied part of Macedonia as well as in the areas of Kosovo and Serbia under Bulgarian control. Similar to the parallel Austrian expedition, the Bulgarian initiative mobilized representatives of different research fields who, after the mission's completion, presented the army authorities with their reports. Next to ethnographic, linguistic, and geographical studies, the academic team had the task of investigating the "new lands" from an archaeological point of view, while the data collected by all participants were supposed to support the "fatherland's interests in the future international peace talks" (Petrov 1993b, 17–18).[18]

Thus, Bulgarian *Kunstschutz*, and wartime academic involvement in general, was of a particular genre: instead of "protecting" foreign cultural heritage and spreading political influence among other nations, it was concerned with finding proof of the supposed Bulgarian identity of the

---

[17] The creation of this commission was consulted with their Bulgarian allies: see Langer (2019, 117–27). The linguist Gustav Weigand, a specialist in Balkan Romance languages but also a staunch supporter of the Bulgarian cause in Macedonia, participated in the commission. At the same time, Bulgarian authorities jealously declined the request of the Austro-Hungarian mission to work in the Bulgarian-occupied area (Baric 2017, 66–67).

[18] A year later, it had a follow-up in the region of Dobrudja (formerly annexed by Romania) with the participation of some of the scholars from the previous expedition. The researcher who was tasked with the archaeological study there was Karel Škorpil, the discoverer of Pliska.

occupied areas and with elaborating arguments supporting Bulgarian territorial claims. While the ethnographic research of these areas was of primary concern, participants such as the historian Vasil Zlatarski dedicated special attention to cultural monuments in Macedonia and Kosovo from a clearly patriotic angle. In his description of the Treskavec Monastery near Prilep (thirteenth-fourteenth century), Zlatarski contested its Serbian foundation and hypothesized Bulgarian origins; in the fourteenth-century Marko's Monastery near Skopje, the historian was eager to reject the claims that Bulgarians had vandalized Serbian inscriptions and murals representing Serbian saints (Petrov 1993b, 51–52). Being also a member of the team, Yordan Ivanov, the author of *Bulgarian Antiquities in Macedonia*, researched the Saint George Church in Staro Nagoričane near Kumanovo—a foundation of the Serbian King Stefan Uroš II Milutin— with the idea that Bulgarian Tsar Mihail Shishman should have been buried there.[19] Nevertheless, concerning archaeology and art history, the most important figure in this and other Bulgarian expeditions in the "new lands" was certainly Bogdan Filov.

Archaeologist and classical scholar who had received his professional training in Germany, and founding father of art history in Bulgaria, Filov was by that time the director of the National Museum in Sofia. Since 1912, he had already toured several times Bulgarian-occupied or newly annexed territories to study and document archaeological and historical monuments.[20] As Fani Gargova argues, although Filov's agenda was "clearly nationalistic," in his travel diaries from those missions and reports submitted to the Bulgarian General Staff, his tone is rather neutral and "controlled by scholarly judgment" (Gargova 2017, 158–59). Moreover, the scholar was not exclusively interested in antiquities related to Bulgarian history as he paid special attention to ancient Graeco-Roman and early Christian sites and monuments in Macedonia. Later, in 1918, he conducted with Karel Škorpil the first excavations of the Trebeništa necropolis

---

[19] Ivanov's claims were later questioned (Ovcharov 1994, 108–12). Otherwise, Ivanov's report is focused on the "Bulgarian" population in western Macedonian confines and the Albanians living there: a sensitive question against the background of the uneasy relations with Austria-Hungary regarding the demarcation of the common border in the area.

[20] One of his expeditions, in 1914, was within the 1878 Bulgarian territories where he was accompanied by Josef Strzygowski and by the American Byzantinist Thomas Whittemore (Gargova 2017).

near Ohrid Lake (Iron Age to fourth century BC)—a site discovered by chance by a Bulgarian army unit.[21]

Filov's approach to heritage was not parochial: he sought rather to legitimize the *droit de cité* of Bulgarians among "civilized" European nations through the valorization of the remains of former civilizations going back to Early Christianity, and even to Thracian antiquity. It was exactly during the Great War that he conceptualized the existence of ancient "Thracian art," distinct from the Greek one (Filov 1917). In his writings and activity, one can notice sincere eagerness to protect the heritage of different historical periods that was endangered by war—including Ottoman, as attested by his plea for the preservation of the famous sixteenth-century Selimiye Mosque in Edirne (Petrov 1993a, 17). Nevertheless, the results of his missions in Macedonia and other areas under Bulgarian control remain ambiguous. He explicitly stated as one of his tasks "to take away" (*pribera*) monuments of greater interest under the pretext that they were endangered (Petrov 1993b, 70). Indeed, he and his colleagues from the 1916 academic team referred to a number of artifacts that they were able to pack and send to the National Museum and Library in Sofia: from Roman epigraphic and sculptural monuments to different ethnographic items and archives from the recent history of Macedonia, as well as medieval and Ottoman-period icons, ecclesiastical objects, Greek and Slavic inscriptions, manuscripts and incunabula.[22]

Bulgarian wartime academic and military activity led to a massive relocation of heritage objects from the occupied territories to Sofia. Among the most famous ones were the inscription of the emblematic Tsar Samuel from the village of German in the Prespa area (late tenth century), the cloak given as a present to the Ohrid Archbishop by the Byzantine Emperor Andronikos II Palaiologos (late thirteenth-early fourteenth century) as well as a crown of the Ohrid Archbishops (eighteenth-century Venetian creation). Being relevant to the rule of Tsar Samuel and the later archbishopric, artifacts from Ohrid were obviously seen as important material proofs legitimizing the Bulgarian reading of the history of Macedonia. Nevertheless, their relocation provoked the protests of the

---

[21] After 1918, the necropolis was studied by Serbian archaeologist Nikola Vulić and other Yugoslav (after 1945—Macedonian) researchers.

[22] See, the lists of items provided by the ethnographer Anton Popstoilov (Petrov 1993b, 293–326). This mission was approved by the Ministry of Public Instruction: TsDA, 177k, 1, 475, 10–11, 21–22.

locals.[23] It must be noted that representatives of Western missions working on the Balkans during the Great War also appropriated archaeological findings—despite the will of some of them to respect the Second Hague Convention of 1899 forbidding wartime pillage (Baric 2017, 65). This practice of the Germans in Macedonia and Dobrudja caused the dissatisfaction of Filov who was otherwise their Bulgarian interlocutor (Petrov 1993b, 72; Koneva 1998, 108). For the Bulgarian military and scholars, the stakes were different: instead of the spoliation of foreign heritage, they perceived themselves as rescuers of "Bulgarian" antiquities in Macedonia from Serbian and Greek enemies. Yet, in World War I, Bulgarian motivations visibly changed toward revanchism (Koneva 1998, 104–6). Thus, in a number of cases, Bulgarian practices were rather akin to indiscriminate plunder: instead of protecting heritage, Bulgarian military and academic missions turned into a hazard for it.

Two monasteries in Greek East Macedonia are characteristic examples. By the beginning of the twentieth century, Timiou Prodromou Monastery near the city of Serres and the one of Panagia Eikosifoinissa in the diocese of Drama (both founded in the Byzantine era) remained firmly loyal to the Patriarchate of Constantinople; for that reason, they were considered as fanatically Greek centers by Bulgarian scholars (Strezov 1891, 835; Kănchov 1894, 516). In March 1917, Eikosifoinissa was attacked and plundered by a Macedonian paramilitary group led by Todor Panitsa but under the guidance of Vladimír Sís—a Czech journalist and partisan of the Bulgarian cause in the Balkans. With the assistance of the Bulgarian army authorities, Sís had been sent by the Bulgarian Academy of Sciences to the Drama and Serres monasteries in order to study and take pictures of old manuscripts—a mission that was soon modified to "collecting antiquities."[24] Several months later, after Sís was sent again by the academy,[25] similar robbery and damage occurred in Prodromou Monastery. After the war, facing accusations by the Inter-Allied commission investigating war crimes in East Macedonia, Bulgarian military authorities denied involvement and tried to blame the incidents on local Turks.[26] But the plunder committed by Panitsa and Sís is confirmed by a Bulgarian army commander who

---

[23] TsDA, 177k, 1, 475, 43–44.

[24] See NA-BAN, 1k, 2, 358, 10–16; NA-BAN, 1k, 2, 377, 12–13.

[25] NA-BAN, 1k, 2, 371, 22–28.

[26] TsDA, 176k, 3, 646, 46. My deepest gratitude goes to Dr. Martin Valkov for drawing my attention to the files kept at the Central State Archive of Bulgaria (TsDA).

visited somewhat later Eikosifoinissa and noted that he "found it completely ransacked and its monks scattered. There was no doubt that along with the book treasure, the money treasure had also been taken" (Azmanov 1995, 176–7).

As a result of the robbery, hundreds of manuscripts and books, and also icons and works of ecclesiastical art were taken to Bulgaria, while the parchment collection of Eikosifoinissa was destroyed.[27] Part of the antiquities sent to Sofia were inventorized by the army authorities in Drama: forty-six "simple" icons, five gilded and three enameled icons, one hundred twenty manuscript books, two hundred eighty printed books, eight gilded gospels, two gift boxes, ninety sanctuary lamps, fifteen candlesticks, eleven carved crosses, eleven metal crosses, thirty-two reliquaries with holy relics, eight empty reliquaries, all kinds of vestments and attributes.[28] While after the war, with the Treaty of Neuilly-sur-Seine (November 1919), Bulgaria was bound to restitute antiquities to Greece, Romania and the Serb-Croat-Slovene Kingdom, it declined the repeated Greek claims regarding those from the Drama and Serres monasteries. The art objects have been kept in a "secret fund" for decades (along with those from Ohrid and other places in Macedonia), before some of them finally went on display at the National History Museum in Sofia, while most of the manuscripts were hosted by the Centre for Slavo-Byzantine Studies "Ivan Duychev" (Rousseva 2009, 2011). Yet, some of the relics mysteriously reached western collections and libraries, including those of Princeton and Duke Universities.

During the next Bulgarian occupation, in World War II, both monasteries underwent another spoliation (Kotzageorgi-Zymari 2002, 80–82). Panagia Eikosifoinissa was burnt down in June 1944. During most of the war, the internationally renowned archaeologist and art historian Bogdan Filov was the Prime Minister of Bulgaria. As such, he was to a great extent responsible for the Bulgarian participation in the war on the side of Nazi Germany as well as in the Holocaust. Thus, archaeological expertise, art history studies, politics, and wartime devastation merged in the same figure.

---

[27] See TsDA, 177k, 1, 475, 25, 31.

[28] NA-BAN, 1k, 2, 377, 29. More manuscripts, books (including Turkish), and artifacts coming from Northern Greece are mentioned in NA-BAN, 1k, 2, 371, 38; NA-BAN, 1k, 2, 377, 8–28 and 30–31.

The Birth of "Old Bulgarian Art"

Meanwhile, following his wartime expeditions between 1912 and 1916, Filov had the intention to write "a special work on the archaeological monuments of Macedonia" (Petrov 1993a, 198). The result was in fact the first academic work dedicated to "Early/Old Bulgarian art." Published in 1919 in German, French, and English, it visibly targeted foreign audiences in Bulgaria's difficult post-war moment. The main message of the work is condensed in a quotation from the Russian Byzantinist Fyodor Schmidt: although influenced by Constantinople, Bulgarian art was not a form of Byzantine art—it did not originate in Byzantium. It was an original cultural phenomenon, one "so strong and vigorous" that it continued to flourish and produce valuable works "even under Turkish rule" (Filov 1919, VIII). Even though Filov, in a contradictory way, situated "Old Bulgarian art" within the context of Byzantine art (like "German" or "French art" within the Romanesque and the Gothic), his emphasis was by all means on its originality.

In fact, Filov's thesis was largely made possible thanks to theories launched by the great European authorities in (Byzantine) art history. Wasn't it Gabriel Millet who had discovered the local variations and even national schools within Byzantine art? Filov's "de-Byzantinization" of Bulgarian medieval heritage was operated primarily through references to Oriental roots—so dear to his colleague and mentor Strzygowski but also emphasized by Millet. Filov went so far as to search for the origins of Bulgarian applied arts in the famous stone façade of Mshatta Palace on display in Berlin's Pergamon Museum (Filov 1919, 79). Indeed, Filov's argument looked convincing in the case of Pliska-Preslav art: the scholar discovered Oriental imprints not only on the monumental architecture of the First Bulgarian state but also on other works associated with it, which became truly iconic in the interwar Bulgarian cultural context. Such was the famous rock relief of the Madara Horseman not far from Pliska (eighth century), where Filov identified Persian (Sassanid) archetypes, and the hoard of golden vessels known as the Treasure of Nagyszentmiklós. Discovered as early as 1799 in the Habsburg Banat and having played an important role in nineteenth-century Hungarian nationalism as "the treasure of Attila," the early medieval hoard has been ascribed different identities (Magyar, Avar, Byzantine, Persian, etc.). While it has been seriously questioned abroad (Bálint 2010), after Filov the Bulgar identity of the treasure became almost unshakable in Bulgarian studies. Filov's thesis about the Sassanid roots of Bulgarian art also proved to be authoritative in the country's academia, although it provoked controversies already in the interwar period. In any case, by arguing for the originality of Bulgarian art, Filov sought to rescue the reputation of Bulgarian ancestors: instead of uncultured nomads of obscure Asiatic stock, pagan Bulgars turned out to be "highly developed civilization" (Filov 1919, 4) and mediators of prestigious ancient cultures.

At the same time, Bogdan Filov traced a perfect historical continuity from this "civilization" to art production under Ottoman rule, passing through the period of the Second Bulgarian state. The task was demanding: in the architecture of the latter, Filov noticed a "striking break with the ancient tradition" (Filov 1919, 16). The "magnificence" of the buildings from the first state was "lacking" in the thirteenth-fourteenth century constructions. According to Filov, instead of monumentality, more attention was given to decorative refinement and ornaments. Here, the Bulgarian scholar referred in particular to the ceramic decorations of the church exteriors from that period—the same that Millet had ascribed to the "Greek school" of Byzantine architecture. Filov admitted that Byzantine influence was so powerful that "finally Bulgarian art became one with the art of Byzantium" (Filov 1919, 17) but warned that Byzantine art should not be understood as "Greek" or emanating from one center.

In fact, Filov's interpretations amounted to a selective appropriation of heritage: under "Early" or "Old Bulgarian architecture," the academic put together various medieval pre-Ottoman and Ottoman-period buildings existing on contemporary Bulgarian territory. Such was the case of the churches of Mesimvria/Nesebăr (eleventh-fourteenth century) whose Byzantine character was downplayed in favor of hypothetical links to the architecture of the Bulgarian medieval capital Tărnovo. Yet, Filov admitted that the latter "offers no very good example" of the decorative idiom of the thirteenth-fourteenth-century building technique, while "we find it employed in a remarkably artistic way in the churches at Mesembria" (Filov 1919, 20).

Most notably, Filov stepped outside the contemporary borders of Bulgaria in an effort to include Macedonia in the inventory of "Old Bulgarian art." Led by the mainstream Bulgarian historiographic narrative (according to which Tsar Samuel continued the Bulgarian statehood while moving its centers to Macedonia), Filov listed the Basilica of Saint Achillius in Prespa and the cathedral church of Saint Sophia in Ohrid as examples of Bulgarian art. While Gabriel Millet and other scholars also believed Saint

Achillius to be built by Samuel, Filov hastily dated the oldest part of Saint Sophia to "the beginning" of the eleventh century so that it could coincide with the period of the same ruler. Similar to Millet, Filov compared Saint Achillius to the earlier grand basilica in Nesebăr: but while for the French art historian their similarity made them "belong to the Byzantine Middle Ages" (Millet 1916a, 18), in the eyes of the Bulgarian scholar it only confirmed the Bulgarian identity of both of them. Without much discussion, Filov referred also to thirteenth- and fourteenth-century churches in Ohrid and elsewhere in Macedonia as pieces of Bulgarian architecture—while obviously silencing the fact that they were most probably built during periods of Byzantine and Serbian rule. In this case, Filov thought it to be enough to indicate the importance of Ohrid in the Bulgarian "spiritual" history.

Published five years later, the Bulgarian version of the monograph is marked by a number of modifications that are highly indicative of the nationalist trend in his work. The Sassanid origins of "Old Bulgarian art" are visibly emphasized at the expense of its Byzantine framing: Filov added a whole chapter on "Old Bulgarian and Byzantine art" where he attacked the deniers of the original character of the former. When he addressed the "decline" of architecture under the Second Bulgarian state in comparison with the pagan period during the First state, he blamed it on Christianity and "Byzantinism": Byzantine influences brought about a loss of creativity within the Bulgarian people/race (*pleme*) and a deterioration of its authentic culture.[29] Moreover, Filov suggested that the Saint Achillius Basilica in Prespa should be attributed to the ninth century and the rule of Prince Boris I who Christianized Bulgaria. He also moved the dating of Saint Sophia in Ohrid to the "tenth-eleventh century," so that it could coincide with Bulgarian rule in Macedonia (Filov 1924, 20).

A few years later, Filov credited the construction of Saint Sophia likewise to the rule of Boris I in the ninth century (Filov 1930a, 30–31). Therefore, he contested the data suggesting that the cathedral was built by the Ohrid Archbishop Leo in the mid-eleventh century—that is after the destruction of Samuel's state, under Byzantine rule. In general, Saint Sophia's case is representative of the Balkan "art wars": like most medieval architectural monuments, it had many phases of construction whose chronology became easily a political question. Thus, while Bulgarian scholars

---

[29] Filov (1924, 28). This point would be soon ingeniously developed by the historian Petăr Mutafchiev: see Mishkova (2023, 133–39).

sought to date the church to the periods of Bulgarian domination in Macedonia, their Greek and Serbian colleagues preferred to see it as a monument commissioned by Archbishop Leo.[30] Similar is the case of the churches in the city of Kastoria in Western Greek Macedonia. While the earliest among these are likely to have been built under Bulgarian rule, as we shall see, Greek scholars tended to attribute them to periods of Byzantine rule.

Referring to the churches of Kostur (Kastoria) with their striking brick decoration, Filov managed to turn upside down Millet's theory of the "Greek school": according to him, it was not Greece that spread its provincial architectural idiom in the Balkans, but the "Old Bulgarian art" in Macedonia that influenced Greece. While, in his earlier publications, Filov deplored the completely Byzantinized character of the architecture of the Second Bulgarian state, in 1930 he "orientalized" it as well, through analogies with Mesopotamian and Armenian monuments. In this way, he achieved a double result: on the one hand, he re-evaluated it categorically in the canon of the Orient-based "Old Bulgarian art." On the other hand, he turned Millet's argument about the Oriental influences within the "Greek school" against his theory: finally, the "Greek school" looked much more Bulgarian than Greek. On these grounds, the Bulgarian scholar contested the Serbian belonging of the fourteenth-century churches and monasteries in Macedonia: Millet's *école de la Serbie byzantine* in fact followed Bulgarian traditions and even employed Bulgarian masters (Filov 1930a, 57–58).

Thus, the internationally renowned Bulgarian archaeologist produced both a geographically and historically homogenized image of "Old Bulgarian art." Since the arrival of the Bulgars in the early medieval Balkans up until the nineteenth century under Ottoman rule, and from the Black Sea coast to Ohrid and the Prespa Lakes in Macedonia, basically the same art existed—the traces of foreign political, ecclesiastic, and cultural traditions being devalued or removed altogether. One can also already recognize most of the "tricks" that would be perfected by other Bulgarian scholars in their approach to "Old Bulgarian art": arbitrary chronological dating (so that the respective works of art can coincide with the period of a Bulgarian ruler); neglecting periods of foreign rule or ecclesiastic jurisdiction in Macedonia—or on present Bulgarian territories

---

[30] See the polemical work of the Berlin-based Bulgarian art historian Assen Tschilingirov (Chilingirov 2013).

(with the argument that, nevertheless, it was Bulgarian masters who created those works—or that the places in question were essentially Bulgarian anyway); neglect of obvious parallels with other, "non-Bulgarian," Balkan traditions and monuments; on the contrary—erasing striking regional and/or chronological differences within what is seen as "Bulgarian" art in a way that certainly reminds of Millet's essentialism of "Serbian" art.

Another point supported by Filov would also enjoy longevity in Bulgarian art history. Already during his 1916 expedition in Macedonia (Petrov 1993b, 72), he emphasized that the churches of Varoš, the medieval quarter of Prilep, were similar in plan and building technology to those in Tărnovo as well as in Arbanasi: an old village near the capital of the Second Bulgarian state, founded by Albanian/Epirote settlers in the early Ottoman period (Kiel 1985, 111–2). Its sixteenth–eighteenth-century monuments were used by Filov in a largely retroactive way in order to reimagine medieval architectural features that have been lost in Tărnovo itself. More importantly, by neglecting the possibility of other powerful vectors of influence, Filov posited Tărnovo as a major cultural metropolis irradiating the territories of Bulgaria and Macedonia. As he noted in a publication from 1930 regarding the thirteenth–fourteenth-century painting, "[i]t is beyond doubt that the center […] is to be sought in the then capital of the Bulgarian state, namely in Tărnovo" (Filov 1930b, 60).

Thanks to the Russian-French art historian André Grabar (1928), this point had already evolved into the theory of a specific "Tărnovo artistic school." Still, Filov remained prudent in some respects: he admitted possible activity of Byzantine masters in Tărnovo; he supposed this possibility even regarding the thirteenth-century murals of the Boyana Church (Filov 1930b, 74–75), which were much praised by him and, as we shall see, by other scholars in Bulgaria. Moreover, Filov stated that the miniatures in the fourteenth-century illuminated Gospels of Tsar Ivan Alexander—a work that will be later celebrated as an example of "Renaissance trends" in Bulgarian art—were undoubtedly "copied after some Greek original."[31] By the same time, some of his colleagues in Sofia were much less cautious and demonstrated an unequivocally nationalistic approach.

---

[31] Filov (1930b, 94). He dedicated a whole study to the Gospels and their Byzantine genealogy (Filov 1934).

Traits, Trajectories, and Territories of the "Bulgarian school"

This approach is exemplified by the art historian Andrey Protich who, in the 1920s, succeeded Bogdan Filov as director of the National Museum in Sofia. His work is thoroughly dominated by the idea of "national art" and in many cases he arrived at quite doubtful conclusions. The one that provoked the anger of his Serbian colleagues was the thesis of the existence of a particular "Southwestern school" in Bulgarian mural painting in the thirteenth and fourteenth century, next to the supposed "Tărnovo school" (Protich 1925). While the latter was allegedly Byzantinized, Protich considered that the former was a true "Bulgarian national painting," characterized by "realism." Here, Protich launched the surprising theory that the painters from the "Southwestern school" followed model portraits of real persons and multiplied them in the images of saints in churches. Although he discovered the origins of this "school" in monuments in Western Bulgaria (Berende, Boyana, Zemen), he spread its area over the art of Macedonia under Byzantine and Serbian rule, and even claimed that it influenced monuments in Serbia, Constantinople, and Wallachia. Protich, himself born in Macedonia, visibly sought to demonstrate the Bulgarian ethnic character of the region and of its monuments created under "foreign" domination. The scholar also believed that, through the "Southwestern school," Bulgarian art rejuvenated Byzantine art after the Latin conquest of Constantinople.

Somewhat later, Aleksandăr Rashenov, pioneer of monument restoration in Bulgaria, formulated the existence of a "Bulgarian school in the Byzantine style." In fact, he completely "Bulgarianized" Millet's "Greek school" with the thesis that the decorative style in Byzantine architecture using bricks and glazed ceramic elements was born in Bulgaria—although he dated it to the eleventh century, that is, probably under Byzantine rule (Rashenov 1932). Rashenov was convinced that the ceramic decoration of churches had Slavic roots. He speculated that it typically spread in territories with a Slavic/Bulgarian population (including, as he thought, Peloponnese and Epirus).

In fact, most of these points have been already systematized by Nikola Mavrodinov, the main ideologist of the "Old Bulgarian art" in that period. At the age of twenty-seven, Mavrodinov, who had studied art history and archaeology in Liège, Belgium, tried to formulate the distinctive features of the "Bulgarian architectural school" in the medieval period (Mavrodinov

1931, 151–8). Regarding the architectural heritage of Macedonia and other Balkan areas, his argumentation rested upon several interpretative strategies: a protochronic search for "the first" emergence of one or another architectural element or form; privileged analogies between architectural monuments in East Bulgaria and those in quite distant geographical territories—at the expense of possible analogies between the monuments in the latter territories; respectively, reconstruction of highly hypothetical trajectories of influence from East Bulgaria over Macedonia; finally, a deliberate reduction of the notion of "Serbian art" to heritage outside Macedonia.

Thus, Mavrodinov believed that he had found the first case of external decoration with glazed ceramic elements called *phialostomia* in Greek (quatrefoils and cup-shaped round vessels) in the Saint Demetrius Church in Tărnovo (dated by Mavrodinov to 1186). Moreover, referring to discoveries made by Karel Škorpil, he declared that these elements continued an older decorative tradition that started in the First Bulgarian state, with the painted ceramics of Preslav. As this kind of decoration appeared later in Macedonia (as well as in the Morava area of Serbia), Mavrodinov concluded that it came from Bulgaria (Mavrodinov 1931, 123). Similar was his approach based on comparisons of church plans. Mavrodinov believed that churches in Macedonia, in particular those dating from the period of Serbian rule in the fourteenth century, followed the plan of a church in Nesebăr (Saint John the Baptist, tenth-eleventh century) (Mavrodinov 1931, 80, 83–93). What is more, he explained the presence of bell towers in the architecture of the Morava area in Serbia (in particular, Lazarica in Kruševac, late fourteenth century) with the existence of "strong East Bulgarian influences" there. The archetypes in this case were allegedly the tower of Saint Mother of God Church (Petritsiotissa) in Stenimachos/Asenovgrad in South Bulgaria as well as those in Nesebăr. Mavrodinov imagined that this influence was mediated by the fourteenth-century Bulgarian state of Vidin, although he noted that in the latter "unfortunately, we do not have so far a single discovered monument" (Mavrodinov 1931, 92).

The scholar's argument was certainly contradictory in some ways. While he admitted that the *opus mixtum* masonry was older than the Bulgarian art, he imagined it as a typical Bulgarian feature: thus, regarding the alternating layers of stones and bricks in the fourteenth-century Marko's Monastery near Skopje, he claimed that its masonry was "purely East Bulgarian" (Mavrodinov 1931, 126). On this basis, he rejected altogether Millet's concept of "Byzantine Serbia." In Mavrodinov's opinion, the fourteenth-century churches in Macedonia did not have "anything to do" with Serbian architecture (that he identified with the Raška and Morava "schools"), as they were built by "local Macedonian masters."[32] Moreover, as we shall see, he scandalized Serbian scholars with his claim that, even in Gračanica, "we do not notice the hand of a Serbian architect" (Mavrodinov 1931, 88). It is a question of the famous fourteenth-century monastery near Priština/Prishtinë in Kosovo, founded by the Serbian King Stefan Uroš II Milutin and celebrated as the apex of Serbian medieval architecture by scholars such as Đurđe Bošković (Ignjatović 2016, 247–8).

Thus, the door was open to a wholesale appropriation of architectural heritage hitherto attributed to other countries. Mavrodinov insisted that even the old architecture of Raška in Western Serbia, the one with Romanesque features (of Dalmatian origin), "is rooted in Bulgaria": the twelfth-century church of Studenica allegedly followed the plan of the one in Asenovgrad (Mavrodinov 1931, 141–2). The later Morava architecture with its brick decoration was even easier to "Bulgarianize": it was "rooted in the Bulgarian and Macedonian architecture of the thirteenth and the first half of fourteenth century" (Mavrodinov 1931, 144–5).[33] Mavrodinov also attested Bulgarian influences over the oldest medieval architecture of Romania: a topic that was already researched by Bogdan Filov (1925). But his protochronic method led him even to conclude Bulgarian influences over the architecture of Constantinople—in the late thirteenth–fourteenth-century Palace of the Porphyrogenitus (Tekfur Sarayı) (Mavrodinov 1931, 139). In this way, the old thesis about the Byzantine character of Bulgarian medieval architecture was completely reversed: instead of models transferred from the Byzantine capital, it was

---

[32] Mavrodinov (1931, 83). See also the fieldwork studies in Skopje and Kumanovo areas conducted by Mavrodinov during the Bulgarian occupation of Macedonia in World War II (Mavrodinov 1942, 1943a). According to Mavrodinov's conclusions concerning the Saint George Church in Staro Nagoričane, not only it was built by Bulgarian masters but also the earlier church on the same spot was not Byzantine but Bulgarian.

[33] Some monuments from the Morava area of Serbia had entered the inventory of *Old Churches and Monasteries in the Bulgarian Lands* published by the art historian Vera Ivanova, Nikola Mavrodinov's wife and daughter of Yordan Ivanov (Ivanova-Mavrodinova 1926). The same area had been under Bulgarian occupation in World War I, and Bulgarian scholars were urged to provide historical and ethnographic "proofs" of its alleged Bulgarian character.

the latter that received architectural know-how that had appeared for the first time in Bulgarian territories.

Soon, Nikola Mavrodinov developed his theory of the "Bulgarian school." He particularly insisted on architectural forms such as the blind arcades, or "pseudo-constructive niches" with decorative character, that allegedly appeared for the first time in the Ossuary of the Bachkovo Monastery in South Bulgaria (eleventh century). From Bulgaria, the element spread to neighboring countries, including Romania (the Cotmeana Monastery, fourteenth century) (Mavrodinov 1935, 295). This time, Mavrodinov managed to find a "secure" East Bulgarian archetype even in the case of the *cloisonné* masonry that was otherwise typical of Macedonia: it appeared in the Saint Stephen Church in Nesebăr, next to the relevant churches in Ohrid, in the village of German (Prespa area) and in Kastoria. From there, it moved to Greece and thus entered the vocabulary of Millet's *école grecque*. The mixed masonry of arches (stones and bricks) appeared in tenth-century Nesebăr and reached both Macedonia and Constantinople (Tekfur Sarayı) only in the fourteenth century (Mavrodinov 1935, 308–10). The decoration with glazed ceramic elements: it originated in ninth-tenth-century Preslav, adorned Nesebăr at the Black Sea coast, moved to the capital of the Second Bulgarian state, and reached the fourteenth-century church of Donja Kamenica—on contemporary Serbian territory but probably founded either by the Bulgarian Tsar Mihail Shishman or by one of his sons. From there, the glazed ceramic cups and quatrefoils entered Macedonia: thus, Mavrodinov managed to find the mediator of "East Bulgarian" influences in the Vidin area that was missing in his 1931 monograph.

Mavrodinov's conclusions were clear: outside Bulgaria, the existence of this type of decoration over church exteriors was "due only to Bulgarian influence"; Bulgaria also created the brick decoration that spread everywhere in the fourteenth century (Mavrodinov 1935, 312–3, 318). In these cases, Mavrodinov speculated about some predilection ("love") for exterior decoration, allegedly typical for "the Bulgarian architect" (Mavrodinov 1935, 320).

As "chauvinist" as it may seem, Mavrodinov's theory was not idiosyncratic. Part of his conclusions were based on (hypo)theses launched by the Russian scholar Nikolay Brunov whom Mavrodinov readily cited. To some extent, his theory also exposed some weak points in the work of great authorities in the field of Byzantine art such as the overestimation of Constantinople as a source of models—or Millet's attempt to blend together in his *ancien art serbe* architectural idioms that were not only strikingly different but also isolated from each other both geographically and historically. What is more, Mavrodinov's and Rashenov's fascination by the rich exterior decoration of medieval churches as a "national" architectural trait had close parallels in other national contexts. Ironically, at the same moment, their Serbian colleagues also celebrated the rich decoration and polychromy of façades as a feature of national genius (Ignjatović 2016, 720–5). Thus, both in Serbia and Bulgaria, decorative idioms were accepted as a style close to popular artistic traditions and also to painting: they were named *slikarski* (in Serbian), *zhivopisen stil* (in Bulgarian), that is, "pictorial style." Yet, the doctrine of the "Bulgarian school" also provoked reasonably expected retaliation.

SERBIAN RIPOSTES

Following the disaster of World War I, the victorious reincarnation of Serbia as the center of a large South Slav kingdom, a cornerstone of the post-Versailles geopolitical status quo, was clearly not in Bulgaria's favor. Serbian scholars soon found part of "their" national heritage damaged by Bulgarian wartime activities. Newly acquired by Belgrade, the previously Bulgarian Poganovo Monastery (fourteenth-fifteenth century) had lost its iconostasis, a valuable fourteenth-century bilateral icon, and other relics that had been moved to Sofia. In the fourteenth-century church of Psača, not far from Kriva Palanka in Macedonia, Bulgarians reportedly destroyed inscriptions mentioning Serbian founders (Popović et al. 1933). Regarding the much-disputed region of Macedonia, the Serbian academic reply to Bulgarian claims did not wait long. In 1919, the year of Millet's *L'ancien art serbe*, the Serbian linguist Aleksandar Belić published likewise in Paris an authoritative volume on Macedonia propagating the Serbian point of view. Belić was a member of the delegation of Serbian scholars participating in the Versailles Peace Conference, and his task was to legitimize his country's claims on linguistic, ethnographic, and historical grounds (Ignjatović 2016, 686–7). The volume included also a chapter on "The Monuments of the Old Serbian Art in Macedonia," which was written by the art historian Vladimir Petković, a close acolyte of Millet during his tours in Serbia and Macedonia.

He soon became one of the most active Serbian polemicists debunking the theses launched by Bulgarian art historians. As was to be expected, Petković denied Bulgarian cultural presence in Macedonia—or rather in

"Southern Serbia," according to the official terminology he used in a book published several years later. He emphasized that the "[o]nly people that kept Southern Serbia conquered for a certain period of time but which left absolutely no trace in it, nor a single monument marked the time of their conquest in Southern Serbia, were the Bulgarians" (Petković 1924, III). By contrast, Serbian rulers built "innumerable churches" there, and Serbian art took deep roots and lived its heyday in the area. Thus, Petković described Macedonia as the "classical land of Serbian art" and even more than that, he believed that the "Serbian Church in Southern Serbia" used to be the "center of the Orthodox [Christian] world" and the main vector of Orthodox Christianity for the neighboring Balkan peoples (including Bulgarians) and areas such as Mount Athos, the Peloponnese, and even Russia and the Christian Orient (Petković 1924, VIII, X–XI; Ignjatović 2016, 484–5).

Expectedly, publications by Bulgarian scholars provoked harsh critiques by Petković and other Serbian scholars. In two articles, Petković attacked Andrey Protich for his claims of a "Southwestern school" in Bulgarian painting (Petković 1926a, b). He claimed that, already before the thirteenth-century "school" postulated by Protich, Serbs had built magnificent churches and repeated his thesis that, unlike the numerous "Serbian" churches in fourteen-century Macedonia, no Bulgarian monument existed there. He rejected the possibility of influence from the "inferior" Bulgarian art with its "insignificant little churches" (*beznačajne crkvice*) over the "superior" Serbian art (Petković 1926a, 155; Ignjatović 2016, 474). Here, Petković ridiculed in particular Protich's focus on the village church in Berende with its tiny dimensions as one of the cradles of the "Southwestern school," and as a model of monumental buildings under Serbian rule. Last but not least, Petković claimed that the churches indicated by Protich (Boyana, Kremikovtsi, etc.) were themselves built by rulers of Serbian origin: an argument mirroring the emphasis on a Bulgarian origin for Serbian rulers used by Bulgarian scholars.[34]

More sober, but still strongly critical, was the review of Nikola Mavrodinov's monograph from 1931 published by Đurđe Bošković (Bošković 1933). The Serbian art historian exposed a number of flaws in Mavrodinov's work: arbitrary dating of churches, highly hypothetical and

---

[34] See, for instance, Mavrodinov's presentation of the fourteenth-century church in Matejče not far from Skopje (Mavrodinov 1943a) where he mostly discussed Helena, the Bulgarian wife of the Serbian Tsar Stefan Dušan.

even incorrect reconstructions of buildings based on preserved foundations, hazy terminology and suspicious or erroneous typologies of plans, and misunderstanding of plans and structures. Bošković rejected Mavrodinov's ethno-centric approach regarding the "Bulgarian" origin of ceramic decorations of churches. But, most of all, he attacked the arbitrary analogies made by Mavrodinov between constructions in East Bulgaria, on the one hand, and in Macedonia and Serbia, on the other. Mavrodinov's statements about Gračanica (where, according to the Bulgarian scholar, "we do not notice the hand of a Serbian architect") and about the alleged "Bulgarian roots" of Raška and Morava architecture were expectedly presented as absurd. Bošković's verdict was harsh: "With the comparisons he makes here, Mr. Mavrodinov shows that he is far from having grasped the basic concepts of architecture and archaeology. Instead of deciding to write such an ambitious discussion, which will cause no little confusion in those who would read it with confidence, he had better have picked up a few good textbooks on the structures and history of Byzantine architecture and mastered them first. This would have been more useful both to him and to scholarship" (Bošković 1933, 226).

In this way, Serbian researchers dismissed the theory of "Old Bulgarian art" and the claims about its existence in Macedonia and Serbia: as the historian Aleksandar Jovanović would later similarly conclude concerning the southern Serbian territories, "[n]ot a single one of these monuments marks the presence of Bulgarians" (Ignjatović 2016, 567). Moreover, Serbian scholars from the interwar period constructed a whole doctrine about the national superiority of medieval Serbian art—in particular, in comparison with Bulgaria. The most famous geographer of the Balkans, Jovan Cvijić, also contrasted Serbian creativity to the Bulgarian "blind imitation" of Byzantine culture (Ignjatović 2016, 642). Scholars such as Vladimir Petković actually sought to bring the "battle" to Bulgarian territory by appropriating important monuments there as Serbian creations: in the first place, Rila Monastery (perceived as a national sanctuary by the Bulgarians), but also the church of the Zemen Monastery or one of the (already Serbian) Poganovo Monastery. As a result, next to Macedonia, a second "front" of Serbo-Bulgarian "art war" formed on both sides of the common political border. Among the monuments that provoked controversies was also the church in Donja Kamenica in the area of the Serbian city of Knjaževac mentioned by Mavrodinov: a number of Serbian specialists (among them Bošković) did not accept a Bulgarian ruler as the founder and proposed a Serbian noble instead (Frfulanović 2001).

Surprisingly or not, a third "front" also appeared—in Romania. Both Serbian and Bulgarian (art) historians tended to look upon Romanians as "latecomers" in Balkan medieval history—despite the claims of long historical continuity formulated by scholars such as Nicolae Iorga with his famous dictum *Byzance après Byzance* regarding Wallachia and Moldavia as the true inheritors of Byzantine legacy.[35] Both Bulgarian and Serbian academics insisted that this legacy was mediated in the Romanian medieval context in a Slavic manner by their respective countries and cultures. Concerning architecture, the thesis of Serbian influence had been accepted by leading Romanian (art) historians such as Gheorghe Balş, who even described the fourteenth-century Cozia Monastery (founded by the Wallachian voivode Mircea the Elder) as an example of the Morava group of monuments (Balş 1911, 41–42). The importance of the "Morava school" in the emergence of Wallachian church architecture was later confirmed by the great authority of Gabriel Millet (1933). Meanwhile, at the Second International Congress of Byzantine Studies, held in 1927 in Belgrade, particular attention was dedicated to Serbian influences in Romanian art. In Serbian scholarship, the latter was largely reduced to an "imitation" or a "copy" of Serbian medieval monuments (Ignjatović 2016, 201, 481).

Yet, as already mentioned, Bulgarian scholars such as Mavrodinov and Filov started insisting on the formative character of the "Old Bulgarian" influences in medieval Wallachian and Moldavian architecture. Ironically, Bulgarian and Serbian specialists concurrently discovered the features of "their" respective "national art" in the same fourteenth-century Romanian monuments, such as the Princely Church of Saint Nicholas in the medieval Wallachian capital Curtea de Argeş. Moreover, Bulgarian claims were to some extent supported by the Romanian scholar Orest Tafrali, who rejected Serbian influences in Curtea de Argeş in favor of Bulgarian and Byzantine models (Nastasă 1997, 171). Not surprisingly, Tafrali's work provoked angry reactions from his Serbian colleague Miloje Vasić (Ignjatović 2016, 203, 481).

---

[35] On Romanian perceptions and appropriations of Byzantine legacy, see Mishkova (2023, 109–22, 154–65, 264–85). Specifically on Bulgarian-Romanian "history wars"—Daskalov (2015).

Greek Ripostes

Although Serbian scholars saw their Bulgarian colleagues as "blinded by chauvinism," they did their best to follow their academic output (Ignjatović 2016, 474). By contrast, Greek academics rarely commented on Bulgarian publications. The reasons for that certainly go beyond the language barrier, which did not play such a role between Bulgarians and Serbs. Greek scholars had successfully "nationalized" Byzantine art—a thousand-year phenomenon that had left innumerable traces on three continents being also the object of a grand, prestigious, and transnational field of study. Against this background, the particularistic claims of national originality advanced by Bulgarian or Serbian scholars certainly looked irrelevant.

A characteristic example is a short note by Andreas Xyngopoulos, the first Ephor of Byzantine antiquities in Thessaloniki, concerning an article by Andrey Protich. Published in *Mélanges* dedicated to Charles Diehl, the founding father of Byzantine Studies in France, Protich's work discussed the Sassanid and Byzantine origins of Bulgarian art. According to Xyngopoulos, it was an "unfortunate and unmethodical attempt" to apply Strzygowski's theories to Bulgarian material. In Protich's analyses of mural paintings, "the misunderstanding proves to be complete and the propaganda purpose of the article becomes obvious, reaching the limits of pure absurdity especially when the writer claims that Bulgarian painting influenced not only Russians, Serbs and Romanians but also the very art of Constantinople from the fourteenth century!" (Xyngopoulos 1931, 354).

Yet, in two cases, Bulgarian claims provoked an answer, although it mostly came after World War II in the new context of strained Greek-Bulgarian relations. Greek reactions were related: first, to the "Bulgarization" of Byzantine heritage in Bulgaria itself (especially regarding Mesimvria/Nesebăr, but also monuments in Bulgarian Thrace such as those in Stenimachos/Asenovgrad or Bachkovo); second, to Bulgarian claims of heritage in Greek Macedonia—especially in Kastoria and the Prespa area. In the first case, Bulgarian scholars visibly tended to overestimate the importance of periods of Bulgarian medieval rule and to marginalize the larger Byzantine context of the local monuments. Moreover, they demonstrated a double standard: while Bulgarian art historians regularly insisted that it was Bulgarian masters who worked on churches under Byzantine or Serbian rule, they progressively downplayed the possibility that Byzantine Greek masters could work under Bulgarian rulers.[36] In the second case, Greek scholars were eager to deny any trace of Bulgarian rule or possible Slavic/Bulgarian heritage.

Georgios Sotiriou, director of the Byzantine Museum in Athens and president of the Christian Archaeological Society, was involved in both debates. Sotiriou accused Bulgarian scholars of "falsifying" the "historical origin of the Byzantine monuments of Mesimvria (Messembrie), [that are] purely Greek, bearing Greek inscriptions, with names of Greek donators" (Sotiriou 1945, 73). He not only rejected the claim that Bulgarian masters would have created those monuments but he also denied the existence of such masters, at least until the nineteenth century. Thereby, he questioned the existence of the "so-called Bulgarian national art" and also attacked the inclusion of Macedonia in its canon.[37]

This inclusion relied on two emblematic monuments located on Greek territory that had been discussed in particular by Yordan Ivanov, the pioneer of the study of "Bulgarian antiquities" in Macedonia. These were the Basilica of Saint Achillius located on a homonymous island in the Little Prespa Lake, and the medieval church in the village of German/Agios Germanos nearby. As already mentioned, the construction of the basilica was attributed by Bulgarian scholars either to Tsar Samuel or to Prince Boris I in the ninth century; moreover, they believed it was part of a larger urban settlement—Samuel's capital Prespa—and credited it as the seat of the Bulgarian Patriarchate under Samuel (Ivanov 1910). The church in the village of German was particularly important, possessing a marble plaque that was moved to Sofia during World War I. Bearing an epitaph ordered by Tsar Samuel, the plaque was discovered by chance in 1888 and published for the first time by Fyodor Uspensky, the director of the Russian Archaeological Institute of Constantinople. This discovery sealed definitively in the Bulgarian narrative the image of the Prespa area—in particular its Greek part—as a major medieval Bulgarian center. Sotiriou tried to debunk this claim: he contested the identity of the Saint Achillius Basilica as Samuel's patriarchal cathedral and indicated the absence of urban constructions on the islet and at the lake shore that could confirm the existence of a city (Sotiriou 1949).

---

[36] Other scholars admitted the importance of Bulgarian rule in cases like Nesebăr and even the "building boom" under it, but still indicated the strong Constantinopolitan imprint on its heritage (Ćurčić 1989, 63).

[37] Sotiriou (1942, 476), quoted in Hadjimihali (1950, 21).

The same monuments were later discussed by the archaeologist Stylianos Pelekanidis. Regarding the church in German/Agios Germanos, he dated it to the period after Samuel and the destruction of his state by Basil II the Bulgar Slayer. For that reason, he questioned the much later Greek inscription in the temple indicating that it was founded by the eighth-century Constantinople Patriarch Germanos and repainted at the beginning of the eleventh century (under Samuel). While Bulgarian scholars agreed that the church was not from the eighth century, they identified German(os) as the Bulgarian Patriarch German during Samuel's reign. Pelekanidis rejected this hypothesis and questioned the authenticity of the "strange" tombstone ordered by Samuel (*periergoteras epitymvias plakos*). He reminded that it was discovered "during the well-known active movement for the Bulgarization of Macedonia," that is, in the period of Greek-Bulgarian conflict in late Ottoman Macedonia (Pelekanidis 1960, 52–53).

Regarding the Saint Achillius Basilica, he contested Ivanov's reading of Byzantine sources. He attacked the thesis that the temple was built by the Bulgarian Prince Boris I, as well as the version according to which Samuel founded the church in order to host the relics of Saint Achillius that he had transferred from the city of Larisa (Pelekanidis 1960, 62–69). Pelekanidis also exposed the "myth" of the Bulgarian Patriarchate in Prespa advanced by the Russian Pavel Milyukov and by Yordan Ivanov. Regarding the islet that was supposed to be one of Samuel's capitals, he confirmed the absence of traces of important civil constructions and expressed doubt that Ivanov had ever visited the place he described. Finally, he dated the basilica to the third decade of the eleventh century, that is, after the end of Samuel's state. Ironically, the Greek architect and archaeologist Nikolaos Moutsopoulos claimed later the discovery of Tsar Samuel's bones in Saint Achillius Basilica and thus boosted greatly the Bulgarian thesis (Moutsopoulos 1999).

In his work on the Byzantine heritage of Kastoria, Pelekanidis demonstrated a similar approach. He dated the oldest churches there—Saint Stephen, Taxiarchis Mitropoleos, and Panagia Koubelidiki—to the mid-ninth century in order to align with a period of Byzantine rule (Pelekanidis and Chatzidakis 1985, 84). Their first Greek researcher Anastasios Orlandos had also dated them to a Byzantine period but to the one after Samuel (Orlandos 1938).[38] Pelekanidis's tone became overtly nationalist

---

[38] By contrast, scholars outside Greece and Bulgaria believed that the three churches should be attributed to the late ninth and early tenth centuries, that is, to a period of Bulgarian rule (Epstein 1980). Pelekanidis's tendentious dating is noticed by Kiel (1985, 29).

in the conclusion of his monograph on Prespa. He stated that the area experienced its religious and cultural heyday after its "liberation" from "the Bulgarian yoke" and that "the indigenous Hellenic population" never lost its traditions and "national consciousness" (Pelekanidis 1960, 134).

In fact, this statement sounded more like a political incantation. Greece had not long ago survived a traumatic period of foreign occupation (including a new Bulgarian one) and of civil war. Until the latter, the rural areas of Prespa and Kastoria were massively Slav-speaking and a Greek national allegiance of the locals was far from being obvious. During World War II, Bulgaria tried to spread its influence among this population in the Italian- and German-occupied areas of Macedonia, where it dispatched liaison officers and translators. In Kastoria, for a certain period of time in 1941, this was the mission of a historian from Sofia, named Ivan Duychev, who was personally sent there as a translator by Prime Minister Bogdan Filov. Soon, the patriotic activity of Duychev among local "Bulgarians" provoked Greek protests and Italian concern, and he had to leave: in his diary, Duychev exclaimed "I'll be back! With victory!" (Angelov 2018, 115). Indeed, in 1942–1943, next to other Bulgarian academics, he toured Northern Greece, including the monasteries of Mount Athos.

Duychev later became the leading Byzantinist of Bulgaria and to a large extent reshaped the Bulgarian mainstream approach to the Byzantine legacy. Departing from the traditional parochialism of Bulgarian medieval studies, with his research on "Slavo-Byzantine" commonality, he "laid the groundwork for the reassessment of the nature of Byzantine culture and its symbolic appropriation" (Mishkova 2023, 235). It was exactly this tension between universalist aspirations and national appropriation that was particularly visible in one kind of art studies.

Political Uses of Medieval Painting

As the example of Protich's "Southwestern school" demonstrates, church painting was no less instrumentalized than architecture in Balkan "nationalizations" of medieval art. In Bulgaria, this field of expertise was to a large extent developed thanks to a future world authority in Byzantine art history who later succeeded Gabriel Millet's tenure as academic chair in Paris. This was the Kiev-born André Grabar, who similarly to his teacher Nikodim Kondakov, moved to Sofia after the October Revolution. Following his nomination at the Bulgarian National Museum, Grabar authored a seminal study on the thirteenth-century murals in Boyana Church near Sofia (Grabar 1924). It was followed by another monograph on "Bulgarian religious painting"—a ground-breaking publication where Boyana Church also held center place (Grabar 1928).

With these publications, the Russian-French Byzantinist not only sketched the Bulgarian mainstream interpretation of Boyana and of medieval painting in general, but also inspired a popular historical "myth" in Bulgaria (Antonova 2012, 45). Grabar attributed the monument to a specific "Bulgarian art school" whose center was allegedly the capital Tărnovo. Although he promptly discovered the Byzantine models of Boyana's iconography, he believed that this was the most important monument of the "Old Bulgarian art" and also supposed that the painters were Bulgarians. More importantly, Grabar held that Boyana's painting had an exceptional place in art history with its "naturalistic" and "humanist" trend. According to him, "Boyana is perhaps the only example attesting a real effort towards naturalism that was ever attempted in Byzantium in the framework of Byzantine art" (Grabar 1928, 155). Moreover, he emphasized that it was not a matter of Western/Gothic influences which were minimal in Boyana: it was a unique monument that was ahead of the first instances of the Italian Renaissance. It was painted seven years earlier than the birth of Giotto, stated Grabar.

This was the starting point of a true apotheosis of Boyana in Bulgarian art history as a brilliant precursor of Renaissance art. Nikola Mavrodinov openly declared that Boyana represented a Renaissance earlier than the one of Duccio and Giotto (Mavrodinov 1943b, 58). In a monograph in German, Filov even declared that the painter of Boyana surpassed Giotto with regard to the individualization of images, while Mavrodinov compared him with Leonardo and stated that the art of Boyana was largely superior to Western art from the same period (Mavrodinov 1966, 120, 141; Antonova 2012, 48). These claims were credited with a series of qualifiers regarding the thirteenth-century murals: art with a popular basis, close to life and reality (hence, different from the "lifeless" and "repetitive" canon of Constantinople)—even "revolt against the mystical medieval art" (Mavrodinov 1966, 143).

This line of interpretation developed greatly during socialism, especially after a new edition of Grabar's 1924 essay was published in 1978, with a markedly ethno-centric preface by Ivan Duychev that was focused on the alleged Bulgarian identity of the masters (Antonova 2012, 47–48). It must be noted that Boyana was not the only imagined example of a

"Bulgarian Renaissance." While the archaeologist Krăstyu Miyatev characterized the "primitive" murals in the church in Zemen as a demonstration of a "naïveté, [which is] almost childish," this did not prevent him from claiming their "Renaissance" character: along with those in the later Poganovo Monastery, they represented a "popular" and "naturalist" painting, distinct from the Byzantine models and akin to Italian and Flemish Primitives (Miyatev 1927; Miyatev 1936). A similar approach was applied to the paintings in the thirteenth-fourteenth-century rock-hewn churches of Ivanovo, "the real Renaissance of the artistic worldview of Antiquity" (Mavrodinov 1966, 160), or to the Gospels of Tsar Ivan Alexander—especially after a luxurious monograph on the matter by Lyudmila Zhivkova, the daughter of Communist Party and state leader Todor Zhivkov.[39] In her work on the church in Donja Kamenica, Lilyana Mavrodinova discovered in it a "new humanism" akin to Duccio's and Giotto's masterpieces (Mavrodinova 1969, 28). Meanwhile, her father Nikola Mavrodinov had discovered the first Bulgarian Renaissance in the late ninth and tenth century, in accordance with the mainstream historical narrative about the "Golden Age" of Tsar Simeon (Mavrodinov 1959, 139–40). Mavrodinov also emphasized the Bulgarian ethnic character of these "Renaissances" using racial characteristics: the head of young Christ in Boyana was allegedly typical for Western and Northern Bulgaria, while in Ivanovo the "Greek type" with a characteristic nose was absent (Mavrodinov 1966, 161).

As idiosyncratic as it may seem, the "Renaissance" theory in Bulgarian art history is nevertheless not unique. Its basis was certainly the international thesis about the successive Byzantine "Renaissances" (Macedonian, Komnenian, Palaiologan), itself resulting from the initial Classicist bias of Byzantine Studies. As Anna Adashinskaya explains, the "primary merit of Byzantium was considered for a long time to be the preservation of Classical tradition and the transmission of ancient artistic forms to Italian humanism" (Adashinskaya 2022, 31). Gabriel Millet had extensively discussed the interaction between Byzantium and Italy during the Dugento and the Trecento, while in the same context he also addressed the particularities of a specific "Macedonian school" in Byzantine painting (Millet 1916b, 630–83).

---

[39] See Zhivkova (1980, 71–76). Unofficially, the creation of this work is attributed to Ivan Duychev.

Against this background, the Bulgarian national appropriation of the Renaissance was challenged by Serbian scholars. They also discovered in "their" medieval art "signs of Renaissance prior to the one in Italy"—as the historian Pero Slijepčević put it (Ignjatović 2016, 738). These signs were identified for instance in the paintings of the thirteenth-century monasteries of Mileševa and Sopoćani (Adashinskaya 2022, 39). In the long run, the fresco of the "White Angel" (*Beli anđeo*) from Mileševa become a popular emblem of the national artistic genius in Serbian visual culture (Pavićević 2005)—much like the image of the noble Desislava from the Boyana Church in Bulgarian visual culture.

Inspired by Millet's emphasis on Macedonian painting, Serbian specialists also referred to the fourteenth-century monuments in Macedonia. Both in his chapter in Aleksandar Belić's propagandist volume on Macedonia and in his own monograph on "Serbian monuments" in "Southern Serbia," Vladimir Petković claimed that Italian art developed under Serbian influence and was indebted to it. According to him, Italian Trecento could be understood "only in relation to the Serbian church art in Southern Serbia" (Petković 1924, XI; Ignjatović 2016, 739–40). At the same time, Petković conspicuously rejected the possibility of a particular "Macedonian school" in painting: visibly in order to be on the safe side, he fragmented fourteenth-century painting into several smaller "schools." While on this occasion he addressed a critical remark to Millet, Petković preferred to assign all responsibility for the "mystification" of the "Macedonian school" to scholars in Bulgaria, particularly to André Grabar (Petković 1930, II). In response, Vladimir Petković disdainfully rejected Bulgarian claims of originality: he emphasized that Serbian rulers had built churches on Bulgarian territory as well and stated that the murals in Mileševa were "by far superior" to those in Boyana. Denouncing Protich, he added that the "modest painting" of the Zemen Monastery in Bulgaria could not possibly inspire the great murals in Dečani, Peć, Gračanica, and Lesnovo (Petković 1926a, 155).

On the Bulgarian side, there was a similar valorization of Macedonian monuments. Nikola Mavrodinov suggested that the art in Ohrid from the period of Samuel could have generated "the whole modern painting five centuries before the Italian Renaissance." Unfortunately, Basil II the Bulgar Slayer, the "rude and uncultured ruler," put an end to this trend (Mavrodinov 1946, 54). Mavrodinov also insisted that a Macedonian (Bulgarian) painter from Ohrid had worked in the Basilica of Saint Francis in Assisi and influenced Giotto's artistic idiom (Mavrodinov 1946,

139–140). Ironically, Mavrodinov almost repeated Petković by stating that "the Italian Trecento is based entirely on Macedonian painting" (Mavrodinov 1946, 192; Adashinskaya 2022, 39). Apart from Saint Sophia in Ohrid and the Boyana Church, Mavrodinov emphasized the church of Saint Panteleimon in Nerezi near Skopje among the Bulgarian precursors of the Renaissance—a monument otherwise attributed to the Byzantine Komnenian "Renaissance" in international scholarship.

Finally, he completely marginalized any non-Bulgarian Byzantine artistic tradition in Macedonia: to the extent that it existed, it was an adaptation of a Bulgarian Macedonian tradition. In his opinion, the latter had "conquered" Byzantine Thessaloniki and he offered as an example Manuel Panselinos, perhaps the most famous painter from the Palaiologan period, who was allegedly inspired by Bulgarian Macedonian models. Another major painter from Thessaloniki, Eutychios had also "appropriated the old local Macedonian tradition," which was "more human" than the Byzantine one (Mavrodinov 1946, 129, 133). Still, Mavrodinov insisted that the masters from Ohrid understood the Renaissance of Antiquity "differently from the Greeks" and referred to the local thirteenth-century Saint Clement Church/Panagia Perivleptos. According to his evaluation, the latter was not only representative of the Macedonian (Bulgarian) Renaissance but also continued a longer artistic trend going back to the period of the First Bulgarian state (Mavrodinov 1946, 135, 138).

Mavrodinov's ethno-nationalist speculations soon proved to be dramatically wrong. A few years after his publication, Yugoslav specialists discovered in Saint Clement/Panagia Perivleptos signatures of the artists who painted it: these were Michael Astrapas and Eutychios, the famous Byzantine Greek painters who were already known for their work in Staro Nagoričane and other important churches commissioned by Serbian rulers.

As far as Greek scholarship is concerned, it had largely taken for granted that Byzantine art was a repository of Classical Hellenic legacy. Hence, Greek scholars did not need to imagine any more special link to the European Renaissance than those discussed in international scholarship. In his praise of Manuel Panselinos, Andreas Xyngopoulos demonstrated a rather sober approach to earlier erudite comparisons of the painter from Thessaloniki with Giotto and Raphael (Xyngopoulos 1956, 17, 27). Yet, he demonstrated a more nationalist approach when facing denials of Greek artistic activity under Serbian medieval rulers.

A controversy had formed—again—thanks to Vladimir Petković due to his allegations that the presence of Greek inscriptions in medieval Serbian churches could not be considered proof of the activity of Byzantine masters (Petković 1930, III). In a way, quite similar to Bulgarian scholars such as Filov, Petković explained that masters simply wished to demonstrate their proficiency in a prestigious language that was even regarded as sacred in the Orthodox Christian tradition—similarly to Latin in the West. Xyngopoulos agreed that inscriptions in churches were not always a reliable indication of the "nationality" of masters, but he presented the opposite argument: Greek-speaking painters could have executed inscriptions in Serbian according to the desire of the donator. Petković had stressed that in Staro Nagoričane, where nearly all inscriptions were in Greek, those next to "Serbian national saints" were in Serbian: his conclusion was that this distinction could have been done only by a Serbian painter. Xyngopoulos replied that precisely this fact—that the inscriptions in this case were in Serbian—demonstrated that the painters were Greek. According to his logic, while the masters habitually wrote in their mother tongue, they were obliged to indicate Serbian saints in Serbian so that the local clergy and congregation could recognize them (Xyngopoulos 1955, 64).

While Petković had also questioned the Greek identity of painters who had signed their works in Greek, Xyngopoulos stressed that signatures of painters were an authentic epigraphic source about their ethnic belonging. Commenting on the case of John—Metropolitan Bishop of Prilep and painter of the fourteenth-century Saint Andrew Church in Matka Canyon near Skopje, who signed his name in Slavonic but executed all inscriptions in Greek—the Greek art historian accepted that John could have been "Serb." Yet, he added that he could write in Greek as well, since Prilep used to be a "Greek" city. Moreover, he stated that the inscriptions were done in Greek because local monks, as well as the majority of the people of medieval Skopje, were also "Greeks" (Xyngopoulos 1955, 66–67).

Andreas Xyngopoulos also endeavored the ultimate "nationalization" of Gabriel Millet's "Macedonian school," active in late thirteenth- and fourteenth-century Macedonia and Serbia. He posited Thessaloniki as the only important creative center of this "school," one that had spread its influence over the entirety of Macedonia and the Balkans for several centuries. The way Xyngopoulos described the distinctive style of Macedonian Byzantine painting is to a large extent reminiscent of the praise it received in Bulgaria (as essentially Bulgarian) and in Serbia (as Serbian painting): it was characterized by "realism" and a "love of movement and life" that were rooted in the art of Antiquity (Xyngopoulos 1955, 7–8). Similar to other Balkan scholars, he distinguished Macedonian painting from the academic art of Constantinople on these grounds. Xyngopoulos discovered the first instances of the Macedonian Byzantine style in monuments such as Nerezi and Bachkovo—regarded by Bulgarian specialists as representative of Bulgarian art. The Greek scholar emphasized the influence of Thessaloniki in Serbia and attributed the heyday of medieval painting under King Milutin to the activity of masters from the Byzantine city. Unsurprisingly, this exclusive focus on Thessaloniki was criticized by Yugoslav scholars—in particular by the Macedonian art historian Cvetan Grozdanov who, similarly to his Serbian colleague Gojko Subotić, stressed the importance of another artistic center in the medieval Balkans: the "Ohrid school."[40]

The Macedonian Heritage—To the Macedonians

An academic of high international profile, Cvetan Grozdanov is also representative of the Macedonian art history that was established after World War II—and of its pattern of "nationalization" of local medieval heritage. On the one hand, as an academic discipline, Macedonian art history was formed in a Yugoslav context largely as an offspring of Serbian scholarship. This aspect predetermined some of its features, such as a relatively greater inclusivity regarding Byzantine cultural influences and legacy, unlike the particularistic accent in Bulgaria over the "Old Bulgarian art." Yet, although Macedonian medieval art was researched by Grozdanov in the context of Byzantine art, he imagined Macedonia rather as the main cultural mediator between Byzantium and the Slavic world (Grozdanov 1983, 9). Similar to the mainstream Macedonian historical narrative, Macedonian medieval art history also adopted and reinterpreted a series of major points of the Bulgarian historical narrative: its focus on the figures of the Slavic enlighteners Cyril and Methodius and their disciples, all of them regarded as national saints, on Samuel's state, on its capital Ohrid as a spiritual center, etc. Nevertheless, the "national" actor who was behind all these cultural and political phenomena was no other but the "Macedonian Slavs."

[40] See Grozdanov (1980, 180–181). It must be noted that Yugoslav authors likewise emphasized the importance of other artistic centers such as Kastoria. Incidentally, their findings concerned also monuments traditionally studied by Bulgarian scholars (Bakalova 2007, 497–503).

Thus, while Grozdanov agreed with Bulgarian scholars that Samuel founded the Saint Achillius Basilica in Prespa as a cathedral church, he interpreted it not as a center of a Bulgarian Patriarchate but of the Ohrid Archbishopric, which was allegedly established by Cyril and Methodius, long before the Byzantine emperor Basil II, and thus functioned as a Macedonian autocephalous Church under Samuel (Grozdanov 2006, 58–59; Grozdanov 2007). Grozdanov stressed that Samuel's state was one of Macedonian Slavs, despite its "official designation," and protested against the appropriation of Macedonian heritage—in particular, against the naming of "our creative exploit" after designations of "ephemerous, foreign state creations" (Grozdanov 2006, 61). Although Grozdanov visibly did not include among the latter Samuel's state (that lasted for a period of twenty years or to just under fifty years, according to the most optimistic dating), the lack of a continuous Macedonian medieval statehood was certainly one of the factors that encouraged the scholar to study a particular topic: the iconography of saints whose cult flourished in Macedonian territories.

In his works on the portraits of Cyril and Methodius, Clement and Naum of Ohrid, and other saintly figures from Macedonia (or related to it), Grozdanov asserted a long historical continuity of a specific Macedonian memory and identity both in the pre-Ottoman medieval era and during the Ottoman period. Nevertheless, although he emphasized their local Macedonian character, Grozdanov traced multiple trajectories and appropriations of these cults in the Balkans. Next to Ohrid and Prespa, it was not the major Byzantine centers Constantinople and Thessaloniki that were the primary actors from this point of view but Kastoria and Mount Athos, the Serbian monasteries in Raška and Kosovo or the Habsburg Serbian center Sremski Karlovci and the Aromanian/Greek/Albanian Moschopolis (Voskopojë) in the Ottoman period.

One of the implications of this research indirectly questions Bulgarian scholarship: in fact, excepting Western Bulgaria, most of this country looks rather peripheral in the circulation of images of Slavic enlighteners and other Orthodox Christian saints celebrated as "Bulgarian national saints" in the Bulgarian historical narrative.[41] While the figures of Slavic enlighteners seem to have been popular in Albania, the portraits of some of them are nearly or entirely absent in present-day Bulgarian territories

---

[41] This applies even to the foremost "Bulgarian national saint"—John of Rila (Kiel 1985, 308–22).

until the emergence of the Bulgarian national movement in the nineteenth century.[42] Thus, contrary to Greater-Bulgarian mappings of "Old Bulgarian art," Cvetan Grozdanov, and in general Macedonian art historians, suggested a map of cultural interactions generally side-lining Bulgaria. Ironically, in the Bulgarian academic context, the importance of the cult to Clement, Naum, and other "national" saints in Macedonia and Albania only confirmed the Bulgarian identity of the former and the longevity of an alleged Bulgarian legacy in the latter: on the same grounds, Yordan Ivanov had emphasized the Bulgarian "historical rights" over Albania (Petrov 1993b, 136–9).

The recognition of the Macedonian national narrative and its definitive construction in the framework of socialist Yugoslavia obliged Serbian scholars to revise the identity categories they used. In their publications from the late 1940s and the 1950s, even Gabriel Millet's former collaborators felt obliged to treat medieval heritage in Macedonia separately from the one in Serbia. Thus, Đurđe Bošković reformulated quite tendentiously Millet's triad (the Raška school, the Serbo-Byzantine school, the Morava school) whereby the second element was renamed the "Kosovo-Metohija school." Hence, the fourteenth-century monuments in Kosovo were strikingly separated from those in Macedonia—the reason why he would be later accused of surrendering to "Titoistic mythology" and offering part of Serbian medieval heritage to "Macedonian Slavs" (Stevović 2018, 5; Stevović 2021, 305–07).

In the first editions of his influential work on "monumental and decorative architecture" in medieval Serbia, the architect Aleksandar Deroko also preferred to be cautious. He justified the inclusion of Macedonia in his book stating that he would consider only those monuments that were built under Serbian rule since they could not be isolated to a specific entity. Otherwise, the development of architecture in Macedonia as a whole was to be studied by "Skopje's scholarly center" (Deroko 1962, 12–13, 19). Nevertheless, his book contained a conspicuous map of the architectural heritage of medieval Serbia: it included the territories of Macedonia and Montenegro as well as areas of Bosnia-Herzegovina, Dubrovnik in Croatia,

---

[42] As also demonstrated by the works of the Bulgarian academic Ralitsa Rousseva (2023). By contrast, her colleague from the socialist period Atanas Bozhkov preferred to water down the question and studied the images of Cyril and Methodius (less popular in the Balkans compared to Clement and Naum) in a longer historical and "pan-European" context including Italy, Czechia, Russia, etc. (Bozhkov 1989).

Shkodër in Albania, and Kyustendil in Bulgaria (Deroko 1962, 20). Based on this mapping of an architectural Greater Serbia, his approach later reversed to traditional Serbian academic theses (Ignjatović 2019). Nevertheless, being part of a larger Yugoslav context, Serbian historians of medieval art and architecture proved to be relatively accommodating concerning the existence of a separate Macedonian art history, while their progressive opening toward the transnational academic context of Byzantine Studies rendered largely irrelevant the old identity concerns.

The situation in Bulgaria was similar, but only to a certain extent. Under socialism, the studies of medieval "Bulgarian art" downplayed the irredentist focus on Macedonia from the interwar period. The "old bourgeois" research was declaratively banished and at least in one respect its appealing resurrection was problematic. In February 1945, Bogdan Filov, the founder of professional archaeology and art history in Bulgaria and of the theory of "Old Bulgarian art," was executed as the former Prime Minister responsible for the Bulgarian wartime alliance with Nazi Germany. This fact had clear implications regarding his intellectual legacy: it was to be used cautiously. Initially, communist-ruled Bulgaria also recognized Macedonian national identity. Thus, in the preface to the 1946 edition of his *Old Bulgarian Painting*, Nikola Mavrodinov tried to distance himself from the "Greater-Bulgarian chauvinism"—in the moment of the self-determination of the "Macedonian people" in the framework of Tito's Yugoslavia (Mavrodinov 1946, 6–7).

EPILOGUE

Yet, although he stressed the particular character of the "Macedonian school" in architecture and painting, Mavrodinov underlined its "close connection" to Bulgaria and the body text of his book was far from asserting any Macedonian distinctiveness anyway. The two volumes of his posthumous monograph *Old Bulgarian Art* largely recycled his pre-war theses, although in a Marxist-Leninist key and with more detailed archaeological data. In the mid-1960s, it was possible to read, in the same book, that Ohrid and Mount Athos were part of "our lands" (Mavrodinov 1966, 56). By the same time, the old mainstream historical narrative about Macedonia was already rehabilitated in Zhivkov's Bulgaria. Research on medieval cultural heritage certainly continued to pursue its national mission, but it was encouraged by the authorities on another level: instead of irredentist concerns, it rather served the official strategy of national homogenization and patriotic indoctrination within the country.

During the socialist period, the apotheosis of medieval "Bulgarian art" did not leave room for any Byzantine influences or contexts, let alone the framing of medieval heritage as something other than Bulgarian. The same was largely instrumentalized for propaganda purposes both inside the country and abroad especially around the grandiose celebrations of the 1300-Years Jubilee of the Bulgarian state in 1981: exhibitions such as *1000 Years of Bulgarian Icons*, *Medieval Bulgarian Civilization*, and *Treasures of the Rila Monastery* toured the world's museums (Dragostinova 2021). For the same purpose, Atanas Bozhkov, a leading art historian, produced an essentialist image of "the Bulgarian icon" (Bozhkov 1984): a catch-all category covering images from the ninth to the nineteenth century of diverse origins, including paintings that ended up in Bulgaria as a result of World War I. The "Renaissance trends" in "Old Bulgarian" culture and the "Bulgarian contributions" to European civilization became topics of predilection destined for larger audiences.

Focusing on major centers of Bulgarian medieval states—Pliska, Preslav, Madara, Tărnovo—the official cultural policy also had an important material impact on heritage sites. In Tărnovo, specialists from the late socialism rebuilt medieval fortifications and churches in a rather nineteenth-century type of fantasist "restoration." It had begun in the 1930s, with the efforts of Aleksandăr Rashenov who reconstructed the so-called Baldwin's Tower after the model of a tower preserved in the medieval site of Cherven (about 70 km away). The new reconstructions were also rather hypothetical and, in some cases, they verge on falsification (Kiel 1985, 223, fn. 37). The city itself was renamed Veliko (i.e., Great) Tărnovo in 1965. Thus, the old claim about the lack of monumentality in the architectural heritage of the Second Bulgarian state vanished definitively. Questioned by foreign scholars (Kiel 1985, 246–7), the theory of the "Tărnovo artistic school" was definitively enthroned during socialism (Bozhkov 1985) despite its obvious defects: in painting, it relied on poorly demonstrated links between a limited number of monuments (mostly Boyana) and traces of almost destroyed murals in Tărnovo itself. In architecture, as Krăstyu Miyatev reminded, even churches built by founders related to Tărnovo (e.g., Boyana) clearly differ from Tărnovo's "architectural school" (Miyatev 1965, 232).

In some cases, the socialist policies of heritage changed radically older perceptions: for instance, in the case of Melnik that was nearly non-existent in Bulgarian scholarship prior to socialism, while its important medieval heritage was almost completely lost. Similar to Nesebăr and Asenovgrad, the "heritagization" of Melnik went in parallel with its "de-Byzantinization": the town was now celebrated as the stronghold of the thirteenth-century Bulgarian despot Alexius Slav. The so-called Byzantine house located in its center—one of the rare cases of medieval residential architecture in the Balkans next to Mystras—was renamed "Boyar's house," suggesting that it belonged to the same or another Bulgarian ruler (Marinov 2015).

The ideological construction of "Old/Medieval Bulgarian art" had also another political implication that goes beyond the limits of the present study: this was the idea to demonstrate the uninterrupted continuity of Bulgarians and their cultural identity during the long Ottoman period. Indirectly, this was an aspect likewise related to the national homogenizing policy of the regime targeting the Muslim minorities in the country. Traditionally, Bulgarian art history shared the "theory of catastrophe" that was also common in Serbian and Greek scholarship: according to the theory, the Ottoman invasion of the Balkans destroyed the magnificent monuments of a brilliant civilization, brought local arts to a standstill, and even cut short the first instances of a "Renaissance" before the one in Italy. A characteristic example was Andrey Protich, who dedicated his most important monograph to what he saw as the "denationalization" of Bulgarian art under the "Turkish yoke" (Protich 1930). In 1985, this theory was bluntly criticized by the Ottomanist Machiel Kiel whose work *Art and Society of Bulgaria in the Turkish Period* was aggressively met by Bulgarian scholars as a brutal political attack (Todorova 1986). While Kiel's work was certainly problematic in many respects, it exposed a continuity in art production before and after the Ottoman conquest that was also acknowledged by Bulgarian specialists and thus paradoxically coexisted in Bulgarian scholarship with the "theory of catastrophe."

In fact, a considerable part of the canon of "Old Bulgarian" architecture, "Old Bulgarian" mural painting, and—even more—of the inventory of "the Bulgarian icon" or "the Bulgarian" applied arts (metalwork, woodcarving) covers antiquities from the Ottoman period, not from the pre-Ottoman medieval Bulgarian statehood. Next to the alleged or real Ottoman destruction of monuments, already Filov emphasized also the vitality of Orthodox Christian art under Turkish rule and even illogically used it for his demonstration of the national peculiarity of Bulgarian art: as he claimed, since there was no Byzantium anymore, the very existence of Bulgarian artistic production during the Ottoman period proved that it was not a simple branch of Byzantine art (Filov 1924, 117). With this idea of national continuity, Filov published a history of Bulgarian art under Turkish domination (Filov 1933). Not surprisingly, the Greek ethnographer Angeliki Chatzimichali criticized Filov regarding woodcarving from the Ottoman period: in her opinion, Greek masters had created the masterpieces of this kind of art in Bulgaria and all over the Balkans (Hadjimihali 1950). The Greek historian Kosmas Myrtilos Apostolidis (born in Philippoupoli/Plovdiv) also contested what he saw as Bulgarian appropriation of woodcarving (Pelekanidis 1960, 22). In any case, the emphasis on continuity tended to completely remove the Ottoman cultural context as irrelevant to the analysis of Christian artistic creations dating back to the same period.

Last but not least, it must be noted that the works on art and architecture under Ottoman rule—including during the so-called Bulgarian National Revival in the nineteenth century—are another important channel of appropriation of Macedonia in the Bulgarian heritage canon. Some of the most important Balkan "schools" and masters of church handicrafts originated from Ottoman Macedonia. Painters, woodcarvers, and master builders from the region figured prominently in a major work on Bulgarian "Revival masters," published by Asen Vasiliev, one of the scholars who conducted extensive fieldwork research in Bulgarian-occupied Macedonia and Mount Athos during World War II (Vasiliev 1965). As a whole, the Bulgarian notion of "Revival art" remained deeply contradictory: one and the same period of art history was understood both as a continuation of medieval "Bulgarian art," and as an innovative break with the Middle Ages—even as a "Renaissance." In fact, the Bulgarian term for "Revival" (*Văzrazhdane*) could be also understood as "Renaissance" and, indeed, this is how the designation of the Western European cultural phenomenon has been often translated into Bulgarian. Hence, a number of dubious analogies in academic publications between eighteenth- and nineteenth-century Orthodox Christian art in Bulgaria and the (several centuries earlier) European Renaissance.[43]

The fall of the communist regime in 1989 was followed by a new vogue of publications on "Bulgarian antiquities in Macedonia," authored mostly by mediatic historians and archaeologists (Ovcharov 1994; Dimitrov 2000). Nikola Mavrodinov's theories were also resuscitated in the most

---

[43] On the Bulgarian and, in general, Balkan narratives of national "Revival," see Vezenkov and Marinov (2015).

nationalist interpretations that are still searching for "the first" *cloisonné* masonry, "the first" brick decoration of churches, and "the first" glazed ceramic decorative elements—of course, in Bulgarian monuments (Tuleshkov 2001). But, while new generations of art historians dedicated themselves to questions of professional research devoid of nationalist emotions, the "Old Bulgarian art" had already left the realm of art history and had become a matter of indoctrinated popular imagination—a piece of banal nationalism.

REFERENCES

ARCHIVAL SOURCES:

NA-BAN (Archive of the Bulgarian Academy of Sciences), 1k, 2, 358; 1k, 2, 371; 1k, 2, 377.
TsDA (Central State Archive—Sofia), 176k, 3, 646; 177k, 1, 475.

BIBLIOGRAPHY:

Adashinskaya, Anna. 2022. Renaissances in Byzantium and Byzantium in the Renaissance. The International Development of Ideas and Terminology in Late Nineteenth- and Early Twentieth-Century Europe. In *Periodization in the Art Historiographies of Central and Eastern Europe*, ed. Shona Kallestrup et al., 31–47. New York & London: Routledge.
Angelov, Dimiter. 2003. Byzantinism: The Real and the Imaginary Influence of a Medieval Civilization on the Modern Balkans. In *New Approaches to Balkan Studies*, ed. Dimitris Keridis et al., 3–23. Dulles: Brassey's.
Angelov, Svetozar. 2018. Prof. Ivan Duychev i misiyata mu v Kostur prez 1941 g. In *Universitetski cheteniya po arhivistika*, vol. VI, 109–126. Sofia: David.
Antonova, Klemena. 2012. Stenopisite ot Boyanskata tsărkva v bălgarskata nauchna literatura (Oshte edin pogled vărhu problema za Renesansa). *Hristiyanstvo i kultura* 8 (75): 43–58.
Azmanov, Dimităr. 1995. *Moyata epoha 1878–1919*. Sofia: Sv. Georgi Pobedonosets.
Bakalova, Elka. 2007. Srăbskite ucheni za monumentalnata tsărkovna zhivopis ot XV vek v Bălgariya. *Zbornik radova Vizantološkog instituta* XLIV: 493–518.
Bakalova, Elka. 2012. Art History in Bulgaria: Institutional Frameworks, Research Directions and Individual Scholars. In *Art History and Visual Studies in Europe. Transnational Discourses and National Frameworks*, ed. Matthew Rampley et al., 287–304. Leiden & Boston: Brill.
Bálint, Csanád. 2010. *Der Schatz von Nagyszentmiklós. Archäologische Studien*. Budapest: Balassi.

Balş, Gheorghe. 1911. *Une visite à quelques églises de Serbie*. Bucharest: Charles Göbl.

Baric, Daniel. 2017. «De la tranchée où l'on fouille à celle où l'on se bat». Français et Autrichiens sur le front de la science entre Balkans et Dardanelles. *Bulletin de l'Institut Pierre Renouvin* 2 (46): 61–76.

Born, Robert, and Beate Störtkuhl. 2017. *Apologeten der Vernichtung oder »Kunstschützer«? Kunsthistoriker der Mittelmächte im Ersten Weltkrieg*. Köln: Böhlau.

Bošković, Đurđe. 1933. N. Mavrodinov: Ednokorabnata i krăstovidnata tsărkva po bălgarskite zemi do kraya na XIV v. *Prilozi za književnost, jezik, istoriju i folklor* 13 (1–2): 216–228.

Bozhkov, Atanas. 1984. *Bălgarskata ikona*. Sofia: Bălgarski hudozhnik.

Bozhkov, Atanas. 1985. *Tărnovska srednovekovna hudozhestvena shkola*. Sofia: Nauka i izkustvo.

Bozhkov, Atanas. 1989. *Izobrazheniyata na Kiril i Metodiy prez vekovete*. Sofia: Nauka i izkustvo.

Chamardjieff, Janaki. 1904. *L'architecture en Bulgarie*. Sofia: n.p.

Chilingirov, Asen. 2013. *Ohridskata "Sv. Sofiya" i neynata datirovka*. Sofia: Heron Pres.

Chlepa, Eleni-Anna. 2022. *The Byzantine Monuments in Modern Greece. Ideology and Practice of Restorations, 1833–1939*. Athens: Kapon.

Ćurčić, Slobodan. 1989. Architecture in the Byzantine Sphere of Influence Around the Middle of the Fourteenth Century. In *Dečani i vizantijska umetnost sredinom XIV veka*, ed. Vojislav Đurić, 55–68. Belgrade: SANU.

Curta, Florin. 2013. With Brotherly Love: The Czech Beginnings of Medieval Archaeology in Bulgaria and Ukraine. In *Manufacturing Middle Ages. Entangled History of Medievalism in Nineteenth-Century Europe*, ed. Patrick Geary and Gábor Klaniczay, 377–396. Leiden & Boston: Brill.

Daskalov, Roumen. 2015. Feud over the Middle Ages: Bulgarian-Romanian Historiographical Debates. In *Entangled Histories of the Balkans*, ed. Roumen Daskalov and Alexander Vezenkov, vol. 3, 274–354. Leiden & Boston: Brill.

Daskalov, Roumen. 2021. *Master Narratives of the Middle Ages in Bulgaria*. Leiden & Boston: Brill.

Denchev, Stoyan, and Sofiya Vasileva. 2010. *Dărzhavna politika za kulturnoistoricheskoto nasledstvo na Bălgariya 1878–2005*. Sofia: Za bukvite.

Deroko, Aleksandar. 1962. *Monumentalna i dekorativna arhitektura u srednjevekovnoj Srbiji*. Belgrade: Naučna knjiga.

Dimitrov, Bozhidar. 2000. *Bălgarski starini v Makedoniya*. Sofia: Aniko.

Dimitsas, Margaritis. 1896. *I Makedonia en lithois ftheggomenois kai mnimeiois sozomenois*. Athens: Afoi Perri.

Dragostinova, Theodora. 2021. *The Cold War from the Margins. A Small Socialist State on the Global Cultural Scene*. Ithaca & London: Cornell University Press.

4 ART WARS: THE CREATION OF BULGARIAN ART HISTORY AND THE BALKAN... 213

Epstein, Ann Wharton. 1980. Middle Byzantine Churches of Kastoria: Dates and Implications. *The Art Bulletin* 2 (62): 190–207.
Filov, Bogdan. 1917. Denkmäler der thrakischen Kunst. *Mitteilungen des Kaiserlich Deutschen Archäologischen Instituts, Römische Abteilung* 32: 21–73.
Filov, Bogdan. 1919. *Early Bulgarian Art*. Bern: Paul Haupt.
Filov, Bogdan. 1924. *Starobălgarskoto izkustvo*. Sofia: Naroden muzey.
Filov, Bogdan. 1925. Starorumănsko i starobălgarsko izkustvo. *Zlatorog* VI (4): 191–200.
Filov, Bogdan. 1930a. Starobălgarskata tsărkovna arhitektura. *Spisanie na BAN* XLIII: 1–59.
Filov, Bogdan. 1930b. Starobălgarskata zhivopis prez XIII i XIV vek. *Bălgarska istoricheska biblioteka* 3 (1): 52–96.
Filov, Bogdan. 1933. *Geschichte der bulgarischen Kunst unter der türkischen Herrschaft und in der neueren Zeit*. Berlin & Leipzig: De Gruyter.
Filov, Bogdan. 1934. *Miniatyurite na Londonskoto evangelie na tsar Ivan Aleksandra*. Sofia: n.p.
Frfulanović, Dragana. 2001. Čija je crkva u Donjoj Kamenici. In *Zbornik radova Filozofskog fakulteta* XXVIII–XXIX, 299–343. Priština-Blace.
Gargova, Fani. 2017. Medievalism, Byzantinism, and Bulgarian Politics through the Archival Lens. In *The Middle Ages in the Modern World*, ed. Bettina Bildhauer and Chris Jones, 152–167. Oxford: Oxford University Press.
Geary, Patrick, and Gábor Klaniczay. 2013. Introduction. In *Manufacturing Middle Ages. Entangled History of Medievalism in Nineteenth-Century Europe*, ed. Patrick Geary and Gábor Klaniczay, 1–9. Leiden & Boston: Brill.
Grabar, André. 1924. *Boyanskata tsărkva*. Sofia: n.p.
Grabar, André. 1928. *La peinture religieuse en Bulgarie*. Paris: Paul Geuthner.
Grozdanov, Cvetan. 1980. *Ohridskoto dzidno slikarstvo od XIV vek*. Ohrid: Naroden muzej.
Grozdanov, Cvetan. 1983. *Portreti na svetitelite od Makedonija od IX–XVIII vek*. Skopje: RZZSK.
Grozdanov, Cvetan. 2006. *Kurbinovo i drugi studii za freskoživopisot vo Prespa*. Skopje: MANU.
Grozdanov, Cvetan. 2007. *Živopisot na Ohridskata arhiepiskopija*. Skopje: MANU.
Hadjimihali, Anghéliki. 1950. *La sculpture sur bois*. Athens: n.p.
Hajdu, Ada. 2017. The Search for National Architectural Styles in Serbia, Romania, and Bulgaria from the Mid-nineteenth Century to World War I. In *Entangled Histories of the Balkans*, ed. Roumen Daskalov et al., vol. 4, 394–439. Leiden & Boston: Brill.
Henning, Joachim. 2007. The Metropolis of Pliska or, How Large Does an Early Medieval Settlement Have to Be in Order to Be Called a City? In *Post-Roman Towns, Trade and Settlement in Europe and Byzantium*, ed. Joachim Henning, vol. 2, 209–240. Berlin & New York: De Gruyter.

Ignjatović, Aleksandar. 2016. *U srpsko-vizantijskom kaleidoskopu, Arhitektura, nacionalizam i imperijalna imaginacija 1878–1941.* Belgrade: Orion Art.

Ignjatović, Aleksandar. 2019. Legacy of the Triad: Architecture in Medieval Serbia between Style and Ideology in the Work of Aleksandar Deroko. *Serbian Architectural Journal* 11 (1): 115–140.

Ivanov, Yordan. 1908. *Bălgarski starini iz Makedoniya.* Sofia: BKD.

Ivanov, Yordan. 1910. Tsar Samuilovata stolitsa v Prespa. Istoriko-arheologicheski belezhki. In *IBAD*, vol. I: 55–80.

Ivanova-Mavrodinova, Vera. 1926. Stari tsărkvi i manastiri v bălgarskite zemi (IV–XII v.). In *GNM* 4 (1922–1925): 429–582.

Kănchov, Vasil. 1894. Pătuvane po dolinite na Struma, Mesta i Bregalnitsa. In *SbNUNK*, vol. X: 469–535.

Kanitz, Felix. 1862. *Serbiens byzantinische Monumente.* Wien: n.p.

Kiel, Machiel. 1985. *Art and Society of Bulgaria in the Turkish Period.* Assen/Maastricht: Van Gorcum.

Kitromilides, Paschalis. 1998. On the Intellectual Content of Greek Nationalism: Paparrigopoulos, Byzantium and the Great Idea. In *Byzantium and the Modern Greek Identity*, ed. David Ricks and Paul Magdalino, 25–33. Aldershot: Ashgate.

Klaniczay, Gábor et al. 2011. *Multiple Antiquities—Multiple Modernities: Ancient Histories in Nineteenth Century European Cultures.* Frankfurt & New York: Campus.

Kondakov, Nikodim. 1909. *Makedoniya. Arheologicheskoe puteshestvie.* Saint Petersburg: IAN.

Koneva, Rumyana. 1998. Krazhbata na tsennosti i săkrovishta mezhdu balkanskite dărzhavi po vreme na voynite na poluostrova (1912–1918)—izraz na balkanska vzaimnost? In *Darove i săkrovishta: duhovna priemstvenost na Balkanite*, ed. Petăr Vodenicharov, 103–111. Blagoevgrad: YUZU.

Kott, Christina. 2006. *Préserver l'art de l'ennemi ? Le patrimoine artistique en Belgique et en France occupées, 1914–1918.* Peter Lang.

Kotzageorgi-Zymari, Xanthippi. 2002. *I voulgariki katochi stin Anatoliki Makedonia kai ti Thraki, 1941–1944.* Thessaloniki: Paratiritis.

Langer, Benjamin. 2019. *»Fremde, ferne Welt«. Mazedonienimaginationen in der deutschsprachigen Literatur seit dem 19. Jahrhundert.* Bielefeld: Transcript.

Lory, Bernard. 2015. The Ottoman Legacy in the Balkans. In *Entangled Histories of the Balkans*, ed. Roumen Daskalov and Alexander Vezenkov, vol. 3, 355–405. Leiden & Boston: Brill.

Lory, Bernard, and Petrit Nathanaili. 2002. Le monastère de Saint-Naum (Sveti Naum/Shën Naum). *Balkanologie* VI (1–2): 35–40.

Madgearu, Alexandru. 2007. The Dridu Culture and the Changing Position of Romania among the Communist States. *Archaeologia Bulgarica* 11 (2): 51–59.

4 ART WARS: THE CREATION OF BULGARIAN ART HISTORY AND THE BALKAN... 215

Makuljević, Nenad. 2013. The Political Reception of the Vienna School: Josef Strzygowski and Serbian Art History. *Journal of Art Historiography* 8: 1–13.

Marchand, Suzanne. 2009. *German Orientalism in the Age of Empire: Religion, Race, and Scholarship.* Washington, DC & Cambridge: Cambridge University Press.

Marchetti, Christian. 2013. *Balkanexpedition. Die Kriegserfahrung der österreichischen Volkskunde—eine historisch-ethnographische Erkundung.* Tübingen: TVV.

Marinov, Tchavdar. 2015. Constructing Bulgarian Heritage: The Nationalisation of the Byzantine and Ottoman Architectures of Melnik. In *Balkan Heritages: Negotiating History and Culture*, ed. Maria Couroucli and Tchavdar Marinov, 77–109. Farnham: Ashgate.

Marinov, Tchavdar. 2017. The 'Balkan House': Interpretations and Symbolic Appropriations of the Ottoman-Era Vernacular Architecture in the Balkans. In *Entangled Histories of the Balkans*, ed. Roumen Daskalov et al., vol. 4, 440–593. Leiden & Boston: Brill.

Maufroy, Sandrine. 2010. Les premiers congrès internationaux des études byzantines: entre nationalisme scientifique et construction internationale d'une discipline. *Revue germanique internationale* 12: 229–240.

Mavrodinov, Nikola. 1931. *Ednokorabnata i krăstovidnata tsărkva v bălgarskite zemi do kraya na XIV v.* Sofia: n.p.

Mavrodinov, Nikola. 1935. Vănshnata ukrasa na starobălgarskite tsărkvi. *IBAI* 8: 262–330.

Mavrodinov, Nikola. 1942. Arheologichni i hudozhestveno-istorichni izsledvaniya na Makedoniya, I. *Makedonski pregled* 2: 1–25.

Mavrodinov, Nikola. 1943a. Arheologichni i hudozhestveno-istorichni izsledvaniya na Makedoniya, II. *Makedonski pregled* 4: 88–129.

Mavrodinov, Nikola. 1943b. *Boyanskata tsărkva i neynite stenopisi.* Sofia: Bălgarska kniga.

Mavrodinov, Nikola. 1946. *Starobălgarskata zhivopis.* Sofia: BID.

Mavrodinov, Nikola. 1959. *Starobălgarskoto izkustvo. Izkustvoto na Părvoto bălgarsko tsarstvo.* Sofia: Nauka i izkustvo.

Mavrodinov, Nikola. 1966. *Starobălgarskoto izkustvo. XI–XIII v.* Sofia: Bălgarski hudozhnik.

Mavrodinova, Lilyana. 1969. *Tsărkvata v Dolna Kamenitsa.* Sofia: Bălgarski hudozhnik.

Millet, Gabriel. 1916a. *L'école grecque dans l'architecture byzantine.* Paris: Ernest Leroux.

Millet, Gabriel. 1916b. *Recherches sur l'iconographie de l'Évangile aux XIVe, XVe et XVIe siècles.* Paris: Fontemoing et Cie.

Millet, Gabriel. 1919. *L'ancien art serbe. Les églises.* Paris: De Boccard.

Millet, Gabriel. 1933. Cozia et les églises serbes de la Morava. In *Mélanges offerts à M. Nicolas Iorga par ses amis de France et des pays de langue française*, ed. Nicolae Iorga, 827–856. Paris: J. Gamber.

Milyukov, Pavel. 1899. Hristianskiya drevnosti Zapadnoy Makedonii. *IRAIK* IV: 21–151.

Minea, Cosmin. 2022. From Byzantine to Brâncovenesc. The Periodization of Romanian Art in the Second Half of the Nineteenth Century. In *Periodization in the Art Historiographies of Central and Eastern Europe*, ed. Shona Kallestrup et al., 48–67. New York & London: Routledge.

Mishkova, Diana. 2023. *Rival Byzantiums. Empire and Identity in Southeastern Europe*. Cambridge: Cambridge University Press.

Miyatev, Krăstyu. 1927. Monumentalnata zhivopis v drevna Bălgariya. In *GSU VI Bogoslovski fakultet*, 131–146. Sofia: Hudozhnik.

Miyatev, Krăstyu. 1936. *Poganovskiyat manastir*. Sofia: CBD.

Miyatev, Krăstyu. 1965. *Arhitekturata v srednovekovna Bălgariya*. Sofia: BAN.

Moutsopoulos, Nikolaos. 1999. *I vasiliki tou Agiou Achilleiou stin Prespa*. Thessaloniki: Paratiritis.

Mutafov, Chavdar. 1927. Rodna arhitektura. *Arhitekt* 1: 19–23.

Nastasă, Lucian. 1997. Orest Tafrali şi studiile de bizantinologie. *Cercetări istorice* XVI: 157–172.

Naxidou, Eleonora. 2019. Ot Ohrid do Solun: Margaritis Dimitsas i negovoto 'makedonsko pătuvane'. In *Solun i bălgarite: istoriya, pamet, săvremie*, ed. Yura Konstantinova et al., 88–109. Sofia: BAN.

Orlandos, Anastasios. 1938. Ta vyzantina mnimeia tis Kastorias. *AVME* D': 2–216.

Ovcharov, Nikolay. 1994. *Prouchvaniya vărhu srednovekovieto i po-novata istoriya na Vardarska Makedoniya. Novo sled Yordan Ivanov*. Sofia: Universitetsko izdatelstvo.

Pantelić, Bratislav. 2016. The Last Byzantines: Perceptions of Identity, Culture, and Heritage in Serbia. *Nationalities Papers* 44 (3): 430–455.

Pavićević, Aleksandra. 2005. Šta radi i gde sedi "Beli anđeo"? *Glasnik EI SANU* LIII: 185–193.

Pelekanidis, Stylianos. 1960. *Vyzantina kai metavyzantina mnimeia tis Prespas*. Thessaloniki: IMChA.

Pelekanidis, Stylianos, and Manolis Chatzidakis. 1985. *Kastoria*. Athens: Melissa.

Perdrizet, Paul. 1907. Melnic et Rossno. *Bulletin de correspondance hellénique* 31 (1): 20–37.

Petković, Vladimir. 1924. *Stari srpski spomenici u Južnoj Srbiji*. Belgrade & Zemun: Makarije.

Petković, Vladimir. 1926a. A. Protich *Yugozapadnata shkola v bălgarskata stenopis prez XIII i XIV v. Prilozi za književnost, jezik, istoriju i folklor* 6 (1): 153–156.

Petković, Vladimir. 1926b. A. Protitch. *Un modèle des maîtres bulgares du XV et XVI siècle. Prilozi za književnost, jezik, istoriju i folklor* 6 (1): 150–153.

4 ART WARS: THE CREATION OF BULGARIAN ART HISTORY AND THE BALKAN... 217

Petković, Vladimir. 1930. *La peinture serbe du Moyen Âge*. Belgrade: Musée d'histoire de l'art.

Petrov, Petăr. 1993a. *Bogdan Filov. Pătuvaniya iz Trakiya, Rodopite i Makedoniya 1912–1916*. Sofia: Universitetsko izdatelstvo.

Petrov, Petăr. 1993b. *Nauchna ekspeditsiya v Makedoniya i Pomoravieto 1916*. Sofia: Sv. Georgi Pobedonosets.

Popović, Pera, et al. 1933. *Staro Nagoričino. Psača. Kalenić*. Belgrade: SKA.

Protich, Andrey. 1925. Yugozapadnata shkola v bălgarskata stenopis prez XIII i XIV v. In *Sbornik v chest na Vasil N. Zlatarski*, 291–342. Sofia: n.p.

Protich, Andrey. 1930. *Denatsionalizirane i văzrazhdane na bălgarskoto izkustvo prez turskoto robstvo ot 1393 do 1879 god*. Sofia: n.p.

Pyatnitsky, Yuri. 2011. An Imperial Eye to the Past: Byzantine Exhibitions in the State Hermitage Museum, 1861–2006. *Tyragetia* V (2): 71–98.

Rashenov, Aleksandăr. 1932. Bălgarska shkola văv vizantiyski stil. *IBAI* 6: 206–220.

Rohdewald, Stefan. 2022. *Sacralizing the Nation through Remembrance of Medieval Religious Figures in Serbia, Bulgaria and Macedonia*. Vol. 1–2. Leiden & Boston: Brill.

Rousseva, Ralitsa. 2009. Belezhki vărhu atributsiyata, avtorstvoto i ktitorite na nyakoi proizvedeniya na tsărkovnoto izkustvo ot manastira „Sv. Bogoroditsa Kosinitsa", săhranyavani v NIM. *INIM* XX: 165–187.

Rousseva, Ralitsa. 2011. Istoriya, atributsiya i analiz na proizvedeniya na tsărkovnoto izkustvo ot taka narecheniya „spets-fond", săhranyavani v Natsionalniya istoricheski muzey, Sofiya. (II). *INIM* XXIII: 253–286.

Rousseva, Ralitsa. 2023. Razvitie i razprostranenie na ikonografiyata na Sv. Naum Ohridski Chudotvorets (XIV–XIX v.). In *Tvărdina na pravoslavieto. Proslava na Sveti Naum Ohridski*, ed. Iskra Hristova-Shomova, 29–67. Sofia: Universitetsko izdatelstvo.

Samara, Samia. 2016. Les politiques de protection et de sauvegarde des sites archéologiques et des monuments historiques en Grèce (1830–2013) : le cas d'Athènes. PhD diss., Paris X.

Sotiriou, Georgios. 1942. *Christianiki kai vyzantini archaiologia*, A'. Athens: n.p.

Sotiriou, Georgios. 1945. I techni ton vyzantinon mnimeion tis Mesimvrias. In *I Mesimvria tou Euxeinou, A'*, ed. Georgios Megas, 161–173. Athens: Estia.

Sotiriou, Georgios. 1949. O vyzantinos naos tou Ag. Achilleiou tis Prespas kai ai voulgarikai peri tis idryseos toutou apopseis. *PAA* 20: 8–14.

Stevović, Ivan. 2018. Medieval Art and Architecture as an Ideological Weapon: The Case of Yugoslavia. *Problemi na izkustvoto* 2: 3–8.

Stevović, Ivan. 2021. *L'ancien art serbe. Les églises* jedan vek kasnije. In *Gabriel Mije i istraživanja stare srpske arhitekture*, ed. Dubravka Preradović and Miodrag Marković, 289–312. Belgrade: SANU.

Strezov, Georgi. 1891. Dva sandzhaka ot Istochna Makedoniya. *Periodichesko spisanie na BKD* XXXVI: 809–860.

Todorov, Georgi. 2001. Razbitoto sărtse na grad Sv. Sofiya, unishtozhavaneto na sofiyskite svetini pri kmeta Dimităr Petkov (1888–1893). *Kultura*, March 1, 2001. https://newspaper.kultura.bg/bg/article/view/5142.

Todorov, Petar. 2021. Production of Territoriality in the Balkans: The Border and the Monastery St. Naum. In *Boundaries and Borders in the Post-Yugoslav Space: A European Experience*, ed. Nenad Stefanov and Srdjan Radović, 167–188. Berlin & Boston: De Gruyter Oldenbourg.

Todorova, Maria. 1986. Machiel Kiel, Art and Society of Bulgaria in the Turkish Period. Van Gorcum, Assen / Maastricht, 1985, 400 p. *Vekove* 4: 81–85.

Tuleshkov, Nikolay. 2001. *Arhitekturnoto izkustvo na starite bălgari*. Vol. 1. Sofia: Marin Drinov, Arh & Art.

Üre, Pınar. 2014. Byzantine Heritage, Archaeology, and Politics Between Russia and the Ottoman Empire: Russian Archaeological Institute in Constantinople (1894–1914). PhD diss., LSE.

Vasiliev, Asen. 1965. *Bălgarski văzrozhdenski maystori. Zhivopistsi, rezbari, stroiteli*. Sofia: Nauka i izkustvo.

Vezenkov, Alexender, and Tchavdar Marinov. 2015. The Concept of National Revival in Balkan Historiographies. In *Entangled Histories of the Balkans*, ed. Roumen Daskalov and Alexander Vezenkov, vol. 3, 406–462. Leiden & Boston: Brill.

Xyngopoulos, Andreas. 1931. *A Protic. Les origines sassanides et byzantines de l'art bulgare. Epetiris Etaireias Vyzantinon Spoudon* 8: 354–354.

Xyngopoulos, Andreas. 1955. *Thessalonique et la peinture macédonienne*. Athens: Myrtidis.

Xyngopoulos, Andreas. 1956. *Manuel Panselinos*. Athens: Athens' Editions.

Zhivkova, Lyudmila. 1980. *Chetveroevangelieto na tsar Ivan Aleksandăr*. Sofia: Nauka i izkustvo.

CHAPTER 5

Defending Our Lands in Ancient and Medieval Studies: The Albanian Case

Alexander Vezenkov

In this chapter, I will examine how historiography and, in particular, historical studies of the distant past have been instrumentalized in contemporary territorial disputes in the Balkans. I will present the Albanian case as a typical phenomenon of engaged national historiographies, especially concerning those of this region, and not as some exotic exception. In fact, it would not even be possible to speak of an exception, inasmuch as the Albanian narrative of the distant past has developed as an ongoing dispute with the historiographies of neighboring countries, which have already produced their own versions, in some respects mirroring them, in others imitating them. Then, in turn, historians from neighboring countries responded to Albanian interpretations with additional counter-arguments. I will try to show how historical arguments were used to justify the Albanian nation's right to Kosovo, a large part of the western and northwestern parts of the present-day Republic of (North) Macedonia, southern Epirus, and the south-eastern parts of the present-day Republic of

A. Vezenkov (✉)
Institute of Balkan Studies and Centre of Thracology at the Bulgarian Academy of Sciences, Sofia, Bulgaria
e-mail: alexander.vezenkov@gmail.com

© The Author(s), under exclusive license to Springer Nature Switzerland AG 2025
D. Mishkova, R. Daskalov (eds.), *Balkan Historiographical Wars*,
https://doi.org/10.1007/978-3-031-90113-3_5

Montenegro. Or, to put it more precisely, how the disputes surrounding these territories have involved, among many other scholars, those engaged with the study of history.

Initially, Albanian claims to these territories were based entirely on the modern ethnic situation—during the nineteenth and twentieth centuries, an Albanian population lived there, in some areas they formed a majority, even an overwhelming majority. The concept of a "Greater Albania" is a product of modern nationalism. It crystallized in the final decades of Ottoman rule, toward the end of the nineteenth and the beginning of the twentieth century, and has not even a remote analog in the more distant past. Subsequently, however, a number of historical writings "discovered" this Albanian space in all past epochs and presented it as exclusively Albanian.

The use of historical arguments on the Albanian side is a response to earlier uses of such arguments by their neighbors. A number of Serbian historians insisted that Kosovo was not only under Serbian rule in the Middle Ages, but that the vast majority of the population was Orthodox Serb, pointing to the many Orthodox churches and monasteries in the region as material evidence. They claimed that the settlement of Albanians took place during the centuries of Ottoman rule, which tolerated them at the expense of the Serbs. This argument was used to support the annexation of lands already inhabited by Albanians by Serbia. In parallel, various Greek writers pointed to the Greek character of Epirus, using as arguments not only the presence of a Greek-speaking Orthodox population in the area and the "Greek self-consciousness" of (part of) the Albanian-speaking Orthodox population, but also the Greek character of Epirus in Antiquity and the Middle Ages. The projection of "Greater Albania" into the distant past is merely a response to these arguments, but one that is elaborated, supported by "scientific evidence," and repeated many times. This anachronistic projection strongly colors the Albanian historical narrative, and the paradox is that during the last decades of the communist regime and in the years after its fall, Albanian historiography was much more insistent in using such arguments than Serbian and especially Greek historiography.

As with all conflicts that are paralleled by a "historiographical war," those related to Albania are not about reopening old wounds and reactivating conflicts from centuries ago. Therefore, one should not search into the distant past for the "roots" of present-day conflicts. On the contrary, today's conflicts are projected into the past, reaching into the distant past (medieval, even ancient), for which they are entirely anachronistic. Territorial disputes, at least as far as the Balkan region is concerned, are as a rule recent—the political formations of the Middle Ages, considered the forerunners of the respective modern states, rarely fought over the same territories that are disputed in modern and more recent times. Very often national historiographies, in their desire to support national claims to one or other disputed territory, attempt to demonstrate that they belonged to the respective state and/or were inhabited by (the forefathers of) their respective communities in the distant past, going as far back in time as possible.

These "historiographical wars" have no practical relevance to contemporary territorial disputes—the drawing and adjusting of modern inter-state boundaries is not based on proven ownership of territory in the distant past by nations. Propaganda based on "historical arguments" is only a symptom of a heightened interest and accompanies other, much more powerful, political instruments. However, these "historiographical wars" leave a serious mark on the historiographies themselves, diverting much of the research effort into the construction of meaningless constructs.

Historical arguments in the territorial disputes in the Balkans first appeared in newspapers, magazines, and amateur writings, and only later were they developed in academic historiography. There was a boom of such publications around the Balkan Wars and the First World War and they continued during the interwar period. A new wave of such publications began in the 1960s. It was in this second wave that Albanian historiography fully participated. Apart from this delay, the efforts of Albanian nationalists, and then of Albanian academic historiography, to prove their nation's historical rights to what they now consider "Albanian lands" are not fundamentally different from what the national elites of other nations in the region began to do long before them. In their essence, the "historiographical wars" over Kosovo and Epirus are very similar to those over other disputed regions such as Transylvania or Dobrudja.

I will try to systematize the main arguments in the disputes, so the picture I will draw here is of course oversimplified. Given the fact that these arguments were used on numerous occasions, the references are only indicative. First, I will present the emergence of the notion of "Albanian lands" in modern times and the subsequent adoption of this notion by Albanian historiography dealing with the more distant past, namely Antiquity and the Middle Ages. Furthermore, I will examine the key role of the theory of the Illyrian origin of the Albanians and of Illyro-Albanian

222 A. VEZENKOV

continuity in the projection of the modern concept of "Albanian lands" in the remote past. Finally, I will systematize the cases in which Albanian historiography dealing with the Late Middle Ages developed its theses as a direct mirror response to the claims of historians from neighboring countries.

TERRITORIAL DISPUTES AND HISTORICAL ARGUMENTS

The territorial question arose for the Albanians at a relatively early stage in the development of Albanian nationalism as a result of external pressure— the claims of their neighbors, the relatively recently established Christian states in the Balkans, to territories more or less populated by Albanians. From the Albanian point of view, the question of the "Albanian lands" was first raised as a demand that these territories should not be ceded to neighboring countries, either when they seceded from the Ottoman Empire or when the newly established Balkans states expanded at the expense of Ottoman territories. Such concerns emerged as early as the 1860s, and became particularly strong after the Russian-Turkish War of 1877–1878, when, at the end of the war, the Preliminary Treaty of San Stefano (March 1878) stipulated that the Bulgarian Autonomous Principality should include areas with significant Albanian populations (Korça, Bitola/ Manastir, Ohrid, Struga, Debar, Kičevo, Gostivar, Tetovo, Skopje). In 1881, after protracted negotiations, Montenegro was granted an extension to the south around the town of Ulcinj, but it also had other demands that remained unsatisfied. Greece demanded not only Thessaly (most of which it received by treaty in 1881) but also Epirus, and actually acquired the southernmost part of it around the town of Arta.

At this stage, the defense of the "Albanian lands" enjoyed the sympathy of the Ottoman authorities, inasmuch as the Albanian leaders insisted at first place on preserving the Empire's territories. Within the Ottoman Empire, once the new Christian states had seceded, Albanian (proto-) nationalism combined with Ottoman interests, and in doing so Albanians could pretend for relatively vast (still) Ottoman territory. Subsequently, plans for broader autonomy, and especially those for Albanian independence, had to be oriented toward a more clearly defined and smaller territory.

The map of "Greater Albania" appeared in the last decades of the nineteenth and early twentieth centuries and was based primarily on the enumeration of regions inhabited by Albanians, that is, Albanophones (including bilinguals). The map of the national space was created in conjunction with the Ottoman administrative map and in its most popular version included the vilayets with a predominant, or at least significant, Albanian population—Shkodra, Janina, Manastir/Bitola, Kosova, and in some cases the Salonica Vilayet, which was the basis for the demands for the creation of a unified "Albanian vilayet" from 1878 onward (Akte të Rilindjes Kombëtare 1978, 123, 126, 129, 132, etc.). Hence the expression "the four Albanian vilayets," which is common in the Albanian national narrative. In fact, it is precisely this expression that helps us to situate the emergence of the concept of Greater Albania in time. The vilayets as administrative units in their then form did not exist in the past—they were introduced on an experimental basis in 1864 and generalized by the Law on Vilayets in early 1867; more specifically, the Kosovo Vilayet appeared in 1877 with its separation from the Bitola Vilayet. The first demands spoke of "three vilayets" (Akte të Rilindjes Kombëtare 1978, 63). It should be mentioned that the notion of "Albanian vilayets" clashes with the widespread thesis in Balkan national historiographies, including the Albanian one, that the vilayets were deliberately created to contain mixed populations in order to prevent separatist movements. However, intentionally or not, Ottoman administrative units usually did not include religiously and/or ethnically homogeneous populations.

The project of one big Albanian vilayet, as well as the talk of four or five "Albanian vilayets" was maximalist like all national projects. The Albanian historiography of the communist period usually tends not to mention the claims to the Salonica Vilayet, which otherwise are often found in the primary sources of the period (Clayer 2007, 463). Albanian historians mention critically the ambitions of large Albanian landowners (*feudals*) who claimed, for the future nation-state, lands where their own holdings were located (e.g., Thessaly), even though they were not predominantly inhabited by Albanians (Buda 1986b, 134).

On the other side, in the late nineteenth to early twentieth centuries, the territorial ambitions of neighboring states encroached on Albanian-populated areas. To a certain extent, this was justified by the mixed nature of the population: of the "Albanian vilayets," that of Janina was also "Greek," that of Kosova also "Serbian," that of Bitola and to a certain extent Kosova (the vilayet was larger than present-day Kosovo) also "Bulgarian/Macedonian." Because the Albanians, like the Turks, were predominantly Muslim, they were initially excluded from the calculations for dividing the Ottoman lands among the small Balkan states. Albania's neighbors supported their claims with "historical arguments"—not only had they ruled these territories politically, ecclesiastically, and culturally in the past, but their population was also, for example, Greek or Serbian. Accordingly, the Albanians, again like the Turks, were almost automatically considered latecomers—after all, Islam appeared relatively late in the region.

In essence, the Greek claims were the most far-reaching because they could be based not only on the mixed nature of the population in the disputed territories, but also on pro-Greek sentiments among Orthodox Albanians; in the nineteenth century, hypotheses of a common "Pelasgian" origin of Greeks and Albanians were also instrumentalized with a view to incorporate Albanians into a larger Greek state.

Serbian interest in the south—in Kosovo and present-day Macedonia—is believed to have been strengthened by the cutting off of other hopes for territorial expansion, specifically the Austro-Hungarian occupation of Bosnia and Herzegovina (1878), though this interest already existed during the previous decades. Simultaneously, Serbian ambitions included a quest for access to the Adriatic Sea (at least a transport corridor with a railway to Medova Bay in order to escape from economic dependence on Austria-Hungary). As a "historical" argument, it was pointed out that the Serbian medieval state Zeta had an outlet to the Adriatic, and Montenegro's political independence prompted Serbia to seek this outlet south of it, in lands with a compact Albanian population (Draškić 2000, 132). Montenegro, for its part, had ambitions for further south-southeastward expansion.

Projects for a Greater Bulgaria also included areas of Macedonia with large Albanian populations. However, the Bulgarian threat appeared only sporadically during military conflicts (1878; 1915–1918; 1941–1944). Projects for an autonomous or independent Macedonia repeated the Bulgarian map of "Macedonia"—it was maximalist and included ethnically mixed territory (Marinov 2013, 297–8). At least in theory, the ambition for an autonomous or independent Macedonia was a supranational project, but here too the interests of the Albanians were ignored in practice.

During the late nineteenth century Albanian intellectuals and political leaders also started looking for arguments in the past. Already at this stage, the focus turned to Antiquity and Prehistory, with the theories of autochthony of the Albanians combined with claims to some of the disputed territories, above all to Epirus. Pashko Vasa (Wassa Effendi) in his *The Truth on Albania and Albanians* (1879) identified Illyrians, Epirotes, and ancient Macedonians as the ancestors of the Albanians. Sami Frashëri, in his famous book *Albania, What It Is, What It Was, and What It Will Be* (1899) presents the Albanians as an ancient and indigenous people with extensive possessions in the past, which allowed him to claim Epirus as well. The thesis of the Albanians as one of the old, or even the oldest, people in the Balkans was also shared by authors from Austria-Hungary and Italy, the two countries that supported the Albanian cause and the creation of an Albania with larger borders.

The delineation of Albania's borders in 1913 was justified on the one hand by ethnic realities (by Austria-Hungary and Italy, who supported Albanian interests), on the other hand by the "right of the victors" of the Balkan Wars, namely Serbia, Montenegro, and Greece (which enjoyed the diplomatic backing of Russia). Generally speaking, the "right of the victors" prevailed, and about half of the Albanian-speaking population remained outside the new Albanian state, with by far the largest part being annexed to the Kingdom of Serbia.

In 1913, the demarcation was made by two commissions for the northern and southern border. The border with Serbia and Montenegro (the later annexed Plav/Plavë) was confirmed in principle in December 1913, but for a long time the precise delineation remained unspecified. The real problem was the considerable and dense Albanian population included in Serbia, which led to an Albanian uprising in September–October 1913. During the following years, there were several attempts to adjust the border, again usually to the detriment of Albania, the most notorious of these being the transfer of the Monastery of St. Naum near Lake Ohrid (as well as a wooded area around Vermosh) to the Serbo-Croatian-Slovenian Kingdom in 1925.

For the delineation of the Greek-Albanian border, the main criteria were the spoken language plus economic, geographical, and strategic criteria. Eventually, at the London Conference in August 1913, most of the disputed territories in Epirus were annexed to Albania. Because of the larger Greek population in (now Albanian) Northern Epirus, an ephemeral pro-Greek Autonomous Republic of Northern Epirus was proclaimed on 24 February 1914. After the outbreak of World War I, the area was occupied by Greece, but after the failure of the Asia Minor campaign, Greece was forced to withdraw in 1921. Eventually, in January 1925 the original border (with some minor changes) was formally reconfirmed.

The official census data from the respective countries give a general idea of how different the situation was in the north and the south. The 1921 census in the Serbo-Croatian-Slovenian Kingdom showed 439,657 Albanians, and their number steadily increased in the following decades. The 1920 census in Greece recorded only 8195 Albanians, and that of 1928 some 15,598 Muslim Albanians, not counting separately either the Orthodox Albanians in Southern Epirus, nor the Arvanites in other parts of the country. For all the reservations about the minority figures in the official statistics, which are understated to varying degrees, there is a marked difference in the numbers of Albanian communities in Greece and the Serbo-Croatian-Slovenian Kingdom. Without justification, some Albanian authors have subsequently spoken of Epirus as if Albanians were "as numerous" as in Serbia/Yugoslavia (Doja 1999b, 160).

This discrepancy is reflected in the ethnic composition of the new Albanian state. Though considerably truncated and therefore more ethnically homogeneous, Albania still had a large Greek minority, reflecting the greater degree of satisfaction of Albanian claims in Epirus and their complete disregard in the drawing of the border with Serbia (partly also with Montenegro) and later with the Serbo-Croatian-Slovenian Kingdom. Census data in Albania after the Second World War show that there were several times more Greek-speaking citizens in the country than the members of all the Slavic-speaking minorities put together; in what concerns ethnic self-identification the ratio was approximately 10:1 in favor of the Greeks.

During the Balkan wars, historical arguments were used by the Serbian side, both in the country's official positions and in targeted publications (Tomitch 1913), but these arguments had no independent significance in the demarcation of borders. Even Albanian historiography of the communist period only mentions the use of historical arguments by the Serbian and Greek sides, and does not claim that they played a role (Buda 1986b, 133, 139). In practical terms, only the demands from the Serbian side for the inclusion of some Orthodox churches and monasteries within its borders (the case of the monastery of St. Naum near the lake of Ohrid) had relatively more impact. However, even in this case, it would be more appropriate to say that a Christian state was given precedence over a newly established, smaller and weaker, predominantly Muslim country.

Not only during the years of the Balkan Wars and World War I, but also during the interwar period, there were no special developments in the historical arguments on the Albanian side. As a continuation of this situation, the political emigré community after World War II professed territorial maximalism, but "lagged behind" in the use of historical arguments

5 DEFENDING OUR LANDS IN ANCIENT AND MEDIEVAL STUDIES... 227

compared to the propaganda and historiography of the communist regime (*Albania: A short summary* 1968, 3–4).

Some contributions were made from the Italian side. In the 1920s, Italian archaeological research began in Albania, addressing also the problem of the origin of the Albanians, which was considered the most important issue by Italian scholars at the time (Ugolini 1928, 19). Italian support for Albanian irredentism gained greater strength on the eve and during the early years of World War II. Italians stimulated research and publications on Albania in all fields, including history, archaeology, and other disciplines that could provide arguments in favor of Albanian irredentism, such as the Illyrian character of Epirus (Mustilli 1943).

Irredentist propaganda during the war combined geographical and historical arguments. For example, in the bilingual brochure "Shënime përmbi Epirin / Appunti sull'Epiro" published in Tirana in 1940, Epirus was said to be a "geographical, strategic, economic and ethnic entity," with a "natural frontier" and most importantly "completely separated from Greece." At the same time, reference was made to those ancient authors who wrote that Epirus was not part of Greece. It was claimed that the Epirotes did not interfere in Greek affairs and, in general, that "Epirus has always been an integral part of Albania," that the ancient names of Tesprotia, Mollosia and Atamania were of Illyrian origin, that the Greeks used to call the Epirotes "barbarians," that the family of King Pyrrhus was Illyrian, and that one can only speak of Greek influence on Epirus in Antiquity and the Middle Ages, as there was in many other places (quoted after Manta 2004, 272–4). In the same pattern, though with fewer examples, another bilingual brochure from the same series "Shënime mbi Çamërinë / Appunti sulla Ciamuria" tells about the Albanian affiliation of Chameria, which has always been Albanian since ancient times, and that the Chams were of "Illyrian race, i.e. pure-blooded Albanians" (quoted after Manta 2004, 289–91).

A real possibility of expanding Albania's borders under Italian control appeared after the occupation of Greece and Yugoslavia in the spring of 1941. This was done at the expense of occupied Yugoslavia, without satisfying all Albanian ambitions. Some of the mixed areas in present-day Macedonia, as well as the most south-eastern parts of present-day Kosovo (Kaçanik/Kačanik, Kamenica) were annexed to Bulgaria, while a large area around Mitrovica remained under German control. The situation in Epirus was very different from that of Kosovo and Western Macedonia. The Italians themselves saw that, contrary to their initial expectations, there was not much enthusiasm for the annexation of Epirus or even a part of it, namely of Chameria, to "Greater Albania," and abandoned this idea and the propaganda for it. Italian scholars, under the auspices of the authorities, prepared two volumes dedicated to the "liberated Albanian lands," but only the one on Kosovo was published (*Le terre albanesi redente, I. Kossovo* 1942), while the second, dedicated to Epirus, proved politically redundant and remained unprinted (Martucci 2012; Martucci 2014; Lafe 2014, 130). This was another tacit acknowledgment of the different situation in Kosovo, Western Macedonia, and the southernmost parts of Montenegro on the one hand, and Southern Epirus on the other.

Despite these examples of the use of historical arguments in propaganda, most references were still related to contemporary ethnic realities. For instance, when Bulgaria and Albania (annexed by Italy) became neighbors on the territory of occupied Yugoslavia, the Bulgarian side emphasized the ethnic composition of the population, claiming that in most of the disputed territories annexed by Albania, Bulgarians (meaning the Slav population) outnumbered Albanians (*Numero dei Bulgari* 1941). In addition, the Bulgarian government negotiated directly with the Italians and also sought German support, effectively ignoring the Albanians.

After the Second World War, Albania's pre-war borders were merely reaffirmed. Overall, the Albanian case is a relatively simple one, with borders that have remained (almost) unchanged since the establishment of the modern nation-state in 1913. Accordingly, the use of historical arguments remains with the same priorities, with Kosovo taking the lead over Epirus both during the Italian annexation in World War II and in Albanian propaganda and academic historiography in the following decades.

The major change in the political map after World War II was the federalization of the new Yugoslavia. According to the new political map of the federal state, Albanians constituted a majority in most municipalities of the autonomous region of Kosovo, while a number of Albanians remained in some neighboring enclaves to the east of Kosovo, in the main part of the Republic of Serbia (in the municipalities of Preševo/Presheva, Bujanovac/Bujanoci, Medveđa/Medvegja). Albanians were compactly concentrated in several small enclaves along Montenegro's south-eastern border with Albania and the autonomous region of Kosovo. In Macedonia, Albanians primarily inhabited the western and north-western parts of the country, forming a common space with Albanians in Kosovo and Albania itself. Although Kosovo, does not only include all the Albanians living in

Yugoslavia, not even all of those living in Serbia, it certainly stands out and therefore naturally came to dominate the debates.

ALBANIAN LANDS IN ALBANIAN ACADEMIC HISTORIOGRAPHY

It was only after World War II that academic historiography developed and became gradually institutionalized in Albania: in 1946 the first such center was established, called the Institute of Sciences after 1948, with a history section. In 1955 it became part of the Institute of History and Linguistics, attached in 1957 to the then-founded State University of Tirana. The number of publications also grew, and in 1964 the University of Tirana's Bulletin for Social Sciences (*Buletin i Universitetit Shtetëror të Tiranës – Seria e shkencave shoqërore*), was transformed into separate journals for historical (*Studime historike*) and philological studies (*Studime filologjike*), plus a third one for articles in foreign languages (*Studia Albanica*). With the establishment of the Academy of Sciences in 1972, the now-independent Institute of History became part of it. The new Albanian historiography built on the previous works of foreign scholars, and initially an important role was played by researchers who had studied abroad before the war, a process that took place under political control and the imposition of official communist ideology; also of importance was the country's increasing isolation (Schmitt 2005; Idrizi 2020; Bezha 2021). It should be emphasized that the Albanian historians of these first generations were relatively familiar with the historiographies of other countries in the region. They made use of their publications and even adopted some of their conclusions, but deeply disagreed with others.

After the war, Albanian academic archaeology was also established and developed rapidly. The starting point was the study of numerous archaeological sites within Albania itself, but later Albanian archaeologists drew general conclusions about a much wider area. Like archaeological studies in other Balkan countries, those in Albania were primarily concerned with ethnic issues, with ethnicities conceived as distinct groups (Kaiser 1995, 104, 106; Tsonos 2009). In parallel, ethnographic and folkloristic studies were developed and institutionalized, and some publications tended to go further back in time.

Albanian academic publications of the first ten to fifteen years after the Second World War entered into disputes with foreign historians for both national and ideological reasons, but without specifically discussing the territorial scope of the "Albanian lands." Thus, as early as the 1950s,

Albanian historians set out to "prove" that the Illyrians had a relatively high level of economic and cultural development; that the Illyrians had states, while this phenomenon was neglected by foreign scholars; and that there was a continuity of the population in the present territory of Albania. They argued that in the Middle Ages there were feudal relations in the country, which were not imported; they also insisted on the existence of medieval Albanian statehood (Pollo and Buda 1959, 97, 99).

Initially, the narrative of the more distant past was almost exclusively confined to the country's present borders. Thus, the first "academic" history of Albania (work on which began in 1952, and the first volume was published in 1959) states from the outset that it deals with the developments within the present borders of the country, and only goes beyond them when the events in question had a direct impact on them (*Historia e Shqipërisë* 1959, 14). This is also true of the second volume of the book (it covers the history of the country from 1839 to 1944), which was prepared at the same time but published in 1965. This first *History of Albania* rejects some theses of Yugoslav historiography, namely the late settlement of the Albanians in the Balkans, pointing in opposition to the Latin terminology of Albanian Christianity, which indicates its earlier acceptance in this territory, that is, long before the arrival of the Slavs (*Historia e Shqipërisë* 1959, 31–32). Also at the First Conference on Albanian Studies in 1962 there were papers on the autochthony of the Albanians and on the Illyrian-Albanian continuity—the problem was presented from the point of view both of linguistics (*Konferenca e parë e studimeve albanolojike* 1965, 89 ff) and of history (*ibid.*, 441 ff), but not on the unity of the "Albanian lands," nor specifically on Kosovo or Epirus. Similarly, archaeological excavations and publications on their findings were, for obvious reasons, confined to sites within the country's borders (*Les Illyriens et la genèse des albanais* 1971, 253).

Traditionally, historical research in Albania has focused mainly on the recent past, especially the most recent history, which is presented in much greater detail. As far as modern and contemporary history is concerned, even during the first decades of the communist regime, historical studies included the fate of Albanians living outside the actual borders of the country. This is the case in the publications on the national movement of the nineteenth century, which emphasize that it spread to all areas inhabited by Albanians. The uprisings in Kosovo are examined, as well as those in Southern Epirus (Mile 1962; Mile 1966), and special importance is given to the Prizren League of 1878–1881 (Frashëri 1956), and the

5 DEFENDING OUR LANDS IN ANCIENT AND MEDIEVAL STUDIES... 231

activities of late nineteenth- and early twentieth-century figures active outside the borders of present-day Albania, such as Hasan Prishtina in Kosovo (Haxhiu 1964), are considered. The history of the communist movement during the Second World War also goes beyond the country's borders and includes the fighting on Yugoslav territory. Such publications speak of the "fraternal struggle" against the German forces; they are critical of the pre-1944 slogans of "ethnic Albania" and "Greater Albania" (Merkaj 1964, 106–7), as well as of the "chauvinist and discriminatory policies" of the Yugoslav Communist Party (*Historia e Shqipërisë* 1965, 816–20).

After the Albanian-Soviet split in 1961, a new interpretation of the Slavic invasions was elaborated and imposed. In the first volume of the *History of Albania*, published in 1959, the Slavic invasion was presented briefly but rather mildly, to the extent that during a discussion of the book's draft the Bulgarian medievalist Vasilka Tăpkova even recommended that "more attention should be paid to the relations between the indigenous population and the Slavic colonizers, which were idealized to a certain extent" (Tăpkova-Zaimova and Paskaleva 1959, 133). During the course of the following decade, a different interpretation crystallized, which at least initially did not aim to portray the relations with the Slavs in dark colors, but primarily to deny their mass settlement in the "Albanian lands" during the Slavic invasion in the sixth and seventh centuries. The influence of the Slavs was limited to a purely military-political conquest—from the ninth century by the Bulgarian Kingdom, and then from the late eleventh century by the Serbian Kingdom. It has been argued that, even during this period, the settlement of a certain number of Slavs did not fundamentally alter the ethnic homogeneity of the Albanian lands (*The History of Albania* 1981, 30).

An increased interest of Albanian historiography in the Albanian lands outside Albania in medieval and ancient history gained strength in the course of the 1960s. Thus, at the Second Conference on Albanian Studies in January 1968 (*Konferenca e dytë e studimeve albanologjike* 1969), several of the papers dealt with territorial issues. They addressed topics that had already appeared in academic publications of the previous few years and would be discussed and elaborated upon many times: on the notion of "Albania" (in all its variations: *Albeinje, Albani*, etc.) and the real extent of the Albanian lands in the Middle Ages (Frashëri 1969; Luka 1969a); on the struggle of the inhabitants of the eastern and northeastern Albanian lands (i.e., Kosovo) against the Turkish conquerors at the end of the fourteenth and in the fifteenth century (Murzaku 1969); and on the toponymy of Slavic origins in the Albanian lands (Myderrizi 1969). At the same time, papers were presented at the conference in which "territorial unity" was understood as the indivisibility of Albania within its recognized borders (Çami 1969). More generally, in the 1960s there were publications that referred to Kosovo and Southern Epirus as Albanian lands, but did not overtly problematize Albania's limited territorial extent after 1913 (Mile 1962, 230).

A very clear interest in the "Albanian lands" in the more distant past outside the country's borders became evident in publications about the Illyrians, especially from the late 1960s onward. A major step was the scientific session on "The Illyrians and the Genesis of the Albanians," held in March 1969 and organized by the Institute of History and Linguistics. In his opening speech the director of the Institute, Androkli Kostallari, stressed that Albanian researchers had reached different conclusions from foreign ones (A[namali] 1969, 195). The most important topics among the works presented, which have been published several times, including in foreign languages, were the origin of the Albanians (Anamali and Korkuti 1971), the continuity between the Illyrian and Albanian languages (Gjinari 1971), the thesis of the Illyrian affiliation of the population in Western Macedonia in prehistoric times (Andrea 1971), and the Illyrian character of the Epirus tribes (Budina 1971).

The next major manifestation was the organization of the First Assembly on Illyrian Studies, which was held in September 1972. In his concluding address, Stefanaq Pollo focused on the Illyrian-Albanian continuity, paying particular attention to the highest achievements of Illyrian culture—urban life and statehood (Pollo 1972, 142). The Illyrian character of Dardania and Epirus was also stressed. In 1972 the journal *Illyria* began to appear, starting with the publication of the materials of the Assembly; it played an important role insofar as in other historical journals publications on modern and contemporary history clearly dominated. In fact, *Studime historike* also published the main papers of both the 1969 scientific session and the 1972 Assembly, which shows the great importance attached to the subject. Chronologically, this wave of academic events and publications devoted to the Illyrians coincided with the interest in the Dacians in Romania and the Thracians in Bulgaria, with the Assembly on Illyrian Studies of September 1972 taking place almost immediately after the First Congress of Thracology (Sofia, July 1972). Leading Albanian historians presented theses about the Illyrian origin of the Albanians also at other international symposia in parallel to scholars from other Balkan countries talking about their alleged ancient predecessors (Mishkova 2018, 158–9).

The expansion of territorial scope in the narrative on ancient history was also evident in the work for a new edition of the *History of Albania*. As early as 1971 it was reported that the sections on the states of Epirus and Dardania had already been prepared (Deçka 1972, 215). By comparison, in the first edition of 1959 there are quite a few mentions of Epirus (the Epirotes are presented as Illyrians) but there is no separate section on Epirus, while Dardania is mentioned only sporadically. The same is valid also for the short histories of Albania published in the meantime in foreign languages, which do not deal with Epirus and Dardania as "Illyrian kingdoms" in their own right, but only mention them in passing (Frashëri 1964; *The History of Albania* 1981, 1 ed. 1974). A new and more comprehensive history of the Illyrians was published in Albanian in 1977 and French in 1985. Its introduction explicitly states that, unlike other previous studies, which presented an incomplete picture of Illyrian history and "neglected entire Illyrian regions, this work provides a new and more complete overview of Illyrian history" (*Les Illyriens* 1985, 9).

However, in the 1977 and 1985 editions of *The Illyrians*, the historical narrative was only mechanically expanded: after presenting the entire history of the Illyrian Kingdom until its fall to Roman rule, the following chapters describe the history of Epirus and Dardania separately (*Les Illyriens* 1985, 139ff). Only in the 2002 *History of the Albanian People* is the political history of all these territories presented in parallel, following a common chronology. In this way, the history of the Southern Illyrians really began to look like the history of a single people who happened to live in several kingdoms (*Historia e popullit shqiptar* 2002).

During the late communist period, the research output on the Illyrians additionally increased. Many specific archaeological sites were studied, in the 1980s the journal *Illyria* was published twice a year, and in September 1985 the Second Assembly of Illyrian Studies was held, without bringing any qualitative change in the grand narrative of the "ancient Albanian lands." The "Illyrian city" and the "Illyrian heritage" remained the most important topics.

From the late 1960s onward, after the constitutional changes in Yugoslavia allowed for the real autonomy of Kosovo, Albanian authors from the region began to play a more active role in defending the theses of the autochthony of the Albanians (with a specific focus on Kosovo), the Illyrian belonging of the Dardanians, and the absence of a significant influx of barbarian tribes (especially Slavs) into the predominantly Illyrian/Albanian populated region of Dardania/Kosovo. Here we can see that the new trends in historical writing—the interest in Kosovo and the interest in the Illyrians—are in fact closely related. Dardania became an important argument in proving the historical rights of the Albanians to Kosovo. Many works by Kosovar authors were republished in Albania itself. At the same time, Albania's cultural (and propaganda) influence in the region increased, especially in the fields of education, science, and culture. In Yugoslavia, some works were published in Albanian which, without going to extremes, adhered to the Serbian/Yugoslav point of view, such as the voluminous bilingual edition *Kosovo – Once and Now* (*Kosovo nekad i danas / Kosova dikur e sot* 1973).

Scholars from Kosovo were unable to attend the Conference on the Formation of the Albanian People in July 1982 but a large number of texts by authors from Kosovo are included in the collective volume *The Albanians and their Territories* (*Shqiptarët dhe trojet e tyre* 1982), which includes various earlier texts. Abridged versions of the later book were translated and published in English (1985) and German (1986). Texts on language and especially on toponymy and anthroponymy dominate here; in territorial terms, the focus of interest on Kosovo is obvious. In the 1990s, two volumes specifically devoted to Kosovo appeared, *The Truth on Kosova* (1993, with modifications from a first edition in Albanian in 1990) and *The Kosova Issue* (1996), which collected papers from a conference held in April 1993 (Kosovo—a Contemporary and Historical Problem). In the first of these volumes, texts by foreign writers from previous eras such as Konstantin Ireček and Milan Šufflay are reprinted, insofar as certain passages from their works were convenient for Albanian propaganda (*The Truth on Kosova* 1993, 69ff). Once again one can see how the same themes and arguments are used over and over again.

These publications appeared simultaneously with a wave of publications in Serbia in the 1980s (*Iliri i Albanci* 1988; *Kosovo i Metohija* 1989, etc.), which coincided with the exacerbation of the situation in Kosovo, and the two themes of the current problems in Kosovo and the distant past of the region (and of Albanians in general) were also raised at the political level. Thus, *The Truth on Kosova* explicitly refers to one such volume on Kosovo published in Belgrade in 1989 (*The Truth on Kosova* 1993, 3). The increasing number of publications on the "Albanian lands" and especially on Kosovo undoubtedly follows an internal logic, but it also coincides with similar developments in other countries in the region. For example, since the 1970s there had been a growing interest in and number of publications on Dobrudja in both Romania and Bulgaria, despite the fact that in this case the dispute between the two countries had long since been successfully settled. The growing number of polemical publications on Kosovo was also part of this more general trend in history writing at a time when communist regimes were becoming more actively and more openly nationalist.

Interestingly, on the Serbian side, in addition to Kosovo, the question of the origins of the Albanians and the Ilir-Albanian continuity was also politicized. In a polemical article, Aleksandar Stipčević explicitly states that while many specialists such as C. Pauli, H. Hirt, G. Meyer, and F. Cordignano rejected the thesis of the autochthonous origin of the Albanians on purely scientific grounds, in the 1980s in Yugoslavia (and more precisely in Serbia) this thesis was rejected for political reasons. Some Serbian/Yugoslav scholars, such as Milutin Garašanin and Fanula Papazoglu, changed their minds and stopped supporting the thesis of the Illyrian origin of the Albanians (Stipčević 1996, 34–36; Anamali 1993, 6–7).

While in Albanian historiography the interest in the Albanians in Yugoslavia and especially in Kosovo had been gradually growing since the 1960s, the question of the Albanians in Greece had been, and continued to be, quite different. On the one hand, this was because of the presence of a Greek minority in Albania itself, in "Northern Epirus" "Southern Albania"—the most numerous minority in the country. On the other, the Muslim Albanians in Chameria, probably around 20,000 at the time, were displaced after the Second World War, further altering the ethnic map of the region in favor of the Greek majority. What remained were Orthodox Albanophones with Greek national identity, a problem that Albanian historiography prefers not to discuss because there is simply nothing to be done about it. The idea of Albanians with Greek identity is just as inconvenient for the notions of ethnicity and national identity in Albanian historiography as "Hellenic Slavophones" is for Bulgarian and Macedonian historiography. As a result, Albanian publications of the communist period were more likely to speak of the Arbëreshë in Italy than of the Arvanites in Greece.

In contrast to Kosovo, there were no Albanians from Southern Epirus to take part in the debates. At the conference on the formation of the Albanian nation in July 1982, Aleks Buda mentioned the contributions of scholars ("colleagues and brothers") from Kosovo, Macedonia, and

Montenegro, but not from Greece (Buda 1986a, 130). Similarly, the April 1993 conference was attended mainly by scholars from Albania and Kosovo, some from Macedonia, Montenegro and Serbia proper (one from each), a few other foreign scholars and Albanian scholars living abroad, but none from Greece (*The Kosova Issue* 1996, 9). The situation on the other side was quite similar: in Greece there are fewer polemical publications on Epirus than on Macedonia, and even on Thrace and Asia Minor, and most of them are written by amateurs.

Still, on the main points Albanian publications on the history of Epirus repeated the logic applied to Dardania-Kosovo: the Illyrian character of the region and its inhabitants in Antiquity (Budina 1971; Islami 1992); the preservation of the Illyrian-Albanian population during the barbarian invasions, including the Slavic ones (Dulaj 1988); and the thesis that Albanians constituted the majority of the population at the time of the Ottoman invasion, which is also attested in the Ottoman tax records (Isufi 2004).

It should be noted that, despite the presence of a number of specialized publications on the Middle Ages and Antiquity, in many of the collective volumes devoted to Kosovo, contemporary issues—on the nineteenth and especially the twentieth century—predominate (*The Truth on Kosova* 1993; *The Kosova Issue* 1996). This is even more pronounced in the Serbian editions, which give a general overview of the Kosovo problem and say much less about the distant past than the Albanian editions (Dragnich and Todorovich 1984; Bataković 2012; see also Verli 2009). For example, the volume *Kosovo and Metohija: Past, Present, Future* (2006) says nothing about Antiquity or even the Middle Ages, and relatively little about the Ottoman period; contemporary issues predominate, with strong anti-Western and anti-NATO sentiments. Similarly, the (pro-)Greek propaganda of the Cold War only mentions the Greek character of Epirus in Antiquity (Sigalos 1963: 8). Some publications in Greece present Epirus as a Greek region from prehistoric times (*Epirus* 2023), but the nationalist narrative is interested mostly in the Ottoman and especially the post-Ottoman period (Vakalopoulos 2012; see also Meta 2009).

The primary interest of Albanian historiography in Kosovo can be explained by at least two objective reasons: firstly, the largest number of Albanians outside Albania itself lived in the autonomous entity thus created, and Albanians formed the majority of the population; secondly, the stakes were higher in Kosovo than anywhere else because real changes could be expected—the Serbian side was pursuing a policy of limiting this autonomy, while the Albanian side was mobilizing to preserve and extend it, possibly with the hope of full independence. Kosovo dominates Albanian polemical publications to the extent that the volume *The Albanians and Their Territories* (*Shqiptarët dhe trojet e tyre* 1982) contains numerous publications on Kosovo, several on other territories of Yugoslavia, but none specifically devoted to Epirus. The above-mentioned collective publications devoted to Kosovo in the following decade also have no equivalent on Epirus.

The fixation of Albanian historiography on Kosovo's past mirrors the Serbian mythologization of the region, with Albanian authors beginning to ascribe a key role in Albanian history to the region as well. From a Serbian perspective, the region was "the cradle" of the Serbian nation, which critics of Serbian national mythology note as inaccurate insofar as Kosovo was annexed by the late twelfth century to the already established Serbian state. In response, Kosovo was seen as the "cradle" of Albanian statehood, both medieval and modern: for the Middle Ages, the state of Balsha/Balšić (second half of the fourteenth century), and for the modern period, the League of Prizren (1878–1881) and the League of Peja (1899–1900) (Doja 1999a, 37–38).

However, Norbert Jokl's thesis that the formation of the Albanian language took place in Kosovo, tempting as it may seem in some respects, has been categorically rejected—Albanian scholars insist that it was a process that developed in the territory of present-day Albania as well as in Kosovo and parts of present-day Macedonia (Domi 1988, 173–5). The temptation to make Kosovo the ancestral homeland of all Albanians is less powerful than the desire to make them "indigenous" in all the lands inhabited by Albanians today.

In fact, the motivation for both Serbs and Albanians to present Kosovo as the "cradle" of their respective nations stems from the desire to contain or preserve a peripheral territory. The Albanians in Kosovo played an active role in the late nineteenth and early twentieth centuries precisely because they inhabited a threatened periphery. Thus, in the summer of 1878, Albanian leaders gathered in Kosovo (the Prizren League), with a relatively large number of delegates from Kosovo and Western Macedonia, as these territories were to become part of Bulgaria under the terms of the preliminary peace treaty of San Stefano.

As in all other national historiographies, even in communist Albania there were some more cautious authors who tried to avoid as much as possible anachronistic theses adopted for political reasons. After 1991, critical studies appeared (like Dritan Egro's works on Ottoman studies in Albania), books and articles by foreign authors that directly criticized the national mythology were translated (initially primarily in the magazine *Përpjekja*, edited by Fatos Lubonja), and critical publications by Albanians in the diaspora were republished (such as the works of Arshi Pipa). On the whole, however, the established school continued to dominate in academic circles, reproducing positions established in the past and referring to the same authors, as can be seen from publications in academic historical journals. The same is true of the new edition of the academic *History of Albania*, which was published under the title *History of the Albanian People* (2002). Identical formulas had already prevailed in Serbia, Bulgaria, and Romania, and in all these cases the history of the "people" covered a wider area than the history of the country. However, this is only an outward manifestation of a process that has been unfolding over the past decades. In parallel, a more radically powerful para-historiography is emerging, in which the Albanians appear even more ancient and their contribution to world history and culture incomparably greater (for instance in the publications of Elena Kocaqi). In addition to denouncing the "falsifications" of the Serbian Academy of Sciences, for example, various amateurs also accuse the official historiography in Albania and Kosovo of reproducing its false statements (Buxhovi 2020, 12). In all this, Albanian historiography is following a path similar to that of other post-communist countries in the region, especially the less developed among them.

THE SPATIAL DIMENSION OF THE ILLYRIAN HYPOTHESIS

Albanian academic historiography, especially during the communist era, tended to attribute to the remote past everything that the regime sought or claimed to have achieved in modern Albania. The political isolation of Enver Hoxha's time is projected onto the entire history of the country, through the constant insistence on the independence of the people and the country, on the heroism in resisting the invaders and later in the fight for liberation; foreign domination, interference and influence are demonized; in the past, Albania appeared to be ethnically homogeneous and (nationally) united; Albanian culture has also been resistant to foreign influences; and it is insisted that the development of the Albanian lands and their inhabitants was parallel to that of developed, civilized countries (Schmitt 2009b, 66). This pattern is applied to each past epoch, often by the same leading historians. In the preface to the three volumes containing the selected writings of the then president of the Academy of Sciences Aleks Buda, it is pointed out that he was the author of studies on all periods of Albanian history "from ancient to modern times" (Buda 1986a, 3).

The "Albanian lands" are projected into the past in the same way, starting from their extent in the late nineteenth and twentieth centuries. In some respects, the narrative makes direct use of contemporary geographical concepts. Kosovo is thus equated with Dardania, albeit with the caveat that ancient Dardania occupied more extensive territories. Even more revealing is the use of terms such as "present-day Macedonia in the Middle Ages" (Rexha 2011), "Western Macedonia" in prehistoric times (Andrea 1971) and in the Middle Ages (Frashëri 2011a; Xhufi 2011a), referring to the present-day Republic of Macedonia or a part of it (first as a federal unit of Yugoslavia, then as an independent state), and not to any geographical concept of Macedonia of the respective period, nor to the state of Philip and Alexander the Great.

Despite Kosovo's clear pre-eminence in propaganda and polemical publications, Albanian historiography is interested in every single disputed region. For example, the medievalist Pëlumb Xhufi has published on the disputed issues regarding the history of Epirus (Xhufi 1995), Kosovo (Xhufi 1996), Western Macedonia (Xhufi 2011a), and Montenegro (Xhufi 2011b). The same goes for the prolific Kristo Frashëri (Frashëri 1969, 2011a, 2011b).

Greater Albania, as conceived in the late nineteenth century, can relatively easily find its predecessor in a not-too-distant period—the two semi-independent pashaliks of the Bushati and Ali Tepelena in the late eighteenth to early nineteenth centuries, which are considered the height of Albanian autonomy and as a kind of unification of the "Albanian lands" during the Ottoman period (Pollo 1990, 236). The territories of these pashaliks did not coincide with the lands now inhabited by Albanian populations: they did not include some of them (in present-day Western Macedonia) and, more importantly, in the south, they went far beyond them. As a result, the term "Albania" (*Shkiperi, Arna(v)utluk*) came to be used in the then Ottoman context as a politico-geographical term without ethnic connotations (Naçi 1976, 63). Most importantly, the two semi-independent pashaliks belonged to a relatively late era and cannot counter the main points of attack of neighboring historiographies, namely their claims that the Albanians settled in the disputed lands during Ottoman rule and that this was often a deliberate policy of the Ottoman authorities.

240   A. VEZENKOV

Albanian historians cannot identify with a sufficiently large medieval state, which puts them at a disadvantage in their disputes with propagandists and nationalist historians from neighboring countries. There is nothing like Stefan Dushan's Serbia, Simeon's or Ivan Asen II's Bulgaria, or even the ephemeral "unification" of Wallachia with Moldavia and Transylvania under Mihai Viteazul (in 1600) or Samuel's state, to which Macedonian historians can refer in addition to Bulgarian ones (see Daskalov in this volume). In the Albanian area, there were only small state formations in the late Middle Ages. Albanian medievalists demonstrate the emergence of an Albanian statehood, but the main problem remains that there was no "Greater Albania" in the Middle Ages. At best, they can speak of a tendency toward political unification into one state—it is argued that there was a similar process under the Balsha/Balšić family (the last decades of the fourteenth century), which was revived and culminated under Skanderbeg (Bogdani 1985).

In fact, the reign of Skanderbeg, which is considered to be the highpoint in the medieval history of Albania, did not extend over a large area. Skanderbeg ruled over a small territory in Northern Albania, and he is regarded a great leader for very different reasons. Emphasis is placed on the length of his struggle because a small nation was able to fight for so long against a vast empire; he is said to have united people from different parts of Albania and to have attracted supporters from other Balkan peoples (Buda 1986a, 251, 266). However, the problem remains that Skanderbeg did not unite all Albanians under his rule, and certainly not all the territories claimed by Albanians in recent times.

More recently, some publications have claimed that Skanderbeg's possessions extended further to the east than previously thought—a thesis repeatedly developed by Kasëm Biçoku. (Biçoku 2006, 2007; Schmitt, 2009a, 350–1). Biçoku himself complained that he was initially refused permission to participate in a symposium in Skopje in November 2005 (to mark the 600th anniversary of Skanderbeg's birth), and was only allowed to attend at the insistence of the director of the Institute of History in Tirana, but in the end his paper "The Eastern Frontier of Skanderbeg's State" was not included in the symposium proceedings (Biçoku 2007, 14). Still, as a whole the discussions about Skanderbeg in Albania are not related to the theme of "Greater Albania" (Schmidt-Neke 2010; see Clayer in this volume).

The fact that there was no sufficiently large Albanian state in the Middle Ages made it necessary to find other solutions that go back even further in time, to Prehistory and Antiquity, and in particular to the history of the Illyrian tribes. This maneuver turned out to be convenient for arguments with Serbian historiography and necessary for arguments with Greek historiography. It is no coincidence that at the scientific session on the Illyrians in March 1969, Albanian scholars spoke more about the extent of the "Albanian lands" than at the Second National Conference on Albanian Studies in January 1968, dedicated to the 500th anniversary of Skanderbeg's death.

The assumption of an ancient indigenous (Paleo-Balkan) origin of the Albanians appeared much earlier and was originally the result of innocent scientific curiosity on the part of foreign authors in the eighteenth and, especially, the nineteenth centuries, who sought to explain the origins of a little-known people and their language. Soon this hypothesis was instrumentalized to show that the Albanians were an indigenous European population and therefore should not be affected by the expulsion of the "Turks" from Europe (Clayer 2007).

Subsequently, the Paleo-Balkan origin thesis was also used to "prove" that the Albanians had inhabited some disputed territories since ancient times. In the nineteenth century, various foreign and Albanian intellectuals considered the Pelasgians to be the ancestors of the Albanians, but the term was too vague and this hypothesis was consequently rejected by scholars. In later territorial disputes it was necessary not only to present the Albanians as the descendants of an "ancient people" who had inhabited the region before anyone else, but also to show that their predecessors had lived on exactly the same lands as the Albanians of today, and the Illyrians fulfilled this condition (see also Clayer 2022, 31, 94). This is why official Albanian historiography easily left aside the old Pelasgian hypothesis and consistently distances itself from the Thraco-Dacian hypothesis of Albanian origins in all its variants. According to the latter hypothesis, the ancestral homeland of today's Albanians would have been to the east of the territories they inhabit today. There is a clear parallel with the Romanian case, where most nationalist historians insist that the Romanians are descendants of the very tribes (Dacians, Getae) that inhabited present-day Romanian lands.

This raises the question of the extent of the territories inhabited by the Illyrians. Above all, it is claimed that "Illyria was a vast country" (*The History of Albania* 1981, 6), that the Illyrians "lived over a vast area," and so on (*Les Illyriens* 1985, 5–7). The problem is that this large area includes broad territories in the north that do not interest the champions of the

Albanian cause, while at the same time it does not include (or at least there is no consensus that it does) some of the most important disputed territories—Epirus and present-day Kosovo. Albanian authors concentrate on the "southern Illyrians" or "Illyrians proper" (*Illyrii proprie dicti*, using the expression of Pliny the Elder), trying to show that it was the Illyrians who were the ancient inhabitants of the now disputed Epirus, Western Macedonia, and Kosovo. Albanian historiography of the 1950s polemicized more openly about Epirus and Epirote. Subsequently, the subject of Kosovo gained strength and occupied a prominent place.

Already in the distant past, the Epirotes were referred to as the ancestors of the present-day Albanians, or as one of their ancestors, along with the Illyrians and the ancient Macedonians. Once it was accepted that the Albanians were descendants of the Illyrians, the Epirotes were simply classified as Illyrians. The first step was to argue that the Epirotes were not Greeks, quoting individual authors such as Thucydides, who called the Epirotes "barbarians"; in parallel, it was argued that their language was not Greek. It was also explained that the use of Greek by the Epirotes was a phenomenon limited to the elite and did not affect the great mass of the people (the same applied to the use of Greek by the Illyrians). It is also insisted that "Epirus "was a geographical name imposed from outside and had no ethnic meaning. Popular publications from the Greek side problematized all these statements one by one (Hatzopoulos 2023).

The second step was to argue directly that the Epirotes were Illyrians, or at least (ethnically and linguistically) more similar to the Illyrians than to the Greeks (Demiraj 2008). Many publications simply assume that the Epirotes were Illyrians and interpret the sources of the period thusly (Basha 2012 and 2013). One linguistic argument is the personal names that occurred both in Epirus and among the Illyrians (Ceka 1965, 86). It should be emphasized that academic Albanian historiography builds on earlier contributions, including from the period of Italian occupation during the Second World War. For example, Albanian authors during the communist period cited publications by Domenico Mustilli from the early 1940s, which supported the thesis of the Illyrian affiliation of the Epirotes (Mustilli 1965; A[namali] 1965; Anamali 1967, 39; Budina 1971, 112).

Subsequently, Albanian scholars added to the selective references to ancient authors and linguistic data (onomastics, toponymy) the results of excavations of Early Iron Age sites, which, according to their interpretations, helped to clarify the Illyrian ethnicity of the Epirus tribes (Anamali and Korkuti 1971, 37). Among the material evidence, both constructions (tombs, fortifications) and everyday objects such as fibulae and double needles are pointed out (Budina 1971, 115–7).

The question of the ethnicity of the Dardanians is also resolved by identifying them as Illyrians, with some ancient authors (Nicola of Damascus; Appian) cited in support (Ceka 1996, 22). The similarities in the material culture revealed by archaeological research in Kosovo and Albania, such as the construction of fortresses (the author writes about "Illyrian-Albanian castles of Late Antiquity and the Middle Ages"), and the cities in general, are used as an evidence (Anamali 1996, 27). In general, it is concluded that the material culture of Dardania did not differ from that of the other Illyrian provinces, and some publications explicitly criticize those who speak of parallels between the Dardanians and other cultures in the region; the political separation of Dardania did not in any way mean that the Dardanians were not Illyrians (Shukriu 1996, 16, 18). Aleks Buda, in his closing address at the July 1982 conference, compared the results of the excavations in Albania with those in Kosovo and concluded that in the provinces of Prevalitania, Dardania, New Epirus, and (the northern part) of Old Epirus there existed a developed material and spiritual culture which, with all its local variations, was essentially unified (*Konferenca kombëtare për formimin e popullit shqiptar* 1988, 504–5). The above enumerated "four (southern) Illyrian provinces" became a handy formulation for defining the "Albanian lands" in Antiquity, just like the "four Albanian vilayets" of the late nineteenth and early twentieth centuries.

The identification of the Dardanians with the Illyrians also largely resolves the question of whether (present-day) western and north-western Macedonia belonged to the Illyrian area. Furthermore, based on archaeological material from Western Macedonia itself, Zhaneta Andrea insists in particular on the parallels in ceramics between south-western Albania and Western Macedonia in the Late Bronze Age, the differences being only minor. This material culture persisted into the Early Iron Age, hence the conclusion that an Illyrian population continuously inhabited the territory of both present-day Albania and present-day Western Macedonia throughout the Bronze and Iron Ages (Andrea 1971). Overall, the Illyrians are described as an ethnic group that inhabited a compact territory with a distinct identity which was therefore well separated from the surrounding peoples.

The image of the Illyrians themselves as the bearers of a highly advanced civilization was further developed. A key element in this narrative is the growing academic output on the "Illyrian cities." In earlier publications they were not specifically presented, while the Greek colonies were described in detail (*Historia e Shqiperisë* 1959, 59–73; Frashëri 1964, 16–22). In just ten years, the subject of the Illyrian city had become central, as can be seen from the first meeting on Illyrian studies. Albanian archaeologists argued with those (foreign) authors who believed that the Illyrians had no urban life and that, insofar as there was urban life in their lands at all, it had been brought in from outside by the Greek colonies (Islami 1972). Later general overviews of Albanian history speak directly of an "urban civilization" among the Illyrians (*The History of Albania* 1981, 14). The question of whether there was an Illyrian urban life acquires political significance, with many on the Albanian side insisting that it was well developed, that is, that the Albanian people were not descended from backward nomads. The importance attached to the "Illyrian cities" is directly related to the thesis of the sedentary nature of the Illyrians (and thus of the Albanians as their descendants), as opposed to the hypothesis that the Albanians were an ethnic group formed from backward, semi-nomadic tribes living in isolated mountainous areas.

Another indicator of the high level of development is the concept of Illyrian statehood, and the subject weighs heavily in the general body of Albanian historiography. The "Illyrian kingdoms" were already present in the 1959 edition of the *History of Albania*, and later the subject was further developed. Albanian authors were dissatisfied with the more cautious formulations of some foreign scholars about "tribal unions" among the Illyrians and insisted on speaking directly of a "state"/"states" among them (Hadri 1976; Garašanin 1980).

After the changes of 1991, some historians stressed that the Illyrians had adopted Christianity as early as the first century, along with the other peoples of the region (Frashëri 1999). Such an early Christianization testifies to the presence of the Illyrians in the area long before the Slavs. Linguistic arguments are also used to prove the early Christianization of the Albanians, and in this case borrowings from foreign languages, namely from Latin, are welcome as evidence (Topalli 2000). Indeed, foreign scholars point to the absence of borrowings from ancient Greek in Albanian as evidence that their predecessors did not live on the Adriatic coast in Antiquity (Matzinger 2009, 28).

The Illyro-Albanian Continuity in All Albanian Lands

All that has been said about the high level of development of the Illyrians (a sedentary people with an urban culture and statehood), the vast territory they compactly inhabited, and the clear distinction from their neighbors is only of value if the Illyrian-Albanian continuity is not questioned. Hence the importance of the period between the seventh century, when the Illyrians are last mentioned, and the eleventh century, when people with the name "Albanoi/Arbanitai" appear in the sources. The fact that this was a period of massive invasions and resettlements makes the problem even more complex. First of all, Albanian scholars wanted to demonstrate continuity, that is, that the same ethnic group, speaking the same language, continued to inhabit the southern Illyrian lands. In addition, they also had to deal with the different names of the inhabitants of the Albanian lands in Antiquity and the Middle Ages (Illyrians/Albanians) and explain the change as a process of transition called the "formation of the Albanian people" (Buda 1988).

An important feature of this continuity is the intact ethnic purity of the Illyrians/Albanians, preserved under foreign rule and during barbarian invasions. This includes periods that are poorly documented, which makes it necessary to deal with the few existing linguistic data and then with the results of archaeological excavations, in both cases with a creative approach. The general assumption is that there were only limited external influences on the culture and language, and minor admixtures in ethnic composition. Let us consider them chronologically.

First of all, it is claimed that the ethnic purity of the Illyrians was preserved in Antiquity. It is insisted that the colonies established by the ancient Greeks on the Adriatic coast from the eighth century BC onward did not lead to Hellenization of the indigenous Illyrian population. The Illyrians had good contacts with the ancient Greeks, Greek was used in writing, but this did not lead to Hellenization; there was some such process among the elite, but "the peasants kept their mother tongue and remained Illyrians." Finding Illyrian names in Greek inscriptions indicated "ethnic consciousness" (Anamali 1993, 8).

Albanian historiography insists that later, under Roman rule, there was no process of Romanization of the Illyrians. The Illyrians resisted the Roman invasion and maintained their identity and traditions under Roman rule, although the conquest itself was brutal and had severe consequences.

Moreover, there was no large influx of migrants from Rome and Italy in general into southern Illyria. Unlike other populations in the Balkans, the Illyrians were not Romanized, as is clear from both linguistic studies (Demiraj 2000; Mansaku 2005) and archaeological evidence (Shpuza 2006). Finally, the Roman occupation actually strengthened unity in the ranks of the Southern Illyrians, and "this was not only a unity of material and spiritual culture and language, but a true ethnic unity, which continued in the following centuries" (Anamali 1993, 9–10). The Dardanians also preserved their characteristics and traditions even under Roman rule (Shukriu 1996, 17). The intact ethnic identity and the constant resistance of the Dardanians were the reason for the creation of a separate province of Dardania in 279 AD (Shukriu 2001).

In sum, the processes of Hellenization and Latinization were superficial and confined to the upper classes (Buda 1986a, 107). The presence of Greek and Latin inscriptions does not mean that the Illyrians were Hellenized, nor that they were later Romanized (Ceka 1965, 85). The main point is that the Illyrians were not Romanized, otherwise they could not be the ancestors of the Albanians, whose language does not belong to the family of Romance languages.

The next crucial point is that there were no significant admixtures and influences from the barbarian invasions, including (and this is becoming increasingly important) the Slavic ones. Albanian historians describe the devastation brought by the barbarians, but from their point of view it is even more important to say that these tribes did not settle permanently and did not change the ethnic composition of the population in the Albanian lands. The barbarian tribes did not leave any significant traces in the material culture either. For example, there was no Avar influence on the ancient Albanian tombs (Spahiu 1969).

Furthermore, it is claimed that the Slavic presence in the Albanian lands dates only from the political conquest by Slavic states from the ninth century onward and not from the Slavic invasion of (the rest of) the Balkans in the sixth and especially the seventh centuries (Anamali 1993, 11–12). No sources from the seventh century speak of Slavic settlement in New Epirus, Dardania, (southern) Prevalitania, or (northern) Old Epirus, that is, precisely in the areas inhabited by Albanians today (Doja 1999a, 35). Archaeological evidence of a Slavic presence in the sixth and seventh centuries is scarce, isolated, and temporary (Buda 1986a, 114). As in present-day Albania itself, the Albanian population in Dardania and Montenegro/

Duklja was "very little affected by the great Avaro-Slav migrations of the sixth and seventh centuries" (Anamali 1996, 25–26; Doja 1999a, 34).

The Illyrian-Albanian language continuity is supported (and challenged) by some highly specialized linguistic arguments, such as word formation, the division of languages according to the satem/centum criterion, and so on. In general, Albanian publications openly favor those authors, even amateurs of the nineteenth century, who accept the Illyrian hypothesis at the expense of all others, including contemporary professional linguists.

Onomastics and toponymy have received particular attention, and understandably so, since they are almost the only surviving traces of the Illyrian language. Toponymy also has the great advantage of being able to locate the Illyrian/Albanian presence on the geographical map. Ekrem Çabej developed a very tempting and widely accepted hypothesis, according to which the names of a number of places in the region known from Roman times developed into their present forms according to Albanian phonetic laws ("without any Slavic intervention"), indicating that an Illyrian/Albanian population lived there continuously (*The History of Albania* 1981, 31).

At the same time, the interest in toponymy was born of the need to respond to those authors who emphasize the presence of Slavic place names in Albania itself, especially in its southern part. The presence of Greek and Slavic toponymy in areas inhabited by Albanians favors the argument that Albanian populations had settled in areas formerly inhabited by Greek or Slavic/Serbian populations. On the Serbian side, it is insisted that Albanian territory is densely covered with Slavic toponymy (Bogdanović 1985, 19). There are some grounds for such a claim, especially concerning southern Albania. In the first edition of the *History of Albania*, this toponymy is still explained by the Slavic invasion, and the Slavic invasion itself is said to have interrupted a process of Romanization, but also to have created a risk of Slavicization (*Historia e Shqipërisë* 1959, 145–6). A little later, Kristo Frashëri also dated the settlement of Slavs in the Albanian plains to the sixth and especially the seventh centuries, repeating the thesis that the Slavs founded many villages and that their names have remained since then (Frashëri 1964, 38–39).

Subsequently, Albanian scholars developed a different interpretation— that it was a toponymy imposed much later, after the political conquest of Albanian lands by medieval Slavic states, and which has nothing to do with an actual settlement of Slavs in these territories as early as the barbarian invasions (although even in this case the Slavs would appear as latecomers compared to the Illyrians/Albanians). The argument is that these Slavic names appear in historical sources only from the eleventh century onward and in most cases were imposed either by the Bulgarian or later by the Serbian Kingdom (Doja 1999a, 35). The most criticized work is Afanasy Selishchev's book on the Slavic population in Albania (Selishchev 1931). In addition, it is claimed that the place names of Slavic origin were actually not so numerous, and that the "microtoponymy" was Albanian. A cleverly chosen argument is the presence of toponymy of Turkish origin—given the fact that there was no Turkish population in Albanian villages, the presence of Turkish names in toponymy supports the plausibility of the thesis that place names could have been administratively imposed (Domi 1982, 303–4). In addition, Albanian authors are annoyed by the use of Slavic toponymy by their neighbors, for example in Macedonian history textbooks (Dalipi 2020, 223).

One of the most problematic theses for Albanian historiography is the portrayal of Albanians by foreign historians as latecomers to at least some of the territories they inhabit. Hence the constant reluctance to study and present "migration(s)" and "(semi-)nomadism." This concerns, on the one hand, the theories that Albanians migrated from a more distant territory (the speculations about the Caucasian origin of Albanians and, above all, the hypothesis that Albanians migrated from other parts of the Balkan peninsula), but also the thesis that Albanians initially inhabited only a smaller mountainous territory in what is now Albania, from where they later migrated to neighboring regions.

One of the oft-repeated arguments against the thesis of the autochthony of the Albanians in their present territory is the lack of a genuinely Albanian maritime vocabulary. Lirak Dodbiba, in a dispute with foreign authors from previous generations such as Gustav Weigand and Norbert Jokl, argues that other languages also lost much of their own maritime terminology to a Mediterranean *koine* imposed by the Venetians and Genoese (Dodbiba 1966, 61), likewise he gives examples of preserved words of the original maritime vocabulary in Albanian (Dodbiba 1976).

In the same context, there is the problem of the common features of Albanian with several other languages of the region in the so-called Balkan Linguistic Union, especially with Romanian, which implies a common origin and/or a long common habitation of the speakers of these languages (Çabej 1969). It is argued that these common features first appeared in

Albanian and that Albanian influenced the other Balkan languages (Beci 1985, 140; 2021).

More numerous and more detailed are the reactions to the claims that in the late Middle Ages and especially during the Ottoman period the Albanians spread from a core area in what is now Northern and Central Albania to adjacent territories. The answer of Albanian scholarship mirrors the claims of historians from neighboring countries, and again goes far back in time: the Albanians did not spread to new lands; on the contrary, the territory inhabited by Illyrians/Albanians shrank over the centuries. Already Sami Frashëri, in his famous book *Albania—What It Was, What It Is, and What It Will Be* (1899), mentioned that in the past the Albanians inhabited a larger territory. In the scholarly literature, this thesis is associated with Ekrem Çabej, who insists in several of his publications that the present Albanian territory is not the result of expansion, but of "constant shrinkage" (Çabej 1993, 22). Leading authors of the communist era (*Les Illyriens* 1985, 8; Buda 1986a, 143) and academic writers after the beginning of the transition (Biçoku 1996, 47) repeat his thesis. However, this "shrinking" did not include even a temporary de-Albanization of disputed territories such as Kosovo, Western Macedonia, or Epirus. Moreover, the Illyrian-Albanian population remained relatively compact during this process of shrinking and did not mix with other arriving peoples.

Albanian historiography is particularly sensitive to the thesis that Albanians migrated from the mountainous regions of present-day Albania, especially its northern part, to the plains and valleys of Kosovo, Western Macedonia, and Epirus. Albanian historians study and openly discuss the migrations of Albanians to more distant places—to the Peloponnese, Attica, Boeotia and Euboea (approximately thirteenth to sixteenth centuries), to Southern and Central Italy (fourteenth to eighteenth centuries), to colonies on the territories of present-day Bulgaria (fifteenth to seventeenth centuries), Romania (seventeenth to nineteenth centuries), and Egypt (eighteenth to early twentieth centuries), but not the migrations to much closer regions such as Kosovo or Epirus (from the thirteenth to fourteenth centuries onward). For political reasons, these particular migrations of the Albanians are not studied (Schmitt, 2009b, 76). Greater Albania should not be the product of migrations from some kind of "smaller" Albania.

The use of the name "Albania" and "Albanian" in the Middle Ages is interpreted in the same way. The name "Albania/Arber" was first used to designate a relatively limited area in what is now central and northern

Albania (roughly the area between the cities of Tivar-Prizren-Ohrid-Vlora), and then gradually began to be used for a wider area. The interpretation proposed by some foreign scholars is that modern Albanians originated in said territory and then migrated to neighboring lands, as a result of which the name began to refer to a wider area. Earlier studies in Albanian historiography analyzed primarily the appearance and later the change of the name from "Arbër" in all its variants to "Shqiperi" (Shuteriqi 1956; Myderrizi 1965). Gradually, Albanian scholars also developed their own explanation for the spread of the name to a larger territory: the name originated among some Albanians and then spread to other territories that were already inhabited by Albanians or, rather, had been inhabited by Albanians since time immemorial (Luka 1969a; Bozhori 1972; Biçoku 1992; Xhufi 2001; Rexha 2005; Mala and Qerimi 2009; Frashëri 2010).

Albanian scholars also insist that the name "Arber" (and its derivatives) was not used to refer to present-day Kosovo and Western Macedonia, not because they were not inhabited by Albanians, but because these inhabitants were identified with the state that owned the respective regions. However, some Albanian scholars referred to individual sources from the fourteenth century onward, according to which Macedonia and Epirus were considered part of Albania (Drançolli 1996, 64).

Not all foreign scholars are subject to criticism. On the contrary, Alain Ducellier's article on the concept of Arbanon and the Albanians in the eleventh century received an extensive favorable review by Kolë Luka. Ducellier's article rejected Georg Stadtmüller's view that the name "Arbanon" was confined to the Mati area, and argued that it referred to a much wider region. The review stresses that in many respects Ducellier's theses coincided perfectly with those of Albanian historians (Luka 1969b, 147–48). Alain Ducellier, whose publications were regularly included in Albanian editions, is the only foreign author in the collection *The Albanians and Their Lands* (*Shqiptarët dhe trojet e tyre*, 1982, 192)

In response to the thesis that the Albanians initially inhabited a relatively limited area and only spread later, Albanian historians pointed out that the history of Serbia itself began with a small core, namely Raška near Novi Pazar, from which it later spread to neighboring regions. The Serbian possessions in Duklja/Montenegro and Dardania/Kosovo during the (late) Middle Ages were part of this expansion (Xhufi 1996, 41, 44).

The racist remarks of some foreign authors, and especially Serbian propaganda, that the number of Albanians had increased rapidly due to an extremely high birth rate, also met with an implicit response from Albanian historians. They claimed that already the Illyrians were "one of the most numerous" peoples of ancient Europe (Anamali in *The History of Albania* 1981, 4), "one of the largest populations in Europe" (Anamali 1993, 5), that the Illyrian provinces were "fairly heavily populated," with three million out of the seven million inhabitants of the Balkan Peninsula living in them; and that the Albanians were also a numerous people in the Middle Ages (Frashëri in *The History of Albania* 1981, 24). Later on, the Albanians in the Middle Ages were "one of the largest peoples in the Balkans" (Biçoku 1996, 47–48). At the same time, Albanian authors exploited the theme of the heroism of a small people against incomparably stronger and more numerous opponents. In complete contradiction to the above quotes, it is emphasized that the Albanians at the time of Skanderbeg had relatively limited economic and human resources (Buda 1986a, 264).

The differences between the Albanian dialects are also used as an argument that the Albanians were not involved in any significant migrations during the Middle Ages. It is claimed that their formation is the result of a process of development over many centuries in the same place: "The great differences between the Ghegs and Tosks in language and customs prove that the Albanians have lived in their territories since ancient times" (Çabej 1993, 21). Bahri Beci argues that the dialectal differences go back to the period before the arrival of the Slavs and that differentiation took place in the Early Middle Ages or Late Antiquity (Beci 1985, 134, 140, 145). Jorgji Gjinari goes the furthest back in time, suggesting that the division between the Gheg and Tosk dialects was recent, but sees deep roots in the geography of the subdialects, which he suggests emerged during Roman rule and coincided with the boundaries of the Roman provinces of various periods between the first and sixth centuries (Gjinari 1971, 180–1). This view remains isolated and Bahri Beci, quoted above, criticizes it as unproven (Beci in *Les Illyriens et la genèse des albanais* 1971, 250). It should be stressed that the very fact that these discussions are based on today's map of Albanian dialects means that the actual extent of the "Albanian lands" is automatically projected into the past.

In other cases, the problem of the Antiquity of Albanian dialects has been approached quite differently. In order to emphasize the unity of the nation, the official position during the communist period was that the dialectal differences between Ghegs and Tosks were not profound and that the dialectal divide emerged relatively late, in the context of "feudal fragmentation." Some authors even link the final formation of the two groups and their dialects to the "two great Albanian pashaliks" (the

Bushati and the Tepelena) of the late eighteenth and early nineteenth centuries, which was not considered convincing by most linguists (Desnitskaya 1968, 46–47, 50, 53). Since both questions are extremely important, some experts arrived at the compromising formulation that the differences between Albanian dialects are relatively small, but very old.

New arguments are added by archaeologists, based on very different material, but arriving at the same conclusions as linguistics and earlier historical studies (Anamali 1988). The role of archaeology can be seen in two directions. Firstly, it provides additional arguments for the Illyrian-Albanian continuity and even began to play a leading role in this respect. Albanian authors began to criticize foreign supporters of the Thracian hypothesis of the Albanians' origin, saying that the latter relied only on written sources and linguistic data, while ignoring archaeological findings (Buda 1986a, 109). Second, Albanian archaeologists claim to have found a similar material culture in all "Albanian lands," both in Antiquity and in the Middle Ages (Historiografia shqiptare në dhjetëvjetorin 1967, 36). Assuming that a similar (many say identical) material culture is a sign of settlement by the same ethnic group, leading Albanian archaeologists conclude that the Illyrian-Albanian continuity took place in all territories inhabited by Albanians today. Ethnology provides additional arguments. Studies of traditional dress show relatively few differences in the Illyrian area, but also continuity in a number of elements in the dress of present-day Albanians (Gjergji 1969, 1985).

The Albanian lands are presented as a homogeneous space. All studies of material culture (e.g., buildings, various objects, clothing), as well as those of Albanian dialects, stress that the differences between the different parts of the "Albanian lands" were relatively small. The lack of political unity has been explained by developmental patterns: the only gradual overcoming of tribal differences in the process of creating a unified Illyrian state, as well as feudalization during the Middle Ages. As for the centuries of foreign domination, both the Romans and the Ottomans have been accused of dividing the Albanians into several administrative units in order to weaken them and prevent possible resistance (*The History of Albania* 1981, 19; Naçi 1976, 61).

The homogeneity of the national space also included well-developed transport links. Even in modern times, road connections in Albania were difficult, but medievalists discovered a well-developed road network with good connections between Albanian ports on the Adriatic and the "fertile plains in the east" and also routes in a north-south direction (Baçe 1985;

Biçoku 1996, 48–49). A supposedly developed urban economy also contributed to the intensive connections between the different parts of the Albanian lands (Malltezi 1985). Alain Ducellier was more cautious, saying that the Albanian space was "both very vast and very fragmented" (Ducellier 1996, 59).

The grand narrative of the Albanian Middle Ages moves smoothly from "Illyrians" to "Albanians" by elaborating the concept of the "formation of the Albanian people." As we have seen, the Illyrians are not only the ancestors of the Albanians, there is practically no difference in human material—the "ethnogenesis of the Albanians" is the overcoming of tribal ties and the transition to the next level of ethnic unity. According to the official ideology of the communist period, the ethnogenetic process could only develop in a class-based society, and the Albanian people/nationality (*kombësisë*, which corresponds to "narodnost" in Russian, and could be also translated as "nationality") was formed in the era of feudalism (Buda 1986a, 143). The main theses can be found in a systematic form in the publications of the Conference on the Formation of the Albanian People held in July 1982 (*Problèmes de la formation du peuple albanais* 1985; *Konferenca kombëtare për formimin e popullit shqiptar* 1988). The dating of the arrival of any Slavic population to the latest possible moment was very helpful in presenting the admixture of ethnically foreign elements as minimal: "The Slavic occupation of the northern and northeastern Albanian lands began in the eleventh century, when the Albanian culture and language had already been formed" (Pulaha 1985, 13–14, 17–18; 1993, 34).

The question of migrations is directly related to another controversial issue—the idea of the Albanians as a backward, isolated, (semi-)nomadic community, as is the case in the historiographies of neighboring countries. The migration thesis is associated with the underdevelopment of the Albanians, while the autochthonous thesis is associated with the portrayal of the Albanians as a highly developed and civilized people. Accordingly, Albanian historiography argues that the formation of the Albanian people during the Middle Ages was the result of the development of an agricultural society with its own urban culture, rather than of isolated tribes in the mountains (Buda 1986a, 93, 116–7). Earlier, the preservation of the Illyrians from Hellenization, and especially Romanization and Slavicization, was not due to the self-enclosure of backward nomads, but to an established (sufficiently high) spiritual and material culture that resisted external influences. This was obviously a reaction to the thesis of (the survival of) the Albanians as an isolated shepherd people living in the mountains, excluded from Greek and Roman influence. The Albanians had to be presented as a sedentary people, and statements that they were mainly engaged in animal husbandry and semi-nomadism were rejected as negative stereotypes (Schmitt 2009b, 74).

The notion of the Albanians as a people, which remained (semi-) nomadic until very late is challenged by evidence of the development of agriculture in Albanian lands in the late Middle Ages. Spiro Shkurti presents the Albanians as an agricultural people with a level of development comparable to that of their neighbors, and pays particular attention to "urban agriculture" and the cultivation of perennial crops such as olives and vines, which implies a permanently settled population (Shkurti 1997, 103ff and 139ff). The author disputes the claims of the "Serb" Jovan Cvijić, the "Russian" Afanasy Selishchev, and the "German" Georg Stadtmüller that the Albanians of the late Middle Ages were cattle breeders who did not cultivate, that they were not settled, that they had no towns and no state organization. On the contrary, according to Shkurti, there were no areas in the Albanian lands where the population was only engaged in animal husbandry, but everywhere they were also engaged in agriculture (ibid., 16). In general, the book demonstrated the existence of agriculture in Albanian areas without discussing the ethnic communities to which the farmers belonged. Linguistic evidence is also provided that Albanians have been involved in agriculture since ancient times (Shkurtaj 1976).

The circulation of coins is quoted by Albanian scholars as another indicator of a developed Albanian society in the Middle Ages. The data on Byzantine coins found on the territory of present-day Albania from Late Antiquity to the end of the High Middle Ages (fifth to eighth centuries) show a rather intensive circulation (although with temporary declines), including the areas outside the major cities and even in the mountains. It is claimed that the monetarization of the economy throughout the Albanian territories contradicts Stadtmüller's account of the isolated life of the Albanian population in that period, and at the same time the fact that this phenomenon was uninterrupted also demonstrates the "ethnic continuity of the autochthonous population" (Spahiu 1985, 175). The circulation of coins is also cited as evidence of the sophistication of Albanian society in Skanderbeg's time (Buda 1986a, 232).

The description of the Albanians as semi-nomads who plundered and terrorized the peaceful agricultural (Slavic) population finds its counterpart in the works of Albanian authors describing the Slavic invasions of the Byzantine provinces in the Balkans in the sixth and seventh centuries (*History of Albania* 1981, 26–28). After decades of publications about the Illyrians and their highly developed material and spiritual culture, about the "Illyrian urban civilization," and about their kingdoms, after the Illyrian-Albanian continuity was accepted as axiomatic the Slavs found themselves in the unfavorable role of savage tribes disturbing the life of the long-settled and civilized ancestors of the Albanians.

PRE-OTTOMAN AND OTTOMAN ALBANIA: INTERPRETATIONS AND COUNTER-INTERPRETATIONS

The use of historical arguments in Albanian historiography began as a response to the use of such arguments by their neighbors, especially Serbian scholars and propagandists. A number of specific themes, especially concerning the disputes with the Serbs about the Middle Ages, were taken up and developed, mirroring those developed by foreign historians. The themes of violence, colonization, and assimilation are almost mirrored on the Serbian and Albanian sides, in each case drawing on observations and grievances of the late nineteenth and especially the twentieth centuries, projected far back in time.

The theme of violence for both sides begins with contemporary examples—in Yugoslavia Albanians blamed the Serbian majority in the Republic of Serbia, Serbs blamed the Albanian majority in the autonomous province of Kosovo; Albanians blamed the foreign nation-state and the authorities in Belgrade, Serbs blamed foreign interventions ("the Great Powers," "the West"), but also the communist regime (for those who see it as imposed from outside) for tolerating the Albanians. Then the violence of the neighbor was projected into the past. From the Serbian point of view, the Albanian invasion of Kosovo took place by force, in conditions of chaos and autocracy during the Ottoman era (Samardžić 1990, 196–7). Albanian historiography focuses on periods when these areas were ruled by Serbs. Descriptions of violence by Serbian and then Yugoslav authorities from 1878 onward (the expulsion of Albanians from the Nish area) and especially after the Balkan Wars include discrimination, land confiscation, expulsion, and restrictions on Albanian education. To a large extent, these grievances are mechanically traced back to the Middle Ages. Albanian scholars write of the forced imposition of Orthodoxy and the Slavicization/

Serbianization of the local population as a policy that continued during the Ottoman period: "The role of the Serbian Orthodox Church in anti-Albanian policies has been extremely prominent in all periods of history from the eleventh century down to the present day" (Krasniqi 1996, 78). According to the Serbian counter-thesis, in the Middle Ages there was "unusual religious tolerance" in Serbia; Catholics were not persecuted because part of the Serbian population belonged to the Roman Church (Samardžić 1990, 182–3) and relations between Serbs and Albanians were not conflictual (Bogdanović 1985, 21).

Another issue used by both sides is colonization. Interest in this issue was triggered by the policy of settling Serbs in the territories annexed after the Balkan wars. But although the systematic colonization of Serbs in Kosovo is a contemporary issue, for Albanian authors its analysis begins in Antiquity (Osmani 2010, 7). The Albanian side sees it as an organized colonization of Slavs in Kosovo by the Serbian conquerors in the Middle Ages; conversely, Serbian authors speak of a systematic colonization of Albanians in Kosovo by the Ottoman authorities.

The issue of assimilation is also treated in the same way by the Serbian and Albanian sides—it is claimed that part of one's own community was assimilated, and in more traditional publications it is denied that such a process took place in the opposite direction. Thus, according to the Serbian version, the Albanians did not succumb to assimilation, and the proportion of the Albanian population in medieval Kosovo corresponds to the relatively rare use of the term "Arbanasa" and the limited number of Albanian names in medieval documents relating to the region (Bogdanović 1985: 39); that is, there were no "Serbianized/Slavicized Albanians" in addition to those referred to as "Albanians", as the Albanian interpretation claims. During the Ottoman period, a large mass of new Albanian migrants were added to the initially "small number of Albanian shepherds in the highlands and summer pastures" (Mikić 2006, 18–19). In addition, many Serbs converted to Islam and part of them were Albanized (Miljković 2006, 14). Serbian authors speak of the Serbs accommodating the Albanians who terrorized them in the region by accepting not only Islam but also the Albanian language—it is claimed that as a result, 30–40% of the Albanians in Yugoslavia were of Slavic origin, usually referred to pejoratively as "Arnautaši" (Samardžić 1990, 200).

Since political borders between nation-states are expected to follow the ethnic composition of the population, debates about the past are not so much about political domination as about the ethnic composition of the population in the regions currently in dispute. Albanian historiography does not argue about the extent and duration of Byzantine, Bulgarian, or Serbian rule over "Albanian lands," but insists primarily on the Albanian affiliation of the vast majority of the population, regardless of who ruled them and for how long.

Similarly, Serbian historians focus on the question of the ethnic composition of the population in Kosovo. From the Serbian point of view, the shifting of the border of medieval Serbia to the south should not be seen as the reason for the settlement of Serbs in Kosovo (which is the thesis of Albanian historiography), but as the unification of areas where a Serbian population had already lived for a long time (Bogdanović 1985, 28–29, 34). The same fixation on the question of ethnicity can be seen in the Bulgarian-Macedonian disputes (see Daskalov in this volume). The interpretations from Greece focus on cultural affiliation, and perhaps that is why historiographies such as Albanian, Macedonian, or Bulgarian find it difficult to argue with the Greek one.

Religious differences and conflicts of the past are understood and presented through the prism of today's national disputes—Albanian historiography has been particularly inventive in this regard, to some extent in response to equally inventive writers from neighboring countries. Since the late nineteenth century, Albanian nationalist thinkers, in their efforts to create an image of national unity, have always played down religious differences among Albanians: Muslim or Christian, Orthodox or Catholic, Albanians were first and foremost Albanians. In addition, the use of some national names is downplayed with the argument that it was only religious affiliation that was concealed behind them. The names "Serb" and "Turk" at that time denoted religious affiliation: "Serb" for instance meant belonging to the Serbian Orthodox Church (Rizaj 1996, 70, 73). Given the fact that religious affiliation was in many cases imposed from above, its imposition also appeared to be an attempt at national assimilation. Thus, the Serbian Church was seen as a "national church" that deliberately baptized children with Slavic names, and the imposition of Orthodoxy, therefore, meant the Slavicization of the (Albanian) population (Krasniqi 1996, 75–76).

In contrast, some publications in recent decades have given religious affiliation the role of a marker of ethnic/national identity. Thus it has been argued that in Late Antiquity Christianity strengthened the ethnolinguistic identity of the Illiro-Albanian population, and that its adoption helped the Albanians (as well as the Greeks) not to be swept away by barbarian invasions, including Slavic invasions (Doja 1999b, 166).

Albanian publications also insist that belonging to the Catholic Church in medieval Kosovo correlated with ethnic affiliation: all those referred to as "Catholics" or "schismatics" (in Serbian sources) were Albanians (Xhufi 1996, 43). The persecution of "schismatics" by the medieval Serbian state and church was very fierce precisely because ethnic differences were behind it and motivated the persecutions. Church sources usually spoke of "Latins" and "schismatics," but in some cases they also mentioned the Albanian ethnicity of the persecuted Catholics. Like the struggle of the Czech Hussites, that of the Albanians against the Serbs in the fourteenth century had a national content under a religious cover (Xhufi 1993, 49, 52).

If sectarian affiliation was a marker of ethnic identity, voluntary conversion could be a means of preserving it: adoption of Catholicism was a means of protection against Serbianization (Xhufi 1996, 42). After the Slavs adopted Eastern Orthodox Christianity from Constantinople, some Albanian clans in the north who had originally belonged to the Eastern Church did not hesitate to convert to Catholicism in order to resist assimilation by the Slavs (Doja 1999b, 166). The Serbian side accuses Catholic missionaries of helping to settle Albanian colonies in Kosovo (Miljković 2006, 13).

While Catholicism is presented as a strong marker of Albanian ethnicity, Albanian historians also promoted the innovative thesis (criticizing older authors such as Ireček) that a substantial part of the Orthodox inhabitants of Kosovo were in fact Albanians (Pulaha, 1985, 38). The talk of the "Orthodox Albanians in Kosovo" has no basis in the existing sources, and is intended to portray the Orthodox population of Kosovo as Albanians, "erroneously" referred to in the sources as Serbs (Malcolm 2009, 231).

As in other Balkan historiographies, the process of Islamization during the Ottoman period is seen in Albanian communist historiography as coercive, more precisely as a result of economic coercion. This is true of both specialized studies (Pulaha 1985, 49) and general overviews of Albanian history (Frashëri, 1964, 101; *The History of Albania* 1981, 90). Gradually, a new accent was added: when Albanians converted to Islam, the new religion became a marker of ethnicity, because in Kosovo Islam spread among the Albanian Orthodox and Catholics, but not among the "Slav minority" (Tërnava 1982, 489–90; Pulaha 1993, 38). Actually, the acceptance of Islam (and before that Catholicism) is again regarded as a matter of external pressure, but according to this newer interpretation the pressure came from the Slavs/Serbs, that is, from the actual adversary in the late twentieth and early twenty-first centuries, and the acceptance of the new religion was a means of countering this pressure.

Albanian historiography ironizes the Serbian argument about the presence of the many Orthodox churches and monasteries in Kosovo in two mutually exclusive ways. On the one hand, it is pointed out, with reference to foreign scholars such as Ireček, that only a small number of the churches were newly built by the Serbs themselves; most of them were pre-existing and merely renovated, including Catholic churches that were converted into Orthodox ones (Krasniqi 1996, 76). On the other hand, the appearance of Orthodox churches is portrayed as part of a deliberate strategy to Serbianize Kosovo—Pëlumb Xhufi speaks of "monasteries that were hastily built there" (Xhufi 1996, 42).

For traditional Albanian historiography, as for the conservative writers of Serbian, Greek, Bulgarian, or Macedonian historiography, the Ottoman conquest is presented as a dramatic and catastrophic setback, the cause of the Albanians' own underdevelopment. From then on, the centuries of Ottoman rule were the "Dark Ages" for the nation and the main reason for its backwardness at the beginning of its independent statehood, and right up to the present day. This, of course, fits in with the way all foreign dominations are portrayed, but Albanian historiography has additional motives for such an interpretation of Ottoman rule. The fact that the anti-Ottoman resistance was also the climax of Albania's medieval history under Skanderbeg contributes to this. It is claimed that Albania was also of great strategic importance because it lies on the route between Asia and Europe—the anti-Ottoman resistance of the Albanians stopped the Ottoman invasion. Two other reasons are relevant to the present work.

First, the emphasis on the destructive nature of the Ottoman conquest indirectly supports the thesis of a highly developed pre-Ottoman Albanian society with a clear national consciousness, the fruit of a relatively high level of economic and intellectual development. It is argued that, just as in other Balkan historiographies, the Ottoman conquest explains the disappearance of a huge part of their medieval heritage; it transformed Albania into a *tabula rasa* in terms of local historical monuments and documents. Otherwise, it is claimed that, until the beginning of the fifteenth century, Albania was at a level of socio-economic and cultural development comparable to the other countries in the Balkan-Adriatic region. The Ottoman conquest led to the decline of urban life, to depopulation, and to migration from the plains to the mountains—just as in the historical narrative of the other Balkan countries and exactly the opposite of their claims about the Albanians themselves (Buda 1986a, 230–6). Moreover, the Ottoman conquest thwarted the completion of the legitimate process of unification of the Albanians into one state (Frashëri 1964, 60). As a result of the regression that followed the Ottoman conquest, clan ties that had largely disappeared during the Middle Ages were reactivated in northern Albania in the fifteenth to sixteenth centuries (Pulaha 1975a and 1975b; Buda 1986a, 120–1).

Second, Albanian historiography attempts to address the accusation that Ottoman power privileged the Albanians (especially those who converted to Islam) and facilitated their territorial expansion (either by terrorizing the Serbian/Orthodox population or, sometimes, by settling Muslim Albanians in certain rebellious regions). In response, Albanian writers strongly deny any positive influence of Ottoman power on the expansion of the Albanians into larger territories. On the contrary, they point to cases in which Serbs, not Albanians, benefited from the Ottoman conquest. For example, the Balšićs (an Albanian dynasty according to Albanian historians) lost their power over Kosovo after being defeated by the Ottomans, and then the region passed (again) into the hands of Serbian rulers (1392–1395 under Vuk Branković; from 1397 under the Lazarevićs), who were, however, vassals of the Ottomans (Bogdani 1993, 59–60). The Serbs continued to have their own church under Ottoman rule, which also put them in a more favorable position than the Albanians.

The centrality of the Battle of Kosovo in Serbian historiography also challenged Albanian historiography to deal with it in greater detail. The latter insisted on a significant Albanian participation in the anti-Ottoman coalition, led by George II Balsha and Theodor II Muzaka (Frashëri 1964, 61; 2005; Muhadri 2021, 269ff). This participation has a twofold role. First, it places the Albanians among the opponents of the Ottoman conquest rather than among its beneficiaries. Second, it points to a (massive) Albanian presence in these areas. In support of the latter, the existence of Albanian folk songs about the Battle of Kosovo is pointed to—as a rule, folk songs were only created by first-hand witnesses of the events, indicating that the Albanian authors of these songs lived in Kosovo at the time (Pulaha 1985, 26).

Finally, Albanian historiography tried to prove that at the time of the Ottoman invasion, the population in all the disputed territories was predominantly Albanian (Thëngjilli 1982). Initially, evidence for this claim came from royal charters mentioning Albanians or using traditional Albanian names, from narrative sources (foreign diplomats and travelers), and so on. From the 1960s and especially from the 1970s, intensive use of detailed Ottoman tax registers from the fifteenth and sixteenth centuries began—sources rich in information that each historiography uses for its own purposes. Bulgarian historiography, for example, focuses on the question of human losses due to Ottoman conquest and/or Islamization, and tries to argue for the indigenous origins of the vast majority of Muslims in the country, in contrast to Turkish historiography, which is particularly interested in settlers from Anatolia. Albanian historiography uses these registers to prove that the population in disputed areas was predominantly Albanian. Selami Pulaha's publications stand out here, and most of his contributions concern Kosovo (Pulaha 1984). This is largely in response to Serbian historiography, which draws the opposite conclusion from the same sources.

On the Serbian side, the argument is simple and convincing: Ottoman registers show clear Serb predominance in almost all parts of Kosovo (Zirojević 2018; Samardžić 1990, 186). For example, the names in the 1455 inventory of the Branković region were 95.88% Serbian, while in most places Albanian names were very few, even less than 1%. Even in regions with more Albanian names, the toponymy is Slavic, which, according to the Serbian interpretation, indicates the settlement of Albanians in villages, towns, and neighborhoods previously inhabited by Slavs/Serbs (Miljković 2006, 8, 10–11).

Albanian authors rightly note that Slavic names are not necessarily borne only by Slavs. They point to various cases of people with Slavic personal names and Albanian patronymics (and vice versa), of people with names of Slavic root but with phonetic modifications characteristic of the Albanian language (e.g., Pjetri, Dimitri) and of Albanian names with Slavic suffixes (-ić), of settlements and urban districts with Albanian names inhabited by Slavs (and vice versa), and so on (Pulaha 1985, 39–47). The presence of names from the Christian calendar, which were not normally used by Slavs, is also emphasized because they were most plausibly borne by Albanians (Xhufi 1993, 50). Ottoman registers also show an Albanian population in present-day Macedonia—a land inhabited by Illyrians/Albanians since ancient times (Rexha 2011).

From the collection of all kinds of data on Albanians in these registers, Albanian historiography jumps to the conclusion that they were a "majority of the population." Authors publishing abroad are more cautious, claiming that the Ottoman registers show that Albanians constituted "an important part" of the population of Kosovo (Doja 1999a, 40). In general, Albanian authors make some adequate remarks regarding the interpretation of toponymy and especially onomastics, they find and systematize numerous examples of the presence of Albanians in the region, but in no way prove their claim that they constituted a majority.

According to the Serbian version, the settlement of Albanians began gradually in the sixteenth century, and until the end of the seventeenth century the Albanian-Serbian ethnic border coincided with the present border between Serbia and Montenegro on the one hand and Albania on the other (Miljković, 2006, 10, 12). The settlement of Albanians was not only accompanied by violence, but is also presented as a deliberate policy of the Ottoman authorities to transfer Albanian Muslims to rebellious territories (Mikić 2006, 22).

The Serbian version of the Albanization of Kosovo focuses on the displacement of Serbs after the Austro-Turkish War of 1683–1699, and especially after the withdrawal of Austrian troops in 1790—the so-called Great Migration (*Velika Seoba*); and later again after the war of 1735–1739. The Albanian counter thesis focuses primarily on problematizing the myth of the "Great Migration" itself—relatively few Serbs migrated, not all Serbs who migrated to the Habsburg Empire were from Kosovo, and many of the Christians who left the region were in fact Albanians (Rizaj 1983; Pulaha 1985). The different versions of the Serbian migration from Kosovo are some of the best-known and best-researched examples of conflicting interpretations of the region's past (Malcolm 2009).

On the Albanian side, counter-examples are given of Albanian migration from Kosovo to other regions. Another important argument from the Albanian side is that Ottoman tax registers show a relatively small demographic potential in the mountains and a larger one in Kosovo—this rules out the possibility that migrations from the mountains to the plains could have Albanized the latter; examples are also given of the many mentions in the registers of new settlers in Kosovo with Slavic names, demonstrating the migration of Serbs to Kosovo (Pulaha 1985, 66, 69). The only migration of Albanians to Kosovo that Albanian historiography likes to talk about happened at a different time and from entirely different places— Albanians, refugees from areas newly annexed by Serbia (the region of Nish), migrated to Kosovo, especially after 1877–1878 (Uka 1991).

The conclusions of the studies of Ottoman tax records are integrated into the long perspective of national history. For example, Selami Pulaha's book, or rather collection of studies, on the Albanian population in Kosovo in the fifteenth and sixteenth centuries begins by referring to Kosovo as an important hotbed of the Albanian national movement in the nineteenth century, and only a few pages later returns to Dardania in Antiquity (Pulaha 1984, 6, 10).

CONCLUSION

Albanian historiography, like any other national historiography, gets involved in disputes with opponents who are very different from each other, namely with representatives of national historiographies and propaganda from neighboring countries, whose approaches and priorities differ from country to country. Serbian historiography deals with the Middle Ages, Greek historiography starts from Antiquity; Serbian authors insist on ethnicity, Greek on language and culture, which attract people from different backgrounds; there are also disputes with foreign scholars who are not committed to any foreign national cause, but whose research conflicts with the established Albanian national narrative. The argumentation of Albanian writers begins as a response to various specific "attacks" or simply inconvenient opinions, but quickly develops into a standard explanatory pattern that applies to every occasion.

Thus, in the long run, the big problem of the historiographical wars is not only the clash between different national schools and the time and effort spent in fruitless disputes, but above all the entrenchment of each national historiography within a self-contained world. The same arguments are repeated over and over again, and once developed and adopted in the national narrative, there is little to build on. Ready-made answers are easy to find, and often the same author "professionally" argues with foreign historians about the Albanian affiliation of different regions in different periods.

Discussions about the past are conducted in different disciplines—history, linguistics, archaeology, and sometimes ethnology; narrowly specialized arguments are put forward, but the studies involved arrive at the same conclusions. The problems of different epochs are explained in the same way—continuity is always found, the influence of any foreign power turns out to be superficial, the settlement of foreign elements is negligible, regional differences are small, while the national space itself is well demarcated from the surrounding peoples. Most importantly, the territory inhabited by Albanians today has remained essentially unchanged since ancient times. If there has been any change, it has been due to the expulsion and assimilation of Illyrians/Albanians from other neighboring territories.

National historiography creates a coherent narrative of the past, but in its desire to respond to a variety of criticisms and challenges it sometimes gives different interpretations of the same problem and contradicts itself: religion is of little importance within the Albanian community itself, it does not divide it, but it is also a strong marker vis-à-vis other peoples and protects Albanians from assimilation; the dialectal differences among Albanians are not deep, but their roots are very far in the past (at least from the early Middle Ages) and thus prove their autochthony; the Illyrians and Albanians in the Middle Ages were a numerous people, but in the struggles of Skanderbeg they are presented as a heroic small nation.

Historical arguments for the autochthony of the Albanians in their present territories first appeared in popular propaganda writings, then were taken up and processed by academic historiography, and gradually enriched by references to a variety of primary sources and scholarly research. This leads to the paradox that, after decades of work by academic institutions in Albania, scholars reproduce some of the main claims made by Albanian intellectuals from the late nineteenth century or from propaganda pamphlets published during the Italian occupation in World War II. However, they have been developed, enriched, and given a scientific form, and foreign opinions can be dismissed not only as "anti-Albanian" but also as "anti-scientific."

References

A[namali], S[kënder]. 1965. Le prof. Domenico Mustilli de l'Université de Naples a visité les centres archéologiques d'Albanie. *Studia Albanica* II (2): 208–209.

A[namali], S[kënder]. 1969. Session scientifique sur le problème illyrien et la genèse des Albanais. *Studia Albanica* VI (1): 195–201.

Akte të Rilindjes Kombëtare Shqiptare 1878–1912: memorandume, vendime, protesta, thirrje. 1978. Ed. Stefanaq Pollo, Selami Pulaha. Tirana: Instituti i Historisë.

Albania: A Short Summary of Its History and Its Political and Territorial Problems. 1968. Madrid: El Economista.

Anamali, Skënder. 1967. Problemi i kulturës së hershme mesjetare shqiptare në dritën e zbulimeve të reja arkeologjike. *Studime historike* XXI (IV): 35–41.

Anamali, Skënder. 1988. Problemi i formimit të popullit shqiptar në dritë e të dhënave arkeologjike. In *Konferenca kombëtare për formimin e popullit shqiptar,*

5 DEFENDING OUR LANDS IN ANCIENT AND MEDIEVAL STUDIES... 265

të gjuhës dhe të kulturës së tij. 2-5 korrik 1982, 337–355. Tirana: Akademia e Shkencave e RPS të Shqipërisë.

Anamali, Skënder. 1993. The Illyrians and the Albanians. In *The Truth on Kosova,* ed. Kristaq Prifti et al., 5–18. Tirana: Encyclopedia.

Anamali, Skënder. 1996. Kosova and the Ethnic Territories of the Former Yugoslavia in the Early Middle Ages. In *The Kosova Issue—A Historic and Current Problem,* ed. Jusuf Bajraktari et al., 25–29. Tirana: Eurorilindja.

Anamali, Skënder, and Muzafer Korkuti. 1971 Le problème illyrien et celui de la genèse des albanians à la lumière des recherches archéologiques albanaises. In *Les Illyriens et la genèse des albanais. Travaux de la session du 3-4 mars 1969,* 11–39. Tirana: Université de Tirana, Institut d'histoire et de linguistique.

Andrea, Zhaneta. 1971. Liens culturels et ethniques entre la Macédoine de l'Ouest et l'Illyrie du Sud-Est durant le bronze récent (à la lumière de la céramique peinte). In *Les Illyriens et la genèse des albanais. Travaux de la session du 3-4 mars 1969,* 77–83. Tirana: Université de Tirana, Institut d'histoire et de linguistique.

Baçe, Appolon. 1985. Les routes albanaises au Moyen Age (du VIIe au XVe siècles). In *Problèmes de la formation du peuple albanais, de sa langue et de sa culture: choix de documents,* 176–189. Tirana: 8 Nëntori.

Basha, Nermi. 2012 and 2013. Epiri dhe bota ilire në veprën e Jul Cezarit, 'Mbi luftën civile' *Studime historike* LXVI (XLIX), 3–4 (2012): 5–25 and LXVII (L) 1–2 (2013): 7–18.

Bataković, Dušan T. 2012. *Serbia's Kosovo Drama: A Historical Perspective.* Beograd: Čigoja štampa.

Beci, Bahri. 1985. L'ancienneté des dialects de l'albanais, temoignage de l'habitat ancien des albanais. In *Problèmes de la formation du peuple albanais,* 129–145.

Beci, Bahri. 2021. *Rreth rolit të shqipes në formimin e bashkësisë gjuhësore ballkanike: bashkësia gjuhësore ballkanike në dritën e të dhënave të gjuhës shqip.* Tirana: Akademia e Shkencave e Shqipërisë.

Bezha, Anastas. 2021. The Trajectory of the Albanian Historiography: Between the Austrian Albanologie (Volkskunde) and the Communist Albanologie (National-Stalinism/Etnographiya). *Études sur la Région Méditerranéenne* 31:117–139.

Biçoku, Kasëm. 1992. Les regions ethniques Albanaises au Moyen Age et la propagation du nom national 'Arber,'. *Studia Albanica* XXIX (1–2): 11–23.

Biçoku, Kasëm. 1996. The Albanian Territories and Their Regional Ties in the Middle Ages. In *The Kosova Issue—A Historic and Current Problem,* ed. Jusuf Bajraktari et al., 47–53. Tirana: Eurorilindja.

Biçoku, Kasëm. 2006. Kufiri lindor i shtetit të Skënderbeut. *Studime historike* LXI(XLIV) (1–2): 131–145.

Biçoku, Kasëm. 2007. L'Étendue à l'Est des possessions des Kastrioti. *Studia Albanica* XLI (1): 14–36.

Bogdanović, Dimitrije. 1985. *Knjiga o Kosovo*. Belgrade: Srpska akademija nauka i umetnosti.

Bogdani, Pranvera. 1985. Les tendances à l'unification étatique des territoires albanais dans la seconde moitié du XIVe siècle et au début du XVe. In *Problèmes de la formation du peuple albanais, de sa langue et de sa culture: choix de documents*, 305–320. Tirana: 8 Nëntori.

Bogdani, Pranvera. 1993. Kosova under the Albanian Feudal State of the Balshas. In *The Truth on Kosova*, ed. Kristaq Prifti et al., 55–62. Tirana: Encyclopedia.

Bozhori, Koço. 1972. Vëzhgime rreth shtrirjes së emërtimit Arbanon në kohën byzantine. *Studime historike* XXVI (IX) (4): 135–140.

Buda, Aleks. 1986a. *Shkrime historike*, vol. 1. Tirana: 8 Nëntor.

Buda, Aleks. 1986b. *Shkrime historike*, vol. 2. Tirana: 8 Nëntor.

Buda, Aleks. 1988. Etnogjeneza e popullit shqiptar në dritën e historisë. In *Konferenca kombëtare për formimin e popullit shqiptar, të gjuhës dhe të kulturës së tij. 2-5 korrik*, 15–30. Tirana: Akademia e Shkencave e RPS të Shqipërisë.

Budina, Dhimosten. 1971. L'appartenance ethnique illyrienne des tribus epiriotes. In *Les Illyriens et la genèse des albanais. Travaux de la session du 3-4 mars 1969*, 111–129. Tirana: Université de Tirana, Institut d'histoire et de linguistique.

Buxhovi, Jusuf. 2020. *Dardania: antika, mesjeta*. Prishtina: Faik Konica.

Çabej, Eqrem. 1969. Al. Rosetti, Sur les éléments autochtones du roumain, dans 'Studia Albanica' 1 (1969) 133–135. *Studia Albanica* VI (1): 141–142.

Çabej, Ekrem. 1993. The Problem of the Autochtony of Albanians in the Light of Place-Names. In *The Truth on Kosova*, ed. Kristaq Prifti et al., 19–25. Tirana: Encyclopedia.

Çami, Muin. 1969. Lufta antiimperialiste e Vlorës—faktor vendimtar për ruajtjet e paravësisë dhe të tërësisë tokësore të shtetit shqiptar. In *Konferenca e dyte e studimeve albanologjjike*, v. 1, 353–357. Tirana: Universiteti Shtetëtor i Tiranës, Instituti i Historisë dhe i Gjuhësisë.

Ceka, Hasan. 1965. Përputhje onomastike ilire-epiriote. *Studime historike* XIX(II) (2): 85–92.

Ceka, Neritan. 1996. The Dardanians in Antiquity. In *The Kosova Issue—A Historic and Current Problem*, ed. Jusuf Bajraktari et al., 21–24. Tirana: Eurorilindja.

Clayer, Nathalie. 2007. *Aux origines du nationalisme albanais. La naissance d'une nation majoritairement musulmane en Europe*. Paris: Karthala.

Clayer, Nathalie. 2022. *Une histoire en travelling de l'Albanie (1920–1939)*. Paris: Karthala.

Dalipi, Qerim. 2020. Periudha e mesjetës në librat e historisë të arsimit të mesëm në Republikën e Maqedonisë. *Albanologjia* 13–14:221–232.

Deçka, N[iko]. 1972. Rezultatet e punës shkëncore të Institutit të historise për vitin 1971. *Studime historike* XXVI(IX) (1): 215–217.

Demiraj, Shaban. 2000. A Propos De La Romanisation Des Anciens Peuples De La Peninsule Balkanique. *Studia Albanica* XXXIII (1–2): 1–6.

5 DEFENDING OUR LANDS IN ANCIENT AND MEDIEVAL STUDIES... 267

Demiraj, Shaban. 2008. *Epiri, pellazgët, etruskët dhe shqiptarët*. Tiranë: Infobotues.
Desnitskaya, Agniya. 1968. *Albanskiy yazyk i ego dialekty*. Leningrad: Nauka.
Dodbiba, Lirak. 1966. Le lexique maritime de l'albanais et ses éléments non empruntés. *Studia Albanica* II (2): 63–84.
Dodbiba, Lirak. 1976. Le lexique maritime de l'albanais et son rapport avec l'ethnogenèse. *Iliria* 5:87–91.
Doja, Albert. 1999a. Formation nationale et nationalisme dans l'aire de peuplement albanais. *Balkanologie* III (2): 23–43.
Doja, Albert. 1999b. Ethnicité, construction nationale et nationalisme dans l'aire albanaise: Approche anthropologique du conflit et des relations interethniques. *Ethnologia Balkanica* 3:155–179.
Domi, Mahir. 1982. Çështje të toponimisë në burime të huaja. In *Shqiptarët dhe trojet e tyre*, ed. Selami Pulaha, Seit Mansaku and Andromaqi Gjergji, 299–305. Tirana: 8 Nëntori.
Domi, Mahir. 1988. Probleme të historisë së formimit të gjuhës shqipe, arritje dhe detyra. In *Konferenca kombëtare për formimin e popullit shqiptar, të gjuhës dhe të kulturës së tij. 2-5 korrik 1982*, 31–63. Tirana: Akademia e Shkencave e RPS të Shqipërisë.
Dragnich, Alex N., and Slavko Todorovich. 1984. *The Saga of Kosovo: Focus on Serbian-Albanian Relations*. Boulder: East European Monographs.
Drançolli, Jahja. 1996. The Albanian Population of Kosova and Other Areas of Former Yugoslavia during the XV–XVII Centuries. In *The Kosova Issue—A Historic and Current Problem*, ed. Jusuf Bajraktari et al., 63–68. Tirana: Eurorilindja.
Draškić, Sreten. 2000. *Evropa i albansko pitanje (1830–1921)*. Belgrade: Srpska književna zadruga.
Ducellier, Alain. 1996. Les albanais et les espaces intérieurs des Balkans à la fin du Moyen Age. In *The Kosova Issue—A Historic and Current Problem*, ed. Jusuf Bajraktari et al., 55–62. Tirana: Eurorilindja.
Dulaj, Edmond. 1988. Konceptet 'Epir' dhe 'epiriot' në shequjt XIII–XVI. In *Konferenca kombëtare për formimin e popullit shqiptar, të gjuhës dhe të kulturës së tij. 2-5 korrik 1982*, 139–146. Tirana: Akademia e Shkencave e RPS të Shqipërisë.
Epirus: 4000 hronia ellinikis istorias kai politismou. 2023. Ed. Michael Sakellariou. Athens: Ekdotiki Athinon. (1st ed. 1997).
Frashëri, Kristo. 1956. *Lidhja e Prizrenit (1878–1881)*. Tirana: s.n.
Frashëri, Kristo. 1964. *Histoire d'Albanie (bref apercu)*. Tirana: s. n.
Frashëri, Kristo. 1969. Trojet e shqiptarëve në shek. XV. In *Konferenca e dyte e studimeve albanologjike*, v. 1, 109–119. Tirana: Universiteti Shtetëtor i Tiranës, Instituti i Historisë dhe i Gjuhësisë.
Frashëri, Kristo. 1999. Debuts Du Christianisme Dans Les Territoires Albanais. *Studia Albanica* XXXII (1): 15–28.

Frashëri, Kristo. 2005. Shqiptarët në betejën e Kosovës. In *Beteja e Kosovës 1389: (Përmbledhje studimesh)*, ed. Luan Malltezi, 113–122. Tiranë: Akademia e Shkencave e Shqipërisë, Instituti i Historisë.

Frashëri, Kristo. 2010. L'appellation des albanais au Haut Moyen Age. *Studia Albanica* XLVII (2): 3–23.

Frashëri, Kristo. 2011a. E vërteta mbi shqiptarët e Maqedonisë dhe shtrembërimet e Enciklopedisë së Shkupit. *Studime albanologjike* 52 (4): 227–237.

Frashëri, Kristo. 2011b. Shtrembërime të historisë së Epirit nga Akademia e Athinës. *Gazeta Shqiptare*, 07/08/2011.

Garašanin, Milutin V. 1980. L'historiographie yougoslave sur l'Etat illyrien (à propos de la communication de Ali Hadri dans Iliria IV, Tirana, 1976). *Godišnjak Centra za balkanološka ispitivanja* XVIII (16): 207–210.

Gjergji, Andromaqi. 1969. Elemente të përbashkëta të veshjes së fiseve të ndryshme ilire dhe vazhdimësia e tyre ne veshet tona populore. *Studime historike* XXIII(VI) (2): 127–131.

Gjergji, Andromaqi. 1985. Le costume, expression des particularités culturelles de notre peuple au Moyen Age. In *Problèmes de la formation du peuple albanais, de sa langue et de sa culture: choix de documents*, 190–198. Tirana: 8 Nëntori.

Gjinari, Jorgji. 1971. De la continuation de l'illyrien en albanais. In *Les Illyriens et la genèse des albanais. Travaux de la session du 3-4 mars 1969*, 173–181. Tirana: Université de Tirana, Institut d'histoire et de linguistique.

Hadri, Ali. 1976. L'historiographie yougoslave sur l'Etat illyrien. *Iliria* IV:273–279.

Hatzopoulos, Miltiadis B. 2023. Ta oria tou Ellinismou stin Epeiro kata tin Arhaiotita. In *Epirus: 4000 hronia ellinikis istorias kai politismou*, ed. Michael Sakellariou, 140–145. Athens: Ekdotiki Athinon.

Haxhiu, Ajet. 1964. *Hasan Prishtina dhe lëvizja patriotike e Kosovës*. Tirana: s. n.

Historia e popullit shqiptar. Vol 1 2002. Ed. Kristaq Prifti. Tirana: Akademia e Shkencave e Shqipërisë, Instituti i Historisë / Toena.

Historia e Shqipërisë, vol. 1. 1959. Tirana: Universiteti shtetëror. Instituti i historisë dhe i gjuhësise.

Historia e Shqipërisë, vol. 2. 1965. Tirana: Universiteti shtetëror. Instituti i historisë dhe i gjuhësise.

Historiografia shqiptare në dhjetëvjetorin e Universitetit Shtetëtor të Tiranës. 1967. *Studime historike* XXI (IV), (3): 35–41.

Idrizi, Idrit. 2020. Between Subordination and Symbiosis: Historians' Relationship with Political Power in Communist Albania. *European History Quarterly* 50 (1): 66–87.

Iliri i Albanci. 1988. Ed. Milutin Garašanin. Beograd: SANU.

Islami, Selim. 1972. Naissance et développement de la vie urbaine en Illyrie. In *L'Illyrie II. La ville illyrienne*, ed. Muzafer Korkuti et al., 7–23. Tirana: Universiteti i Tiranës.

5 DEFENDING OUR LANDS IN ANCIENT AND MEDIEVAL STUDIES... 269

Islami, Selim. 1992. L'Épire ancienne (Réflexions sur le problème ethnique). *Studia Albanica* 29 (1–2): 93–100.

Isufi, Hajredin. 2004. Aspekte të islamizimit në Çamëri. *Studime historike* XVIII (XLI) (3–4): 17–32.

Kaiser, Timothy. 1995. Archaeology and Ideology in Southeast Europe. In *Nationalism, Politics, and the Practice of Archaeology*, ed. Philip L. Kohl and Clare Fawcett, 99–119. Cambridge: Cambridge University Press.

Konferenca e dyte e studimeve albanologjike, v. 1-2. 1969. Tirana: Universiteti Shtetëtor i Tiranës, Instituti i Historisë dhe i Gjuhësisë.

Konferenca e parë e studimeve albanolojike, Tiranë, 15-21 nëndor 1962. 1965. Tirana: Universiteti Shtetëtor i Tiranës, Instituti i Historisë dhe i Gjuhësisë.

Konferenca kombëtare për formimin e popullit shqiptar, të gjuhës dhe të kulturës së tij. 2-5 korrik 1982. 1988. Tirana: Akademia e Shkencave e RPS të Shqipërisë.

Kosovo and Metohija: Past, present, future. 2006. Ed. Kosta Mihailović. Belgrade: SANU.

Kosovo i Metohija u srpskoj istoriji. 1989. Belgrade: Srpska književna zadruga.

Kosovo nekad i danas / Kosova dikur e sot. 1973. Ed. Mihajlo Maletić. Belgrade: Ekonomska politika.

Krasniqi, Mark. 1996. The Role of the Serbian Orthodox Church in Anti-Albanian Policies in Kosova. In *The Kosova Issue—A Historic and Current Problem*, ed. Jusuf Bajraktari et al., 74–80. Tirana: Eurorilindja.

Lafe, Genc. 2014. La questione irrisolta della Çamëria nella complessità dei rapporti greco-albanesi. *Palaver* 3 (2): 115–143.

Le terre albanesi redente, I. Kossovo. 1942. Roma: Reale Accademia d'Italia.

Les Illyriens et la genèse des albanais. Travaux de la session du 3-4 mars 1969. 1971. Tirana: Université de Tirana, Institut d'histoire et de linguistique.

Les Illyriens: aperçu historique. 1985. Ed. Selim Islami. Tirana: Académie des sciences de la RPS d'Albanie.

Luka, Kolë. 1969a. Emni Albeinje-Albani dhe shtrirja e Arbërit në shekullin XI—fillimi i të XII-tit. In *Konferenca e dyte e studimeve albanologjike,* v. 2, 155–160. Tirana: Universiteti Shtetëtor i Tiranës, Instituti i Historisë dhe i Gjuhësisë.

Luka, Kolë. 1969b. Alain Ducellier, L'Arbanon et les Albanais au XIe siècle, dans 'Travaux et Mémoires', du Centre de Recherche d'Histoire et Civilisation Byzantines, vol. 3, Paris 1968, pp. 354–368. *Studia Albanica* VI (1): 147–155.

Mala, Muhamet, and Muhamet Qerimi. 2009. Paraqitja dhe shtrirja e etnonimit Arbër, Arbanon në Bizant. *Studime historike* LXV(XLVIII) (1–2): 7–26.

Malcolm, Noel. 2009. The 'Great Migration' of the Serbs from Kosovo (1690): History, Myth and Ideology. In *Albanische Geschichte: Stand und Perspektiven der Forschung*, ed. Oliver Jens Schmitt and Eva Anne Frantz, 225–251. Munich: Oldenbourg.

Malltezi, Luan. 1985. Les villes et leur rôle dans les relations économiques entre les régions albanaises dans les XIIIe-XVe siècles. In *Problèmes de la formation du*

270 A. VEZENKOV

peuple albanais, de sa langue et de sa culture: choix de documents, 225–241. Tirana: 8 Nëntori.

Mansaku, Seit. 2005. La Romanisation Linguistique dans le Sud-Est de L'Europe et la Survie de la Langue Albanaise. *Studia Albanica* XXXVIII (1): 45–56.

Manta, Eleftheria K. 2004. *I Musulmani Tsamides tis Epeirou: 1923–2000*. Thessaloniki: Idrima meleton Hersonisu tou Emou.

Marinov, Tchavdar. 2013. Famous Macedonia, the Land of Alexander: Macedonian Identity at the Crossroads of Greek, Bulgarian and Serbian Nationalism. In *Entangled Histories of the Balkans: Vol. 1: National Ideologies and Language Policies*, ed. Roumen Daskalov and Tchavdar Marinov, 273–330. Leiden: Brill.

Martucci, Donato. 2012. *Le terre albanesi redente, II. Ciameria*. Marzi: Comet Editor Press.

Martucci, Donato. 2014. 'Le terre albanesi redente'. La Ciameria tra irredentismo albanese e propaganda fascista. *Palaver 3*(2): 145–174.

Merkaj, Sali. 1964. Mbi Luftën e Ushtrisë Nacional-Çlirimtare shqiptare jashtë kufijve të Atdheut më 1944. *Studime historike* XVIII (I) (4): 105–131.

Matzinger, Joachim. 2009. Die Albaner als Nachkommen der Illyrer aus der Sicht der historischen Sprachwissenschaft. In *Albanische Geschichte: Stand und Perspektiven der Forschung*, ed. Oliver Jens Schmitt and Eva Anne Frantz, 13–36. Munich: Oldenbourg.

Meta, Beqir. 2009. Historiografia greke për marrëdhëniet grekoshqiptare. *Studime historike* LXV (XLIII) (1–2): 313–332.

Mikić, Djordje. 2006. Ottoman and Albanian Violence against the Serbs of Kosova and Metohija. In *Kosovo and Metohija: Past, present, future*, ed. Kosta Mihailović, 17–40. Belgrade: SANU.

Mile, Ligor K. 1962. *Kryengritjet popullore në fillim të Rilindjes sonë (1830–1877)*. Tiranë: Universiteti shtetëtor i Tiranës, Instituti i historisë e gjuhësise.

Mile, Ligor K. 1966. Rreth lëvizjes kryengritëse shqiptare në çerekun e dytë të shek. XIX, e sidomos rreth kryengritjes së Kosovës së vitit 1844. *Studime historike* XX(III) (2): 105–127.

Miljković, Ema. 2006. The Population of Kosovo and Metohija under Ottoman Rule. In *Kosovo and Metohija: Past, Present, Future*, ed. Kosta Mihailović, 5–15. Belgrade: SANU.

Mishkova, Diana. 2018. *Beyond Balkanism: The Scholarly Politics of Region Making*. London and New York: Routledge.

Muhadri, Bedri. 2021. *Kosova në Mesjetë, shek. XI-XV*. Prishtina: Instituti i Historisë "Ali Hadri".

Murzaku, Thoma. 1969. Lufta e banorëve të tokave lindore dhe verilindore shqiptare kundër pushtuesve turq në fund të shek. XIV dhe gjatë shek. XV. In *Konferenca e dyte e studimeve albanologjike*, v. 1, 195–203. Tirana: Universiteti Shtetëtor i Tiranës, Instituti i Historisë dhe i Gjuhësisë.

Mustilli, Domenico. 1943. Gli Illiri nell'Epiro. *Rivista d'Albania* III:129–143.

5 DEFENDING OUR LANDS IN ANCIENT AND MEDIEVAL STUDIES... 271

Mustilli, Domenico. 1965. I dati archeologici per la preistoria dell'Albania. *Studia Albanica* II (1): 55–57.

Myderrizi, Osman. 1965. Emëri i vjetër kombëtar i Shqipërisë në tekstet e vjetra shqip me alfabetet latin dhe arab. *Studime historike* XIX(II) (1): 159–172.

Myderrizi, Osman. 1969. Toponomastika jonë dhe disa çështje të histories së popullit tone. *Konferenca e dyte e studimeve albanolojike* 2:161–163.

Naçi, Stavri. 1976. Rreth konceptit 'Shqipëri' në gjysmën e dytë të shek. XVIII—fillimi i shek. XIX. *Studime historike* XXX(XIII) (2): 59–65.

Numero dei Bulgari in Albania e nelle regioni occidentali della Macedonia. 1941. Sofia: Dărzhavna pechatnitza.

Osmani, Jusuf. 2010. *Kolonizimi serb i Kosovës*, 2. ed. Prishtinë: [s.n.].

Pollo, Stefanaq. 1972. Konkluzione rreth punimeve të kuvendit i të studimeve ilire. *Studime historike* IX (3): 141–144.

Pollo, Stefanaq. 1990. *Në gjurme të historisë Shqiptare, v. 1*. Tirana: Akademia e Shkencave e RPS të Shqipërisë, Instituti i Historisë.

Pollo, Stefanaq, and Aleks Buda. 1959. Historiografia shqiptare gjatë pushtetit popullor (1944–1959). *Buletin i Universitetit Shtetëror të Tiranës, Seria Shkencat Shoqërore* XIII (4): 95–108.

Problèmes de la formation du peuple albanais, de sa langue et de sa culture: choix de documents. 1985. Tirana: 8 Nëntori.

Pulaha, Selami. 1975a. Kontribut për studimin e ngulitjes së katuneve dhe krijimin e fiseve në Shqipërinë e veriut në shekujt XV–XVI. *Studime historike* XXIX(XII) (1): 75–110.

Pulaha, Selami. 1975b. Mbi gjallerimin e lidhjeve farëfisnore dhe krijimin e fiseve në Shqipërinë e veriut në shekujt XVI–XVII. *Studime historike* XXIX(XII) (2): 121–145.

Pulaha, Selami. 1984. *Popullsia shqiptare e Kosovës gjatë shek. XV–XVI (Studime dhe dokumente)*. Tirana: 8 Nëntori.

Pulaha, Selami. 1985. *L'autochtonéité des Albanais en Kosova et le prétendu exode des Serbes à la fin du 17ᵉ siècle*. Tirana: 8 Nëntori.

Pulaha, Selami. 1993. On the Presence of Albanians in Kosova during the 14th–17th Centuries. In *The Truth on Kosova*, ed. Kristaq Prifti et al., 33–47. Tirana: Encyclopedia.

Rexha, Iljaz. 2005. Shtrirja e vendbanimeve mesjetare mbi bazën e etnonimit Arban-Alban në Ballkan. *Studime historike* LIX(XLII) (3–4): 7–30.

Rexha, Iljaz. 2011. Vendbanimet dhe populsia albane gjatë mesjetës në hapësirën e Maqedonisë së sotme (Sipas burimeve sllave dhe osmane). *Gjurmime Albanologjike—Seria e shkencave historike* 41–42:167–218.

Rizaj, Skënder. 1983. Mbi të ashtuquajturën dyndje e madhe serbe nga Kosova në krye me patrikun Arsenije Çarnojeviq (1690). *Gjurmime Albanologjike-Seria e shkencave historike* XII:81–103.

272 A. VEZENKOV

Rizaj, Skënder. 1996. The Truth about the So-called Deportation en Masse of the Serbs from Kosova in 1690. In *The Kosova Issue—A Historic and Current Problem*, ed. Jusuf Bajraktari et al., 69–73. Tirana: Eurorilindja.

Samardžić, Radovan. 1990. *Kosovsko opredeljenje: Istorijski ogledi*. Belgrade: Srpska književna zadruga.

Schmidt-Neke, Michael. 2010. *Skanderbegs* Gefangene: Zur Debatte um den albanischen Nationalhelden. *Südosteuropa* 58 (2): 273–302.

Schmitt, Oliver Jens. 2005. Genosse Aleks und seine Partei oder: Zu Politik und Geschichtswissenschaft im kommunistischen Albanien (1945–1991). In *Beruf und Berufung. Geschichtswissenschaft und Nationsbildung in Ostmittel- und Südosteuropa im 19. und 20. Jahrhundert*, ed. Markus Krzoska and Hans-Christian Maner, 143–166. Münster: Lit.

Schmitt, Oliver Jens. 2009a. *Skanderbeg. Der neue Alexander auf dem Balkan*. Regensburg: Friedrich Pustet.

Schmitt, Oliver Jens. 2009b. 'Die Monade des Balkans'—die Albaner im Mittelalter. In *Albanische Geschichte: Stand und Perspektiven der Forschung*, ed. Oliver Jens Schmitt and Eva Anne Frantz, 61–80. Munich: Oldenbourg.

Selishchev, Afanasy. 1931. *Slavyanskoe naselenie Albanii*. Sofia: Makedonski nauchen institut.

Shkurtaj, Gjovalin. 1976. Të dhëna gjuhësore për lashtësinë e bujqësisë ndër shqiptarë. *Studime filologjike* XIII (3): 149–160.

Shkurti, Spiro. 1997. *Der Mythos vom Wandervolk der Albaner: Landwirtschaft in den albanischen Gebieten (13.-17. Jahrhundert)*. Wien, Köln, Weimar: Bohlau.

Shqiptarët dhe trojet e tyre. 1982. Ed. Selami Pulaha, Seit Mansaku and Andromaqi Gjergji. Tirana: 8 Nëntori.

Shukriu, Edi. 1996. Ancient Dardania. In *The Kosova Issue—A Historic and Current Problem*, ed. Jusuf Bajraktari et al., 15–18. Tirana: Eurorilindja.

Shukriu, Edi. 2001. Le Royaume Dardan. *Studia Albanica* XXXIV (1): 1–24.

Shuteriqi, Dhimitër. 1956. Mbi disa çështje t'Arbërit dhe mbi emrin Shqipëri. *Buletin i Shkencave Shoqërore* X (3): 189–224.

Sigalos, Louis. 1963. *The Greek Claims on Northern Epirus*. Chikago: Argonaut.

Spahiu, Hëna. 1969. A ka gjurma të kulturës avare në lëndën e varrezave të hershme shqiptare. *Studime historike* XXIII(VI) (1): 179–188.

Spahiu, Hëna. 1985. La circulation monétaire du Ve au XIIIe siècle, indice des relations économiques sur le territorire albanais. In *Problèmes de la formation du peuple albanais, de sa langue et de sa culture: choix de documents*, 168–175. Tirana: 8 Nëntori.

Stipčević, Aleksandar. 1996. Il problema della continuità iliro-albanese e la sua atualità politica oggi. In *The Kosova Issue—A Historic and Current Problem*, ed. Jusuf Bajraktari et al., 31–40. Tirana: Eurorilindja.

Tăpkova-Zaimova, V[asilka] and Paskaleva, V[irdzhiniya]. 1959. Obsăzhdane na 'Istoriya na Albaniya'. *Istoritcheski pregled* XV (1): 130–137.

Tërnava, Muhamet. 1982. Përhapja e islamizmit në territorin e sotëm të Kosovës deri në fund të shekullit XVII. In *Shqiptarët dhe trojet e tyre*, ed. Selami Pulaha, Seit Mansaku and Andromaqi Gjergji, 481–493. Tirana: 8 Nëntori.

The History of Albania from its origins to the present day. 1981. Ed. Stefanak Pollo and Arben Puto. London, Boston and Henley: Routhledge & Kegan Paul (1st ed.: *Histoire de l'Albanie, des origines à nos jours*. 1974. Roanne: Horvath).

The Kosova Issue—A Historic and Current Problem. 1996. Ed. Jusuf Bajraktari et al. Tirana: Eurorilindja.

The Truth on Kosova. 1993. Ed. Kristaq Prifti et al. Tirana: Encyclopedia. 1st ed. in Albanian 1990.

Thëngjilli, Petrika. 1982. Disa aspekte të kombësisë shqiptare në burimet osmane të shek. XV–XVI. In *Shqiptarët dhe trojet e tyre*, ed. Selami Pulaha, Seit Mansaku and Andromaqi Gjergji, 315–333. Tirana: 8 Nëntori.

Tomitch, Jovan. 1913. *Les Albanais en Vieille-Serbie et dans le Sandjak de Novi-Bazar*. Paris: Hachette.

Topalli, Kolec. 2000. Lashtësia e krishterimit ndër shqiptarë sipas dëshmive të gjuhës shqipe. *Studime filologjike* 54 (3–4): 109–117.

Tsonos, Akis. 2009. *Skavontas stin Albania*. Ioannina: Isnafi.

Ugolini, Luigi M. 1928. *Antica Albania nelle ricerche archeologiche italiane*. Roma: Ente nazionale industrie turistiche.

Uka, Sabit. 1991. *Shpërngulja e shqiptarëve nga Serbia Jugore më 1877–1878 dhe vendosja e tyre në Rrafshin e Kosovës*. Prishtinë: Zëri.

Vakalopoulos, Konstantinos Ap. 2012. *Istoria tis Epeirou. Apo tis arhes tis othomanokratias os tis meres mas*. Athens: Ant. Stamoulis.

Verli, Marenglen. 2009. Qëndrime në historiografinë dhe publicistikën serbe e jugosllave të viteve 80-të për disa momente të historisë së popullit shqiptar. *Studime historike* LXV(XLVIII) (1–2): 333–346.

Xhufi, Pëllumb. 1993. Albanian heretics in the Serbian Mediaeval Kingdom. In *The Truth on Kosova*, ed. Kristaq Prifti et al., 48–54. Tirana: Encyclopedia.

Xhufi, Pëllumb. 1995. Rrethanat etnike në Epir gjatë mesjetës. *Studime historike* LXI(XLIV) (1–4): 5–21.

Xhufi, Pëllumb. 1996. The Albanians in the Serbian Nemanja kingdom. *The Kosova issue—A Historic and Current Problem*, ed. Jusuf Bajraktari et al., 41–46. Tirana: Eurorilindja.

Xhufi, Pëllumb. 2001. Vështgime mbi emrin 'Shqipëri' dhe 'shqiptar' në mesjetë. *Studime historike* LV(XXXVIII) (3–4): 7–22.

Xhufi, Pëllumb. 2011a. Maqedonia Perëndimore në historinë shqiptare të shek. VII–XV. *Studime historike* LXIV(LII) (1–2): 7–24.

Xhufi, Pëllumb. 2011b. Përkime Shqiptaro-Malazeze Në Mesjetë. *Studime historike* LXV(XLVIII) (3–4): 31–54.

Zirojević, Olga. 2018. *Brate moj, hane: Kosovo u svetlu turskih izvora*. Beograd: Prosveta.

CHAPTER 6

In Search of an Acceptable Past: The Bosnian Middle Ages and National Ideologies

Nedim Rabić

This chapter analyzes three different approaches to the study of medieval Bosnian history: Serbian, Croatian, and Bosniak.[1] The focus is intentionally placed on representative instances of national interpretations of medieval Bosnian history. In the various South Slavic mainstream traditions, the medieval period in Bosnian history has been viewed and treated in a variety of ways. Scholarly interest in Bosnia's medieval history dates back to the early days of the South Slavic national movements and, predictably, was not guided by scientific motivations alone. Professional study developed only after World War II. However, interest outside of Yugoslav historiography was limited and concentrated on a few key subjects, with the history of

---

[1] This chapter was presented for an internal discussion at the Center for Advanced Study in Sofia on November 4, 2023. I would like to express gratitude to my Bulgarian colleagues Alexander Vezenkov, Tchavdar Marinov, and Evlogi Stanchev for their enriching conversations as well for suggestions and useful insights. I am tremendously grateful also to Diana Mishkova and Roumen Daskalov for their thoughtful and detailed reading of multiple versions of the chapter, which significantly improved this chapter.

N. Rabić (✉)
Institute of History, University of Sarajevo, Sarajevo, Bosnia and Herzegovina

© The Author(s), under exclusive license to Springer Nature Switzerland AG 2025
D. Mishkova, R. Daskalov (eds.), *Balkan Historiographical Wars*,
https://doi.org/10.1007/978-3-031-90113-3_6

275

heresy in Bosnia receiving the most attention, both domestically and internationally. Currently, the Bosnian Middle Ages garners interest from all three nationalities in Bosnia and Herzegovina. Although many historiographical questions are widely agreed upon, others remain contentious. In this chapter, I will discuss the most significant issues that sparked these historiographical "wars" among historians and intellectuals from former Yugoslavia. Issues such as the national filiation of medieval Bosnian history, the identity of its key figures, and the debates surrounding the religious nature of medieval Bosnia are central to the different national versions of this history and as such form knots of continuing disputes.

Interest in medieval Bosnia and its heritage emerged simultaneously with and was closely related to interest in the medieval forerunners of other Balkan nation-states—itself underpinned by projects of national awakening and modern state-building. This convergence had several important consequences. Since the medieval history of Bosnia was shaped in the neighborhood of Croatia and Serbia, the question of its affiliation arose and became a central theme in national historiography and identity politics. Thus, the Bosnian medieval past became a "battlefield" where battles were fought primarily over ethnogenesis and historical rights. Because of this, it was exposed to political and ideological confrontation from the very beginning. At the same time, the Bosnian medieval past began to be studied within the framework and as an integral part of the history of other medieval countries. Within such projections, Bosnia came to be considered as either a Serbian or a Croatian country, while Bosnian heritage itself was interpreted from the national point of view of these two historiographies.

The aim of this chapter is to offer an overview of rival historiographical narratives based on selected contentious issues—namely, the "ownership" of Bosnian medieval history, the nature of the Bosnian Church, and the coronation of the first Bosnian king, Tvrtko I—while highlighting the most important protagonists and outlining the most significant historiographic currents. My intention is not to determine what the medieval Bosnian past was like, but what attitude the Serbian, Croatian, and, later, Bosniak national historiographies had toward it. Attention is also drawn to the changing political context in Southeastern Europe, and especially in the Western Balkans, an area intersected by various ethnic, cultural, and religious differences without clear boundaries between them.

The "discovery" of the Bosnian Middle Ages by individual representatives of the emerging national historiographies in the second half of the nineteenth century was preceded by a longer period of interest by European Enlightenment historiography in the seventeenth and eighteenth centuries. These surveys of Bosnian medieval history, before it was "discovered" by national pretenders, do not differ much from synthetic reviews of other European countries. This began to gradually change when, with the establishment of national academic institutions among Croats and Serbs, the history of Bosnia began to be perceived, interpreted, and constructed in a political and cultural sense within their respective national historiographic frameworks. In the absence of an intellectual base for its own systematic development, the history of Bosnia and Herzegovina became "easy prey" for neighboring historiographies. Against the backdrop of the geopolitical tensions during the 1870s the fate of the Ottoman Empire, in particular its westernmost province of Bosnia and Herzegovina, came up again on the agenda of the great powers. The decision of Austria-Hungary to occupy the province led to the establishment of different national narratives in the context of a new political configuration. The occupation played a key role in the development of national identities among the different national groups in Bosnia and Herzegovina—Serbs, Croats, and Bosniaks. This period witnessed the rise of national movements and the formation of political parties that sought to represent the interests of these different national groups within the framework of the Austro-Hungarian administration. In the second half of the nineteenth century, scholarly interest in Bosnia's medieval past came from two regional centers—Zagreb and Belgrade, and was pursued much more systematically through newspapers, churches, and schools. As Barbara Jelavich points out, after 1878 the question of Bosnia and Herzegovina "became the ultimate issue for Croats and Serbs of all political persuasions" (Jelavich 1992, 32–33). It was in these two centers that the main national narratives were created that sought to establish the early existence and continuity of the "nation" in history and its claim to present or coveted territory.

Strange as it might seem against this background, there is little material attesting to historiographical wars concerning the Bosnian Middle Ages during this period. There was almost no open debate or direct confrontation of opinions. Instead, two parallel "historiographical worlds" developed, in which the medieval past of Bosnia was considered, respectively, Croatian or Serbian, without the presence of notable debates between representatives of one or the other view. Very rarely would Croatian and Serbian historians confront each other regarding Bosnia. One such isolated example is the clash between the Serbian historian Stanoje Stanojević (1874–1937) and the Croatian historian Ferdo Šišić (1869–1940) during a very politically turbulent event: the annexation of Bosnia and Herzegovina in 1908 by the Austro-Hungarian monarchy and the outbreak of the so-called annexation crisis of 1908–1910. Ferdo Šišić's lecture titled "Herzeg-Bosnia on the occasion of the annexation—geographic, ethnographic, historical and state-legal considerations" (published in 1909 in German), which recalled an anecdote about the dialogue between Romans and Gauls in front of the gates of the eternal city, elicited a response from Stanojević, who stated:

> What is your right to Rome? Our right is at the tip of our swords, answered the Gallic commander. The Serbs will give the same answer to the Croats on the day when the great battle for Bosnia and Herzegovina takes place. Our right is our people's strength. The right of our people's strength and the right of our bayonets will be more important and stronger than your right, which can be weighed with a scale. (Cit. in 2002, 72)

Although Stanojević's quote does not refer to medieval Bosnia, but to contemporary Bosnia and Herzegovina within the Habsburg Monarchy, the stated claims come from historians who dealt with the medieval history of Bosnia in their works, and reflections of their attitudes can be traced there as well as in the works of their successors until today.

The growth of historiography during the last two centuries has rendered an extensive bibliography on medieval Bosnia. Already the earliest modern historical studies of Hungary, Croatia, and Serbia in the nineteenth century, at the height of romantic historiography, included chapters on Bosnia in the Middle Ages. The national thrust of Croatian, Serbian, and Hungarian historians to appropriate the medieval Bosnian past should not come as a surprise given the overall political climate of the second half of the nineteenth century. The concepts and approaches adopted during this period served as the foundation for the development of critical national historiographies. The authors that espoused the standards of the "scientific" school in historiography, in contrast to their predecessors, claimed rigorous use of source material and were able to impart their works with a more durable quality despite the persistence of national Romantic leanings. Their extraordinary erudition and proficient knowledge of foreign languages (particularly Latin and Greek) coalesced with their engagement with current political events to form a single whole.

Although succeeding generations received professional education and used more sophisticated scientific methods, key topoi of national Romanticism persisted and are still in use today (Dautović 2018, 65–73).

In his book *Explaining Yugoslavia*, English sociologist John B. Allcock observed that "the peoples of the South Slav region carry with them their history, not only as an objective past which conditions action in the present, but also as a subjective past. This shapes their consciousness and provides the material out of which they weave accounts of both the past and the future" (Allcock 2000, 413–4). Without discussing the specific merits of this statement, we can nevertheless agree that history, generally understood as a morally exemplary narrative and a matrix of national identity and values, plays a prominent role among the peoples of Southeastern Europe. Possible reasons for such a perception among the peoples of the former Yugoslavia to this day are the intensity and problematic nature of the changes that occurred in these lands during the last two centuries, especially during the 1990s. Several radical transformations in state structures and configurations heightened the search for continuity with the past. Uncertain times seem to have strengthened the people's need to keep their link to the past alive (Džaja 2003, 39–40). In this chapter, based on the above-mentioned selected topics, I will analyze how historians have contributed to the revival of historical heritage, tradition, and historical myths.

Contemporary historiography has established the connection between historical science and the emergence of nationalism. "Modern history was born in the nineteenth century, and it was conceived and developed as an instrument of European nationalism." During this period, according to Patrick J. Geary, the understanding of the past turned into a "dump of toxic waste, full of toxic nationalism," and clearing this "waste" has become the biggest challenge facing today's historians (Geary 2007, 27). The development of national ideologies in the Balkans followed a similar course as in Western Europe. The Middle Ages were interpreted as the golden age of national tradition, as the time of "national rulers" and "national culture." Based on such perceptions, the fundamentals of identity and cultural and political progress were established during this pivotal era. On the terrain of Bosnian medieval history, "three particular nationalisms clashed over questions of geographical borders and the modern national identities of that part of the inhabitants who estranged themselves from the medieval paradigm by deeper acculturation in the cultural and social system of an alien government than the rest of the inhabitants"

(Džaja 2017, 58). At issue here are the national narratives of Serbia and Croatia concerning Bosnia and the Ottoman era, which developed in mutual opposition to one another. Later on, the Bosniaks would join the clash.

The Development of South Slavic Historiography and the Position of the Bosnian Middle Ages

The cultural conditions on the eastern Adriatic coast were positively impacted by the influence of Italian humanist historiographers. The amateur historians of the period between the sixteenth and eighteenth centuries incorporated into their works primary sources now lost and unknown works of other authors, which continue to serve as references to this day. Nicolas Ragnina (1490–1577) is a prominent historical figure whose contribution primarily centers around Bosnia. However, it is worth noting that his work does not offer a precise portrayal of Bosnia's interactions with neighboring countries (Ragnina 1883). In contrast, Mauro Orbini (c. mid-sixteenth century to 1614) stands apart as the author of the initial comprehensive history of the Slavs (Orbini 1601). With an emphasis on Slavic patriotism, the work of the abbot of Mljet includes a large number of works by his contemporaries and predecessors, from which he compiled a chapter on Bosnia, alongside other Slavic countries (Orbini 1968, 1999). Only four years following Orbini's publication, the writings of Jakov Lukarević (1551–1615) were released in Venice. Lukarević's focus was primarily on his hometown Dubrovnik, but he still found sufficient incentive to write about Bosnia (Luccari 1605). Ivan Lucić (1604–1679), a native of Trogir, played a significant role in elucidating the political climate of his times (Lucius 1666). While Lucić did not focus as much on Bosnia's history as previous writers, his work is noteworthy because he incorporated valuable archival material, referenced extensively, that is no longer available. While his work provides limited insight into the conditions in Bosnia, it offers a more comprehensive understanding of the role of the Bosnian ruler Tvrtko in Dalmatia, particularly during the early stages of his reign—a crucial period for comprehending his rapid political ascent (see Gál 2018, 114–26). The youngest among these authors, Junije Rastić (1755–1815), derived his understanding of Bosnia from original testimonies found in the Dubrovnik archive, in addition to extensively utilizing the works of Orbini and Lukarević (Restii 1893).

The Franciscans began documenting significant historical events in Bosnia through chronicles at an early stage. However, their interest in medieval history only intensified in the seventeenth and eighteenth centuries. During this time, two local writers, namely the anonymous author of the Fojnica Chronicle and Nikola Lašvanin, emerged and contributed to the historical accounts of Bosnia (Lašvanin 1981). However, apart from published works, there are no additional sources available that throw substantial light on or enhance significantly our understanding of the Church in medieval Bosnia. The primary sources utilized for their research consist mainly of the historical writings of the Irish Franciscan Luke Wadding († 1657) and the Italian historian Odoric Raynaldi (1595–1671). Consequently, the Bosnian Franciscans did not possess any literature or sources that were previously unknown. Following them, a succession of church historians emerged who, in their writings, offered details about the ecclesiastical state in Bosnia. These include J. S. Assemani, V. Greiderer, J. Harduin, E. Martene, U. Durand, and numerous others (see Džambo, 1991, 9–25).

The historiography of the French- and German-speaking regions on the opposite side of the European continent sustained an ongoing fascination with the past of the South Slavic peoples. Undoubtedly, curiosity about Bosnian history was constrained by these authors' commitment to a more all-encompassing perspective on the prevailing notion of global history (Gross 1996, 101–2). Charles du Fresne du Cange (1610–1688) was a leading figure among them, who in his chapter on Bosnia devoted significant space to Bosnian history and its rulers (Du Cange 1746). Du Cange primarily derives information for this chapter from the works of Orbini and Lukarević. Around the same time, the Habsburg monarch's objective of annexing Bosnia, then a province of the Ottoman Empire, strongly influenced the development of historiography. The Habsburgs were the first to assert historical rights over Bosnia; their interest in the region grew significantly following the Ottoman Empire's decline during the latter half of the eighteenth century. Such claims were supported by the works of Ludwig Albrecht Gebhardi (1735–1802), who wrote the first history of Bosnia in German, and Maximilian Schimek's (1748–1798) much more extensive works, which were written on orders from the Habsburg Court (Gebhardi 1781; Gebhardi 1805; Schimek 1787). Both authors' presentation of Bosnian medieval history is incomplete or one-sided and fails to meet the standards of critical methodology established by that time. Furthermore, contemporary political and cultural biases frequently colored their interpretations (Radojčić 1960, 155–6).

Enlightenment historiography in the second half of the eighteenth century, particularly in the German-speaking regions, greatly influenced local writers. The latter's works now involved a more prominent engagement with critical research, which revitalized the study of South Slavic history. Jovan Rajić (1726–1801), Franjo Ksaver Pejačević (1707–1781), and Johann Christian von Engel (1770–1814), a highly esteemed figure in the German-speaking region, were members of this group of researchers. In an effort to handle the extensive empirical knowledge gathered over the previous centuries, they attempted to standardize the collected materials and employ source criticism as their central methodological procedure (Radojčić 1960, 157). Their activities coincided with a period of significant publishing endeavors and a heightened fascination with the South Slavic populations, whose destinies were increasingly under scrutiny. In this setting, a new phase of presenting knowledge about medieval Bosnia began. At the end of the eighteenth century, the former medieval states of Bosnia and Serbia were still part of the Ottoman Empire, which largely preempted the fundamental methodological assumptions of history writing. Since within the framework of the Ottoman Empire the borders between these medieval states vanished, historians had more freedom in the way they approached their history. Thus, the idea emerged that these two medieval states (Bosnia and Serbia), which had previously operated as separate political entities with different political and ecclesiastical structures, should be treated as interconnected. Engel's book *Geschichte von Serwien und Bosnien* is a notable example (Radojčić 1960, 157). In later times, and until the present day, Bosnian history would be often included in historiographic works devoted to the "Serbian lands."

Engel's work was significantly impacted by the Serbian historian Archimandrite Jovan Rajić's *History of the Slavic Peoples* (Rajić 1794–1795), where Bosnia's past was presented through the lens of Serbian history, emphasizing the links between both countries. Rajić's research, in which he integrated a substantial number of Byzantine and local sources, had great significance for the advancement of South Slavic historiography during the nineteenth century (Radojčić 1952). It signified a reaction against Austro-Hungarian ambitions as these transpired through the writings of Gebhardi and Schimek, yet employed identical ideological approaches (Ćirković 1964a, 15). The idea that medieval Bosnia be considered part of Serbia—an idea that gained prominence in nineteenth-century historiography—entered the scene through the works of Rajić in the east and through Engel in both the west and east. In a similar vein, one should mention Franje Ksaver Pejačević's *Historia Serviae* (1799) published after Rajić's and Engel's works, which presents a concise yet impactful summary of Bosnian history as a subsidiary of Serbian history. The twelfth chapter of the book *On the Organization of the Kingdom and Religion of the Serbs in Bosnia* (De statu regni et religionis Serblorum per Bosnam) is dedicated to the medieval history of Bosnia, and it is laid out in the Serbian context, as the title itself demonstrates. While the author's attempt to unite the Eastern and Western churches may have influenced his reading, his book still provided valuable and previously overlooked information from older writers, demonstrating a discerning approach to literature and sources. It is important to acknowledge also the significant impact of Ignaz Aurelius Fessler (1756–1839) and Johann Mailath (1786–1855) (alongside Engel who was considered the most credible) on European and South Slavic historiography during the nineteenth century. Their works were widely used as key sources of information on medieval Bosnia (Fessler 1816; Mailath 1828).

THE INVENTION OF MEDIEVAL BOSNIA AS A "SERBIAN LAND"

Let us return to Jovan Rajić, the pioneer of modern Serbian historiography. The impact he had on later generations is immensely significant. Despite being written in a complex and obscure "Russian-Slavic" language, his *History* (Rajić 1794–1795) was frequently reprinted and translated during the nineteenth century (Denić 1996, 68). The work was originally intended as a comprehensive account of Slavic history, rather than focusing on any specific nation. In reality, it can rather be seen as a positive celebration of Serbian national history. Rajić himself says of his contribution that it "contains a short history that evokes the idea of the Serbian race," although in the case of Bosnia he speaks of the "Slavic-Bosnian people." Since Rajić received his education as a historian during the mid-eighteenth century, his ideas were primarily shaped by authors who focused on the Slavic or South Slavic population as a collective entity rather than on specific Slavic groups. According to Stjepan Antoljak, Rajić was therefore among the first to present the individual history of those South Slavs, who had created their own independent states and not just territorial and tribal principalities (Antoljak 2004, 288). Rajić wrote about the history of the Bulgarians, Croats, and Serbs, touching even on earlier eras when their states did not yet exist in the same form as they did later in the Middle Ages. On the other hand, Serbian historian Nikola Radojčić (1882–1964) was of the opinion that Rajić intended to write the history of the various Slavic peoples, whether they had states or not, and notes the following about the omission of Bosnia from his list: "From his *History*, the development of Russia, the destiny of Bulgaria and the history of the Croats can also be learned, and from Serbian history, mostly only the development of Raška. Why Rajić neglected the history of other Serbian states and regions except Raška, I cannot say with full certainty" (Radojčić 1952, 81; Ćirković 2007, 73–74). A possible answer to Radojčić's question could be that during Rajić's era, the idea that Bosnia was a "Serbian land" had not yet been clearly formulated. Despite his adamant denial of folk tradition as a reliable historical source, his primary shortcoming is his inability to distinguish between primary and secondary sources (Denić 1996, 49–50). It is interesting that the histories of the Bulgarians, Serbs, and Croats appear for the first time with Rajić as a "single entity" whereas the history of Bosnia is relatively underrepresented. His work remained almost the only source of knowledge about Serbian history until the second half of the nineteenth century (Georgijević 1946, 5–12).

Before Serbian historiography as a whole listed Bosnia among the "Serbian lands," this was gradually done by other Serbian intellectuals, the most famous among whom were the educational reformer Dositej Obradović (1742–1811) and the linguist Vuk Stefanović Karadžić (1787–1864), both of whom declared the entire linguistic culture of Bosnia as being in "the purest Serbian language" (Džaja 2003, 42–43). Subsequently, the Serbian statesman Ilija Garašanin formulated a comprehensive plan outlining Serbia's foreign and national policy, which he named "Načertanije." The document presented a strategic blueprint for the future growth and advancement of Serbia, mirroring the national ambitions and geopolitical outlook of the Serbian leadership during that period. Like any other document, "Nachertanije" is a declaration of its era; as such, it must be read, understood, and assessed within that framework. Any departure from the temporal framework or observation removed from the larger historical process results in unavoidable errors, and is frequently used by historians who value national or ideological truth over historical truth. Although it was written in 1844, it was only made known to the scientific community in 1906 (Bataković 2014, 203). The

6 IN SEARCH OF AN ACCEPTABLE PAST: THE BOSNIAN MIDDLE AGES... 285

document outlines a strategic plan to unify Bosnia with Serbia. Taking the Bosnian Franciscans as the main supporters of propaganda activity in Bosnia and Herzegovina,[2] Garašanin emphasizes their role "for the idea of uniting Bosnia with Serbia." This would, in his opinion, lead to the "liberation of Bosnia from Austrian influence and convert this country more towards Serbia" (Vukićević 1906, XI; Valentić 1961, 135–6).

The second half of the nineteenth century marked an increasing engagement with medieval history—an interest spurred by the discovery and publication of sources. Despite the accumulation of new knowledge, however, outdated preconceptions persisted. History, as a popular subject of study in the rest of Europe at that time, was gradually making progress in the South Slavic regions. In this respect, the nineteenth century can be divided into two parts. The first half was still dominated by amateur history writing. The second half, led by, on the Croatian side, the historians Franjo Rački (1828–1894), Šime Ljubić (1822–1896), Tadija Smičiklas (1843–1914), and Vjekoslav Klaić (1849–1928), and from the Serbian side by historians Ilarion Ruvarac (1832–1905) and Stojan Novaković (1842–1915), created the conditions and prepared the ground for a professional and erudite historiography. Characteristic of this period is the systematic work on the publication of primary sources as a prerequisite for distancing oneself from folklore and folk tradition and the outdated attitudes of older authors (Antoljak 2004, 415–7; Antolović 2016, 350–2). The efforts made during this time to publish source material have never been surpassed. By shedding light on Bosnia's medieval past, the aforementioned writers laid the foundations for future generations of historians. Despite the methodological gap that separates them from the present day, their works remain a source of reference and a starting point for upcoming researchers (Ćirković 1978, 67–68).

Historiography on Bosnia during the latter part of the nineteenth century has to be considered in light of the Austro-Hungarian Monarchy's occupation of Bosnia and Herzegovina from 1878. Despite certain claims in Yugoslav historiography that the new government acted retrogradely (Wenzel 1996, 68–71), the study of Bosnian medieval history advanced significantly. An immensely significant project was the founding of the National Museum (Zemaljski muzej) in Sarajevo in 1888, followed by the

---

[2] Garašanin planned to use the Franciscans for the Serbianization of Bosnia. Meetings were also held in Belgrade between Garašanin and Bosnian Franciscans, but no agreement was reached. See Bratislav Teinović (2016, 31–91).

launching of its periodical, *Glasnik Zemaljskog muzeja* in 1889. This journal was originally published in all South Slavic languages, both in Latin and Cyrillic and, since 1893, in German under the title *Wissenschaftliche Mitteilungen des Bosnisch-Herzegowinischen Landesmuseums*. For the first time, satisfactory conditions were created for the publication of source materials and studies on the Bosnian Middle Ages in one periodical, bringing together the best-known names in the field. This journal featured critical texts written by outstanding historians such as K. Jireček, L. Thalloczy, I. Ruvarac, and F. Šišić, among others (Dautbegović 1988, 7–34).

"Serbian lands" is a term that in Serbian historiography refers to the Serbian medieval states that existed until the time of the Ottoman conquest of the Balkans in the fourteenth and fifteenth centuries. This includes the Serbian principality from the early Middle Ages (ninth to tenth centuries), as well as lands that were later an integral part of the Serbian kingdom, such as Duklja, Travunija, Zahumlje, and Raška. After the gradual disintegration of Dušan's empire during the reign of his son and successor, King Uroš, the Serbian lands split into separate provinces. However, during the second half of the nineteenth century, without particular reasoning, Serbian historians began to include medieval Bosnia among the Serbian lands. Although it is difficult to determine exactly when this happened, it was certainly accelerated by political events. Rarely has any historian explained why he considers Bosnia to be one of the medieval Serbian lands. Such a concept was considered sufficient in itself and no particular argumentation was actually ever presented systematically.

The concept of "Serbian lands" in historiography had several phases, and although not only Serbian authors participated, they contributed the most to its establishment. The idea that Bosnia was an integral part of these lands can be linked to the historian Konstantin Jireček (1854–1918). As an Austro-Hungarian historian of Czech descent and the creator of Bohemian Balkan and Byzantine Studies, as well as an outstanding scholar of the medieval history of Bulgaria and Serbia, Jireček marked a significant turning point in the study of the past of the South Slavic peoples. His rigorous "positivist" use of unpublished archival material, especially that from the major Dubrovnik archive, sets him apart from all other historians who had researched the history of the South Slavs up to that point. He added a great deal of new insights into and new interpretations of Serbian history. Although his writings do not center on Bosnian history, one can still discern his interpretation of significant developments in the country's past (Ćirković 1980). Despite the efforts of Serbian historiographers to present Bosnia within the framework of the Serbian national concept, their attempts remained insufficient until the appearance of Jireček's history of the Serbs, where medieval Bosnia also found a place (Jireček 1978). Jireček's main argument was that Bosnia was originally a Serbian country in its creation during the tenth century, enabling the continuation of Serbian traditions even after the formation of a separate Bosnian *banate* and for centuries afterward. His erudition and extraordinary reputation among the Serbs incited his successors and students to take the same approach toward Bosnian medieval history. Outside of Serbia, Jireček became a key figure in the popularization of this idea.

According to the national concept of Greater Serbia at the end of the nineteenth century, the Austro-Hungarian monarchy encompassed a significant area that included several of the "Serbian lands": Bosnia and Herzegovina, Vojvodina with Srem, as well as some parts of Dalmatia. The concept of South-Slav unification focused solely on the specific interests of Serbia: it envisioned a large Serbian state as a center of power in the Balkans once Serbian military victories and strategic alliances with the older Balkan nations had forced the dying Habsburg and Ottoman empires out of the region. Serbia successfully accomplished the second half of this objective by terminating Ottoman governance and incorporating Macedonia and Kosovo into its territory after the Balkan Wars (Pesic 1996, 6). Pursuing a nationalist ideology, one of Serbia's war-aims during World War I was to unify all Serbs and Serbian territories, which encompassed Bosnia and Herzegovina, and Vojvodina—territories that until then were under Austro-Hungarian rule. Serbia formally articulated its war goal as the comprehensive consolidation of all South Slavs into a single nation-state.

The work of Jireček's student Stanoje Stanojević (1874–1937), one of the most significant Serbian historians at the beginning of the twentieth century, should be read in this context. In his *History of the Serbian People* published in 1908, Stanojević included Bosnia in its entirety within Serbian history. According to him, Bosnia belonged to Serbia at the time of Prince Časlav (c. 930–960), as it did later during the dynasty of Duklja (1042–1101). Bosnia achieved its independence after the death of King Bodin in 1101. Although the Nemanjićs could not subjugate Bosnia, the process of ethnogenesis, according to Stanojević, was by then complete. In other words, since it inhabited the territory of the Serbian state in the middle of the tenth century, the population in Bosnia was said to be Serbian. In Stanojević's *History*, therefore, Bosnia is an important factor

(Mitrović 2017, 142). Unlike the situation in Serbia under the Nemanjić dynasty, to whose members Stanojević attributed great organizational and unifying abilities, that in Bosnia was completely different. While the Serbian ruler Stefan Nemanja (1166–1199), after oscillating between Catholicism and Orthodoxy, finally decided in favor of Orthodoxy and thus laid the foundations for the future development of Serbian history, the indecision of the Bosnian rulers contributed to the creation and expansion of heresy which, according to Stanojević, made it impossible to unite with the other Serbian lands.

The appearance of Stanojević's *History* coincided with the annexation of Bosnia by Austria-Hungary (1908), and as time went on, its importance grew in Serbia, while it was censored in Habsburg territory. It should be noted that between the two world wars, this book was of decisive importance for the positioning of Bosnia in Serbian academic circles. This concept more or less "survived" the creation of socialist Yugoslavia, maintaining its relevance among Serbian historians. That the position of medieval Bosnia in relation to other Serbian lands remained unchanged is evidenced by the large historiographical project "History of the Serbian People" initiated during the 1980s, in which the most influential Serbian historians participated and where one reads: "There is no basis for the opinion, which is still present today, that Bosnia was a neighboring area of Serbia that was occasionally included in the composition of the Serbian state. Bosnia was an area within Serbia, limited to the valley of the same name river, and only later, probably beginning in the eleventh century, the name Bosnia spread to the western part of the former Serbia" (*Istorija srpskog naroda I* 1981, 62). A decade later, already after the dissolution of socialist Yugoslavia, at an International Conference held at the Serbian Academy of Sciences and Arts in 1994, Serbian historians discussed, among other things, the topic "Bosnia and Herzegovina and other Serbian lands." The vitality of this concept has remained largely present among contemporary Serbian historians.

CROATIZATION OF THE BOSNIAN MIDDLE AGES

The emergence of modern nationalism in Croatia can be attributed to the repercussions of the Napoleonic Wars. In 1809, Napoleon created the 'Illyrian Provinces' from the territories ceded by the Austrians. This French stronghold in the Western Balkans encompassed portions of Slovenia, Croatia, the Military Frontier (a militarized zone bordering the realm of the Ottoman Empire and stretching from southern Croatia in the west to Transylvania in the east), and Dalmatia. The term "Illyrian Provinces" refers to the Roman province of Illyricum during classical antiquity. As a result of the French Republic's enforcement of its legal code and administrative practices, the Croats and Slovenes gained firsthand experience with the new economic and political liberties that had swept through much of Western Europe. One benefit included the ability to use the Croatian language. Consequently, the Croatian national awakening adopted the name "Illyrianism" as a continuation of Napoleon's Illyria. Zagreb served as the focal point of the Illyrian movement, attracting predominantly Croatian adherents (Jelavich 1983, 162).

The idea that Bosnia and Herzegovina was an exclusively Croatian land developed in the wake of the Greater Serbia narrative, and reached its final stage at the turn of the twentieth century. Unlike the Serbian, the Croatian narrative in this phase was not based solely on the identity of language and folk culture, but on historical rights. According to this representation, the whole history of medieval Bosnia and the population that inhabited Bosnia in the Middle Ages belonged to the "Croatian political and cultural pattern" (Džaja 2014, 23). Put simply, the inhabitants of medieval Bosnia, who were called Bosnians in local sources, and *Bosnenses* and *Bosignani* in Latin and Italian sources (see Isailović 2019, 51), shared an awareness of their alleged Croatian affiliation and preserved this awareness even after the Ottoman conquest of the Bosnian Kingdom. According to the Croatian narrative, during the four-hundred-year-long Ottoman rule of Bosnia and Herzegovina, the Islamized Bosniaks distanced themselves from the neighboring Serbs culture and tradition and, together with the Catholic Croats, represented a unique nation that was divided only by religious affiliation. This view, roughly sketched here, was most consistently and thoroughly presented by the Croatian Franciscan, Dominik Mandić, in his trilogy on the history of Bosnia and Herzegovina, published in Chicago and Rome between 1960 and 1967 (Mandić 1960, 1962, 1967).

The national rebirth of the Croats began around 1830 with the Illyrian movement. Illyrianism is founded on the belief that the South Slavs, who settled on the Balkan Peninsula during the seventh century, are direct descendants of the ancient Illyrians. The movement began as cultural Slavism shared by Croats and Serbs, but eventually evolved into a Croatian national idea. The focus of the Illyrian view of history was originally on the unity of the Slavic tribes and their equality, as was then believed along with other great medieval populations of European history such as Germans and Franks (Bijedić 2011, 100–1). The name, derived from the designations of the Roman province of Illyricum and the Napoleonic province of Illyriennes, denoted nationality, area, and language. Originating in the sixteenth century, Illyrianism expanded from Dalmatia to other Croatian regions and beyond, was modified during the following three centuries in response to political and other objectives, and affected not only the historical awareness of the Slavic Balkan peoples, but also the idea of Pan-Slavism during the nineteenth century. According to the Illyrian concept of history, a significant role of the Slavic peoples was to defend Europe from the Turkish invasions. Hungary's aspirations to entirely annex Croatia in order to obtain access to the sea and to culturally (particularly linguistically) absorb Croatia were critical to the emergence of Croatian nationalism. The Illyrian national movement in Croatia was mainly concerned with resisting these Hungarian objectives and advocating national independence. According to the Croatian interpretation of Illyrianism, the name "Illyrian" was to be associated with "Croatian," and the goal was to build an Illyrian monarchy or large Illyria. This expanded state, justified by ethnic and linguistic affinity, aimed to gather the South Slavic lands possessed by the Danube Monarchy and to return Bosnia, which was still under Ottoman control at the time, to the rule of Christian rulers (Jelavich 1983, 163–4).

This idea was elaborated by Josip Juraj Strossmayer (1815–1905), bishop of Đakovo, and Franjo Rački (1828–1894), the first president of the Yugoslav Academy. The two were among the most prominent figures in Croatian political and cultural life in the nineteenth century, and advocated cultural Yugoslavism, that is, the intellectual and cultural unity among all South Slavs. In the moderate nationalist programs of the Party of Rights (Stranka prava), territorial demands were made based on ethnic and historical criteria. In the event of Ottoman withdrawal, the party would lay claim to the "people beyond the rivers Una and Sava, who once shared the same fate with the Croatian kingdom," because this people belonged to Croatianness "not only because of the alliance in the past, but also because of the bond of geographical location and the same blood" (Behschnitt 1980, 237; Bijedić 2011, 101). Strossmayer's and Rački's political project envisaged the unification of Croats, Serbs, Bulgarians, and Slovenes into a Yugoslav federation, as well as to liberate the southern Slavs in Bosnia-Herzegovina from Ottoman rule (Slišković 2020, 136–8).

Ante Starčević (1823–1896), a Croatian politician and founder of the Croatian "Party of Rights," advocated the incorporation of Bosnia-Herzegovina and other provinces into Croatia by historical right. According to the picture of Croatia that Starčević envisioned in 1867, "the entire population between Macedonia and Germany, between the Danube and the Adriatic Sea, has only one nationality, only one life, the Croatian life" (cit. in Behschnitt 1980, 259; Bijedić 2011, 101–2). Based on his Croat-centered Pan-Slavism, historical claims, and political strategy, Starčević declared that Croatia encompassed the entire South Slavic region with the exception of Bulgaria. For Starčević, only Croatia had a right, based on history and nationality, to Bosnia-Herzegovina, because the Muslim upper class and the landowning nobility were the "oldest and purest part" of the Croatian nobility (see Sundhaussen 1982, 27). For a period, Starčević envisaged Sarajevo as the hub of his Croatia, which would be independent of Austria and would coincide with nearly the entire area of what was later to become the first Yugoslavia (see 2014, 223).

The publication of extensive collections of sources from the archives of Venice and Dubrovnik, in addition to diplomatic material, created the necessary conditions for the appearance of the first comprehensive synthesis on medieval Bosnia, which was written by Vjekoslav Klaić (1849–1928) (Klaić 1882). Klaić's synthesis was highly regarded in European historical circles, and its translations into German and Hungarian played a significant role in enhancing the visibility of Bosnian medieval history (Klaić 1885; Klaić 1890). The vast majority of Croatian authors at that time tried to "strengthen the impression of the influence of Croatia" (Jelavich 1992, 173) in Bosnia, and Klaić was the most prominent among them and enjoyed status as a respected historian. While most authors in their historical accounts of Croatia, Slavonia, Dalmatia, and Istria simply noted facts that seemed completely self-explanatory to them and did not require special justifications, in the case of Bosnia and Herzegovina they proceeded differently. It was considered obvious that, regarding Bosnia and Herzegovina, they must defend Croatian positions and Croatian rights (Jelavich 1992, 172–3).

The Croatian acquisition of Bosnian territory was also pursued through the use of historiography. There it was dated back to the time of Slavic settlement and the first mention of Bosnia in the sources (Goldstein 2003, 109–37). The work of the fourth Byzantine emperor of the Macedonian dynasty Constantine VII Porphyrogenitus (913–959) *De administrando imperio* is the key source for both Serbian and Croatian claims on Bosnia.

Although the work of the informed Byzantine emperor does not provide the kind of evidence that nationalists would desire, they interpret it very flexibly in favor of the thesis that Bosnia belongs to either Serbia or Croatia. Porphyrogenitus' data suggests that Bosnia was under the dominion of the Serbian duke (*knez*) Časlav, a contemporary of the Byzantine emperor. Although the information is scarce, historians found it possible to discuss at length Serbian ethnogenesis on this basis (Živković 2010, 149–61). During Austro-Hungarian rule of Bosnia, Ivo Pilar, a Croatian historian and politician (1874–1933), was one of the most renowned intellectuals who definitively tied Bosnian medieval history to Croatia. After World War I, several writers followed in his tracks, among them the Croatian historian and numismatist Ivan Renđeo (1884–1962), the Herzegovinian Franciscan and historian Leon Petrović (1883–1945), and the geographer Filip Lukas (1871–1958).

Among the prominent Croatian historians between the two world wars, who wrote extensively about Bosnian history, is Ferdo Šišić (1869–1940). In his well-known synthesis *History of the Croats in the Time of National Rulers*, published in 1925, he frequently associated Bosnia with the Croatian ethnic area (Šišić 1925). Although in his writings the Byzantine emperor Constantin VII Porphyrogenitus mentioned Bosnia as part of Serbia, Šišić argued that, before falling under Serbian rule, Bosnia was part of Croatia:

> Since the description of Constantin refers to his time, i.e. to Serbia under Prince Časlav Klonimirović (d. 931–960), it is acceptable to think that before the fall of Serbia (924) Bosnia was not an integral part of it, entering Serbia only in the time of Prince Časlav, as well as the area around the city of Salines (Sol, Tuzla). We already had the opportunity to show that Bulgarian Khan Boris' Croatian (military) campaign (between 854 and 860) and the passage of papal envoys on their way to Bulgaria through Croatian territory is strong evidence that in the second half of the ninth century Croatia immediately bordered Bulgaria, which could only be somewhere in today's eastern Bosnia. (Šišić 1925, 462)

A number of well-known foreign scholars provided support for these assertions, including Ernst Ludwig Dümmler (1830–1902), who asserted that "Bosnia is also counted as an old land of the Croats, and not as a Serbian land from the beginning" (Dümmler 1856, 373). As pointed out by Šišić, other historians from the second half of the nineteenth century held a similar point of view, such as the Bulgarian historian Marin Drinov (in his *The Southern Slavs and Byzantium in the 10th Century*, 1876), the British historian of Byzantium John B. Bury, and the Hungarian Julius Pauler (Šišić 1925, 462). On the other hand, the aforementioned Serbian historian Stanoje Stanojević (1874–1937), following Jireček and Drinov, tried to apply the "Bulgarian ethnogenesis model" (see Mitrović 2017, 136) to the Serbs. Stanojević believed that Croats and Serbs immigrated to the Balkans more or less at the same time as the initial Slavic settlers, the so-called Bulgarian Slavs, so the entire process of Slavic migration concluded in the seventh century. The Serbs, similar to the Bulgars, succeeded in establishing dominance over their unknown neighboring Slavic tribes and gave them their name; the difference is that the Bulgars that gave their name to the Slavic tribes in the Bulgarian state were of another ethnicity or race (on the ethnogenetic debates of the nineteenth century on Bulgaria see Mishkova 2011, 213–45). For Stanojević, the process of ethnogenesis means, on the one hand, "concentration," that is, the association of different tribes within the same state and, on the other, "leveling," by which he means the creation of a common identity (Stanojević 1908, 39–40). In the case of Serbia and Croatia, this implied the unification of different tribes and territories that almost immediately became aware of being Serbs or Croats, so that, according to Stanojević, the process of ethnogenesis among Serbs was political, not cultural. For this reason, the early history of the Serbian principality is depicted as a continuous struggle with external enemies: Bulgarians, Franks, or Byzantines (Mitrović, 2017, 137–8). Adopting the ideas of the Serbian historian and politician Ljubomir Kovačević (1848–1918), Stanojević attributed special importance to the Serbian prince Časlav, who "managed to unite almost all Serbian tribes and countries, that is, Serbia, Bosnia and four coastal countries: Pagania (Neretva), Zahumlje, Travunija and Duklja" (Stanojević 1908, 39–40).

Dominik Mandić (1889–1973) established the strongest relationship between the Bosnian Middle Ages and the Croatian ethnic area (2008, 186). Mandić's writings were included on the "index prohibitorum" in communist Yugoslavia due to his nationalist beliefs, while citing passages from them could lead to imprisonment. This may explain why this well-known Franciscan and historian, born in Široki Brijeg in Herzegovina, was highly regarded and honored by the Croatian nationalist elites in Bosnia during the time of socialist Yugoslavia, and also after its dissolution. Following his studies in theology and church history in Mostar, Mandić assumed leadership roles in the Franciscan province of

Herzegovina and served as director of a high school in his hometown. In 1939 he was selected as the representative for the Slavic countries of the Franciscan provinces and appointed to the Central Curia of the Franciscan order in Rome. Mandić's early pro-Yugoslav political stance underwent a profound metamorphosis during World War II, leading him to align with the Croatian extreme nationalists. After the war, he facilitated the emigration of many Croatians who opposed communist rule in Yugoslavia. Most of them emigrated through Rome to South America, while he himself emigrated to the United States in 1952. In Chicago, he became the leader of the Franciscan exile group from Herzegovina and dedicated himself to historical studies of that area until his death in 1973 (Bijedić 2011, 113–4).

In the aftermath of World War II, Mandić emerged as a prominent advocate for a distinctively Croatian nature of the history of Bosnia and Herzegovina, particularly concerning the Bosnian Middle Ages. He expressed his views in three voluminous works, the most controversial of which is the *Ethnic History of Bosnia and Herzegovina*, published in Rome in 1967. The fact that his work was "scientifically illegal" among the Yugoslav public, "contributed even more to the creation of [a] mythical-conspiratorial atmosphere around it and its author" (2002, 66). Without going into the book's analysis, his unprecedented Croatization of medieval Bosnia can be illustrated by the extensive chapter titles such as: "According to old contemporary sources, the inhabitants of Bosnia and Herzegovina in the Middle Ages were Croats"; "The social and state organization of medieval Bosnia was Croatian"; "Medieval Bosnia and Herzegovina lived in a cultural community with Croats"; and "Archaeological finds of medieval Bosnia and Herzegovina bear Western and Croatian features" (Mandić 1967, 8, 24, 43, 62).

Franjo Rački particularly emphasized the heresy accusations against the Bosnian rulers and heresy in Bosnian history as a whole, which he more or less exaggerated in his research. Mandić endorsed Rački's views of the heretical nature of Bosnia's medieval history and strongly supported the idea that the Bosnian Church had a dualistic character. He considered the Bogomils to be "neo-Manichean heretics" and believed that the Bosnian Church was an important institution in medieval Bosnia. Yet when reading Mandić's book *The Bogomil Church of the Bosnian Christians* one gets the impression of a distinctively Croatian phenomenon, which was called the Bosnian church ("Crkva bosanska") and not "Croatian church" solely because it appeared in Bosnia. Mandić thus placed the historical subject of the Bosnian Church in a Croatian historical and geographical context, and its members were considered "Croats of the Bogomil faith"; that is, they represented a purely Croatian phenomenon that was given the Bosnian name due to the name of the locality (Šidak 1977, 158).

While not extensively discussed in the public sphere, Mandić's writings were not altogether ignored by the academic community. Some historians, including Nada Klaić (1920–1988), a professor of medieval history at the University of Zagreb, openly disagreed with Mandić, causing a dispute between the two. Mandić disseminated his articles through the emigration periodicals *Hrvatska Revija* and *Hrvatski Kalendar*, whereas Klaić published her articles in scientific journals circulated in Croatia. She objected to Mandić, writing that in his works "all the Goths and Slavs are transformed into Croats and, in this way, he gets Croatia within the desired borders," which eventually led to the myth that Bosnia and Herzegovina is Croatian land (Klaić 1969, 605; Šanjek 2014, 51–52). On the other hand, Mandić expressed his deep disappointment with the "talented historian" Nada Klaić, who as a "Croatian and the granddaughter of the great Croatian patriot and historian Vjekoslav Klaić" had turned "against her Croatian people" (Ančić 2014, 873, 879).

HERESY AS NATIONAL MYTH: THE BOSNIAK NATIONAL PERSPECTIVE

As can be seen from the above, the perception and treatment of the Middle Ages in Bosnian history pit the different South Slavic historiographic traditions against each other. There was an upsurge of interest in medieval Bosnian history after World War II; however, it was primarily centered around specific topics. Due to the unique ecclesiastical circumstances in Bosnia starting from the late twelfth century, the history of the church in Bosnia became a favored subject for both local and international scholars. Most of these studies focused on the "eccentric" characteristics of medieval Bosnia, particularly the existence of a unique religious institution known as the "Bosnian Church" (Šidak 1977, 149–84; Ćošković 2010, 97–125; Dautović 2015, 127–60).

The term "Bosnian Church" originates from the Latin term *ecclesia bosnensis*, which is documented in medieval sources. The Bosnian Church had been associated with heresy since the late twelfth century, initially following the accusations of heresy made by Prince Vukan of Zeta against the

Bosnian ruler Kulin (Fine 1994, 47; Curta 2006, 433). This association existed institutionally in Bosnia until 1459, when the Bosnian king Stjepan Tomaš persecuted its followers, which most likely led to the collapse of this institution, while mentionings about its members can be found in Ottoman sources during the sixteenth century. At the same time, the members of this Church referred to themselves as "Krstjani," a term that can be translated as "Christians." The church's hierarchy was structured into four tiers. At the top was the "Djed" or "grandfather," who served as the head and was also referred to as the "true bishop" in Bosnian sources. Following him were the "Gost" ("great host"), the "Starac" ("elder"), and the "Strojnik" ("steward"). However, the latter term "Strojnik" could be used to describe all ranks except the "Djed." The language used in the liturgy was Slavic, not Latin (Ćošković 2000, 61–83; Ćošković 2005, 217–442, Stoyanov 2005, 173).

The question about the origin of the teaching of the "Bosnian Church" is complicated due to contradictory Latin and Slavic sources. It continues to be the most contentious subject in the historical literature. As I will discuss later, efforts had been made to establish a connection between the "Bosnian Church" and the Cathar, Bogomil, or Manichean movements. Other researchers claimed that there were no similarities between the teachings and practices of these heresies. Recently, certain scholars have proposed the hypothesis that the institution in question was not a heretical church, but rather a schismatic one, and hence a church with regular doctrine without being under the authority of either Rome or Constantinople (Džaja and 2008–09, 237–41).

Already during the seventeenth and eighteenth centuries some European authors emphasized the heretical nature of the Bosnian church. However, it was not until the 1860s that South Slavic authors began to deal with these issues. In 1867, Božidar Petranović (1809–1874), a lawyer and secretary of the Orthodox diocese in Šibenik, published a book titled *Bogomils, the Bosnian Church and Christians: An Historical Treatise* (Petranović 1867), which marked the beginning of what turned out to be a long-lasting historiographical debate. Petranović argued that the Bosnian Church was Orthodox, with a teaching similar to other Orthodox churches in the East (Šidak 1977, 151). Two years later, the above-mentioned theologian and historian Franjo Rački published the first of three articles in the journal *Rad*, released by the Zagreb-based Yugoslav Academy of Sciences and Arts, of which Rački was the president (Rački 1869a, 84–179; Rački 1869b, 121–87; Rački 1870, 160–263). In contrast to Petranović,

Rački possessed an excellent knowledge of Bosnia's history as well as deep proficiency in the sources, particularly in Latin. The Latin writings, which Rački had complete trust in, played a crucial role in his identification of the teachings of the Bosnian Church with those of the Patarens and Cathars. Being highly knowledgeable about dualistic sects, he employed the comparative method to conclude that the Bosnian heretical movement could be classified as moderate dualism (Šidak 1977, 151–3).

These contrasting perspectives on the history and riddles of the Bosnian Church would have a profound impact on later generations of historians. Until the mid-twentieth century, Franjo Rački's theory enjoyed wide acceptance among prominent historians. Petranović also had adherents, particularly among Serbian authors, who saw the Serbian Middle Ages as culturally similar to the Bosnian Middle Ages due to the Orthodox Church's influence. The best known among them were Sima Tomić (1866–1903), pen name Atom, and Vaso Glušac (1879–1955), a literary historian who produced an extensive work on the Bosnian Church in 1924 (Glušac 1924, 1–55; Glušac 1953, 105–38). Both authors, particularly Vaso Glušac, hardened Petranović's more cautious perspective. Tomić completely dismissed the likelihood of any heretical impact on the Bosnian Church, while Glušac categorically denied the existence of heresy in Bosnia in general. The Serbian public gave a warm reception of their concepts with particular acclaim for Glušac's work (Šidak 1977, 154).

While the Serbian-Orthodox aspect of the Bosnian Church was emphasized by Božidar Petranović (and his followers), on his part Franjo Rački did not ascribe it a clear Croatian national identity. This was undertaken by the already-mentioned Ivo Pilar, a Croatian lawyer, who wrote a book titled *Die südslawische Frage und der Weltkrieg. Übersichtliche Darstellung des Gesamt–Problems* (The South Slav Question and the World War. The Presentation of the Entire Problem) under the pen name L. V. Südland, which was published in 1918 in Vienna. In line with the prevalent racial theories of the era, he regarded the population of medieval Bosnia as Croats and considered Bosnia to be part of the Croatian lands (Pilar 1990, 91–95). Pilar advanced the notion that Croats possessed a particular racial and historical superiority that distinguished them from other South Slavs, particularly Serbs. As Dubravko (1956–2017), a Bosnian medievalist and former professor at the Department of History of the Faculty of Humanities at the University of Sarajevo, states, "Südland's concept of the so-called Croatization of Bogomilism remained the most consistently implemented attempt to provide the Bosnian Church with an exclusively Croatian national image" (Lovrenović 2008, 187).

Historical medievalist research was advanced by the work of the Croatian historian Jaroslav Šidak (1903–1986), who, in his doctoral dissertation of 1934, undertook a thorough analysis of the historiography surrounding the Bosnian Church (Šidak 1937, 37–182). Following a detailed examination of the two opposing concepts, Šidak came up with an alternative interpretation. By prioritizing domestic sources, particularly those originating from within the Bosnian Church, the author concluded that the latter was not associated with any dualistic movement or Orthodox monastic order. He considered the Bosnian Church to be an institution that was "according to its teaching in compliance with the Slavic tradition of Cyril and Methodius,"[3] and that during the 1230s it separated from Rome, to whose diocese it belonged, under the name *ecclesia bosnensis*.

The controversies surrounding the Bosnian Church in socialist Yugoslavia revolved primarily around the three above-mentioned interpretations. Until the 1990s, the dualist framework was dominant. In 1954 Šidak himself chose to adopt Rački's dualistic concept as the most appropriate framework for studying the Bosnian Church. Šidak's reinterpretation of the teachings of the Bosnian Church as dualistic and therefore heretical would have significant implications for the historiography of both the church and medieval Bosnian history generally. With minor modifications prominent historians, including Sima Ćirković and Pejo Ćošković, adopted this reading. However, during the socialist period, some doubted the correctness of this interpretation, claiming that "the Bogomilism of the Bosnian Church is the creation of Franjo Rački and Croatian romanticism. It is that beautiful national heresy, of which the Croats were proud, and which competed with Czech Hussitism" (Šanjek 1975, 215; Vaillant 1974, 525).

In recent years most scholars tend to agree that the terms "Bogomil" and "Bogomilism," appropriately associated with other Balkan countries, in the case of Bosnia are incorrect and misleading. They argue that there is no evidence of these terms in medieval Bosnian sources. Recently, there

---

[3] The Cyrillo-Methodian tradition is the cultural and religious legacy of Saints Cyril and Methodius, Byzantine Christian theologians and missionaries. They are best known for their efforts to spread Christianity among the Slavs and develop the Glagolitic alphabet, which was used to translate the Bible and other religious texts into Slavic. Their efforts had a significant impact on the dissemination of Slavic culture, literature, and Christianity throughout Eastern Europe (Betti 2013, 10–34; Dvornik 1964, 195–211).

6 IN SEARCH OF AN ACCEPTABLE PAST: THE BOSNIAN MIDDLE AGES... 299

has been a preference for using the historically documented terms "Crkva bosanska/Bosnian Church" to refer to the institution, and "krstjani/ Christians" to identify its members. However, the term "Bogumili/ Bogomils" (or Bosanski bogumili/ Bosnian Bogomils) continues to be employed, particularly by Bosniak (Muslim) writers, the medievalist Salih Jalimam being most persistent in doing so (Jalimam 1999). The idea that Bogomilism held the utmost prominence as a religion during the medieval period is also prevalent among Bosniak politicians, intellectuals, and the broader public. Bosniak authors prefer the term "Bogomil/Bogomilsm" over "Christian" because the former does not imply a church of "Christians" and therefore avoids the Christian connotations that go against their national Muslim allegiance. Yet, the Bogomilism thesis lacks recognition from the vast majority of professional historians, particularly medievalists, as well as Slavists, who have dedicated significant efforts to studying manuscripts produced within the Bosnian Church (Dautović 2015, 128–31).

This brings us to the, properly speaking, Bosnian input to the historiographic debate. The Bosnian Middle Ages first attracted the attention of Bosniak intellectuals relatively late, following the Austro-Hungarian occupation. Benjamin Kállay (1839–1903), the Minister of Finance who headed the monarchy's administration of Bosnia-Herzegovina from 1882 to 1903, was concerned about the rise of Muslim activism in Bosnia. Kállay's comprehensive Bosnian policy was designed to shield the country from the nationalist political movements in Serbia and Croatia, while simultaneously fostering the concept of Bosnian nationhood as a distinct and cohesive force. Kállay aspired to broaden the scope of the Bosnian identity to encompass individuals from all religious groups. It was crucial for his objectives that the concept of Bosnian national identity be embraced by the Muslim population. Kállay achieved some degree of success with the more amenable Muslims in Sarajevo, as they viewed this line of thinking as a logical extension of the historical pursuit of Bosnian self-governance during the Ottoman era. The founder of the journal *Bošnjak* (The Bosnian) in 1891 was Mehmed-beg Kapetanović Ljubušak (1839–1902), a prominent landowner and major political figure, who was known for his role in associative life. He was also a pioneering scholar who researched the cultural history of Bosnian Muslims. Primarily targeting a Muslim audience, the journal *Bošnjak* aimed to challenge conservative beliefs among the Muslim clergy and counter the efforts of Croat and Serb nationalists claiming that the Bosnian Muslims were actually Croats or Serbs respectively. Kapetanović examined the role of Bosnian Muslims in the contemporary world in light of the Bogomil proto-component of their identity before the Ottoman conquest. He established a connection between the medieval and Ottoman periods, which he claimed provided the legal foundation for the land ownership of the Beys in Bosnia and Herzegovina:

> Let anyone think and write what they want, yet everyone knows it all too well and as clear as the sun that only that nation has a strong foundation and a permanent basis of material and moral life, which has strong and patriotic landowners, who are all the more valuable to each country the further they reach out into the historical ages, preserving the ancientness of the good and bad of their forefathers, preserving their virtues, customs, language - properly speaking, everything that is the eternal and undying soul of the people; and today this is only the Mohammedan element in Bosnia. This is evidenced by our thoroughly preserved wealth, possessions, customs and language, and lords since [the time of] Bogomil, who inherit to this day the same origin: Ljubović, Sokolović, Kositerović, Kulenović, Filipović, Kapetanović, and many others. In Bosnia, the same families that existed from the beginning still remain today, although they now have Muslim names: Mujo, Alija, Mehmed, etc. This is beautifully and well attested by the genealogy, written two centuries ago by Pope Rubčić, which book is still kept in the Franciscans monastery in Kreševo. Of the two hundred or so noble families registered all were, with few exceptions, Mohammedans. (Kapetanović Ljubušak 1886, 8–9)

One of the first Bosniak scholars to treat the medieval Bosnian past was Safvet-beg Bašagić (1870–1934), a historian, orientalist, and skilled poet. In his work titled *A Brief Guide to the Past of Bosnia and Herzegovina from 1463 to 1850*, Bašagić intended to present a neat political, ethnic, confessional, and cultural continuity from the Middle Ages to his own time, when Bosnia was in search of a post-Ottoman national identity after centuries of Ottoman rule. The Habsburg takeover of Bosnia proved challenging for Bosnian Muslims, as it meant parting ways with the four centuries of stability provided by the Ottoman political system and the necessity to adjust to the novel parameters of Western civilization (Bašagić-Redžepašić 1900). Although his historical exposition begins with the year of the collapse of the medieval Bosnian kingdom, subsequent historians were interested above all in Bašagić's argumentation about the continuity between the Middle Ages and the Ottoman period. In opposition to Petranović, who highlighted the confessional connection between the Bosnian Church and the Orthodox Church, Bašagić focused on the supposed Bogomilism within the Bosnian Church and argued for a spiritual link between Bogomilism and Islam. He also tried, similar to Kapetanović Ljubušak, to show the continuity between the medieval Bosnian nobility and the influential Muslim landlords from the late Ottoman and the Austro-Hungarian epoch (Bašagić-Redžepašić 1900, 17–18).

The Bosniak ideology of national integration emerged at a later stage relative to the Serbs and Croats. The "Ottoman experience," related as it was to the historical perception of Muslims as traitors by the Serbs and the Croats, further complicated this process. The Bosniaks faced exclusion from the Slavic community and saw themselves pressed to demonstrate that they were not of Turkish origin and that their adherence to Islam did not preclude their affiliation with Slavdom. They had to go to great lengths to prove either that although they adopted Islam from the Turks, they maintained their distinct identity, or that they belonged to an indigenous population in the Bosnian region before the arrival of the Slavs. The medieval Bosnian kingdom, known for its supposed Bogomilism, supplied the necessary narrative (2008, 199–203; Dautović 2021, 90). In seeking to underscore their distinct identity and distinguish themselves from the Serbs and Croats, the Bosniaks made use of the Bogomil concept. They also employed it as a means to rationalize their adoption of Islam, a tendency that had resulted in allegations of disloyalty to Slavdom. According to this Bosniak narrative, their medieval ancestors before the Ottoman conquest were not Christian, Orthodox or Catholic, but Bogomil. Due to the alleged similarities between Bogomilism and Islam, this was perceived as a facilitating condition for their conversion to Islam. The assertion that Bogomilism resembles Islam was thus put forward with the aim of offering a credible alternative explanation to the persistent allegations that their conversion was treasonous, which often arose in historical research (see Maslo 2020, 273–307).

A frequently encountered contention concerning Bosniaks or Muslims is that they lack a distinct historical identity due to their inability to associate themselves with a medieval history, a history which predominantly features Christian rulers. The mythologized representation of conversion as treason goes back to the beginning of the nineteenth century and is closely related to the ideology of nationalism, which until the end of that century "was primarily a political and socio-cultural phenomenon limited to Europe and its colonial extensions in America. Nationalism did not arise in any culture outside of the West" (Wehler 2001, 15). Serbian historian Bojan Aleksov has investigated the genesis and transformation of these "convert myths" and their influence among Serbian intellectual circles from the nineteenth century to the present (Aleksov 2005, 58–190). Here is one illustration from the Serbian intellectual Georgije Magarašević (1793–1830), the founder of *Letopis Matica Srpska*, the first Serbian literary newspaper, which appeared at the beginning of the nineteenth century:

> What a terrible thing merciless fate has done to our brothers! They are thoroughly trans-formed by their change of religion and law! They don't want to hear any talk about their Slavic origins, but instead persecute their brothers. They are like dry and fallen twigs from the Slavic tree. Their ancestors were forced into conversion under tyrannical regimes and by force of arms, while they now willingly embrace the new faith and extol it. By accepting the foreign law, they have renounced their ancestry and origin. Islamized Serbs, blinded by fanaticism, are much worse than the Turks. (Aleksov 2005, 164–5)

The collapse of communism in the late 1980s and early 1990s witnessed an increased interest in national medieval narratives among the peoples of Yugoslavia. In line with this trend, the flag of the Republic of Bosnia and Herzegovina was adorned with the heraldic motif of the lily, with which the members of the Bosnian royal Kotromanić dynasty identified themselves. During the previous decades, Yugoslav historiography had gradually moved away from the idea that Bogomilism was the defining characteristic of the Bosnian Middle Ages. However, this idea was gaining increased support among the Bosniak population, particularly among intellectuals and politicians. One reason for this was the desire to be recognized as a distinct ethnic group, separate from Serbs or Croats (Steindorff 2007, 112–3). In the aftermath of the international armed conflict in Bosnia and Herzegovina between 1992 and 1995 and the ethnic cleansing of Bosnian Muslims, the Bogomil narrative found a particularly fertile ground. A historical parallel was drawn with the persecution of the alleged Bogomils in medieval Bosnia by Hungary through the crusades during the thirteenth century (Bijedić 2011, 211; on the problem of the Crusades against Bosnia, see Dautović 2020, 63–77).

6 IN SEARCH OF AN ACCEPTABLE PAST: THE BOSNIAN MIDDLE AGES... 303

KING TVRTKO I AND THE ISSUE OF HIS CORONATION

Another focal point of intense debate in medieval Bosnian history concerns the coronation of the first Bosnian king Tvrtko I. Precisely because little is known about the coronation itself due to the limited number of sources, a variety of interpretations emerged. Some of the most frequently asked questions in the debate concern where he was crowned; who he was crowned by; and the origin of the Bosnian crown. These apparently purely historiographical questions carry far more weight than first appears. Depending on the perspective of the individual researcher, the answer carries significant ideological baggage. Before we tackle this issue, we need to take a look at the personality of this Bosnian ruler.

Tvrtko I was the ruler of Bosnia between 1353 and 1391. His parents were Prince Vladislav, brother of Bosnian Ban Stjepan II, and Princess Jelena, daughter of Croatian notable Jurje II Šubić. He was a member of the illustrious Kotromanić dynasty—a Bosnian elite family that had marital relationships with other European courts. He assumed power at the age of fifteen, succeeding his uncle Stjepan II Kotromanić (1322–1353). Bosnia's greatest territorial expansion occurred during the reign of these two rulers, when it extended to the area of Hum, the river Lim, and, at one point, the Adriatic coast from Kotor to Zadar. Tvrtko's reign is widely regarded as the most successful period in medieval Bosnian history. There are several reasons for such a positive evaluation, the most important of which are undoubtedly his territorial expansion, the economic growth under his rule, and his coronation as king, a title that no Bosnian ruler before him had possessed. Despite this, the period of his reign has not been a subject of a comprehensive monograph study since the work of Vladimir Ćorović (Ćorović 1925, to be discussed further down).

Tvrtko I was most likely crowned on Mitrovdan (October 26) in 1377 at the church of St. Nikola in Mili near the town of Visoko, the center of the Bosnian medieval state. After the death of Uroš, son of the most famed Serbian king-emperor Dušan, the Serbian throne became vacant and Tvrtko ascended. He derived his legitimacy from his position as great-grandson, through the maternal family line, of Serbian Prince Stefan Dragutin. The coronation marked the pinnacle of Tvrtko's political power and a turning point in medieval Bosnian history. Tvrtko's ceremonial charter from 1378 states that he was crowned with a *sugubi*, or double wreath, and that his title was "King of Serbia, Bosnia, the Maritime areas, and the Western Regions" (Ćirković 1964b, 343–70). Bosnia's elevation to the status of kingdom represented a major transformation in almost every administrative and legal aspect of the former Bosnian *banate*. The coronation provided the opportunity for an elevated "abstract understanding of the state" by introducing the idea that the king has two bodies—the natural body and the body politic or mystical body, as suggested by the medieval historian Ernst H. Kantorowicz (1895–1963) (Kantorowicz 1957). According to this concept, the ruler's title is seen as separate from his individual, personal identity. The ruler embodies the state not only as a physical person but also as a symbolic representation of the state's continuity and sovereignty. The title of the ruler is inherently linked to the concept of kingship in general, rather than being tied to any particular individual who possesses the title. This division enables the state to maintain its continuity even when there are changes in leadership, such as through the process of succession or other political transitions. It also reinforces the idea of the ruler as a divine or semi-divine figure, whose authority is derived from a higher power and is therefore not bound by mortal limitations. Remarkably, among intellectual circles in Europe in the following centuries, the memory of the Bosnian kingdom would remain firmly embedded, so that even in the seventeenth century the area of Bosnia, despite being under Ottoman rule, would be referred to as the Kingdom of Bosnia or the *regnum Bosine*.

However, and in contrast to Ban Kulin, who ruled at the end of the twelfth century, the memory of King Tvrtko I has vanished from folk tradition. On the other hand, in the early stages of historiography on the area (at that time the Ottoman Eyalet) of Bosnia, connected with the chronicles of Bosnian Franciscans such as Bono Benić (1708–1785), Nikola Lašvanin (1703–1750), and Filip Lastrić (1700–1783), Tvrtko I was treated through an anti-imperialist lens; while these writers advocated for liberation from Ottoman rule, they did not cling to the Austrian side either (Benić 2003; Lašvanin 1981; Lastrić 1977). Soon after, the first outline of a romantic interpretation of the independent Bosnian Middle Ages began to take shape, with the first Bosnian king being presented as the unifier of all South Slavs. Ivan Franjo Jukić (1818–1857), an enlightened Franciscan, wrote the first domestic history of Bosnia in 1851 under the pseudonym Slavoljub Bošnjak (Jukić 1851). The first Croatian professional historians, the already discussed Franjo Rački and Vjekoslav Klaić (1849–1928) followed in his footsteps. According to Klaić, Tvrtko's goal was to separate Bosnia from the Hungarian crown by bringing together Serbian and Croatian territory (Klaić 1882, 194). Klaić was among the

6 IN SEARCH OF AN ACCEPTABLE PAST: THE BOSNIAN MIDDLE AGES...

first to compare the collapse of the Serbian emperor Dušan's state to the events in Bosnia following Tvrtko's death. Similarly, the above-mentioned leading Serbian historian of the interwar period Vladimir Ćorović emphasized the parallels between Tvrtko and Dušan, stating that "King Tvrtko is the greatest ruler of the Bosnian state, as Dušan was of Raška," and highlighted the similarities between Bosnia and Serbia during their reigns (Ćorović 1940, 336).

The significance of the location of the coronation resides in the connection drawn between it and Tvrtko's identity. According to Mauro Orbini (in his book *Il regno degli Slavi* from 1601), Tvrtko was crowned in the Orthodox monastery of Mileševa, which came to be considered as irrefutable proof of his Serbian national and Orthodox religious identity (Orbini 1601, 358; Orbin 1968, 151). Although modern medieval studies have refuted such claims as anachronistic and incorrect, a large number of Serbian historians and intellectuals continue to reiterate this interpretation to justify their national appropriation of Bosnia. The controversy among the authors stems from the confusion of the Bosnian medieval locality Mili or Mile, today known as Arnautovići, situated near Visoko, with the Serbian-Orthodox Monastery Mileševa near Prijepolje. It is interesting to note that different authors have equated Mile with Mileševa from 1369, after a Franciscan martyrology which states that Ivan of Aragon died in the monastery "de Milesevo in Bosna" (Anđelić 1980, 234). Confusion over the name Mile or Mileševa prevailed in Franciscan chronicles and writings. The reason for this could be that the church of Mile was most likely abandoned in the Middle Ages, and its location was eventually forgotten (Lovrenović 2006, 618–9).

Lajos Thallóczy (1857–1916), a Hungarian historian and politician, was the first to question Orbini's assertion about Mileševa, stating unequivocally that the coronation must have taken place elsewhere. Although he supported the Mile site, he was uncertain about the location of that site in Bosnia. Thallóczy's tragic death prevented him from exploring this issue and perhaps resolving the problem of the coronation site (Thallóczy 1906, 419). Concerning Hungarian historiography, one should mention yet another crown-related dispute. It was again Orbini who claimed that Tvrtko I was crowned solely with the approval of the Hungarian king Louis I of the Anjou dynasty (1326–1382)—a claim Hungarian historians cited as irrefutable proof of Bosnia's vassal relationship with Hungary (Orbini 1601, 358; Orbin 1968, 151).

Although historians had been discussing it since Orbini, the question of the location grew in importance only after 1918, at the time of the founding of Yugoslavia. Klaić's synthesis was authoritative until the appearance of the *History of Bosnia* by Vladimir Ćorović, who was born in Mostar (Bosnia and Herzegovina). Ćorović endorsed the view of Tvrtko I's Serbian identity and, at the same time, that he was the ruler who united the South Slavs (Ćorović 1940, 337). As already mentioned, in several of his works, particularly those written after Austria-Hungary's withdrawal from Bosnia in 1918, he emphasized the Serbian character of the Bosnian Middle Ages and, accordingly, Tvrtko's coronation was interpreted in a pro-Serbian manner. *History of Bosnia*, published posthumously in 1940, provides the best exposition of his views and a full-blown elaboration of the concept of Bosnia as one of the "Serbian lands." Although he wrote about the inhabitants of Bosnia that "they are only called 'Bosnians' and 'good Bosniaks'; like that and no other way" (Ćorović 1940, 338), his presentation of Bosnia as a country primarily of Serbs and Croats is emphasized throughout the book: "Its population," he wrote, "consists of Serbs and Croats, Orthodox Slavs, Catholics and Bogomils; therefore, it was neither tribally nor religiously homogeneous" (Ćorović 1940, 337). Ćorović's treatment of Bosnia during Tvrtko's era is clearly linked with the idea of the political and cultural unification of the South Slavs between the two world wars, illustrating its influence on historiography:

> Bosnia had a central position in the Serbo-Croatian countries and was able to include both of our tribes, Serbs and Croats, on both wings (...) He [Tvrtko] was the first to start the activity of attracting neighboring areas to the Bosnian state, when the other tribal elements were prevented from working independently, like the Croats, or busy with other issues, like the Serbs (...) His creation of a true Serbo-Croatian state, conceived at the beginning more territorially than nationally, is one of the most pleasant pages of our history; in spite of the many factors that separated Serbs and Croats, he offered a solution that would certainly bring them closer together. (Ćorović 1940, 337)

Ćorović thus characterized Tvrtko's reign as a form of symbiosis between the Croatian and Serbian components, with a bias toward the latter, in the context of the post-1918 Yugoslav unification.

A collaborative publication of a very different type by several Croatian authors titled *History of the Croatian Lands of Bosnia and Herzegovina*

6 IN SEARCH OF AN ACCEPTABLE PAST: THE BOSNIAN MIDDLE AGES...   307

from Ancient Times to 1463 appeared two years later in 1942. In post-war communist Yugoslavia this book was considered very controversial because it was published under the Ustasha regime in Bosnia and Herzegovina during World War II. The Ustasha was a fascist ultranationalist movement that aimed to establish an independent Croatia, which included Bosnia and Herzegovina. The initiative came about in the early 1930s from the Croatian cultural society *Napredak*, which announced a competition for writing a history of Bosnia and Herzegovina with a particular emphasis on the historical and cultural progress of the Croatian community within Bosnian society. The project was planned to examine the history of Bosnia and Herzegovina until the end of Ottoman rule. However, only the first of the planned three volumes, which covered prehistory and the period until the end of the Middle Ages, was published (Išek 2011, 245–58).

The medieval period continued to be a focus of research after this publication. However, there is a significant difference in perception of the *Napredak*'s *History of the Croatian lands of Bosnia and Herzegovina* in Yugoslav historiography after 1945 compared to after its re-publication in the early 1990s. Although most of the participating authors did not write from a nationalist perspective, in Yugoslav historiography this publication was largely associated with Ustasha ideology. Two reprinted editions of the book appeared in Sarajevo in 1991 and 1998. They are identical to the original, except for the removal of the designation "Croatian lands" and the controversial preface that read:

> Here, Croatian people, is the book of the history of the Croatian lands of Bosnia and Herzegovina from the earliest times to the fall of the Bosnian kingdom (1463). The Croatian cultural society Napredak presents it to you on the occasion of the first anniversary of the restoration of the Independent State of Croatia, when Bosnia and Herzegovina freed itself from foreigners and returned to the bosom of Mother Croatia, from which it had been torn for centuries. The soul of tortured Bosnia and Herzegovina has always strived to find itself together with other Croatian regions. Centuries of continuous suffering did not erase those longings, and now the dreams of the ruler of Bosnia Pavle Šubić Bribirski, the dreams of the great Bosnian king Stjepan Tvrtko I, Duke Hrvoje Vukčić Hrvatinić and other great Bosnian personalities have come true. Their Bosnia is once again part of the Croatian lands, to reassemble the old state unit. (*Povijest Bosne...* 1942, non-paginated preface)

Instead, both new editions feature a modified title: *History of Bosnia and Herzegovina from the Oldest Times Until the Year 1463*. Although the *History of Bosnia* was a collaborative effort, Marko Perojević stands out among its authors due to the extensive range of topics that he dealt with and the length of the text he wrote (he contributed 495 pages out of a total of 829) (Perojević 1942, 196–592). Most significant is his view about Tvrtko I's double crown, namely the assertion that he was ceremoniously crowned with both the Serbian and Bosnian crowns (Perojević 1942, 314–5). Perojević strengthened Rački's assessment of Tvrtko I Kotromanić as the creator of a strong South Slavic state that included "Serbian lands" and "Croatian lands," adding a new national dimension to it: "King Tvrtko is without doubt the greatest ruler of the Bosnian state and one of the greatest rulers of the Croatian past. He left a large, yet unsettled and unconsolidated state. As the Bosnian magnates were getting stronger, it could easily happen that Tvrtko's work would collapse quickly, if his successor was not strong enough" (Perojević 1942, 349).

Among the historians who touched upon the coronation ceremony of Tvrtko I was the Serbian historian Nikola Radojčić in his work *Coronation Ceremony of the Bosnian King Tvrtko I: A Contribution to the History of the Coronation of Serbian Rulers in the Middle Ages*, in which he approached this problem in a broader comparative context involving coronations in Byzantium and Western Europe. However, despite its title, in this extensive work little space is devoted to Tvrtko's coronation ceremony and Bosnian medieval history as a whole. A detail that Radojčić particularly tried to emphasize was that the coronation was performed according to the Eastern Orthodox rite (Radojčić 1948, 80–82; see also Ćirković 1964b, 352). For Radojčić, and his Serbian historiography foregrounding, that fact was important because it reinforced the narrative of historical and cultural connections between the medieval Serbian and Bosnian states. Sima Ćirković (1929–2009), a renowned author in the second half of the twentieth century known for his expertise in Bosnian medieval history, extensively explored the topic of coronation in several of his works (Blagojević 2010, 249–54). In his renowned 1964 publication *The Double Wreath. A Contribution to the History of Kingship in Bosnia* he underscores, similar to Perojević, the dual origin of the crown. Ćirković's works do not espouse strong nationalistic bias, but they are still ideologically influenced by the Serbian historiographical school to which he belonged and which advocates that Bosnia should be considered part of the "Serbian lands." Ćirković also hypothesized that Tvrtko I was not crowned in Mileševa, but in another, unknown, location (Ćirkovic 1964b, 352).

Overall, the study of Tvrtko I's reign was an unpopular topic of investigation in socialist Yugoslavia because the Marxist concept of historiography was not favorable to emphasizing the role of great ruling figures in the "pre-socialist" past. Although the commemoration of jubilees and anniversaries was common in Yugoslav historiography, the 600th anniversary of Tvrtko's coronation in 1977 went relatively unnoticed. A specific contribution to solving the dilemma about the coronation's location was made by archaeologists, such as Pavao Anđelić (1920–1985) and Đuro Basler (1917–1990), who used the pseudonym Juraj Kujundžić. Anđelić excavated the remnants of the church of St. Nikola in Arnautovići, formerly Mili, one of the places believed to have hosted the coronation ceremony (Anđelić 1980, 183–247). Like Anđelić, Basler advocated the Mile-coronation-thesis (Basler 1975/76, 49–61). Following Yugoslavia's dissolution, the debate again came to the fore, now in a new constellation. The Bosnian historian Dubravko took up this issue, assertively arguing that the coronation took place in Mile. In addition to researching the circumstances surrounding the coronation far more thoroughly than other historians, his original hypothesis is that the person who performed coronation itself was the head ("djed") of the autocephalous Church of Bosnia. believes that the different approaches in historiography on this issue were heavily influenced by national-ideological motives, political instrumentalization, and the infusion of historical events with contemporary ideas (Lovrenović 2006, 623–4).

Among the latest works, the critical synthesis *A Concise History of Serbia* by the Serbian historian Dejan Đokić is worth highlighting. In this book Đokić underlines the impact of the master national narratives and ideological assumptions concerning the interpretations of Tvrtko I's coronation, and concludes, "The location of the coronation and the denomination of the priests who conducted the ceremony are not known, but have been a matter of controversy due to the highly politicized modern debates about the origins of Bosnia and the Bosnians, so tragically manifested during the war of the 1990s" (Đokić 2023, 122). At the same time, although more cautiously, Đokić seems to adopt the Serbian viewpoint when stating that "[h]istorians have speculated, not unreasonably, that the coronation took place at the Mileševa monastery located in the 'Serbian land' that

Tvrtko had recently conquered. There are also plausible alternative arguments that the ceremony took place elsewhere and that the clergy involved may have belonged to the local Bosnian church" (Đokić 2023, 123). With this statement, Đokić for the first time among Serbian historians (even though he is not a medievalist) allowed for the possibility that the location of Tvrtko I's coronation could have been in the area of Visoko in central Bosnia. Yet, in the end, he concludes that "no one knows the right answer due to the lack of sources" (Đokić 2023, 123). It barely needs reminding that in the Middle Ages religious and identity boundaries were much more permeable than they are today; in any case, ahistorical modern projections of Tvrtko I's identity are problematic. The historiographic discourse in the last thirty years has not been grounded in an understanding of the medieval period on its own terms, but rather drew on the interpretations of historians from the nineteenth and early twentieth centuries.

Concluding Remarks

To conclude, Bosnian medieval history found itself in the middle of two growing national projects and narratives: the Croatian and the Serbian. These narratives set the stage for a historiographical war on the battlefield of the history of Bosnia, as each of them sought to appropriate medieval Bosnia as an essential component of the Serbian or the Croatian past, with their respective territorial claims. In this battle many outstanding scholars were involved, who were fluent in a variety of languages and utilized different research methodologies. Nevertheless, their interest and passion for history stemmed from service to their nation, which implied not only the cultivation of national pride, but also the demonstration of the nation's "historical rights" over the territory of Bosnia-Herzegovina, and fulfillment of what is generally understood to be the "justification" of one's own nation. The Serbian and Croatian narratives exerted significant influence beyond the field of historiography into popular culture and politics, especially due to the ambivalent religious inter-ethnic attitudes and relations during the Austro-Hungarian occupation of Bosnia and later in socialist Yugoslavia. This influence has persisted to the present day and brought its bitter fruits. More recently, these nationally colored discourses were joined by a Bosniak grand narrative, which has proven to be no less tendentious and misleading with respect to the overall understanding of the Bosnian Middle Ages. One may recall what František Graus wrote, already in 1975, in his book *Lebendige Vergangenheit*, namely that "although the past itself may be over, our view of the past can never be definitive and unambiguous, if only because the observer and his point of view are an inseparable part of its construction" (Graus 1975, VIII).

This overview presented exactly such an attempt to capture the ingrained ideological influences on the historiography of the Bosnian Middle Ages exerted by historians' perspectives on certain historical developments in various historical eras. Each era and concomitant new approaches brought unique insights and biases that reflect broader ideological contexts and currents. Some of the political and ideological perspectives that we examined were unique to a particular historical era and vanished with its end, regardless of whether they served their purpose or not. Other ideologies, most notably the national ones, have proven to be far more persistent and long-lasting, and thus more deeply ingrained in the historiography.

Graus also emphasized the significant role of history writing in the emergence of the "cultural evils" in the nineteenth and twentieth centuries, emphasizing the importance of studying how historical representations shaped by different eras and perspectives became realities. The Bosnian case is an eloquent example of historical representation becoming cultural evil. Yet this need not be so except when instrumentalized to political ends in extremely polarized situations. Having surveyed three national approaches to Bosnian medieval history we cannot but agree with Vitomir Lukić's statement that "cultures are never inherently opposed to one another. They are turned into enemies the moment they become the tool of some demonic idea" (2004, 82).

REFERENCES

Aleksov, Bojan. 2005. Adamant and Treacherous: Serbian Historians on Religious Conversions. In *Myths and Boundaries in South-Eastern Europe*, ed. Pål Kolstø, 158–190. London: Hurst & Co.

Allcock, John B. 2000. *Explaining Yugoslavia*. London: Hurst & Company.

Ančić, Mladen. 2014. Mjesto Bosne i Hercegovine u konstrukciji povijesti Dominika Mandića (Kako danas čitati djela Dominika Mandića). In *Dr. fra Dominik Mandić (1889–1973): Zbornik radova sa znanstvenog simpozija*, 867–883. Mostar.

Anđelić, Pavao. 1980. Krunidbena i grobna crkva bosanskih vladara u Milima (Arnautovićima) kod Visokog. *Glasnik Zemaljskog muzeja* 34:183–247.

Antoljak, Stjepan. 2004. *Hrvatska historiografija*. Zagreb: Matica hrvatska.

312 N. RABIĆ

Antolović, Michael. 2016. Modern Serbian Historiography between Nation-Building and Critical Scholarship: The Case of Ilarion Ruvarac (1832–1905). *The Hungarian Historical Review* 5 (2): 332–356.

Bašagić-Redžepašić, Safvet-beg. 1900. *Kratka uputa u prošlost Bosne i Hercegovine. Od g. 1463–1850.* Sarajevo: Vlastita naklada.

Basler, Đuro. 1975/76. Proglašenje Bosne kraljevinom 1377. godine. *Prilozi* 11–12: 49–61.

Bataković, Dušan T. 2014. *The Foreign Policy of Serbia (1844–1867): Ilija Garašanin's Načertanije.* Belgrade: Institute for Balkan Studies.

Behschnitt, Wolf Dietrich. 1980. *Nationalismus bei Serben und Kroaten 1830–1914. Analyse und Typologie der nationalen Ideologie.* München: R. Oldenbourg Verlag.

Benić, Bono. 2003. *Ljetopis sutješkog samostana.* Sarajevo-Zagreb: Synopsis.

Betti, Maddalena. 2013. *The Making of Christian Moravia (858–82). Papal Power and Political Reality.* Brill: Leiden-Boston.

Bijedić, Elvira. 2011. *Der Bogomilenmythos. Eine umstrittene 'historische Unbekannte' als Identitätsquelle in der Nationsbildung der Bosniaken.* Heidelberg: Südwestdeutscher Verlag für Hochschulschriften.

Blagojević, Miloš. 2010. Sima Ćirković - istoričar i akademik. *Glas Srpske akademije nauka i umetnosti* 414 (15): 249–254.

Ćirković, Sima. 1964a. *Istorija srednjovekovne bosanske države.* Beograd: Srpska kraljevska akademija.

Ćirković, Sima. 1964b. Sugubi venac: Prilog istoriji kraljevstva u Bosni. *Zbornik Filozofskog fakulteta u Beogradu* 8 (1): 343–370.

Ćirković, Sima. 1978. Metodološki problemi proučavanja srednjovekovne srpske istorije. Istorijski glasnik 1–2: 63–68.

Ćirković, Sima. 1980. Die bedeutung Jirečeks für die Geschichte der Serben un der Kroaten. In: Konstantin Jireček, sein Leben, schöpferisches Wirken und sein wissenschaftliches Erbe, ed. Snežka Panova. Wien, 51–60.

Ćirković, Sima. 2007. Rajićeva Istorija i počeci moderne srpske historiografije. In *Sima Ćirković, O istoriografiji i metodologiji*, 63–70. Istorijski institut: Beograd.

Ćorović, Vladimir. 1925. *Kralj Tvrtko I Kotromanić*, Beograd-Zemun: Srpska Kraljevska akademija.

Ćorović, Vladimir. 1940. *Historija Bosne I.* Beograd: Srpska kraljevska akademija.

Ćošković, Pejo. 2000. Ustrojstvo Crkve bosanske. In *Zbornik radova sa Znanstvenog skupa u povodu 500. obljetnice smrti Fra Anđela Zvizdovića*, ed. Marko Karamatić, 61–83. Sarajevo-Fojnica: Franjevačka teologija Sarajevo.

Ćošković, Pejo. 2005. *Crkva bosanska u XV. stoljeću.* Sarajevo: Institut za istoriju.

Ćošković, Pejo. 2010. Četvrt stoljeća historiogafije o Crkvi bosanskoj. *Radovi Filozofskog fakulteta u Sarajevu* 14 (1): 97–125.

Curta, Florin. 2006. *Southeastern Europe in the Middle Ages, 500–1250.* Cambridge: Cambridge University Press.

6 IN SEARCH OF AN ACCEPTABLE PAST: THE BOSNIAN MIDDLE AGES...   313

Dautbegović, Almaz. 1988. Uz stogodišnjicu Zemaljskog muzeja Bosne i Hercegovine u Sarajevu. In *Spomenica stogodišnjice rada Zemaljskog muzeja Bosne i Hercegovine 1888–1988*, ed. Almaz Dautbegović, 7–34. Zemaljski muzej Bosne i Hercegovine: Sarajevo.

Dautović, Dženan. 2015. Crkva bosanska: moderni historiografski tokovi, rasprave i kontroverze (2005–2015). *Historijska traganja* 15:127–160.

Dautović, Dženan. 2018. Mapiranje ideologija u historiografiji o srednjovjekovnoj Bosni. *Preporodov journal*, 208–209: 65–73.

Dautović, Dženan. 2020. Historiographic Controversy about the Crusades against Bosnian Heretics. *Journal of Balkan and Black Sea Studies* 3 (4): 63–77.

Dautović, Dženan. 2021. Regio nullius dioecesis: kako je Bosna ostala bez biskupije? Procesi i posljedice. In: *Prijelomne godine bosanskohercegovačke prošlosti* (1), ed. Sedad Bešlija. Sarajevo: Institut za historiju Univerziteta u Sarajevu, 75–92.

Denić, Čedomir. 1996. Pogledi na dela Jovana Rajića. *Zbornik Matice srpske za istoriju* 54:39–85.

Đokić, Dejan. 2023. *A Concise History of Serbia*. Cambridge–New York: Cambridge University Press.

Du Cange, Charles du Fresne. 1746. *Illyricum vetus et novum, sive historia regnorum Dalmatiae, Croatiae, Slavoniae, Bosnae, Serviae atque Bulgariae*, Posonii.

Dümmler, Ernst Ludwig. 1856. Über die älteste Geschichte der Slaven in Dalmatien (549–928). *Sitzungsberichte. Akademie der Wissenschaften in Wien, Philosophisch-Historische Klasse* 20 (8): 353–430.

Dvornik, Francis. 1964. The Significance of the Missions of Cyril and Methodius. *Slavic Review* 23 (2): 195–211.

Džaja, Srećko. 2003. Bosanska povijesna stvarnost i njezini mitološki odrazi. In *Historijski mitovi na Balkanu*, ed. Husnija Kamberović, 39–66. Zbornik radova Instituta za istoriju u Sarajevu: Sarajevo.

Džaja, Srećko. 2014. Kulturni identitet bosanskohercegovačkih Hrvata. *Povijesni profil. Bosna Franciscana* 40:21–44.

Džaja, Srećko. 2017. Bosansko-hercegovačke povijesne paradigme, nacionalni narativi i pitanje pomirbe. *Bosna Franciscana* 46:55–76.

Džaja, Srećko and . 2008–09. Dubravko. Crkva bosanska (Ni bogumilska, ni dualistička nego šizmatička i državna crkva). *Jukić* 38–39: 237–256.

Džambo, Jozo. 1991. *Die Franziskaner im mittelalterlichen Bosnien. Franziskaner Forschungen*. Werl/Westfalen: Dietrich-Coelde-Verlag.

Fessler, Ignaz Aurelius. 1816. *Die Geschichten der Ungern und ihrer Landsassen*, 3–2, Leipzig: Gleditsch.

Fine, John V. A., Jr. 1994. *The Late Medieval Balkans. A Critical Survey From the Late Century to the Ottoman Conquest*. Ann Arbor: University of Michigan Press.

Gál, Judit. 2018. Iohannes Lucius és hagyatéka = Ivan Lucic-Lucius and his heritage. *Belvedere Meridionale* 30 (1): 114–126.

314   N. RABIĆ

Geary, Patrick J. 2007. *Mit o nacijama. Srednjovekovno poreklo Evrope.* Novi Sad: Cenzura.

Gebhardi, Ludwig Albrecht. 1781. *Geschichte des Reichs Hungarn und der damit verbundenen Staaten.* Leipzig: Dritter Theil.

Gebhardi, Ludwig Albrecht. 1805. *Geschichte der Königreiche Dalmatien, Kroatien, Szlavonien, Servien, Raszien, Bosnien, Rama und des Freystaats Ragusa,* Pesth.

Georgijević, Krešimir. 1946. Kada je Jovan Rajić završio svoju istoriju. *Glas Srpske akademije nauka* 95:5–12.

Glušac, Vaso. 1924. Srednjevekovna 'bosanska crkva'. *Priloz za književnost, jezik, istoriju i folklor* 4:1–55.

Glušac, Vaso. 1953. Problem bogomilstva i pravoslavlje 'Crkve bosanske'. *Godišnjak istoriskog društva Bosne i Hercegovine* 5:105–138.

Goldstein, Ivo. 2003. Granica na Drini – Značenje i razvoj mitologema. In *Historijski mitovi na Balkanu,* 109–137. Institut za istoriju: Sarajevo.

Graus, František. 1975. *Lebendige Vergangenheit. Überlieferung im Mittelalter und in den Vorstellungen vom Mittelalter.* Köln: Böhlau

Gross, Mirjana. 1996. *Suvremena historiografija: korijeni, postignuća, traganja.* Zagreb.

Isailović, Neven. 2019. Pogled iznutra i pogled sa strane – percepcija srednjovjekovne bosanske države i njenih stanovnika u domaćim i stranim izvorima. In *Bosna i njeni susjedi: pristupi i perspektive,* ed. Elmedina Duranović, Enes Dedić, and Nedim Rabić, 33–57. Sarajevo: Institut za historiju Univerziteta u Sarajevu.

Išek, Tomislav. 2011. Izrada Napretkove Povijesti Bosne i Hercegovine. *Prilozi* 40:245–258.

Istorija srpskog naroda I. 1981, Beograd: Srpska književna zadruga.

Jalimam, Salih. 1999. *Historija bosanskih bogomila.* Tuzla: IPP Hamidović.

Jelavich, Barbara. 1983. *History of the Balkans.* Cambridge University Press.

Jelavich, Charles. 1992. *Južnoslavenski nacionalizmi. Jugoslavensko ujedinjenje i udžbenici prije 1914.* Zagreb: Globus nakladni zavod – Školska knjiga.

Jireček, Konstantin. 1978. *Istorija Srba.* I–II, Beograd: Slovo Ljubve.

Jukić, Ivan Frano. 1851. *Zemljopis i poviestnica Bosne.* Zagreb.

Kantorowicz, Ernst H. 1957. *The King's Two Bodies: A Study in Mediaeval Political Theology.* Princeton University Press.

Kapetanović Ljubušak, Mehmed-beg. 1886. "Što misle muhamedanci u Bosni" Odgovor brošuri u Lipskoj tiskanoj pod naslovom: "Sadašnjost i najbliža budućnost Bosne", Sarajevo.

Klaić, Vjekolsav. 1882. *Poviest Bosne do propasti kraljevstva.* Zagreb: Dionička tiskara.

Klaić, Vjekolsav. 1885. *Geschichte Bosniens von den ältesten Zeiten bis zum Verfalle des Königreiches.* Translated by Ivan von Bojrničić. Leipzig: Verlag von Wilhelm Friedrich.

6 IN SEARCH OF AN ACCEPTABLE PAST: THE BOSNIAN MIDDLE AGES... 315

Klaić, Vjekolsav. 1890. *Bosznia története a legrégibb kortól a királyság bukásáig*, Nagy-Becskerek, Pleitz Fer. Pál könyvnyomdája.

Klaić, Nada. 1969. Dominik Mandić, Rasprave iz stare hrvatske povijesti, Rim: Hrvatski povijesni institut, 1963. *Historijski zbornik* 21–22: 605–611.

Lastrić, Filip. 1977. *Pregled starina bosanske provincije*. Sarajevo: Veselin Masleša.

Lašvanin, Nikola. 1981. *Ljetopis*. Sarajevo: Veselin Masleša.

Lovrenović, Dubravko. 2002. Povijest i duh vremena: Tri etnonacionalna pogleda u bosansko srednjovjekovlje. *Forum Bosnae* 18:60–84.

Lovrenović, Dubravko. 2004. Dvije slike Bosne i Hercegovine. *Status* 4:82–84.

Lovrenović, Dubravko. 2006. *Na klizištu povijesti (sveta kruna ugarska i sveta kruna bosanska) 1387–1463*. Zagreb-Sarajevo: Synopsis

Lovrenović, Dubravko. 2008. Od bogumilskog mita do hegemonističkih pretenzija. In *Zbornik o Pavlu Anđeliću*, ed. Marko Karamatić, 169–303. Franjevačka teologija Sarajevo: Sarajevo.

Lovrenović, Dubravko. 2014. Kroatizacija bosanskog srednjovjekovlja u svjetlu interkonfesionalnosti stećaka. *Bosna Franciscana* 40:221–263.

Luccari, Giacomo. 1605. *Copioso ristretto degli annali di Rausa*. Venetia.

Lucius, Ioannes. 1666. *De regno Dalmatiae et Croatiae libri sex*. Amstelaedami: Ioannes Bleau.

Mailath, Johann. 1828. *Geschichte der Magyaren*, II, Wien.

Mandić, Dominik. 1960. *Bosna i Hercegovina. Povijesno-kritička istraživanja*. Chicago: The Croatian Historical Institute.

Mandić, Dominik. 1962. *Bogomilska crkva bosanskih krstjana*. Chicago: The Croatian Historical Institute.

Mandić, Dominik. 1967. *Etnička povijest Bosne i Hercegovine*. Rim: Hrvatski povijesni institut u Rimu.

Maslo, Amer. 2020. 'Bosanski lonac sjećanja': 1463. godina i konstitutivni narodi Bosne i Hercegovine. *Prilozi* 49:273–307.

Mishkova, Diana. 2011. Differentiation in Entanglement. Debates on Antiquity, Ethnogenesis and Identity in Nineteenth-Century Bulgaria. In *Multiple antiquities—Multiple Modernities: Ancient Histories in Nineteenth Century European Cultures*, ed. Gábor Klaniczay, 213–245. Frankfurt am Main: Campus–Verlag.

Mitrović, Bojan. 2017. *Nastanak moderne istorijske discipline u Srbiji i Bugarskoj*. In *Pretpostavke, teze, polemike (1878–1918)*. Novi Sad: Akademska knjiga.

Orbin, Mavar. 1968. *Kraljevstvo Slovena*. Translated by Zdravko Šundrica and edited by M. Pantić, R. Samardžić, F. Barišić, and S. Ćirković. Beograd: Srpska književna zadruga.

Orbini, Mauro. 1601. *Il Regno degli Slavi*, Pesaro.

Orbini, Mauro. 1999. *Kraljevstvo Slavena*. Translated by Snježana Husić and edited by Franjo Šanjek. Zagreb: Golden marketing and Narodne novine.

316 N. RABIĆ

Perojević, Marko. 1942. *Povijest hrvatskih zemalja Bosne i Hercegovine od najstarijih vremena do godine 1463*, 196–592. Sarajevo: Hrvatsko kulturno društvo Napredak.

Pesic, Vesna. 1996. *Serbian Nationalism and the Origins of the Yugoslav Crisis.* Washington, DC: United States Institute of Peace.

Petranović, Božidar. 1867. *Bogomili. Crъkva bosanska i krstjani. Istorička rasprava*, Zadar.

Pilar, Ivo. 1990. *Južnoslavensko pitanje. Prikaz cjelokupnog pitanja*, Varaždin.

Povijest hrvatskih zemalja Bosne i Hercegovine od najstarijih vremena do godine 1463. 1942. Sarajevo: Hrvatsko kulturno društvo Napredak.

Rački, Franjo. 1869a. Bogomili i patareni. *Rad Jugoslavenske akademije znanosti i umjetnosti* 7:84–179.

Rački, Franjo. 1869b. Bogomili i patareni. *Rad Jugoslavenske akademije znanosti i umjetnosti* 8:121–187.

Rački, Franjo. 1870. Bogomili i patareni. *Rad Jugoslavenske akademije znanosti i umjetnosti* 10:160–263.

Radojčić, Nikola. 1948. *Obred krunisanja bosanskog kralja Tvrtka I. Prilog istoriji krunisanja srpskih vladara u srednjem veku.* Beograd: Srpska akademija nauka.

Radojčić, Nikola. 1952. *Srpski istoričar Jovan Rajić.* Beograd: Srpska akademija nauka.

Radojčić, Nikola. 1960. Die wichtigsten Darstellungen der Geschichte Bosniens. *Südost-Forschungen* 19:146–163.

Ragnina, Nicola. 1883. *Annales ragusini anonymi item Nicolai de Ragnina.* Edited by Natko Nodilo, Zagreb: Jugoslavenska akademija znanosti i umjetnosti.

Rajić, Jovan. 1794–95. *Historija raznih slavenskih narodov, najpače Bolgar, Horvatov i Serbov* I–IV, Vienna: Stefan Novaković.

Restii, Junii. 1893. *Chronica Ragusina Junii Restii item Joanis Gundulae.* Edited by Natko Nodilo. Zagreb: Jugoslavenska akademija znanosti i umjetnosti.

Šanjek, Franjo. 1975. *Bosansko-humski krstjani i katarsko-dualistički pokret u srednjem vijeku.* Zagreb: Kršćanska sadašnjost.

Šanjek, Franjo. 2014. Profesorica Nada Klaić kao integralni povjesničar. In Nada Klaić i njezin znanstveni i nastavni doprinos razvoju historiografije. edited by Tomislav Galović and Damir Agičić, Zagreb: Hrvatski nacionalni odbor za povijesne znanosti (HNOPZ) - Društvo za hrvatsku povjesnicu - Filozofski fakultet Sveučilišta u Zagrebu - FF Press: 49–57.

Schimek, Maximilian. 1787. *Politische Geschichte des Königreichs Bosnien und Rama vom Jahre 867 bis 1741*, Wien.

Šidak, Jaroslav. 1937. Problem 'bosanske crkve' u našoj historiografiji od Petranovića do GluŠca. *Rad Jogslavenske akademije znanosti i umijetnosti* 259 (116): 37–182.

Šidak, Jaroslav. 1977. Heretička 'Crkva bosanska'. *Slovo* 27:149–184.

6 IN SEARCH OF AN ACCEPTABLE PAST: THE BOSNIAN MIDDLE AGES... 317

Šišić, Ferdo. 1925. *Povijest Hrvata u vrijeme narodnih vladara*. Zagreb: Nakladni zavod Matice hrvatske.

Slišković, Slavko. 2020. Kako je Strossmayer vidio Bosnu i Hercegovinu. *Zbornik Odsjeka za povijesne znanosti Zavoda za povijesne i društvene znanosti Hrvatske akademije znanosti i umjetnosti* 38:115–145.

Stanojević, Stanoje. 1908. *Istorija srpskog naroda*. Beograd: Geca Kon.

Steindorff, Ludwig. 2007. *Kroatien: vom Mittelalter bis zur Gegenwart*. Regensburg: Pustet.

Stoyanov, Yuri. 2005. Between Heresiology and Political Theology: The Rise of the Paradigm of the Medieval Heretical 'Bosnian Church'. In: Teologie politiche. Modelli a confronto, ed. Giovanni Filoramo. Brescia, 163–180.

Sundhaussen, Holm. 1982. *Geschichte Jugoslawiens 1918–1980*. Stuttgart: Kohlhammer.

Teinović, Bratislav. 2016. Bosanski franjevci između Gaja i Garašanina (1836–1849)–suprotnosti dvije nacionalne politike. *Historijska traganja 15*:31–91.

Thallóczy, Lajos. 1906. Istraživanja o postanku bosanske banovine sa naročitim obzirom na povelje körmendskog arkiva. *Glasnik Zemaljskog muzeja* 18 (4): 401–444.

Vaillant, André. 1974. Les »chretiens« bosniaques. In: *Melanges de l'histoire des religions offerts a Ch. H. Puech*, Paris, 525–530.

Valentić, Mirko. 1961. Koncepcije Garašaninova 'Načertanija' (1844). *Historijski pregled* VII-2:18–27.

Vukićević, Milenko. 1906. *Program spoljne politike Srbije na koncu 1844. god*, Delo 38. Beograd.

Wehler, Hans-Ulrich. 2001. *Nationalismus: Geschichte, Formen, Folgen*. München: C.H. Beck.

Wenzel, Marian. 1996. Povijest Bosne i austrougarska politika: Zemaljski muzej u Sarajevu i bogumilska romansa. *Ersamvs 15*:68–71.

Živković, Tibor. 2010. On the Beginnings of Bosnia in the Middle Ages. *Godišnjak Centra za balkanološka ispitivanja* 39:149–161.

Index[1]

A

Aaron (brother of Tsar Samuel), 69, 77, 83
Achillius (Saint), 184
Adashinskaya, Anna, 200–202
Adrianople (Edirne), 86
Adriatic coast, 280, 303
Adriatic Sea, 224, 291
Ahmeti, Ali, 148
Albania/Albanian(s), 8, 10, 13, 26, 27, 31, 35, 57, 59, 61, 72, 74, 75, 81, 87, 91, 93, 105–154, 177, 178n19, 186, 206, 207, 219–264
Aleksov, Bojan, 302
Alexander the Great, 33, 39, 43n29, 239
Alexius Slav, 209
Alfonso V, 129
Ali Tepelena, 239, 252
Allcock, John B., 279
Anastasiević, Dragutin, 64

Anatolia, 174
Anđelić, Pavao, 305, 309
Andrea, Zhaneta, 232, 239, 243
Andronikos II Palaiologos, 179
Antoljak, Stjepan, 86–90, 92, 283–285
Apostolidis, Kosmas Myrtilos, 210
Appian (of Alexandria), 243
Aragon, 129
Arbanasi, 186
Arbëreshs (Italian-Albanians), 111, 137, 138
Argondizza, Francesco, 130
Armenia/Armenians, 54, 55, 57, 58, 74, 75, 87, 88, 93, 174
Arnautovići (village near Sarajevo), 305, 309
Arta, city of, 174, 222
Asenovgrad/Stenimachos, 176, 188, 189, 195, 209
Asia Minor, 225, 236
Assemani, J. S., 281
Assisi, 202

---

[1] Note: Page numbers followed by 'n' refer to notes.

© The Author(s), under exclusive license to Springer Nature Switzerland AG 2025
D. Mishkova, R. Daskalov (eds.), *Balkan Historiographical Wars*,
https://doi.org/10.1007/978-3-031-90113-3

319

320 INDEX

Athens, 42, 110, 112–115, 163, 166,
168, 172, 177, 196
Attica, 168, 249
Austria-Hungary/Austro-Hungarian
Empire, Austro-Hungarian(s),
106, 120, 121, 149, 178n19,
224, 225, 277, 278, 288, 306
Avars, 246

B

Babinger, Franz, 127, 130, 139, 153
Bachkovo, 195, 204
Balkan range (Stara planina), 61,
62, 67, 72
Balkans/Balkan states, 1–43, 219,
221–223, 225, 226, 229, 230,
233, 240, 246, 248, 249, 251,
255, 256, 258–260, 276, 279,
286, 287, 293, 298
Balli Kombëtar, 139
Balş, Gheorghe, 194
Balsha/Balšić family, 237, 240
Banat, 182
Barić, Henrik, 122
Barletius, Marinus, 112, 115–118,
127, 129, 146
Bašagić-Redžepašić, Safvet-beg,
300, 301
Basil II, the Bulgar-Slayer(Byzantine
emperor), 51, 56, 58, 67–69, 71,
81, 83, 85, 90, 95–97, 176,
197, 202
Basilica of Saint Achillius, 197
Basler, Đuro (Juraj Kujundžić), 309
Beci, Bahri, 249, 251
Beissinger, Mark, 3–5, 4n2, 4n3
Belasitsa mountain, 51
Belgium, 187
Belgrade, 118, 122, 128, 129, 148,
164, 172, 191, 194, 277, 285n2
Belić, Aleksandar, 191, 201

Benić, Bono, 304
Berende, 187, 192
Berlin, 113, 182
Biçoku, Kasëm, 140, 144, 153,
240, 249–252
Biemmi, Giammaria, 118, 127, 130,
133, 146
Bitola/Manastir, 113
inscription, 54, 58, 71–73, 96
vilayet of, 223
Black Sea, 185, 190
Blagoevgrad, 97
Boeotia, 249
Boia, Lucian, 30
Boris I (prince of Bulgaria), 184, 196,
197, 292
Boris II (Tsar of Bulgaria), 68,
69, 71, 72
Boškoski, Milan, 90–92
Bošković, Đurđe, 189, 192, 193, 206
Bosnia and Herzegovina, 207, 224,
276–278, 285, 287–291, 294,
295, 299, 300, 302, 306, 307, 310
Bosnia/Bosniaks, 10, 12–14, 30, 31,
37, 41, 41n28, 275–278,
280–310, 285n2
Bosnian *banate*/Bosnian kingdom,
287, 289, 300, 301, 304, 307
Bošnjak, Slavoljub (Jukić, Ivan
Franjo), 304
Boston, 123, 132
Bougarel, Xavier, 12, 13
Boyana, 187, 192, 199–201, 208, 209
Bozhilov, Ivan, 75–77
Bozhkov, Atanas, 206n42, 208
Brandi, Efthim, 113–115
Brescia, 118
Brunnbauer, Ulf, 33, 36, 40
Buda, Aleks, 131–136, 138–140, 151,
153, 154, 223, 226, 230, 235,
236, 239, 240, 243, 245, 246,
249, 251–254, 260

INDEX 321

Bujanovac/Bujanoci, 228
Bulgaria/Bulgarians/Bulgars, 8n7, 9,
   12, 26, 27, 29–33, 35, 37, 39,
   40, 55–57, 59, 66, 67, 72–74,
   76, 80, 81, 83, 86, 98, 111, 114,
   137, 161–211, 224, 227, 228,
   231, 232, 235, 237, 238, 240,
   248, 249, 257, 259, 261, 284,
   286, 290–293
Bulgarian Durostorum
   Patriarchate, 59, 60
Burebista (Dacian king), 29
Bury, John B., 293
Bushati family, 239, 252
Byzantium/Byzantine (Eastern Roman)
   Empire, 7–10, 8n7, 12, 14, 18, 35,
   164–166, 169, 182, 183,
   199–201, 204, 210, 293, 308

C
Çabej, Ekrem, 247–249, 251
Carol I, 166n6
Carr, Edward H., 22
Časlav Klonimirović, 287, 292, 293
Cathars, 296, 297
Chameria, region of, 227, 228, 235
Charlemagne (Charles the Great), 63, 88
Chatzimichali, Angeliki, 210
Cherven, 208
Chicago, 289, 294
Ćirković, Sima, 282, 284, 285, 298,
   303, 308, 309
Clement of Ohrid, disciple of Cyril
   and Methodius, 32, 79, 98, 205
Cluj, 129
Constantine VII Porphyrogennetos
   (Byzantine emperor), 91, 92,
   291, 292
Constantinople, 71, 82, 86, 93, 172,
   174, 175, 182, 187, 189, 190,
   195, 199, 204, 205, 296

Coquelle, Pierre, 116
Cordignano, Fulvio, 235
Ćorović, Vladimir, 122, 303, 305, 306
Ćošković, Pejo, 295, 296, 298
Cotmeana, 190
Croatia/Croats, 13, 26, 41, 42, 87,
   93, 207, 276–278, 280, 284,
   288–295, 297–299, 301, 302,
   306, 307
Curta, Florin, 96
Curtea de Argeş, 194
Cutolo, Alessandro, 130
Cvijić, Jovan, 122, 193, 254
Cyril and Methodius of Thessaloniki,
   inventors of the Slavic (Glagolitic)
   alphabet, 32, 79, 98, 170, 170n12,
   204, 205, 206n42, 298, 298n3
Czechia, 206n42
Czernovitch (Crnojević),
   Skanderbeg, 117

D
Dalmatia, 39n24, 280, 287, 289–291
Dani, Doan, 134, 140, 147, 150
Danube, 61, 62, 67, 72, 73, 86, 291
Dardania
   kingdom of, 233
   Roman province of, 246
Dardanians, 233, 243, 246
Debar, 222
Dečani, 201
Dečanski, Stefan Uroš III, 168
Deljan, Petăr, 92
Demus, John, 139
Deroko, Aleksandar, 206, 207
Desislava (founder of the Boyana
   Church), 201
Dibra, 140
Diehl, Charles, 195
Dimitrov, Bozhidar, 33
Dimitrov, Strašimir, 138

322 INDEX

Dimitsas, Margaritis, 113, 114, 173
Djordjević, Jovan, 118
Dobrudja, 177n18, 180, 221, 235
Dodbiba, Lirak, 248
Đokić, Dejan, 309, 310
Dölger, Franz, 84
Donja Kamenica, 190, 193, 200
Dragoumis, Nicolaos, 109, 110
Dragutin, Stefan, 303
Drama (city), 180, 181
Drinov, Marin, 53, 57, 58, 60,
    61, 64, 293
Dubrovnik, 207, 280, 286, 291
Du Cange, Charles du Fresne, 281
Duccio, 199, 200
Ducellier, Alain, 250, 253
Duklja, 286, 287, 293
    principality of, 246–247, 250
Dümmler, Ernst Ludwig, 292
Duponcet, Jean Nicolas, 108
Durand, U., 281
Durostorum (today's Silistra), 69
Dušan, Stefan (King of Serbia),
    192n34, 240, 286, 303, 305
Duychev, Ivan, 166, 181, 198,
    200, 200n39
Dyrrachium (Dyrrachion, today's
    Durrës, Albania), 61

E
East Central Europe, 36
Eastern Europe, 3, 36
Edirne, 179
Egro, Dritan, 144, 145, 238
Egypt, 114, 249
Elbasan, 132
Emathia, 112
Epirus, 31, 61, 82, 112, 187
    Epirotes, 112, 224, 227, 233, 242
    New Epirus, Roman province,
        243, 246
    Northern, 225, 235, 243, 246

Old Epirus, Roman province,
    243, 246
    Southern, 219, 226, 228, 230,
        232, 235
Erdoğan, Recep Tayyip, 11
Ermenji, Abas, 139
Europe/European, 13, 18n9, 19n11,
    26, 36, 42, 106, 108–110, 119,
    126, 129, 131, 139, 142, 144,
    145, 148, 149, 151–153
Eutychios (painter), 202

F
Fallmerayer, Jakob Philipp, 8, 110,
    112, 113, 115
Fatih, Sultan, 136
Feraj, Hysamedin, 145, 149
Ferjančić, Božidar, 77
Ferluga, Jadran, 56, 67–69, 71, 77
Fessler, Ignaz Aurelius, 283
Filov, Bogdan, 168n8, 178–187,
    186n31, 189, 194, 198, 199,
    203, 207, 209, 210
Fojnica, 281
France/French, 107–110, 116, 117,
    126–129, 138, 139, 173, 176, 195
Franks, 62, 63
Frashëri, Kristo, 131–133, 136–138,
    140–147, 153, 154, 231, 233,
    239, 244, 247, 250, 251, 258, 260
Frashëri, (Shemseddin) Sami, 225, 249

G
Garašanin, Ilija, 284, 285
Garašanin, Milutin, 235, 244
Gargova, Fani, 178, 178n20
Gaul (Gallia), 88
Geary, Patrick J., 96, 279
Gebhardi, Ludwig Albrecht, 281, 282
Gegaj, Athanase (Athanas), 125–130,
    133, 136

INDEX 323

George II Balsha, 260
Georgia, 174
German (patriarch of Bulgaria), 197
German (village), 52, 58, 93, 179, 190, 196, 197
Germanos (patriarch of Constantinople), 197
Germany/Germans, 107, 109, 110, 113, 116, 117, 119, 127, 129, 130, 135, 138, 141, 153, 174n16, 177–180, 182, 190, 196, 197, 199, 291
Gibbon, Edward, 153
Giotto, 199, 200, 202
Gjinari, Jorgji, 232, 251
Glušac, Vaso, 297
Gökalp, Ziya, 127
Gostivar, 222
Grabar, André, 186, 199–201
Gračanica, 189, 193, 201
Graus, František, 310, 311
Graz, 122, 128
Great Britain, 106
Greece/Greeks, 8, 8n7, 9, 20, 26, 28, 31, 33–37, 39, 40, 40n25, 42, 43, 54, 61, 81, 95, 108–115, 119, 121, 131, 149, 151, 152, 162–168, 166n7, 172, 174–176, 179–181, 183, 185, 188, 190, 195–198, 197n38, 202–205, 209, 210, 222, 224–227, 235, 236, 242, 245, 257, 258
Greiderer, V., 281
Grigorovich, Viktor, 171
Grozdanov, Cvetan, 204–206
Gyuzelev, Vasil, 74, 75, 77, 97

H
Habsburg Empire, 11
Habsburg Monarchy, *see* Austria-Hungary

Hahn, Johann Georg von, 109, 110, 112, 113, 123
Halsall, Guy, 96
Hammer, von, 113
Harduin, J., 281
Helena (Empress of Serbia), 192n34
Herzeg-Bosnia, 278
Herzegovina, 14, 37, 41, 111, 276–278, 285–295, 299, 300, 302, 306, 307, 310
Herzfeld, Michael, 8, 20, 21
Hilandar, 139
Hirt, Hermann, 235
Hobsbawn, Eric, 19, 19n11, 20, 20n12
Hopf, Carl, 109, 110, 112, 113, 115–118, 123
Hoxha, Enver, 132, 143, 151, 238
Hrvoje Vukčić Hrvatinić (Bosnian duke), 307
Hum, 303
Hungary/Hungarians, 105, 129, 278, 290, 291, 293, 302, 304, 305
Hunyadi, Jean, 118

I
Ignjatović, Aleksandar, 164, 165, 189, 191–195, 201, 207
Illyrians, 27, 31, 39n24
Illyricum, 289, 290
Inalcik, Halil, 136–138
Innocent III (Pope), 83, 93
Iorga, Nicolae, 9, 115, 120, 128–130, 194
Ireček, Konstantin, 234, 258, 259
Istria, 291
Italia/Italians, 105–107, 109, 118–120, 124, 126, 128–130, 137
Italy/Italians, 173, 201, 206n42, 209, 225, 227, 228, 235, 242, 246, 264

324 INDEX

Ivan Alexander, 186, 200
Ivan Asen II (King of Bulgaria), 240
Ivan of Aragon (medieval franciscian
    monk), 305
Ivanov, Yordan, 54, 55, 173, 178,
    178n19, 189n33, 196, 197, 206
Ivanova (-Mavrodinova), Vera, 189n33
Ivanovo, 200

J

Janina (Ioannina), vilayet of, 223
Jazexhi, Olsi, 150
Jireček, Constantin (or Konstantin),
    115, 116, 120, 169n10, 286,
    287, 293
Joannes VI Kantakouzenos (Byzantine
    emperor), 92
Joannes Geometres, 95
John (metropolitan bishop), 203
John of Rila, 205n41
John or Joannes (Ivan) Vladislav (ruler
    of Bulgaria), 54, 58,
    71–73, 80, 96
Jokl, Norbert, 237, 248
Jovanović, Aleksandar, 193
Jukić, Ivan Franjo (Slavoljub
    Bošnjak), 304
Justiniana Prima/First
    Justiniana, 56, 91

K

Kaçanik/Kačanik, 227
Kačić-Miošić, Andrija, 117
Kadare, Ismail, 142
Kaldellis, Anthony, 96
Kállay, Benjamin, 299
Kaloyan/Kaloiannes (Tsar of
    Bulgaria), 80, 83, 93
Kamberović, Husnija, 42
Kamenica, 227

Kanitz, Felix, 163n3
Kantorowicz, Ernst H., 304
Kapetanović Ljubušak, Mehmed-
    beg, 299–301
Karadžić, Vuk Stefanović, 284
Karavangelis, Germanos, 176
Kastoria/Kostur, 168, 174, 176, 185,
    190, 195, 197, 198, 204n40, 205
Kastriot, family, 110, 149
Kedrin, 58
Kičevo, 222
Kiel, Machiel, 167, 168, 172, 186,
    197n38, 205n41, 208, 209
Klaić, Nada, 295
Klaić, Vjekoslav, 285, 291, 295,
    304, 306
Kleidion, pass, 51
Klyuch, 51
Knjaževac, 193
Kocaqi, Elena, 238
Koliqi, Ernest, 137
Kolubara River, 62
Kondakov, Nikodim, 172
Korça, 222
Korça, Xhevat, 120–123, 153
Korçë, 113, 123, 132
Kosovo, 13, 14, 26, 31, 32, 37, 117,
    131, 134, 137, 142, 145, 147,
    148, 151, 175, 177, 178, 189,
    205, 206, 287
    autonomous province of, 255
    region of, 221, 228, 233, 234, 236,
        237, 249, 262
    vilayet of, 223
Kostallari, Androkli, 232
Kotkin, Stephen, 3–5, 4n2, 4n3
Kotor, 303
Kotromanić dynasty, 302, 303
Kovačević, Ljubomir, 293
Kremikovtsi, 192
Kriva Palanka, 191
Krujë, 120

INDEX 325

Krum, Bulgar Khan, 86
Kruševac, 188
Kuçi, Ali, 124–127
Kujundžić, Juraj (Đuro Basler), 309
Kulin, 296, 304
Kumanovo, 168, 178
Kyustendil/Velbăzhd, 167, 168, 207

L

Laconia, 174
Larissa, 82
Lastrić, Filip, 304
Lašvanin, Nikola, 281, 304
Lazarević family, 260
Lecomte du Nouÿ, André, 166n6
Leipzig, 113
Leitsch, Walter, 27
Lemieux, Cyril, 106
Leo (Archbishop), 184, 185
Leonardo (da Vinci), 199
Leo the Deacon, 91, 95
Lesnovo, 201
Lezhë, 150
Liège, 187
Lim river, 303
Ljubić, Šime, 115, 285
Ljušić, Radoš, 34
Louis I of Anjou, 305
Louvain, 128
Lovrenović, Dubravko, 278, 291, 293,
  294, 296–298, 301, 305,
  309, 311
Lowenthal, David, 17, 22–25, 23n15,
  24n16, 29, 30n20, 34, 36
Lubonja, Fatos, 142, 145, 146,
  151, 238
Lucić, Ivan, 280
Luka, Kolë, 231, 250
Lukarević, Jakov, 280, 281
Lukas, Filip, 292
Lukić, Vitomir, 311

M

Macedonia/Macedonians/
  Macedonian Slavs, 112, 113,
  131, 147, 148, 161–211,
  287, 291
People's Republic of, (Republic of)
  North, Macedonians, 13, 26,
  27, 31–33, 35, 38–43, 39n23,
  39n24, 40n25, 41n26,
  43n29, 239
Western, 227, 228, 232, 237, 239,
  242, 243, 249, 250
Madara, 208
Madgearu, Alexandru, 15
Magarašević, Georgije, 302
Mailath, Johann, 283
Makušev, Vikentij, 109, 115–118, 135
Manastir, see Bitola/Manastir
Mandić, Dominik, 289, 293–295
Manuel Panselinos, 202
Marinesco/Marinescu, Constantin,
  126, 129
Martene, E., 281
Mati, area, 250
Matka Canyon, 203
Mavrodinov, Nikola, 187–194,
  189n32, 189n33, 199–202,
  207, 211
Mavrodinova, Lilyana, 200
Medova Bay, 224
Medveđa/Medvegja, 228
Melnik/Meleniko, 167, 209
Merxhani, Branko, 127, 146
Mesopotamia, 174
Meteora, 168, 176
Methodius (brother of Cyril,
  inventors of the Slavic
  alphabet), 79, 98
Meyer, Gustav, 235
Michael Astrapas, 202
Michael of Devol, 58
Mihail III Shishman, 168, 178, 190

326 INDEX

Mihai Viteazul (Prince of Wallachia and Moldavia), 240
Mihov, Milen, 94
Milan, 130
Mileševa (Orthodox monastery), 305, 309
Miliarakis, Antonios, 112–114
Mili/Mile (medieval town, Arnautovići near Sarajevo), 303, 305, 309
Millet, Gabriel, 173–176, 182–187, 189–191, 194, 199–201, 203, 206
Milosavljević, Olivera, 148
Milutin, Stefan Uroš II, 178, 189
Milutinović, Dragutin, 164
Milyukov, Pavel, 172, 197
Mircea the Elder, 194
Misirkov, Krste, 39
Mitrovica, 227
Miyatev, Krăstyu, 171n14, 200, 208, 209
Mljet, 280
Moesia/Moesians, 53, 57, 64, 72, 80, 81, 85, 91, 93, 95
Moldavia, 194
  principality of, 9, 240
Montenegro/Montenegrin(s), 37, 106, 111, 116, 126, 149, 177, 207, 222, 224–226, 228, 236, 239, 246, 250, 262
Monti, Gennaro Maria, 130
Morava, 168, 188, 189, 189n33, 193, 194, 206
Moschopolis/Voskopojë, 205
Moscow, 108
Mostar, 293, 306
Mount Athos, 168, 171, 176, 192, 198, 205, 207, 210
Moutsopoulos, Nikolaos, 197
Munich, 162
Musachi, family, 115
Mustilli, Domenico, 227, 242

Mutafchiev, Petăr, 9, 53–55, 57, 60, 64, 184n29
Mutafov, Chavdar, 168, 169
Mystras, 168, 209

N

Nagyszentmiklós, 182
Naples, Kingdom of, 105, 129
Napoleon Bonaparte, 288, 289
Naum (of Ohrid), disciple of Cyril and Methodius, 32, 98, 205
Nemanja, Stefan, 288
Nemanjić dynasty, 288
Nerezi, 202, 204
Nesebăr/Mesimvria/Mesembria, 168, 176, 183, 184, 188, 190, 195, 196, 209
Nicephorus Bryennius (or Nikephoros Bryennios), 68
Nicola of Damascus, 243
Nikephoros Gregoras, 92
Nikola (father of Tsar Samuel), 79
Nish, 255, 262
Njegoš, Petar II Petrović, 176
Noli, Fan (Theofan), 122–136, 151, 153, 154
Novaković, Stojan, 60, 61, 74
Novi Pazar, 250

O

Oakeshott, Michael, 27
Obradović, Dositej, 284
Odessa, 110
Ohly, Kurt, 130
Ohrid, 53, 56, 57, 60, 61, 63–65, 68, 69, 73, 79, 87, 89, 91, 95, 113, 168, 170, 171n13, 173, 174, 179, 181, 183–185, 190, 201, 202, 205, 207
  lake of, 225, 226
  town of, 222

INDEX 327

Orbini, Mauro, 280, 281, 305, 306
Orlandos, Anastasios, 197, 198
Orthodoxy/Orthodox, 106, 115,
    128, 149
Ostrogorski, Georgi (George), 56,
    65–68, 74, 76, 77, 88
Ottoman Empire/Ottomans, 6–8,
    10–15, 18, 30, 34n21, 37, 39,
    41, 105, 107–109, 111–114,
    116, 117, 120, 122, 127, 134,
    136, 137, 139, 144–146, 149,
    150, 152, 153, 220, 222, 223,
    236, 238, 239, 249, 252,
    255–263, 277, 280–282, 286,
    287, 289, 290, 296, 299–301,
    304, 307
Özal, Turgut, 14

P
Padua, 132
Paganel, Camille, 109, 112, 115
Pagania (Neretva), 293
Palermo, 137, 138
Pall, Francisc, 129, 130, 153
Panaitescu, Petre, 57
Panitsa, Todor, 180
Panov, Branko, 88–90, 92–94
Panov, Mitko, 84, 88, 92, 94–97
Papadopoulos-Vretos, Andreas, 109,
    110, 115
Paparrigopoulos, Constantine
    (Konstantin), 8, 37, 39,
    108–114, 164
Papazoglu, Fanula, 235
Paris, 108, 116, 126, 128, 162,
    191, 199
Pastor, Ludwig von, Louis, 116, 117
Patarens, 297
Patsch, Carl, 121
Paul, Walter, 96
Pauler, Julius, 293
Pauli, Carl, 235

Peć, 201
Pechenegs, 80
Pejačević, Franjo Ksaver, 282, 283
Pelasgians, 111, 114
Pelekanidis, Stylianos, 197, 197n38,
    198, 210
Peloponnese/Peloponnesus, 61, 173,
    187, 192, 249
Perdrizet, Paul, 167
Perojević, Marko, 308
Peter I (Tsar of Bulgaria), 52, 55,
    59–61, 63, 65, 67–69, 71–73, 80,
    84, 86, 87, 91, 92
Petković, Vladimir, 191–193, 201–203
Petranović, Božidar, 296, 297, 301
Petrich, 97
Petrides, 112
Petrov, Petăr, 77, 78
Petrović, Leon, 292
Petrović, Predrag R., 149
Philip II (King of Macedonia),
    39, 40, 239
Pilar, Ivo (L. V. Südland), 292, 297
Pipa, Arshi, 10, 238
Pirin, 167
Pirivatrić, Srđan, 69–75, 77, 78
Pisani, Paul (Abbé), 116, 117
Pisko, Julius, 116
Plasari, Aurel, 149
Plav/Plavë, 225
Pliny the Elder, 242
Pliska/Aboba, 169, 170, 170n11,
    177n18, 182, 208
Plovdiv/Philippoupoli, 210
Poganovo, 191, 193, 200
Pollo, Stefanaq, 230, 232, 239
Popović, Jovan Sterija, 118
Popovski, Petar, 148
Popstoilov, Anton, 179n22
Prandis, Efthimios, *see* Brandi, Efthim
Preševo/Presheva, 228
Preslav, 61, 70, 73, 79, 170, 188,
    190, 208

328 INDEX

Prespa/Prespa lake, 58, 61, 73, 168,
170, 179, 183, 184, 190,
195–198, 205
Prevalitania (Roman province),
243, 246
Prijepolje, 305
Prilep, 168, 178, 186, 203
Prishtina, Hasan (bey), 231
Prishtinë/Prishtina/Priština, 137,
138, 147, 189
Prizren, 250
Prokić, Božidar, 53–57, 61–63, 77
Protich, Andrey, 187, 192, 195, 198,
201, 209
Psača, 191
Psellos, Michael, 69, 71
Pulaha, Selami, 138, 253,
258, 260–263
Pulevski, Gjorgjija, 39

R
Rački, Franjo, 285, 290, 294,
296–298, 304, 308
Radojčić, Nikola, 282, 284, 308
Radonić, Jovan, 118, 122, 129
Ragnina, Nicolas, 280
Rajić, Jovan, 282–284
Ranke, Leopold von, 117
Raphael, 202
Rashenov, Aleksandăr, 187, 191, 208
Raška, 168, 175, 189, 193, 205, 206,
284, 286, 305
Rastić, Junije, 280
Raynaldi, Odoric, 281
Renđeo, Ivan, 292
Rhomios, 74–76, 87
Rila, 193
Ripsimia (mother of Tsar Samuel), 54
Ristovski, Blaže, 88, 89, 92
Roman (son of Tsar Peter),
51, 55, 59

Romania/Romanians/Aromanians, 9,
10, 12, 15, 26, 27, 29, 30, 32,
37, 108, 109, 111, 115,
119–121, 126, 129, 164, 166n6,
169, 170, 177n18, 181, 189,
190, 194, 194n35, 195
Romanos I Lekapenos (Byzantine
emperor), 84
Rome/Roman empire, 9, 26, 74, 129,
130, 137, 246, 278, 289, 294,
296, 298
Roth, Klaus, 120
Roudometof, Victor, 24, 25, 40
Rousseva, Ralitsa, 181, 206n42
Ruskin, John, 162
Russia/Russians, 106–109, 111, 115,
135, 163, 170–173, 190, 192,
195, 206n42, 225, 284
Ruvarac, Ilarion, 117, 118, 285, 286

S
Saadeddin, 116
Salines (Sol, Tuzla), 292
Salzburg, 132
Samuel/Samuil (Tsar of Bulgaria), 32,
40, 51–53, 55–91, 93–98, 100,
170, 171n13, 179, 183, 184,
196–198, 201, 205, 240
San Stefano (Yeşilköy), 222, 237
Sarajevo, 285, 291, 299, 307
Schimek, Maximilian, 281, 282
Schmidt, Fyodor, 182
Schmitt, Oliver Jens, 106, 124,
141–145, 147, 148, 153, 154
Scythians, 85, 91, 95
Selishchev, Afanasy, 248, 254
Serbia/Serbians/Serbs, 8n7, 13, 14,
26, 28, 34, 35, 41, 42, 57, 59,
61–64, 74, 75, 87, 88, 91, 93,
111, 115, 117, 118, 120, 139,
148, 149, 151, 152, 163–166,

163n3, 168, 168n8, 169, 173,
175, 177, 187, 188, 189n33,
191–193, 195, 203, 204, 206,
207, 220, 224–226, 229,
234–238, 250, 255–262,
275–278, 280, 282–289,
291–293, 297, 299,
302–306, 308–310
Serres, 180, 181
Sevast'yanov, Pyotr, 171
Shamardzhiev, Yanaki, 168
Shkodër, 115, 118, 120, 124,
126–128, 147, 207
Shkurti, Spiro, 254
Šibenik, 296
Šidak, Jaroslav, 295–298
Simeon I (King of Bulgaria)/Simeon
the Great (Tsar of Bulgaria), 55,
59–63, 65, 68, 69, 73, 75, 76,
84, 87, 170, 200, 240
Sirdani, Marin, 125
Široki Brijeg, 293
Sís, Vladimír, 180
Šišić, Ferdo, 278, 286, 292, 293
Skanderbeg, 240, 241, 251, 254,
259, 264
Skopje, 42, 43n29, 77, 82, 86, 93,
147, 168, 178, 188, 202,
203, 207
city of, 222, 240
Škorpil, Hermenegild, 169n10
Škorpil, Karel, 169, 169n10, 177n18,
178, 188
Skylitzes, Joannes, 58
Slavonia, 291
Slavs/South Slavs, 106, 113, 116,
117, 228, 230, 231, 234, 244,
247, 248, 251, 255, 256, 258,
259, 261, 279, 280, 283, 286,
287, 289, 290, 295, 297, 298n3,
301, 304, 306
Slijepčević, Pero, 201

Slovenes/Slavenes, 89
Slovenia, 288
Smičiklas, Tadija, 285
Snegarov, Ivan, 56, 60, 63, 64, 69
Sofia, 42, 164–167, 172, 178, 179,
181, 186, 187, 191, 196,
198, 199
Sotiriou, Georgios, 196
Southeastern Europe, 7, 36, 276, 279
Soviet Union, 131, 136
Srećković, Pantelija, 117
Srem, 287
Sremski Karlovci, 117, 205
Stadtmüller, Georg, 129, 153,
250, 254
Stanojević, Stanoje, 278, 287,
288, 293
Starčević, Ante, 291
Staro Nagoričane, 178, 189n32,
202, 203
Stipčević, Aleksandar, 235
Stjepan II Kotromanić, 303
Stobi, 177
Stojanović, Dubravka, 26, 28, 34
Strossmayer, Josip Juraj, 290
Struga, 222
Strzygowski, Josef, 162n2, 174,
174n16, 178n20, 182, 195
Südland, L. V. (Ivo Pilar), 297
Šufflay, Milan, 115, 234
Sulstarova, Enis, 149
Sveta Petka, 118
Sviatoslav (Prince of Kievan Rus), 87
Syra, 110

T
Tafrali, Orest, 194
Tăpkova, Vasilka, 231
Tărnovo/Veliko Tărnovo, 167, 171,
176, 183, 186, 188, 199,
208, 209

330 INDEX

Taškovski, Dragan, 33, 79–88, 92, 98, 99
Tetovo, 222
Thallóczy, Lajos (Ludwig von), 115, 305
Theodor II Muzaka, 260
Theophylact of Ohrid, 87
Thessaloniki/Salonika (Salonica), vilayet of, 34, 79, 86, 91, 113, 164, 168, 173, 174, 195, 202–205, 223
Thessaly, 54, 61, 82, 222, 223
Thrace, 62, 78, 81, 86, 95, 177, 195
Thracians, 29, 30
Thucydides, 242
Tirana, 120, 121, 124, 132, 134–141, 148, 150
Tito/Tito (Josip Broz), 52, 207
Tivar, 250
Todorova, Maria, 5, 6, 6n5
Tomaš, Stjepan, 296
Tomić, Sima, 297
Transylvania, 221, 240, 289
Travunija, 286, 293
Trebeništa, 178
Trebizond, 173
Trigger, Bruce, 20
Troebst, Stefan, 42, 43
Trogir, 280
Tschilingirov, Assen, 185n30
Turkey/Turks, 8n7, 10, 11, 13, 14, 28, 105, 108, 137, 144, 149, 180, 223, 224, 241, 257
Tvrtko I Kotromanić, 276, 280, 303–310
Tzimiskes, Joannes (Byzantine emperor), 70

U
Ulcinj, 222
United States of America/United States, 106, 119, 123, 128, 131, 132, 137, 154, 294

Uroš V, Stefan, 286, 303
Uspensky, Fyodor, 169, 196

V
Valentini, Giuseppe (Zef), 124–126, 136, 137
Valtrović, Mihailo, 164
Vardar Macedonia, 65
Varoš (quarter of Prilep), 186
Vasa, Pashko, 224
Vasić, Miloje, 194
Vasiliev, Asen, 210
Velichkov, Konstantin, 168
Venice/Venitian(s), 105, 280, 291
Vermosh, 225
Veroia, 168
Vidin, 188, 190
Vienna, 119, 120, 122, 162, 297
Viollet-le-Duc, Eugène Emmanuel, 162, 166n6
Visoko (town), 303, 305, 310
Vlachs, 54, 57, 80, 85, 87, 91, 93, 113
Vladislav Kotromanić, 303
Vlora/Vlorë, 124, 250
Voizava, 116
Vojvodina, 287
von Engel, Johann Christian, 282, 283
Voynov, Mihail, 66–69, 80
Vukan Nemanjić, 295
Vuk Branković, 260, 261
Vulić, Nikola, 118, 179n21

W
Wadding, Luke, 281
Wallachia, 187, 194
principality of, 9, 240
Weigand, Gustav, 177n17, 248
Western Balkans, 42
Western Bulgarian Kingdom (or Ohrid Kingdom), 57, 60, 70, 82

Whittemore, Thomas, 178n20
Williams, Raymond, 18, 19
Wittenberg, Jason, 4, 5

X

Xhufi, Pëllumb, 153, 239, 250, 258, 259, 261
Xyngopoulos, Andreas, 195, 202–204

Y

Yonchev, Lyubomir, 55, 66, 67
Yugoslavia/Yugoslavs/Serb-Croat-Slovene Kingdom, 7, 13, 26, 28, 39, 40, 42, 119, 121, 128, 131, 132, 137, 138, 148, 151, 181, 206, 276, 279, 288, 291, 293, 294, 298, 302, 306, 307, 309, 310

Z

Zagreb, 277, 289, 295
Zahumlje, 286, 293
Zambelios, Spyridon, 164
Zemen, 187, 200
Zeta (today's Montenegro), 61, 295
Zhivkov, Todor, 78, 79, 200, 208
Zhivkova, Lyudmila, 200
Zlatarski, Vasil, 53–55, 60, 64, 75, 178
Zogu, Ahmet, 119, 122, 124
Zonara, 68

Printed in the United States
by Baker & Taylor Publisher Services